Understanding Data

SECOND EDITION

Understanding Data

SECOND EDITION

B. H. ERICKSON AND T. A. NOSANCHUK

UNIVERSITY OF TORONTO PRESS
Toronto and Buffalo

First Published in North America in this second edition in 1992 by
University of Toronto Press
Toronto and Buffalo

ISBN 0-8020-2877-2 (Cloth)
ISBN 0-8020-7382-4 (Paper)

Cataloguing in Publication Data for this book
is available from the University of Toronto Press

Printed and bound in Great Britain

Contents

Preface to the Revised Edition

It has now been more than 15 years and several thousand students since the original edition of *Understanding Data* was completed. The original premise of the text was that insights gained from data exploration not only would be important in their own right but could carry over to analogous confirmatory statistics. We anticipated that social science students, who are often very weak mathematically, would comprehend the traditional materials better than if taught either through mathematical demonstrations or in a cookbook fashion. As a consequence, the text was built around a set of core elements from John Tukey's (1977) highly innovative text *Exploratory Data Analysis*. In our view the approach works well, a view generally supported by students, other teachers and several reviewers. But 15 more years of teaching, including much trial and error, plus comments from students, other users and reviewers have indicated the need for some changes. Other changes have been mandated by the increased access to personal computers and the more general availability of high quality software for exploratory data analysis.

The overall organization of the text as well as our views about how best to teach the material are largely unchanged. We have added sections on a variety of topics though, including interval estimation (Chapter 9), tabular analysis (Chapter 14), transformation as a way of treating interaction effects (Chapter 16), dummy variable analysis and high influence points (Chapter 20). In addition, nearly every chapter contains a section on using the computer. This has been keyed to MINITAB (release 7), one of the most user-friendly of the many packages available, with good exploratory capabilities. Consequently, we have also slightly de-emphasized handwork in the text although we continue to feel that at least some handwork is important for developing a sense of mastery and control. Several chapters have been substantially reorganized, most notably Chapters 5 and 6 on batch transformations, and several text examples have been simplified, resulting in somewhat clearer exposition.

For teachers experienced only with traditional statistics courses, selecting effective data sets can be a problem. Along with the data being real ('warts and all') and appropriate to the task, experience has shown that good data sets meet most of the following criteria:

1 *Transparency:* the data should make sense to the students; either they are of clear disciplinary interest or they tap general knowledge.
2 *Wide range:* there should be a variety of information associated with the units of analysis, permitting a lot of choice in the direction to take an exploration.
3 *Informative:* data that inform students substantively as well as being useful statistically are great morale builders.
4 *Small and simple:* one (or rarely two) modest data set can take a great deal of time to analyse, so problems that are too large or complex encourage superficial analyses.

No book can be written without incurring enormous debts. Ours are first to John Tukey, for his path-breaking work on data exploration, and to the very many students whose intense commitment has helped to make this approach effective and whose thoughtful feedback has helped to shape this revision. Dean Marshall of Carleton University provided word processing support and Ann Cameron and Elsa Brock did the word processing with care and patience. Special thanks to Greg Graves, Laura Landry and Beth McKibbin for their comments on selected chapters. We acknowledge the support of Minitab, Inc. (3081 Enterprise Drive, State College, PA 16801, USA) in permitting our extensive use of the MINITAB (release 7) statistics package. We are grateful to the Literary Executor of the late Sir Ronald A. Fisher, FRS, to Dr Frank Yates, FRS and to Longman Group Ltd, London, for permission to reprint Tables III and IV from their book *Statistical Tables for Biological, Agricultural and Medical Research* (6th edn, 1974).

1
Understanding Data

Many of the readers of this book, we suspect, are approaching it with a sense of dread. Students, especially in the behavioural sciences, often believe that while other courses may be enjoyed, statistics courses must be endured. We believe that statistics is not only useful and important, but also enjoyable. Students believe this too, after they have overcome some initial stumbling blocks. The first problem to be faced is the problem of numerical illiteracy: unnecessary difficulty in reading numbers.

Look at it this way: students are expected, and expect themselves, to be able to read at very high levels. They read complex ideas as presented by difficult writers, and deal with the ideas intelligently and critically. It may take time and even be painful but the reader, being confident, is spurred by his or her confidence and usually is successful.

But suppose he or she is beginning to read a table of numbers, not a chapter of words. That's quite another story! Many students who are bright with anything but numbers freeze up when numbers come along. They don't even try to cope; instead they immediately succumb to 'data-phobia'. The symptoms of data-phobia are easy to spot when someone is reading an article with tables in it. The poor victim of the phobia reads the text confidently, absorbing the argument and possibly taking issue with it. Then comes a table: and the data-phobe may avert his eyes, stare at the table helplessly without knowing what to make of it, or skim the table very quickly to try to find what the author says is there. The reader rarely gets into the table, but relies on asking, 'What does the author say the table says?' Unless there are really gross departures from this in the table, our data-phobe is likely to find the author's explanation acceptable, even when the reader agrees with nothing else in the paper. It may surprise some readers to learn that authors' interpretations of tables are sometimes incorrect. More commonly, authors will fail to remark on important aspects of their own data, aspects that the reader may be interested in. The author may overlook these features because they do not seem important, or he or she may misjudge their importance, or they may not matter as much in the author's theoretical or evaluative framework as in the reader's. Authors may even ignore these features because they did not notice them, may have run out of time, may be data-phobes themselves, or may not be very good analysts (that's possible!). For all sorts of reasons the reader simply cannot rely on a paper's author to get everything out of the paper's data, and one certainly can't expect that an author will always interpret the data the way the reader would like to.

It is, therefore, up to the reader to read the numbers as carefully as the words; there is a lot to be gained by doing so. But it often doesn't happen – why not? Numbers, after all, are a far more simple and unambiguous form of information than words. If you can read and understand books expressing difficult ideas and using complex language, why can't you read numbers critically? Certainly, there are reasons: for one thing, we've been carefully trained to be literate in the usual sense of being able to use and understand the written word; but very few of us have been trained to be numerically literate. If anything, our training tends to make us fearful rather than enquiring when faced with numerical data. We usually start with a deeply rooted conviction that it is just going to be too hard for us. As a result, we don't try very hard, and don't get very far. When we end up doing poorly our initial expectation is confirmed – a good example of the self-fulfilling prophecy.

One of the major goals of this book is to break up this self-defeating pattern, to demonstrate that data analysis is not difficult. The bulk of data analysis is comparatively simple; the bread-and-butter work that keeps most of social science research going is no more difficult than reading ordinary textual material. Indeed, routine data analysis uses tools much like those used in routine reading: some thought, some common sense, some orderly reasoning, some imagination, some background knowledge of the area. If you have read this far, you can read the rest of the book; if you are verbally literate, you can develop numerical literacy.

At this point you may be thinking, 'It's all very well to talk about common sense and so forth, but statistics is full of mathematics – and that's not like reading words and I definitely will not understand it!' However, it isn't necessary for data analysis to involve complex mathematics. At this level, in an introductory course, we rarely need any maths beyond counting and arithmetic. Our big mathematical weapon turns out to be subtraction! We also make use of a few familiar techniques like drawing graphs. But what you really need is judgement, persistence, paper, a pencil and a willingness to use your eyes and your head. Basic data analysis is easy and you can do it.

There is another misconception about statistics that we would like to demolish. Analysing numbers is not painful and boring: it can be engrossing and a lot of fun. We can't convince you of that just by saying so, but you can and will convince yourself by doing some data analyses and experiencing the pleasures of discovery and understanding at first hand. There is nothing more exciting than learning something about social reality through data, learning it through your own efforts: once you get started, it is hard to stop – like eating peanuts!

We hope to turn you into data-philes rather than data-phobes, into people who can deal with numbers sensibly and critically and who can enjoy the process. We have promised you some simple tools to help you do this. Now it is time to describe the two kinds of data analysis dealt with in this book and to give some idea of the book's overall strategy.

We will discuss two general approaches to understanding data: exploratory and confirmatory. Exploratory techniques make it easy to see into the data, to poke around some information in search of ideas about how things work. These procedures can generate the hypotheses that are sometimes taken to be the starting point of the scientific enterprise. Confirmatory techniques are directed to testing these hypotheses, once we have them, provided that we also have good data that are relevant to the hypotheses. Looking for ideas and trying to test them are two different things, so the two sets of techniques are also different.

We will try to approach problems first through exploration and then through confirmation. There are several reasons for this order. A lot of research is done in this way: the researcher explores an area and then tests the resulting hypotheses that look most promising and sensible. Besides, the exploratory methods are particularly easy to understand, and once you are familiar with the exploratory methods, the parallel confirmatory statistics are far easier to follow.

Exploring Data

The spirit of exploratory data analysis is a lot like the spirit of classic detective work. If you enjoy mysteries you could get into the right frame of mind by reading some Sherlock Holmes stories. Both detection and exploration require tools, some understanding of the material examined, and relentless following up of clues. The detective needs to know the tools of the trade, whether fingerprinting or classification of tobacco ash, in case it is necessary. Similarly, the data analyst should know at least one way of tackling each of the major kinds of data that are likely to be encountered. For this reason you will learn a range of useful basic tools even though this book cannot cover all the available techniques. The detective needs to have background knowledge, from timetables to laws of inheritance, to make sense of the clues. Similarly, the data analyst should be able to call on basic knowledge to interpret clues in numerical form. This does not mean that you must have an advanced degree before reading this book, only that you should use knowledge you already have or can find quickly. For example, if you find that English and French people are different in some way you should be able to think of many reasons for the difference. Or if you find that cities differ in migration patterns, say, you can easily look up some possible reasons, such as size or growth rate, by spending a few minutes with a yearbook. Finally, the good detective finds a way to a solution to the case at hand by following through on clues, by pursuing and checking the possibilities that clues suggest. Similarly, the data analyst checks and pursues insights by trying them out against available information. Sometimes the insight does not work out; that is fine, you have learned something and can test another idea. Sometimes the insight works but not perfectly; that is fine too, as you can look for additional insights to improve your explanation. Sometimes an insight really takes care of a problem by explaining almost all the data you have; and that is terrific, but it doesn't happen very often!

One of the nice things about detective stories is that the detective usually takes time at some point to explain just how he or she interpreted clues and followed them up (few published research articles do this, which is a pity). For example, consider how Sherlock Holmes works in 'Silver Blaze'. First we quote a narrative passage showing Holmes at work, and then give his explanations of what he was doing and why.

> As we stepped into the carriage one of the stable-lads held the door open for us. A sudden idea seemed to occur to Holmes, for he leaned forward and touched the lad upon the sleeve.
>
> 'You have a few sheep in the paddock,' he said. 'Who attends to them?'
>
> 'I do, sir.'
>
> 'Have you noticed anything amiss with them of late?'
>
> 'Well, sir, not of much account, but three of them have gone lame, sir.'
>
> I could see that Holmes was extremely pleased, for he chuckled and rubbed his hands together.
>
> 'A long shot, Watson, a very long shot,' said he, pinching my arm. 'Gregory, let me recommend to your attention this singular epidemic among the sheep. Drive on, coachman!'
>
> Colonel Ross still wore an expression which showed the poor opinion which he had formed of my companion's ability, but I saw by the inspector's face that his attention had been keenly aroused.
>
> 'You consider that to be important?' he asked.
>
> 'Exceedingly so.'
>
> 'Is there any point to which you would wish to draw my attention?'
>
> 'To the curious incident of the dog in the night-time.'
>
> 'The dog did nothing in the night-time.'
>
> 'That was the curious incident,' remarked Sherlock Holmes.

Now what was all that about? 'The incident of the dog in the night-time', which is quite a famous one, is an example of interpreting a clue using background knowledge. As Holmes explains,

> I had grasped the significance of the silence of the dog, for one true inference invariably suggests others. The Simpson incident had shown me that a dog was kept in the stables, and yet, though someone had been in and had fetched out a horse, he had not barked enough to arouse the two lads in the loft. Obviously the midnight visitor was someone whom the dog knew well.

When Holmes asks after the health of the sheep, he is checking an earlier conclusion by looking for further related evidence:

> My final shot was, I confess, a very long one. It struck me that so astute a man as Straker would not undertake to lame the horse without a little practice. What could he practise on? My eyes fell upon the sheep, and I asked the question which, rather to my surprise, showed that my surmise was correct.

We want to be able to find clues, get ideas about them, and follow up on the ideas in search of hypotheses as we explore our data for insights about some problem. We cannot be sure of where our search is going to lead us; if we could, why would we be searching? We may have to make several stabs at the data before we work out a possible interpretation that looks good. Now, just how good does it have to look? Here is a point where our analogy to detection breaks down. In mystery stories the solution the detective works out has to be not only good but perfect: there is only one true version of how the crime was done and that is the version the detective must find and prove. That's fine for fiction, where the author can invent a crime designed just so that it can be solved, but it will not do for real-life data analysis. There is no use looking for perfect interpretations of data: it would be terribly hard to find perfection if it were available, and it isn't. You never look for *the* interpretation of a complex data set, or *the* way of analysing it, because there are always lots of interpretations and lots of approaches depending on what you are interested in. There are many good answers to different questions, not one right answer as in the detective story.

In principle, the one perfect analysis does not and cannot exist. In practice, if you stick to looking for 'the right answer' you are in for a terrible time, constantly bedevilled by loose ends that won't quite fit. You may get so frustrated that you give up because you can't get the right, the perfect, result; consequently you may end up with nothing when you could easily have found half a dozen different ideas that were good even if not perfect. This is one situation in which Voltaire's aphorism, 'the best is the enemy of the good', applies. Don't worry too much about 'the best': look for things that appeal to you, that make sense to you and seem worth following up. Look for good ideas and plan to work with them.

Now just about every data set with anything to it can generate several good leads, but that does not mean that you will find one at the first shot. Your first few hunches may not lead anywhere; or you may have several hunches and want to work a little on all of them to see which is the most promising. One way or another you often have to make several tries on your data.

It follows that your tools have to let you be flexible, which means that they have to be quick and easy to use. The exploratory techniques take very little time to learn or to use. This means that you can (and should) use them often, to investigate a set of numbers from different points of view. If the techniques were time-consuming and difficult they would be less useful for exploration because we just would not use them. We might admire them greatly, but life would be too short for exploring with them. So the first requirement for an exploratory tool is *simplicity*.

What other features should a useful exploratory technique have? Well, let's think about what we are exploring when we use the techniques. If the data on a problem are in beautiful shape it is usually because the exploration stage is long past; we usually explore before going to the expense of collecting good clean data. The explorer, therefore, must use whatever is on hand, and often only 'dirty' data, filled with errors and gaps, will be available. Still, even poor data can generate useful insights if we are unlikely to be seriously misled by occasional wild or erroneous observations. Hence we want our tools to have *resistance*. By this we mean resistance to things that are probably misleading: to extreme cases that may be flukes, measurement errors, or highly special instances that need special attention. For example, suppose we were looking at salaries for junior and senior members of a firm and found that the 'average' (arithmetic mean) income was the same for both groups. Using our background knowledge we decide this is very strange since income usually increases with age or years of service. Perhaps we look more closely and find that the average for juniors has been pulled up by one person with a very large income. We may have misplaced a decimal (giving her 300 000 instead of 30 000 a year) or made some other mistake; or perhaps there is something special about that person, who is the world's leading authority on computers or the boss's son. In any case it seems reasonable to put that observation aside for special attention and conclude that, excepting a few cases, the average senior makes more money than the average junior. This 'setting aside' of extreme cases is one way of making an analysis resistant. There are of course others.

You may be wondering why we spend so much time learning how to cope with bad data. Why not get good data and use the confirmatory tools, which are not very resistant but are popular? Why have two sets of statistics? First of all, exploratory tools are useful for exploring even good data; remember, they are very fast and easy to use. Secondly, there are many situations in which you have to use very imperfect data because of pressures of time, money, etc. You may not be able to wait five years for the results of the next census, for example, or may simply want to follow up a new and rather wild idea at little cost in time, effort and money. Any information when used with proper caution is better than none.

One final feature of exploratory methods is a little harder to pin down here, although it will be obvious after you have worked with exploration for a while. This feature could be called insight. After all, the purpose of exploration is finding good ideas about how the world works, so the tools should help us to get insights. They do, and for the most part they do so by quite literally letting us *see into* the data. A crucial component of every exploratory analysis involves finding ways of looking at the data. Of course you have to do this yourself; a method cannot see or think for you. But the method will help by displaying the data in highly visual ways and by clearing away the parts you think you understand so that you can look harder at what you are still puzzled about.

Confirming Hypotheses

Confirmatory techniques are designed to test hypotheses, not find them. If you have a clearly formed idea and some high-quality data that bear on the idea, then you turn to confirmatory statistics to find out whether or not your idea is acceptable in light of the evidence. Where exploratory work is like detection, confirmatory work is more like the courtroom trial that follows. In confirmation, a possible hypothesis has been found and its truth must be tested; in the court, a possibly guilty person has been found and he must be tried. As we follow this new analogy we will see that confirmation has a different role in data analysis from that of exploration, and this different role is carried out in a different way. Both, however, remain important.

Confirmatory procedures, like courtroom trials, are supposed to gather unbiased evidence, to examine it rigorously in accordance with the standard rules, and to demand very convincing evidence before deciding that something is so. In the courts the relevant data are supposed to accumulate without bias through the efforts of the judge, the prosecution and the defence, the last two working as adversaries; while the scientist is expected to get good unbiased data on his or her own. Actually, science does have something like the adversary system of the courts in that an assertion made by one scientist will be disputed by another if the assertion seems unwarranted. Good unbiased data are essential because we are hoping to draw conclusions about the issue in question: to decide that a person is or is not guilty or that a hypothesis is or is not true. Naturally, our conclusions can't be worth much if our data are not good. The nature of 'good' data, from a confirmatory viewpoint, will be clarified in Chapters 7 and 8.

The conclusions will also be worthless if we take the data and handle them improperly. We want to make inferences from the evidence systematically, as exactly as we can, and in ways that are comparable to other tests or other trials; all this will help us to be accurate and objective in our conclusions. The best way of doing this, in courts and in confirmation, is to use agreed procedures which have been very carefully worked out and have well-understood strengths and weaknesses. That is one reason (not the only one) why confirmatory statistics are so much more rigid and formalized than exploratory ones. In exploration, you feel free to modify or invent techniques to suit your particular problems and your own style of thought; but in confirmation you have a decision to make, one that other people will expect you to be able to defend carefully.

Finally, courtrooms and data analysts try to avoid positive decisions (that a person is guilty or that a hypothesis is correct) unless the evidence is very strong indeed. A mere hint of proof is not enough; if that is all you have, you declare that no one's guilt can be shown or no hypotheses can be proven. This is stringent, and in fact both the court and the scientist enhance this stringency by assuming the *opposite* of what the prosecution or scientist would like to prove, i.e. they assume the defendant is innocent or the cherished hypothesis is false.

The assumption is rejected only if it is distinctly unreasonable in the light of the evidence. In courtrooms this means that an accused is 'presumed innocent until proven guilty beyond a reasonable doubt'; indeed, one rule of thumb declares it is better that a hundred guilty men go free than that a single innocent man be convicted. In science one begins by assuming a 'null hypothesis' – if seeking a link between income level and level of education, for example, the null hypothesis would state that income is not related to education. The opposing hypothesis, that a link exists, is acceptable only if the evidence is overwhelmingly in favour of it as against the null. We will go into all this in more detail, expanding on the courtroom analogy somewhat, when we begin to discuss the logic of confirmatory statistics.

For now, the main thing is to note the importance of making a well-supported decision about how the world works, and to see what making such a decision demands. We must have good data for a basis; in exploration no one objects to having good data, of course, but good data are not essential. We must also have clear-cut rules for reaching decisions, and clear-cut hypotheses to test; in exploration, on the other hand, we may have no hypotheses to start with and we look around for them in ways designed to be free and easy rather than rigorous. Overall, confirmation is much less flexible and much more precise than exploration; they have to be different in these ways to do their different jobs.

As we have seen, the job of exploration is creating ideas, and the beauty of it is its openness and playfulness. The job of confirmation is making careful decisions, and the beauty of it is its power. If a few important assumptions (like random sampling) are met, then one can make very strong statements from modest amounts of data. For example, quite elaborate and informative studies using national samples of fewer than a thousand respondents have been carried out; many important studies use under a hundred. This is quite impressive when you think of how complex social reality is and how hard it would be to study it without statistics. This power has a price tag: you have to follow the rules, you have to spend some time on the calculations (or, better, get a computer to do them) and you have to spend a lot of time and money getting good data. But presumably the price tag is a reasonable one because you are getting a solid test of hypotheses that look important and plausible in the light of previous exploratory or theoretical work.

Now, how do you learn to follow the rules, do the calculations, and so on? In this book we assume that the essential thing is to understand the logic of what goes on when a test is made. This logic is easy to see once you have learned the exploratory approach to a problem; the confirmatory approach is usually just a tighter version of the same thing plus the making of a decision. If you see what is going on, you do not have to settle for 'cookbook' approaches to your data – approaches that you stumble through by rote, not really understanding or learning anything. Nor do you have to steel yourself for massive doses of mathematics to 'help you see how it works'. Few students see anything that way so we have left most of the mathematical derivations out of the main text. We are interested in having you develop a feeling for and understanding of the tools. And how do you understand? By seeing what the tools actually do to the data, which again is something we learn through exploration.

We will make no attempt in this book to survey all of the confirmatory statistics; there are far too many for any single course, for one thing. Instead we will concentrate on a relatively small number of the more basic and popular techniques, discussing their logic and some of their properties as well as presenting relatively simple computing forms. Most of the more complicated ways to test hypotheses use the simple approaches we will deal with as starting points, so you can work up to the more dazzling techniques as the need arises. In short, we stress confirmatory statistics that are easy to do, easy to understand, generally used and basic to more advanced methods.

Confirmation and Exploration Together

So far we have stressed the differences between the two kinds of statistics, hoping to clarify each of them. But it is important to realize that they are complementary as well as different: you can't do without either one, and the good analyst is the one who can work with both together. The easiest way to work with them together is to use them in alternation. We have already said that people often start on a problem with exploration, get some ideas, and then move to confirmation to test the ideas. And what comes after testing the hypothesis? More exploratory work, of course! There is almost always something unexpected and interesting, or something that doesn't fit, and a good researcher can't resist asking why 'if you know all the answers you haven't asked all the questions'. A lot of important new ideas are found in exactly that way, by following up the odds and ends (or 'deviant cases'). So exploratory work is naturally followed by confirmation because you want to test good-looking ideas once you see them, and confirmatory work is naturally followed by exploratory because you will want to push an explanation a little further if you can. The process doesn't terminate until the researcher runs out of time, energy, information or interest. Both ways of looking at data are essential parts of doing science; neither is better or more important than the other.

The alternation between exploration and confirmation can take place from minute to minute in the researcher's mind, or from decade to decade as the status of a problem changes, or over longer periods of time as a whole discipline changes gears. In the case of long-term change we get something like the alternation Kuhn (1970) sees between 'normal' and 'revolutionary' science. In normal science, paradigms provide our hypotheses so confirmatory statistics are generally more important, although exploration still plays a role. However, in revolutionary science what is primary is the discovery and interpretation of the unexpected, a very important pay-off from the exploratory approach.

Even though both approaches are essential, they do not both get the same amount of publicity. Confirmation gets more attention and recognition because it is more formalized, which means that it looks more rigorous and impressive. Besides, it shows up in the most polished phase of research, the testing of clear hypotheses with clean data, which is the phase that usually gets published. The formality and familiarity of confirmatory statistics make them very useful for public communication of findings. By contrast, exploratory analyses are fluid and require more explanation to an outsider, so they tend to be done privately to help the researcher clarify her ideas in her own mind. Exploratory tools are not only less standard and more private, they are also almost unknown to many researchers. But don't let that fool you: exploratory tools belong in your tool kit.

There are many fine standard sources for confirmatory statistics; two that we have used are Hays (1981), *Statistics* and Brownlee (1960), *Statistical Theory and Methodology in Science and Engineering*. All of the exploratory material in this book is drawn from the innovative work of John Tukey. Most of the material, plus additional refinements and more advanced exploratory tools, can be found in his book *Exploratory Data Analysis*. On some minor points we have followed an earlier version, *Exploratory Data Analysis: Preliminary Edition*. Sometimes our language is a little different from his, largely because we have tried to use standard terms whenever possible. Information on his terms and usages can be found in the 'Exploratory and confirmatory' sections following most chapters. We plan to cover rather less of both approaches than can be found elsewhere, but hope to clarify both by showing how they can fit together.

In this introduction we have often talked about analysing data, getting ideas from data, seeing things happen in or with data, and so on. None of this is going to occur without data! So data there will be, believe us, and lots of data! All the remaining chapters contain examples based on real data, and the homework is based on real data too. Nothing else would be suitable; after all, you are taking the course to learn how to analyse data and you don't learn that from anything else but analysing data.

You may wonder why we bother to say such obvious things. The reason is that it seems they are not so obvious: have a look at the problems in most standard statistics textbooks and see how many of them are based on simplified problems of questionable relevance, such as picking coloured balls out of urns or estimating how long you will have to wait until the next bus arrives. Artificial examples and assignments like these can be fast to compute, and they can be set up so that there are 'right answers', but they are not very helpful in learning how to use statistics in social science research. Data analysis is something that has to be done, and done for actual situations, to be understood. We think that it also has to be done for real situations to be enjoyed. Genuine data about social life are often messy, complicated, time-consuming – and fascinating.

One final word about doing data analyses: you do them to learn how to use tools and, more importantly, to learn about data and how to understand them. To accomplish this aim, make sure your work is never just a bunch of calculations. It is what the calculations, displays and so on tell you that counts, so you should always *discuss* your results in words at some length. We have found a good rule of thumb to be that every assignment or examination should have at least as many pages of verbal discussion as of calculations or graphs or other non-verbal analyses. The discussion can be quite simple, little more at first than writing down what you can see easily. This takes practice for many students who feel that it is a waste of time to write down what is obvious. It is not, for a number of reasons, one being that subtler things are easier to see once you have cleared away the intellectual underbrush. What you will have to say will rarely seem earth-shattering, but saying it clearly is an important step in penetrating deeply into the data.

Using the Computer

Every technique that we cover in the text can be done by hand or calculator. Not only is it possible to do things by hand, but this is generally a good thing to do at least once. It can help you understand how things work and it also provides a sense of control by demystifying this new and, for some, scary technology. As against this, analysis is a very labour-intensive activity and the computer can help by reducing both labour and errors. Most statistical packages these days offer a variety of both exploratory and confirmatory statistics. We have keyed the text to one particular package, MINITAB (release 7) which is very user-friendly. Be aware that, while other packages have similar analysis capabilities, the data format and command structure described here are unique to MINITAB.

Entering Data

There are two commands for entering data, READ and SET. READ is the more general command and we present that here.
    Say that you have the following data to enter:

```
22    88    99
12    10    77
11    3     9
```

You have three columns of data (C1 = 22, 12, 11; C2 = 88, 10, 3; etc.), each consisting of three rows. Using the READ command, you will enter these data row by row – that is, you will enter the data as three lines and on each line you will enter three numbers, each separated by a space. (Note that it is not important to line these numbers up, one directly beneath the other. The computer reads the space, or a comma between numbers, as a sign to move to the next column in the worksheet.) The procedure for READing this data into the computer is reproduced below:

```
MTB> READ THE FOLLOWING DATA INTO C1, C2, C3
DATA   22    88    99
DATA   12    10    77
DATA   11    3     9
DATA   END
```

```
3 ROWS READ
MTB> PRINT C1, C2, C3
ROW    C1    C2    C3
1      22    88    99
2      12    10    77
3      11     3     9
MTB> STOP
```

Correcting Errors

To err is human, to correct . . . After entering your data, check for errors by using the PRINT command. If you find any, they can be corrected by either LET or INSERT. If you have made one or a few scattered errors, LET permits you to substitute values in particular rows and columns:

```
MTB> LET C1(10)=9
```

If you have put an incorrect value in column 1, row 10 and the correct value is 9, this command will make the correction.

If you have missed an entire row, use the INSERT command. If, for example, you left out two rows of numbers between row 1 and 2, then procedure to correct it would be as follows:

```
MTB> PRINT C1–C3
ROW    C1    C2    C3
1       1     3     3
2       2     4     5
3       8     9     0
4      12    13    14
MTB> INSERT BETWEEN ROWS 1 AND 2 OF C1–C3
DATA  9     9     9
DATA  7     7     7
DATA END
2 ROWS READ
MTB> PRINT C1–C3
ROW    C1    C2    C3
1       1     3     3
2       9     9     9
3       7     7     7
4       2     4     5
5       8     9     0
6      12    13    14
```

Of course, if you have left out a column, just use the SET command.

How to Save Data Files and Work Files

We use two types of files in MINITAB – data files and work files. When you enter a data set into the computer, you save it in a data file. This is done by using the command SAVE. The actual syntax is SAVE 'FILENAME', where FILENAME is any name you choose, enclosed within single quotes. You save the file after you have entered all the data. For example, if you wanted to save the data below and call it Example, the procedure would be as follows:

```
MTB> READ C1–C3
DATA   22   88   99
DATA   12   10   77
DATA   11    3    9
DATA   END
3 ROWS READ
MTB> SAVE 'EXAMPLE'
MTB> STOP
```

These data would now be saved in the computer and could be accessed at any time with the command RETRIEVE. Simply type in RETRIEVE 'EXAMPLE'. Note that the filename is again enclosed in single quotes.

A work file, often called OUTFILE, is used to perform various statistical procedures on the data that have been saved in data files. You can save a work file using the command OUTFILE. The syntax is OUTFILE 'FILENAME', where FILENAME is again any name you choose, and is again enclosed in single quotes. The OUTFILE command saves all output that *follows* (SAVE saved the data preceding the command) – that is, every command entered and results received after the OUTFILE 'FILENAME' command is used will be saved in the file called FILENAME. If, for example, you want to determine the mean of each column in the data file EXAMPLE, and save it as an outfile called MEAN, you could do the following:

```
MTB> OUTFILE 'MEAN'
MTB> RETRIEVE 'EXAMPLE'
MTB> PRINT C1–C4
ROW    C1   C2   C3
1      22   88   99
2      12   10   77
3      11    3    9
MTB> MEAN C1
       MEAN = 15.000
MTB> MEAN C2
       MEAN = 33.667
MTB> MEAN C3
       MEAN = 61.667
MTB> STOP
```

Everything following the command OUTFILE has been saved in the computer under the filename MEAN. It is now possible to get a copy of this file on paper. If you have problems with these (or other) commands, just type HELP after the MTB> prompt.

Section I
Exploratory Batch Analysis

Chapters 2 to 6 introduce the idea of 'batches' and show some basic ways to explore batch data. Three aspects of batches are stressed: levels, spreads and shapes (or central tendency, dispersion and distribution in more common language). Section II will turn to the confirmatory analogues to some of the ideas in Section I.

At the end of this first section, right after Chapter 6, there are several sets of batch data. Your instructor may assign one of these sets as homework or as exam material.

2
Organizing Numbers

Perhaps the single most important thing in data analysis, both exploratory and confirmatory, is learning to look hard at data. It may sound embarrassingly simple-minded, but it isn't. We must learn to look not only at a data set but also into it. We have probably all had the experience of looking at a large complex table without really knowing how to begin to extract the juice from it. We stare sightlessly long enough to placate our consciences and then turn gratefully to the text where we are told what the table says. And if it is hard to see very far into a table where the numbers are already organized in some useful way, how much harder it is to see anything in a set of numbers that have not been analysed at all! We have to find ways of putting numbers into arrangements of some sort which let us look at them, and then we must learn to see them effectively. In this chapter we start right at the first stage of inquiry with some simple ways of organizing numerical information.

Picking Your Numbers

Consider the rich array of numbers in Table 2.1, which gives some suicide rates for various countries by sex and age. There is a lot there; enough, in fact, to serve as example material for this chapter and the next few chapters as well. We could just stare hard and think hard, and we would dig some interesting things out that way. Try it now for a few minutes before reading on.

No doubt you have seen several important things; for example, you have probably noticed that the male rates are higher than the female ones. Country and age seem to be important too. But if we want to get further than very general impressions like these, we must look harder at some of the numbers; we can't see everything about all of them at once.

We first decide to look only at male rates (leaving the female rates as a possible homework assignment). The male and female rates are clearly different, with most male rates higher than the corresponding female rates, so it will probably be useful to look at the sexes separately. This leaves us with male rates for various age groups and various countries; it might seem natural,

Understanding Data

Table 2.1 Mortality from suicide, 1971: rates per 100 000

Country	Sex	Age				
		25–34	35–44	45–54	55–64	65–74
Canada	M	21.6	27.3	31.1	33.5	23.5
	F	7.8	11.5	14.8	12.3	9.2
Israel	M	9.4	9.8	10.2	14.0	27.3
	F	7.6	4.2	6.7	22.9	19.1
Japan	M	21.5	18.7	21.1	31.1	48.7
	F	14.0	10.3	13.2	21.0	40.1
Austria	M	28.8	40.3	52.3	52.8	68.5
	F	8.4	16.4	22.4	21.5	29.4
France	M	16.4	25.2	36.1	47.3	56.0
	F	6.6	8.9	13.0	16.7	18.5
Germany	M	28.3	34.6	41.3	49.1	51.8
	F	11.3	15.6	24.2	25.6	27.3
Hungary	M	48.2	65.0	84.1	81.3	107.4
	F	12.7	18.4	26.9	34.7	47.9
Italy	M	7.1	8.3	10.8	17.9	26.6
	F	3.5	3.7	5.5	6.7	7.7
Netherlands	M	7.8	10.6	17.9	20.2	28.2
	F	4.7	8.2	10.5	15.8	17.3
Poland	M	26.2	29.1	35.9	32.3	27.5
	F	4.4	4.7	6.6	7.3	7.0
Spain	M	4.1	7.0	9.6	15.7	21.9
	F	1.4	1.6	3.8	5.4	5.7
Sweden	M	27.6	40.5	45.7	51.2	35.1
	F	13.0	17.5	19.6	22.4	17.1
Switzerland	M	21.7	33.6	41.1	50.3	50.8
	F	10.4	15.9	18.2	20.1	20.6
UK (England and Wales)	M	9.6	12.7	14.6	17.0	21.7
	F	5.1	6.5	10.7	13.0	14.1
United States	M	19.6	22.2	27.8	32.8	36.5
	F	8.6	12.1	12.5	11.4	9.3

Source: World Health Organization (1974).

then, to ask what effect age has on suicide rates among males. This is still too big a question to start with; five age groups for 15 countries is a lot of numbers. Starting may be easier if we look hard at just two age groups, develop some ideas, and see how the ideas work for all the age groups later. Which two groups? Such choices depend on the tastes and judgements of the analyst. Here, we decide to do the oldest group (65–74) and the youngest (25–34) on the grounds that a big age difference would be likely to highlight any effects age might have. Other choices would also have been plausible; for example, if you were looking at retirement as a major crisis point in life, you might contrast the 55–64 group to the 65–74 group because the first group is probably mostly men at the end (and often the apex) of their careers while the second group is mostly retired men; if retirement is traumatic, the second group should have markedly higher rates of suicide. The general point here is: pick out the sets of numbers that suit your interests. Don't try to see everything straight away; feel free to concentrate on whatever interests you.

Batches and Units of Analysis

Now that we have started by picking some numbers to concentrate on at first, what do we have? We chose the youngest and the oldest males' rates as a starting point. These numbers have been copied out in Table 2.2 so we can see them more clearly, uncluttered by all the other numbers in Table 2.1. Each of these sets of rates is a *batch*: a set of related numbers. The rates for males 25–34 can be considered a batch because they are all of a kind. The rates for males 65–74 are also all related numbers. If we had suicide rates for Canada, divorce rates for Israel, mean income for Japan, etc., we would have not a batch, but a

Table 2.2 Mortality from suicide, 1971, for males 25–34 and 65–74

	Males 25–34		Males 65–74	
	Unrounded	*Rounded*	*Unrounded*	*Rounded*
Canada	21.6	22	23.5	24
Israel	9.4	9	27.3	27
Japan	21.5	22	48.7	49
Austria	28.8	29	68.5	69
France	16.4	16	56.0	56
Germany	28.3	28	51.8	52
Hungary	48.2	48	107.4	107
Italy	7.1	7	26.6	27
Netherlands	7.8	8	28.2	28
Poland	26.2	26	27.5	28
Spain	4.1	4	21.9	22
Sweden	27.6	28	35.1	35
Switzerland	21.7	22	50.8	51
UK (England and Wales)	9.6	10	21.7	22
United States	19.6	20	36.5	37

Rounding rule: 0–4 down, 5–9 up.

bunch of unrelated numbers. Numbers go together in a batch because they appear to belong together. Each of the numbers stands for the same kind of thing: here, for the number of suicides per 100 000 males of a given age group for various countries. As we will discuss later, the meaning of these figures may vary slightly from country to country; none the less, they are enough alike to be called a batch. Since the numbers in the two batches, each corresponding to an age group, are alike, we may compare the batches. Otherwise, we would have no basis for comparison.

Numbers have to belong to things – here, the suicide rates have to be attached to various countries. The countries are the *units of analysis* or *units of observations*, the things that were observed to get the numbers. In this particular case the countries themselves recorded the suicide statistics and passed them on.

More will be said about batching following Chapter 6, after you have become at home with batches.

Simplifying Numbers

Before starting to organize numbers it often pays to simplify them, especially if an electronic calculator isn't easily available. You can usually gain in ease of calculation without losing anything; you keep all the accuracy you really need, or believe in. In any case, figures often appear more accurate than they really are, and can often be simplified without any loss in accuracy at all.

Consider the suicide rates. There is a strong tendency to regard these data as virtually perfect, because they come from authoritative-sounding sources like national governments or a United Nations agency. However, at least two major problems are associated with these data. First, different nations have different procedures for determining cause of death; for example, if a man deliberately shoots himself but does not die for a week, his death may or may not be classified as a suicide. Secondly, while the rates are calculated on a base 100 000, which sounds like a lot, the groups involved may actually be smaller, thus reflecting only a very few actual suicides. As a result, the rates may fluctuate wildly from one year to the next. For example, Israel had a population of about three million in 1970, and probably less than half were aged between 25 and 74, the ages for which we present figures. How many of these are males between 65 and 74? Probably far fewer than 100 000, with perhaps fewer than 25 actual suicides (remember, the rate is 27.3); a few errors in classification or even random fluctuations could markedly alter this figure. (We could have looked these up, and easily. But 'guestimating' is an important skill for data analysis.)

As a result, small differences between rates should probably be ignored in cases like this. Thus, when we wish to simplify our figures, we shouldn't feel badly if some of the apparent accuracy is lost. In fact, even if the figures are very accurate, we may simplify for ease of calculation as long as we do not obscure the general trends.

Rounding is the most familiar simplifying procedure and can be done in several ways. Table 2.2 illustrates one fairly common way: decimals from .0 to .4 are rounded to the whole number below them, while .5 to .9 are rounded to the next higher whole number. Note that we jotted our rounding choice down at the bottom of the table so we would not forget what we had done to the numbers. A look at the rounded numbers shows that they are not really any less informative than the original figures: the differences from one country to another are still clear. This is because the changes due to rounding are small in relation to the overall range of the numbers: for the younger batch, the rates vary from 4.1 to 48.2, so a change of 0.5 (the largest possible when using this method) is not likely to make an important difference.

Other methods of simplification are available. If you want to be very quick, you can simplify by truncating, or chopping off the ends. In our example, we could have just cut off the decimals so that 21.6 would become 21 and 9.4 would become 9.

Rounding does not have to be restricted to decimal places. For example, we could round off the units as well as the decimal place. Then 21.6 would become 2, 9.4 would become 1, and so on; in short, we would be left with rounded rates per ten thousand. This would be meaningful – rates can be per 100 000, per million or whatever – and is sometimes helpful. Here, it is less helpful because the numbers become uninformative. In Table 2.3 we see what happens to our younger batch: when rounding goes too far, too many numbers end up looking the same when they are actually different in ways that may well turn out to be interesting (e.g. both 21.6 and 16.4 become 2). So how far should you round in a particular case? This is a matter of judgement, like a lot of data analysis; it will depend on the accuracy of the original figures, the range of the figures in the batch, and the use you intend to make of the rounded figures. Common sense and a little experience make this decision an easier one.

Still, even a lot of experience doesn't always guarantee that you will make

Table 2.3   Rounded suicide rates, males 25–34

Original rates; per 100 000	Rounded; per 10 000
21.6	2
9.4	1
21.5	2
28.8	3
16.4	2
28.3	3
48.2	5
7.1	1
etc.	etc.

Rounding rule: 0–4 down, 5–9 up.

the right rounding decision every time. On reading Tennyson's 'The Vision of Sin', Charles Babbage, a pioneer in computing, is said to have written to the poet,

> In your otherwise beautiful poem there is a verse which reads:
> 'Every moment dies a man,
> Every moment one is born.'
> It must be manifest that, were this true, the population of the world would be at a standstill. In truth, the rate of birth is slightly in excess of that of death. I would suggest that in the next issue of your poem you have it read:
> 'Every moment dies a man,
> Every moment one and one-sixteenth is born.'
> Strictly speaking, this is not correct. The actual figure is a decimal so long that I cannot get it on the line, but I believe one and one-sixteenth will be sufficiently accurate for poetry. (From the *Mathematical Gazette*)

Well, we have started; we have chosen the batches we want to begin with and we have simplified the data by rounding. But it is still hard to see much because the data are not organized. Surely it would be convenient to *order* the rates by size so we can look for patterns, for regularities and for departures from these patterns and regularities.

Ordering Batches

There are many ways of organizing the data in Table 2.2. A familiar way is to gather the numbers into categories as in Table 2.4, a tally. Just to remind you of how this works, in Table 2.4 for males 25–34 we see that one country had a rate between 40 and 49, eight countries had rates between 20 and 29, two between 10 and 19, and four between 0 and 9. We get these tallies by going through the raw numbers and marking each one off in the appropriate category. This is quite easy to do (as long as you don't have too many numbers) and it is quite useful too. For example, we can see that the rates for the older batch are higher and also more spread out than the rates for the younger group.

Why do older men have higher rates of suicide? Many possibilities come to mind. The end of one's working life may indeed, as suggested earlier, be a blow for some people, diminishing the sense of self-worth and increasing financial problems. Older people generally have poorer health and fewer social contacts. In general, the problems of life grow and the resources for meeting them shrink. Why are the rates for older men more diverse? Perhaps the experiences of old age are more different, country to country, than those of youth – for example, some countries may have better social services for older people, which in turn might result in lower suicide rates for this group. Older people may also be more diverse in their values and beliefs (including values

Table 2.4   Tally of Table 2.2, rounded figures

Males 25–34		Males 65–74	
100–109		100–109	1
90–99		90–99	
80–89		80–89	
70–79		70–79	
60–69		60–69	1
50–59		50–59	111
40–49	1	40–49	1
30–39		30–39	11
20–29	~~1111~~ 111	20–29	~~1111~~ 11
10–19	11	10–19	
0–9	1111	0–9	

related to suicide) because they grew up in earlier periods when countries were less 'homogenized' by industrialization and higher levels of international communication. You may have some other suggestions.

In general this approach is good for finding gross similarities or differences between batches. On the other hand, it is poor at giving details. Looking at Table 2.4, how can we know just where a case fits in an interval? We can't. The only way we can get this sort of detail is to go from the tally back to the original numbers, which can be a nuisance – especially if these original numbers are somewhere else (perhaps in a reference book we used) or no longer available (perhaps we were counting things as they happened and the behaviour we looked at is now past and gone). Fortunately there is a way to jot down numbers that takes no more time than tallying and does not throw away information; we can get something for nothing, if we spend a few minutes learning more efficient techniques.

Suppose that instead of a range to the left of the 'bar' we have only the leading digit(s), and to the right of the bar we have our next digit. In this way, we retain the quick visual impact of the tally and, moreover, retain the richness of the original table! Tukey refers to this as a *stem-and-leaf* display. Table 2.5 gives stems and leaves of the batches from Table 2.2. Let us look at the first few lines of the stem and leaf for the younger batch to see how this works. The first several lines with stems 5 to 10 have no leaves; this means no countries had rates in the fifties, sixties, etc., for males 25–34. The line with a stem of 4 has a leaf of 8, which means one country had a rate of 48. The stem 3 has no leaves, so there were no rates in the thirties. The stem 2 is very popular, with eight leaves. So there were eight countries with rates in the twenties. We would see that much from the tally, but here we have the graphic quality of the tally and we have not had to sacrifice information. You can read off the original numbers just by tacking the leaves on to their stems.

Table 2.5   Stems and leaves for Table 2.2, rounded figures

Males 25–34		*Males 65–74*	
10		10	7
9		9	
8		8	
7		7	
6		6	9
5		5	621
4	8	4	9
3		3	57
2	22986820	2	4778822
1	60	1	
0	9784	0	

stem:	*leaf:*	*stem:*	*leaf:*
tens	units	tens	units

A stem and leaf is easy to read; it is also easy to make. First put down the stems in order; in Table 2.5 we put down 10, 9, 8 and so on. This is much like listing the intervals for a tally but simpler: instead of 100–109 we write 10, instead of 90–99 we write 9, etc. When the stems are ready, go through the numbers in the data source and record leaves next to their stems as you come to them.

Let's go through an example in detail. We want to make a stem and leaf of the older males' suicide rates. Working down the column of figures in Table 2.2, we meet the numbers in this order: 24, 27, 49, 69, 56, and so on. The first number has a 2 in the tens' place, so its stem is 2; and it has a 4 in the units' place, so the leaf on that stem is 4. Similarly, 27 has a stem of 2 and a leaf of 7. Table 2.6 shows the stem 2 and leaves 4 and 7 placed on a stem and leaf. Table 2.7 shows how the first five rates are added to a stem and leaf.

Actually, this is one of those things that takes longer to describe than to do. Writing numbers down in stems and leaves takes no longer than just copying them. You don't even need a table like Table 2.2, which we use here just to clarify what is happening by taking it one step at a time. You can copy straight from a source (like Table 2.1) to a stem and leaf (like Table 2.5).

Table 2.6   Different leaves on the same stem

	24
	27
stem	leaf
2	47

Table 2.7   Making a stem and leaf

Number	Stem	Leaf	Stem and leaf
24	2	4	6 9
27	2	7	5 6
49	4	9	4 9
69	6	9	3
56	5	6	2 47
			1
			0

stem: tens   *leaf:* units

The first few times you try this it may seem a bit awkward, but a little practice pays big dividends. With minimal expenditure of energy, we have a data representation that is graphic and complete. We can see all that can be seen from a tally, plus some things that are difficult or impossible to see there. For example, if we look hard at Table 2.5 we begin to see that the numbers in both batches cluster a lot. In the younger batch, there seem to be several clusters of numbers. The numbers in the high twenties (Austria, Germany and Sweden, and perhaps also Poland) form one cluster, the numbers in the low twenties (Japan, Switzerland, the USA, Canada, and perhaps France) form another, and the countries with rates of ten or less also seem to cluster. In the tally we could see that there were a lot of rates under ten and a lot in the twenties, but we could not see whether the 'teens' rates went with either of the clusters. We will return to the clusters later.

The stem and leaf is very little work (actually a little less than straight copying when you have learned to do it) and gives lots of information in an organized form. It is one of the basic tools of exploratory analysis, especially batch analysis. Here is a list of steps to follow when doing stems and leaves:

1 Choose your stems. Run your eyes over the numbers you plan to work with. Find the biggest and the smallest and make sure your stems cover that range. In Table 2.2 it was easy to see that the rates went from 4 to 107, so stems from 0 to 10 would handle all the numbers. You don't have to worry about anything but coverage to start with because, as we will see in a moment, it is easy to change your stems if you decide you want to.
2 Order your stems. We like to put the biggest one at the top as in Table 2.5, so that numbers 'higher' on the page are 'higher' in size as well. However, the reverse works perfectly well and computer output is usually in that form.
3 Always make a note of the stem and leaf units. In Table 2.5 we noted: 'stems are in tens, leaves are in units'. Otherwise you can't tell how large the numbers are.
4 Check quickly. To be sure you have not skipped a number, count the number of leaves. In Table 2.5, each stem and leaf should (and does) have 15 leaves because there were 15 countries.

Different Kinds of Stem and Leaf

Changing Stems

The stem and leaf gives us a lot for a little bit of work. It also turns out to be a
flexible tool. To illustrate this, we carry on with the suicide data using different
variations on the basic stem and leaf, each of which shows us something a bit
different. For example, if we look hard at Table 2.5 we see that we do not really
need two sets of stems here because the stems for the two batches are identical.
We can use just one set of stems and put one batch (say the younger) to the left
and the other to the right. This gives us Table 2.8, which contains the same
information as Table 2.5 in a form that makes comparison a little easier. This is
called a 'back-to-back' stem and leaf and is very handy when you want to
compare two rather similar batches for detailed differences.

In our example it is hard to see much that is new in Table 2.8 because we
have already looked rather hard at these batches. Table 2.8 stresses the size
difference; the older men's rates look much higher than the younger men's,
with the former starting almost where the latter end.

The most important variations are variations in the kinds of stems and/or
leaves used. By varying the kind of stem, we can change 'magnification' from a
very compact view to a very detailed one. Compactness comes from putting
more than one stem on a line. We can make Table 2.5 more compact by, say,
cutting the number of lines in half as in Table 2.9, where each line has double
stems. To keep track of which leaf goes with which stem, we can use colons to
divide the leaves; the leaves on the right of the colon go with the stem on the
right. Consider this line from Table 2.9 for the younger batch:

0, 1 | 9784 : 60

Table 2.8 Back-to-back stem and leaf

Males 25–34		Males 65–74
	10	7
	9	
	8	
	7	
	6	9
	5	621
8	4	9
	3	57
22986820	2	4778822
60	1	
9784	0	

stem: tens   *leaf:* units

Table 2.9 Compact view: double stems

Males 25–34			Males 65–74	
10, 11		:	10, 11	7 :
8, 9		:	8, 9	:
6, 7		:	6, 7	9 :
4, 5		8 :	4, 5	9 :621
2, 3	22986820	:	2, 3	4778822 :75
0, 1	9784	:60	0, 1	:

stems: tens   *leaves:* units

The leaves to the right of the colon go with the stem to the right; the rates are 16 and 10. The leaves to the left of the colon go with the stem to the left; the rates are 9, 7, 8 and 4. Compared to Table 2.5, this more compact form makes overall features (like the younger group's less diverse rates) easier to see.

Table 2.10 Detailed view: half stems

Males 25–34		Males 65–74	
10		10	7
10		10	
9		9	
9		9	
8		8	
8		8	
7		7	
7		7	
6		6	9
6		6	
5		5	6
5		5	21
4	8	4	9
4		4	
3		3	57
3		3	
2	9868	2	7788
2	2220	2	422
1	6	1	
1	0	1	
0	978	0	
0	4	0	

stems: tens   *leaves:* units

By using more lines, 'opening up' the stem and leaf, we can get a picture that emphasizes details more. In Table 2.10 we double the number of lines compared to Table 2.5 (our original stem and leaf): each line is now half of a stem. That is, there are two lines for the stem '6'; the upper one gets the upper sixties, 65–69, and the lower one gets the lower sixties, 60–64. In the younger group we can easily see the two clusters in the twenties and also the one around ten; in the older group we see a cluster in the high twenties and, perhaps, another more spread-out cluster around the fifties and high forties.

You may ask, which form is best? Which should I use? There is no one answer: what you use depends on what you want. Sometimes the little details of figures are what count, sometimes not. Sometimes you want a compact stem and leaf and sometimes you want the data spread out well. Since each kind of display shows something a little bit different, you should often find yourself doing several different stems and leaves rather than worrying about what the 'right' one is. You might well want to use Tables 2.5, 2.9 and 2.10: 2.9 for a quick overview, 2.5 for moderate detail, and 2.10 for intensive detail. If you have any one of these, others are easily made from it; you don't have to go back to the original data source.

One final caution: for our example, the most detailed stem and leaf happened to be one with half stems. For a different problem the most detailed version may have single or double stems. The nature of the data and your requirements should be the criteria governing your choice of a kind of stem.

Changing Leaves

So far we have only considered the simplest kind of stem and leaf where each leaf is a single digit. This organization is a good general one that you will use often, but it is not the only kind. For example, you may want to keep more numerical information than Table 2.5 (and its relatives, Table 2.8 to 2.10) provide. You may want to copy out the decimal places from a source like Table 2.1, which is a pretty good idea if the source is one that you would find it a nuisance to consult again, and you think the details may turn out to be interesting. The extra information can be worked into a stem and leaf by using double-digit leaves, as in Table 2.11. This is the same as 2.4 but with more detail. The top line for the older group is

10 | 74

which does not mean two rates of 107 and 104 here, but one rate of 107.4. We do not bother to put the decimal points in the leaves because it is unnecessary, as long as a footnote that explains what you have done is included. If you prefer, you could think of these numbers as rates per million instead of per 100 000 so that the decimal points go away. Then the stems would be hundreds, and the leaves tens and units.

We have lost one piece of information that we had in the original table, the association of a rate with a country. With a little ingenuity, we can manage to

Table 2.11   Table 2.5 with double digit leaves

Males 25–34		Males 65–74	
10		10	74
9		9	
8		8	
7		7	
6		6	85
5		5	60, 18, 08
4	82	4	87
3		3	51, 65
2	16, 15, 88, 83, 62, 76, 17	2	35, 73, 66, 82, 75, 19, 17
1	64, 96	1	
0	94, 71, 78, 41, 96	0	

stems: tens   *leaves:* units and tenths

keep this too. We need only to give up the 'units' information in the leaves and put in their place country identifications, nominal leaves. In Table 2.12 we do this for both the batches 'back-to-back'. In this form, we can most easily think about the clusters we have noted so often. We can immediately see which countries cluster together, and think about what they may have in common that produces similar suicide rates.

Spain, the Netherlands, Italy and Israel come on the same line for both

Table 2.12   Using names as leaves

Males 25–34		Males 65–74
	10	HUN
	9	
	8	
	7	
	6	AUS
	5	FRA, GER, SWI
HUN	4	JAP
	3	SWE, USA
CAN, SWI, SWE, POL, GER,		CAN, ISR, ITA, NET, POL, SPA,
AUS, JAP, USA	2	UK
UK, FRA	1	
SPA, NET, ITA, ISR	0	

stem: tens   *leaves:* first three letters of country names

batches. Their rates are somewhat higher in the older batch, but are still low for that batch. This suggests that these four countries may be similar in some way that keeps suicide rates relatively low. There are a lot of similarities, and different people will find different similarities thought-provoking. One possibility: all four have relatively mild climates. Does warmer weather mean a less stressful life, perhaps because expenses are lower and the climate less depressing? One could follow up on this possibility in various ways. On the one hand, some information about the climates would be useful. How severe are the winters in the 15 countries? On the other hand, we could look beyond the four countries whose similarity caught our eyes: what are rates like in other warm countries?

We could use the nominal leaves to ask other kinds of seminal questions. For example, why is Hungary so much higher in both batches, the highest by far? Why is it that age does not seem to make much difference for Poland and Canada although it does for other countries?

Overview

Where has all this led us to? Well, having our batches organized in even these rudimentary ways has made it possible to look at these numbers painlessly, to start thinking and speculating about them. Many interesting questions have emerged: why are Hungarian rates so high and Spanish rates so low? Why do France and Austria increase so much from one batch to the other? What do Israel, Italy, Spain and the Netherlands have in common? Furthermore, some possible hypotheses have emerged: suicide may be a function of stress points that are related to age and/or may be a function of climate. Other hypotheses could be made, and some simple lines for further research have been suggested: for example, looking up data on climate would help us to check some of our hunches. You can get a lot out of a little data just by looking hard.

We have just gone through the first stage of analysis of a very simple set of data and it has been relatively painless; using the stem and leaf, all we have done is transcribe our data (we must do this in any event) and look at it (no formulae, no complications). Questions and patterns have emerged almost effortlessly. After all, before we can hope to find useful answers to a problem, we must ask questions of our data; the better our data presentation is, the more easily productive questions will emerge. You have also been introduced to the simplest form of data in a body, the batch. Besides the suicide rates seen here, other examples of batch data are: batting averages for various baseball and cricket teams; ages of members of your class; the ages of a set of survey respondents, etc. Remember that the numbers in a batch should belong together: the numbers should emerge from the same process. Sometimes this is obvious: who would try to mix suicide rates with the heights of volcanoes? The two sets of numbers obviously do not belong in the same group. Sometimes deciding what can go into a common batch is less obvious. For example, does

Japan belong in our suicide batches? You might argue that it does not, because its culture is so different; among other things, suicide is traditionally regarded as honourable in certain circumstances, and this tradition remains influential. Or you might argue (as we did) that Japan does belong with the rest because it is a highly industrialized and Westernized nation.

To describe these ideas in another way, a batch consists of numbers generated by the same process: by factors underlying suicide (suicide rates), by demographic processes (ages), by skill and training (batting averages) and so on. If we suspect that the process does not always work the same way, we might break up our batch into several sub-batches. For example, the male suicide batching by age lets us see if suicide rates seem to be at all different for men at differing points in their lives. We could sub-batch further to check out factors that we suspect are related to suicide. We could divide the countries into warm or cold, Catholic or Protestant, politically repressive or politically open, and so on. This would give us some idea whether climate, religion or politics really do make some difference to suicide rates. If we are unable to decide in advance, a couple of approaches can be tried to see what makes the most sense.

In this section we have taken the first steps in a data analysis: looking hard at data, asking questions, some of which we can perhaps answer later. We have also begun to see what is meant by 'doing better', getting more information or clues without proportionally more effort. Minimum effort is an important criterion since we will want to do a great many things, and will only do them if they are not too difficult or time-consuming. People, after all, are not computers: we can weary of a task, or simply become bored. The more we can get done before this point is reached, the more likely it is that we will master the problem.

Large Batches

Even the stem and leaf is a bit slow when you have a very large collection of numbers. What if you have hundreds of numbers in a batch? There are two major ways to cope. First, if you are exploring you don't need hundreds of numbers; fewer numbers would actually be better, easier to work with and see and think about. So don't use them all: select a manageable quantity randomly and save the rest for later use, perhaps to test ideas developed in exploration. A second major way of coping is the computer. There will be more on this shortly.

Peculiarities of Our Example

Our example had some special features; any example would. Just remember that stem-and-leafing is not confined to the kind of batches we happened to use here. We compared batches that had equal numbers of entries (15 per batch), which will not often happen. We might have batched by region, say, and compared rates for European and Asian countries, and we would not be likely to get exactly the same number of each. Further, our batches happened to have the same cases (countries) appearing in each batch. This is interesting for discussion but not at all necessary for batch analysis in general.

We also chose to work with national statistics. We have listed examples of other kinds of batch data above, but national statistics happen to be very handy; you can easily get answers to questions you think up, you can look up urbanization, climate, or whatever you require in almanacs by spending a few minutes in any library.

Exploratory and Confirmatory

This is the first of several 'translation' sections which will appear at the ends of many chapters. The idea is to provide standard, or confirmatory, equivalents of the relatively novel exploratory language (due mainly to Tukey) so that you can describe your work to others in the language they are most likely to understand. Sometimes it really is just a translation; we use some term which is simpler than the standard one, or more evocative, but means the same thing. Sometimes it is a little trickier because we are talking about exploratory tools that have no exact equivalent in the tool kit of standard approaches. The stem and leaf is one of those tools.

There are a couple of standard techniques that are closely related to the stem and leaf and can be very quickly found from stems and leaves. They are not nearly as good as stems and leaves for exploratory work, but they are often

Table 2.13   Males 65–74: alternative presentations

Stem and leaf		Frequency distribution		Histogram	
10	7	100–109	1	100–109	▭
9		90–99		90–99	
8		80–89		80–89	
7		70–79		70–79	
6	9	60–69	1	60–69	▭
5	621	50–59	3	50–59	▭▭▭
4	9	40–49	1	40–49	▭
3	57	30–39	2	30–39	▭▭
2	4778822	20–29	7	20–29	▭▭▭▭▭▭▭
1		10–19		10–19	
0		0–9		0–9	

stems: tens   *leaves:* units

more useful for communication; after all, many people have not heard of the stem and leaf technique, and it is a nuisance to be explaining it all the time. One thing you can get from a stem and leaf is a frequency distribution: the number of cases per interval or category of cases. You can see how to get this by comparing the stem and leaf in Table 2.5 to the corresponding tally in Table 2.4. In the stem and leaf for the younger batch, the stem 0 has four leaves; this means there are four cases from 0 to 9; so the frequency of the interval 0–9 is four. Each line is converted to an interval (just jot down the range of numbers that would be stored on that line); and the number of cases on each line is recorded. Table 2.13 gives a stem and leaf and corresponding frequency distribution for rates for males aged 65–74.

Frequency distributions are useful summaries when you have a lot of cases; in this case stems and leaves become cumbersome. If we had hundreds of cases per line, the stem and leaf would be quite something! The exploratory tools are designed for fast work with a modest number of cases, remember. If we had hundreds of cases we just would not look at them all when we explored, we would select a manageable subsample: at most a hundred, often less.

Another popular tool is the *histogram*. Again, you start with intervals and represent the number of cases per interval, but you do it graphically rather than numerically by putting bars against each category; the length of the bars is proportional to the number of cases in the intervals. The width of the bars is (usually) the same for all of the bars. Table 2.13 presents the suicide data for older men in bar graph form as well as stem and leaf and frequency distribution. Note how easy it is to get from the stem and leaf to the other two. The histogram may look a little difficult at first glance because you have to draw little bars of the right length; for example, in our histogram we have used 3 millimetres per case so we have to make a bar 3 mm long for the interval 100–109, which has one case, 9 mm long for the interval 50–59, which has three cases, and so on. But look at the histogram and look at the stem and leaf: the histogram is just the outline of the stem and leaf's leaves! If you write down your leaves so that they are fairly evenly spaced, the stem and leaf is a histogram: the longer the lines the more cases there are.

So it is clear that the stem and leaf tells you everything the other two displays tell you, and it can be converted to either form quickly to make communication easier. It should also be clear that the stem and leaf is much superior for two reasons: it is quicker to do and it contains far more information. It tells you not only how many cases there are per interval, but also what they are. Thus we intend to use the stem and leaf as our basic tool for preliminary data organization.

Using the Computer

To stem-and-leaf a batch just type 'stem-and-leaf C1' (or whatever column your batch is stored in) or, more simply, 'stem C1' and you will get:

MTB> STEM-AND-LEAF C1
Stem-and-leaf of C1 N = 15
Leaf Unit = 1.0

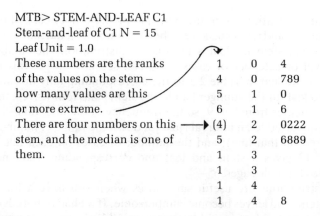

These numbers are the ranks	1	0	4
of the values on the stem –	4	0	789
how many values are this	5	1	0
or more extreme.	6	1	6
There are four numbers on this ⟶	(4)	2	0222
stem, and the median is one of	5	2	6889
them.	1	3	
	1	3	
	1	4	
	1	4	8

The information in the left-hand column will help you to find levels and spreads, the topics for the next chapter, quickly.

The computer is a blessing but it can sometimes be too much of a good thing. It can overwhelm you with numbers; too much, too fast, with too much precision (often specious). In addition, we may expect the computer to tell us everything worth noting. We must be careful when we turn on the computer not to turn off our brains.

HOMEWORK

1 Do-it-yourself Data

It is a little extra work but a lot of fun to collect your *own* data. Count some things, get at least one batch of numbers, stem-and-leaf in a good variety of ways and discuss. Why did you decide to count what you did? What does it mean? What do the stems and leaves tell you? What would you like to do next to follow up on your ideas from the analysis?

In the past students have gathered numbers about all sorts of things. One student, for example, was interested in whether male students or female students had better concentration when they were studying. So he went to the library, spread out some work so he could fit into the background, and discreetly observed male and female students working at the library tables. He watched each person for two minutes, counting the number of times the person looked up from whatever he or she was doing (the idea being that the people who looked up more were concentrating less, probably). So he ended up with two batches: a set of counts for female students and a set of counts for male students. Each count was a number, the number of times that a person looked up. Curious about how it came out? Try it in your own library.

Another student was interested in how traffic patterns around her home changed during the day, so she counted the number of vehicles passing by during five-minute intervals in the morning, the afternoon and the evening. After several days she had several counts of traffic flow for each period: a morning batch, an afternoon batch and an evening batch. One could introduce many variations on this, depending on the amount of time one had and what was most interesting.

Still another student wanted to figure out what television programmers were up to, so she counted several kinds of things, like the number of commercials for programmes of various types. For example, she would watch several documentaries, count the number of commercials in each one, and note several counts; or she would watch police dramas and get several counts of the number of commercials on each of them. Thus she got a documentary batch, a police story batch, etc. (and if anyone complained about all this TV, she was doing her statistics homework!).

Another thing that might be useful is to find out 'where all the money goes'. Carry around a little notebook and jot down the amount of every purchase and the sort of thing it is for (food, stationery, etc.).

These possible mini-studies bring up a point not obvious for the suicide data: interpreting batch data often includes comparisons to background knowledge, whether or not the comparison is explicit. Suppose the student recording television commercials found three in a half hour; is that many or few? Few if our comparison is with North American commercial TV; many if it is with public service TV. We all have a surprisingly large range of knowledge about how big things tend to be, so that we can recognize unusually sized things easily: a four-pound baby is tiny, while a four-pound diamond is too large to be credible. For some kinds of data like suicide rates, few of us have much feeling for size at first. Is a rate of 10 per 100 000 a lot or a little? Who knows? But looking at batch data quickly changes this. We have already seen that Hungary's rates are high and Spain's low, because we have seen these rates in comparison with others. So if you have background comparison knowledge, use it. If you are starting fresh, you will soon learn from the data.

2 Female Suicide Rates
We will not be working with the female rates in the text, so you can work on them for the next several chapters. Pick a couple, put these batches into all the various kinds of stems and leaves, and discuss what you see. For the next chapter's homework you will need all five batches in comparable stem-and-leaf format.

3 Homicide Rates
The data to be analysed are homicide victim rates for females and for males, for 18 nations, with rates averaged over 1980–1984 to help to even out accidental fluctuations from year to year (Table 2.14). For example, the Canadian female rate of 1.66 means that 1.66 out of every 100 000 Canadian women were homicide victims on average every year, for the years 1980–1984.

Table 2.14   Female and male homicide victim rates 1980–1984

	Females	*Males*
Australia	1.42	2.40
Austria	1.34	1.68
Belgium	0.97	1.97
Canada	1.66	3.42
Denmark	1.10	1.24
England and Wales	0.60	0.70
Finland	1.34	4.20
France	0.86	1.42
West Germany	1.10	1.34
Ireland	0.65	1.43
Italy	0.70	3.15
Japan	0.80	1.10
Netherlands	0.58	1.16
New Zealand	1.02	1.66
Norway	0.86	1.50
Sweden	0.88	1.60
Switzerland	1.06	1.28
USA	4.20	15.48

Source: World Health Organization.

General Comments on Homework

All homework assignments have two parts: technical work and discussion. They are equally important and they both must be done. This time, for example, you must get used to the basic batch technique: assorted stems and leaves. But you don't just stem-and-leaf the numbers and stop! Look at the display, think about them, write down the things you see (main features of the data) and the things you think of (questions, speculations, hypotheses). The discussion in the chapter gives you some idea of the sort of thing we mean, although your discussion will naturally stress the data more and the technique less than ours has to.

Numerical work alone is boring for you, indigestible for the reader and ambiguous for the marker (do you really understand what you have done?). For everyone's sake, always discuss.

3
Understanding Numerical Summaries

We have now seen how the stem and leaf can help us get a quick feel for one or two batches of data. Unfortunately, when we have more batches, the amount you can see is limited in some ways. Two stem-and-leaf arrays can be seen if arrayed back-to-back, as in Table 2.8. However, it is difficult to see beyond a mere jumble of numbers if three or more data sets have to be compared, and the interesting problems often involve many batches. For example, Table 3.1 gives suicide rates for all five age groups for males rather than just the oldest and youngest. There are five batches altogether now; that is a lot of numbers and we may have difficulty coping with them. Table 3.2 does about as well as we can do with the tools of the last chapter alone: we have used a single common stem followed by the five columns of leaves side by side. It is possible to see a few things in this maze of numbers if you work at it, but it is hard work and it is difficult to be sure of what you are doing.

We want to have some simple ways of comparing a lot of batches easily. In this chapter we will learn how to compare some important features of batches very easily using numerical summaries. A series of summary numbers can be seen easily while a series of data sets can't. Of course, we can only summarize after deciding what we want summarized; that is, after deciding what features of the batches are important enough to put in a summary and what can be left aside as mere detail. Now, what are some of the major features of batches? Our explorations of the suicide data in the previous chapter suggested several things that are likely to be of interest for many different kinds of data:

1 Level, or how big the numbers are 'on average'. For example, it looked like suicide rates for older males were higher than those for younger males.
2 Spread, or how compact the batches are. For example, the rates for older males appear to be more spread out, more different from one another, than are the rates for younger males.
3 Clumping, or how the batch is clustered into groups of numbers. For example, for the rates of the 25–34 age group in Table 2.5, 12 of the 15 rates are on only two stems.

4 Shape, or how the numbers are distributed. Do they trail off nearly evenly above and below the middle or do they trail off primarily in one direction? For example, the older batch tended to trail upward.

Table 3.1 1971 mortality rates from suicide for males (rates per 100 000; rounded to nearest unit)

	1971				
	25–34	35–44	45–54	55–64	65–74
Canada	22	27	31	34	24
Israel	9	10	10	14	27
Japan	22	19	21	31	49
Australia	29	40	52	53	69
France	16	25	36	47	56
Germany	28	35	41	49	52
Hungary	48	65	84	81	107
Italy	7	8	11	18	27
Netherlands	8	11	18	20	28
Poland	26	29	36	32	28
Spain	4	7	10	16	22
Sweden	28	41	46	51	35
Switzerland	22	34	41	50	51
UK (England and Wales)	10	13	15	17	22
USA	20	22	28	33	37

Table 3.2 Stems and leaves for data in Table 3.1

	25–34	35–44	45–54	55–64	65–74
10					7
9					
8			4	1	
7					
6		5			9
5			2	310	621
4	8	01	161	79	9
3		54	166	4123	57
2	22986802	9275	18	0	4778822
1	60	0913	01805	4867	
0	9784	87			

stem: tens   *leaf:* units

5 Unusual numbers, or numbers that seem rather high or rather low compared to the rest (like Hungary).

If we could satisfactorily summarize these features of batches, broad comparisons of batches would be greatly simplified. We would still be interested in some details, and would expect to return to them from time to time, but a good summary would do for a first look and would also, by implication, tell us which details need special attention because the summary describes them poorly.

As it will turn out, the numerical summaries we will use can do a very good job of summarizing level, spread and unusual values. They will not tell us much about clumping; fortunately that is one thing we can see pretty easily from stems and leaves.

In this chapter we will deal with ways to summarize level and spread. The next chapter will show how these summaries can be made more effective using graphic techniques, and the last two chapters of this section will describe techniques and strategies for working with shape.

Level: The 'Centre' of the Data

Perhaps the single most important feature of data description is the batch *level*: where the batch is centred. Among other things, this provides a quick best guess about the magnitude of values a given process might generate. For example, 'miles per gallon' (or the equivalent in litres and kilometres) gives a best guess as to how far you can travel on a given amount of fuel. Level is also a familiar idea that people use, in a rough-and-ready way, all the time. Comments like 'men are stronger than women' are typical. This doesn't mean that all men are stronger than all women – in fact, the two batches overlap substantially. But men are stronger 'on average'. The general idea of level or centre is familiar, but many people don't realize that this general notion includes many different kinds of levels. For any batch, there are different centres for different purposes. Here we describe four especially useful kinds of level, starting with two familiar ones and then discussing two that are less familiar but very handy.

The Mean and the Median

The most familiar, most frequently used level is the *mean*. To find the mean of a batch, add up the values of all the observations and divide by the number of observations (the *count* of the batches, whose symbol is N). For example, the mean of the 25–34 batch in Table 3.1 is:

$$\frac{\text{total}}{\text{count}} = \frac{22 + 9 + 22 + 29 + \ldots + 22 + 10 + 20}{15} = \frac{299}{15} = 19.933\ldots$$

By the way, how precisely should we report figures like these? For example, should we make this mean 20, 19.9, 19.93, 19.933, or what? As a general rule of thumb, we suggest: keep as many significant digits as there are in the data, or perhaps one more. Here we used numbers with at most two significant digits (units and tens) so the mean would be calculated as 20 or as 19.9. More precision (e.g. 19.93) is really fake precision, since the data themselves were not this precise. Less precision might be too crude here, although it might be acceptable for another data set. Well, what about 19.9 versus 20? This is not too important as a rule; we will sometimes do one thing and sometimes another. When you get to Table 3.3, you will find various levels reported with different degrees of precision: with no decimal places, some with quarters, some with one decimal place. This is of no consequence, since the table has all the information we need for our exploratory work. If you want a guideline (your common sense is really enough) you might try starting analysis with one more significant digit than the data and drop this extra digit if and when you can see you don't need it. If you are already familiar with significant digits and scientific notation, read on. If not, this is a good time to learn, so turn to the section on significant digits in Appendix A.

There is another technical detail worth noting since things like it often crop up for rates. We just found the mean of the rates of countries, not the mean rate of suicide of men in the youngest age group in all countries. To find the overall rate per 100 000 men we would have to allow for the fact that some of these countries have more people than others. Israel with a fairly low rate has many fewer people than Hungary with a high rate but when we average the rates we treat them as if they had the same population base.

The mean is just one kind of level, good for some purposes and not so good for others. For confirmatory work the mean is very useful indeed. It uses all the data; it is easily understood, although sometimes tedious to compute by hand; and it has mathematical properties which are very convenient for confirmatory statistical problems. However, we don't like the mean for exploratory purposes because it is more laborious than other levels and, more importantly, it is not resistant. 'Not resistant' means that a few wild observations or errors can affect its magnitude dramatically. To illustrate, consider the kingdom of Frammistan in which the 999 peasants earn $1 per year while the king collects $1 000 000 000 per year. The mean income of our mythical Frammistanis is more than one million dollars per year, a figure which misleads because it is not even approximately true of anyone in the society.

We might do better here by asking not, 'how much do people earn on the average?' but rather, 'how much does the *average person* earn?' We would then rank the 1000 inhabitants of Frammistan and take the middle observation; here this is the mean of the 500th and 501st, or $1, which gives us a better indication of the income level. This measure is called the *median*, symbolized Md. (By the way, this example is really not as far-fetched as all that; there are many nations in which the top 10 per cent have a share of the total income many times as large as that of the bottom 90 per cent. Kuwait before the invasion is one example.)

The median is the number such that half the batch is greater and half is smaller than it; if we have an odd number of cases, there is a middle one and that is the median, while if there is an even number of cases, there are two middle ones, and the median is half-way between them. Finding the median can be a nuisance if the batch is not ordered, but it is very easy from stems and leaves like those in Table 3.2. For the youngest group, for example, the number N of figures in the batch is 15, so we want the eighth largest or eighth smallest number (the same thing); we just start at the top (or bottom) of the stem and leaf and count towards the centre in order of magnitude (not in the order the numbers are written) until we get to the eighth largest or smallest, here 22. On checking, we see that seven of the batch values are bigger than this and seven are smaller.

Of course, you want to know how to remember how far to count in! That is the only problem in computing a median. It is easy enough if you use a mnemonic device of Tukey's, *grows* to. A number that is not an integer grows to the next higher integer; e.g. 8.25, 8.875 all grow to 9. On the other hand, any integer grows to itself plus one-half; e.g. 8 grows to 8.5, 13 grows to 13.5, etc. Now the median observation (Md) is the observation that $N/2$ grows to. We just did an example for odd numbers: for the suicide batches $N = 15$ so

$$\frac{N}{2} = \frac{15}{2} = 7.5 \to 8$$

(the little arrow means 'grows to'). What about even numbers? Take, for example, the batch

$$3 \quad 7 \quad 16 \quad 19$$

Here N is 4. So

$$\frac{4}{2} = 2 \to 2\frac{1}{2}$$

We count in 2½ from top or bottom and find ourselves half-way between the second and third values, or 7 and 16; their mean,

$$\frac{7 + 16}{2} = \frac{23}{2} = 11.5$$

is the median of the batch. Again the rule works: half the values are above 11.5, half below.

The median is a very familiar level, probably the commonest after the mean. How do the two compare? The mean uses all the information but at the cost of occasionally being 'victimized' by stray observations. To guard against this, the median sets aside both the upper and lower halves of the data, taking only the middle one or two. This makes it very resistant. For example, the means and medians of the five suicide batches are listed in Table 3.3, which also sums up other things we will get to shortly. Note that the mean is higher than the median for four of the five batches; and it is especially higher for the oldest

Table 3.3   Comparison of the levels of five suicide batches

	25–34	35–44	45–54	55–64	65–74
Mean	19.9	25.7	32.0	36.4	42.3
Md	22	25	31	33	35
Tri	20¼	24	29.5	33.5	37¼
Mid	19.7	24.1	30.1	35.1	36.4
q_U	28	35	41	50	52
q_L	9	11	15	18	27

batch. If you look back at Table 3.2 you soon see that the mean is overreacting to the rates for Hungary; the rates for Hungary are so extreme, so large compared to the rest, that the mean is being pulled up a lot by this single value. Of course, the median is not affected; it reflects what happens in the middle of the batches, ignoring what happens at the extremes. This resistance to extreme cases is desirable in exploration, where you often use data of erratic quality. The median uses very few of the data and yet loses less information than you might think; if the data are free of strays then the median generally gives results much like the mean, while if the data do have erratic values then the median often fits our intuitive impression of overall level better than the mean does. Nevertheless, the median does force us to rely on one or two observations, a somewhat uncomfortable situation.

We would like a measure that uses more of the data without relying much on the extreme observations. In the next part of the chapter we present two measures of the level that gives us this sort of compromise.

Middle Means

The basic strategy for using more data than the median while avoiding extremes is to take levels from the usually more reliable middle half of the data. This strategy is one version of the more general approach of trimming off some part of the less reliable extremes. You may well be familiar with one sort of trimmed level in common use, especially in sports like gymnastics or diving. For example, a gymnast's performance is judged by several experts; the highest and the lowest judgements are thrown out, and the score is the mean of the remaining judgements. Often this keeps a gymnast from being unduly penalized because one judge loathes the performance for idiosyncratic reasons; equally, the procedure sometimes keeps a competitor from being unduly rewarded because one judge rates the performance extremely highly.

For our trimming, we want a procedure that will be generally useful for various kinds of data and sizes of batches; trimming off the highest and lowest quarters usually works out well. So we need to know how to find the *quartiles*, those values that quarter a batch. (Sometimes you see two analogous terms: deciles, which divide a batch in tenths, and percentiles, which divide a batch in hundredths.) You already know one quartile, the median, or second quartile, which divides the top two quarters from the bottom two. To find the other two quartiles we break the top and bottom halves of the batch in half again, and it is easy to do this by using the concept grows to. We find what $N/4$ grows to; counting in that amount from the top gives the upper quartile, counting in that amount from the bottom gives the lower quartile. Here is how it works for the youngest suicide batch.

$$N = 15, \text{ so } \frac{N}{4} = \frac{15}{4} = 3\tfrac{3}{4} \rightarrow 4$$

we are at the fourth largest and fourth smallest values. From the stem and leaf we quickly find these numbers: 28 and 9. See how they divide up the batch.
    Counting in:

1	48	
2	29	
3	28	
4	28	Upper quartile = q_U
	26	
	22	
	22	Middle quartile = median = Md
	20	
	16	
	10	
4	9	Lower quartile = q_L
3	8	
2	7	
1	4	

If it happens to be a multiple of 4 then q_U and q_L may not be values in the batch. For example, if we have

$$2 \quad 5 \quad 7 \quad 10 \quad 13 \quad 17 \quad 18 \quad 20$$
$$\qquad \uparrow \qquad\qquad\qquad\qquad \uparrow$$
$$\qquad q_L \qquad\qquad\qquad\qquad q_U$$

then

$$\frac{N}{4} = \frac{8}{4} = 2 \rightarrow 2\tfrac{1}{2}$$

the quartiles are half-way between the second and third values counting in from each end; here

$$q_L = \frac{5+7}{2} = 6 \text{ and } q_U = \frac{17+18}{2} = 17.5$$

The summary Table 3.3 gives q_U and q_L for all five suicide batches.

Now that we know how to find batch middles we can discuss the middle means. The easiest middle mean to compute is the *trimean*, which just uses what we have already found:

$$\text{trimean} = \text{TRI} = \frac{q_U + q_L + 2\,\text{Md}}{4}$$

For the 25–34 age group we know q_U, q_L and Md so the trimean is

$$\text{TRI} = \frac{28 + 9 + 2(22)}{4}$$
$$= \frac{81}{4} = 20\frac{1}{4}$$

The trimean uses more data than the median by including the upper and lower quartiles, which give extra information about the location of the centre, while still avoiding extremes. The trimean weights the median doubly because the median is, after all, close to the centre and the centre is what we are after. Obviously this weight is slightly arbitrary: for example, we could easily have decided to weight the median triply and divide by five. However, this formula will turn out to have some desirable properties, is quick and easy to compute, and gives a measure that combines many of the nice properties of the mean and median.

There are other middle levels, the best known being the *interquartile mean*, or the mean of the numbers between the upper and lower quartiles. It is the mean of the middle half of the data, excluding the quartile values themselves. Using the 25–34 batch again,

$$\text{interquartile mean} = \frac{26 + 22 + 22 + 22 + 20 + 16 + 10}{7}$$
$$= \frac{138}{7} = 19.7$$

Since the interquartile mean is just the mean of the middle, Tukey suggests the less cumbersome title *midmean*, or MID for short. There is just one little thing to be careful about when using this straightforward measure: repeated values. Some or none of the repeated values may be included in the calculation, depending on how many are needed to get half the data (the middle half) into the midmean. For the suicide batches, each of the extreme quarters has four observations, leaving seven for the middle half. In the 25–34 batch, q_U is 28 and 28 occurs twice; neither 28 is used in the midmean because the middle has seven values without the 28s. By contrast, in the 45–54 batch q_U is 41, 41 occurs twice, and one of the 41s must be included in the midmean to get a full seven cases in the middle. With a little practice, you can easily set aside top and bottom quarters from the stem and leaf.

The midmean is somewhat more work than the trimean while giving very similar results (as you can see in Table 3.3), so in general we prefer the trimean.

On the other hand, the midmean is fairly well known under its ponderous name 'interquartile mean'. It is thus a good level if you want to explore levels using a resistant measure and then easily communicate your result to a wide audience.

Both midmean and trimean resist the effects of wild values, use the usually more stable central values, are easy to compute and give about the same results as the more comprehensive arithmetic mean when the data are well-behaved, that is, when the data are smooth and there are no wild outliers, like the Hungary rates here.

All four levels can be compared for the suicide batches by looking at Table 3.3. All three resistant measures (Md, TRI, MID) give similar results, with the trimean and midmean perhaps closest together (they usually are). The mean is clearly different from the resistant trio: again, the mean is much affected by Hungary's unusually high rates. These differences are important because the numbers give us different first impressions of what is happening in the data, once we get past the obvious common message that suicide rates increase with age. The mean seems to be saying that suicide rates increase at about the same rate as we pass from one age group to another except between the 45–54 group and the 55–64 group, where the increase is slightly lower. The more resistant measures appear to show a relatively large increase from 35–44 to 45–54, and a relatively small increase from 55–64 to 65–74. The rates are high and similar for both older groups. This could lead us to speculate that retirement at age 65 may not be as important a factor in suicide as we had suggested earlier. On the other hand, the greater difference from 35–44 to 45–54 might reflect the fact that the older group is exposed to certain difficulties that the younger group does not face; the older men are more likely to lose their jobs with little chance of re-employment, more likely to get ill, less likely to have children at home. The resistant levels give a sensible picture and one that is true to more of the data, while the mean seems to be reflecting the extreme nature of a single piece of the data (Hungary) too much.

All types of levels have their advantages; which to use is a matter of judgement. If you have trouble deciding, try two or three and see what happens. All the levels have problems with some sorts of data; even the resistant measures are not always best. If you do meet some batches to which the exploratory levels do not do justice, remember that many of the rules for the exploratory levels (for example, the weighting of the median when calculating the trimean) are a bit arbitrary and can be adjusted to suit particular needs. You should feel free to make such adjustments but, if you do, make them consistently for any batches that you want to compare. And, of course, tell your reader (and yourself: you might forget) what you are doing.

Get to know all four levels, so you can use the best one for each job; no single measure can be best for all purposes.

Hiatus: Some Necessary Symbols

Since the mean is easy, we use it as a vehicle to introduce some important and recurring symbols. We symbolize our batch values with x, their mean with $\bar{x}$ (read 'x bar'), and the rule for finding the mean with

$$\bar{x} = \frac{\sum_{i=1}^{N} x_i}{N}$$

which is just

$$\text{mean} = \frac{\text{total all the } x \text{ values}}{\text{count}}$$

as above. Here is a glossary of these symbols.

x represents the elements of a set of numbers, here the batch (definitely *not* 'the unknown').

$\bar{x}$ is the mean of x.

i the subscript i is an *index number*; if there are ten observations in a batch, i stands for the numbers 1, 2 ... 10. These index numbers have nothing to do with the value of the x referred to (any more than a house number tells you anything about the residents' age), but rather specify which of the xs is being referred to.

$\sum_{i=1}^{N} x_i$ means 'add up all the x_is, where i goes from 1 to N'. In other words

$$\sum_{i=1}^{N} x_i \text{ means } x_1 + x_2 + \ldots + x_N.$$

N stands for the number of x values that we have, the count.

Most of the time we will just want to add up a bunch of numbers called x so we simplify by leaving out the is that distinguish one x value from another, thus:

$$\text{mean of } x = \bar{x} = \frac{\sum x}{N}$$

The Spread of the Data

As we have seen, knowing the approximate centre of a batch of data is extremely useful. Clearly, this by itself is not enough. We would also like to know something about the amount the batch can be expected to vary about this centre, the *spread* of the data. When spread is low, the level can provide a very good guess; when spread is high, knowing level won't help a lot in predicting any particular outcome. You may have heard the old saw about the man who drowned in a river where the average depth was one foot. Many students have trouble understanding spread at first, confusing it with level. A brief discussion may be useful. Consider a class going through an intensive training programme, say in social work. At the time when they enter the programme, their individual attitudes towards anti-poverty legislation, for example, might be very diverse. At the conclusion of their training, their attitudes could well be more similar to each other – this sort of 'homogenization' being a common result of a training programme. But the average attitude in the group on this topic, the level, might well be the same after training as before. A before–after, back-to-back stem and leaf for this fictitious group might look like this:

Before   After
Training   Training

$$
\begin{array}{r|l}
\text{XXX} & \\
\text{XXXX} & \text{XXXXXXX} \\
\text{XXXXX} & \text{XXXXXXXX} \\
\text{XXX} &
\end{array}
$$

Thus, training has affected the spread but not the level. Or consider a firm that hires men for all sorts of positions, but only hires women for low level clerical jobs. Here, both level and spread of women's incomes would be lower than males'.

Males   Females

$$
\begin{array}{r|l}
\text{XXXX} & \\
\text{XXXXX} & \\
\text{XXXXX} & \\
\text{XXX} & \text{X} \\
\text{XX} & \text{XXXX} \\
\text{XX} & \text{XXXXX}
\end{array}
$$

In short these two qualities are very different from one another and so need to be thought about separately.

Once again, there is a variety of measures available. One extremely simple and well-known measure is the *range* of a batch: the smallest number subtracted from the largest. For the 25–34 batch, a glance at the stem and leaf shows

range $= 48 - 4 = 44$

We label the smallest number X_L (lower extreme) and the largest number X_U (upper extreme) so another definition of range is:

range $= X_U - X_L$

The range is very easy to find; unfortunately it is not very resistant because it is based on precisely those values that are most likely to be erratic: the extremes.

A good combination of resistance, ease of calculation and use of a reasonable amount of the data is again probably to be found in the middle of the distribution. We define the *midspread*, or spread of the middle, to be the difference between the upper and lower quartiles (*dq* for short).

midspread $= dq = q_U - q_L$

For the 25–34 batch, $dq = 28 - 9 = 19$. In more standard language this measure labours under the title 'interquartile range', which is descriptive but cumbersome. The midspread or, alternatively, difference of quartiles, dq, is the principal exploratory measure of spread that we will use.

When we turn to confirmatory statistics, we will find another spread measure to be important, the *variance*. Very roughly speaking, the variance measures spread by looking at how much the batch values differ from their mean. We can see exactly what happens by following through the example in Table 3.4. The first column gives x, the batch values, again for the 25–34 batch. From this we obtain the mean $\bar{x}$, which we earlier found to be 19.9. Next we want to know how much the batch values differ from $\bar{x}$; that is the next column, $x_1 - \bar{x}$, or each of the x values minus the mean (these are often called 'deviations' from the mean). So far so good; the more spread out the batch is, the bigger these deviations will be, so we can measure spread by some summary of the deviations' sizes. Would the mean of the deviations be suitable? No: it is easy to demonstrate that the deviations must add up to zero. Well, we could get rid of the minus signs. One way is to drop them and then take the mean of the results, which gives us the 'mean of the absolute deviations' (MAD). The MAD is a measure of spread, but one hardly ever seen outside of statistics books. The preferred method for handling minus signs is to square the

Table 3.4 Work sheet for variance computation, 25–34 batch: long method

x_i	$x_i - \bar{x}$	$(x_i - \bar{x})^2$
48	28.1	789.61
29	9.1	82.81
28	8.1	65.61
28	8.1	65.61
26	6.1	37.21
22	2.1	4.41
22	2.1	4.41
22	2.1	4.41
20	0.1	0.01
16	−3.9	15.21
10	−9.9	98.01
9	−10.9	118.81
8	−11.9	141.61
7	−12.9	166.41
4	−15.9	252.81

$\bar{x} = 19.9$	$\sum(x_i - \bar{x}) = 0.5^*$	$\sum(x_i - \bar{x})^2 = 1846.95$

$$\text{Variance} = \frac{\sum(x_i - \bar{x})^2}{N - 1} = \frac{1846.95}{14} = 131.93$$

* Theoretically, this sum should be zero. We can use this to check our calculations. Here the sum is 0.5, which is within rounding error of zero; so our calculations are probably correct.

deviations, getting the third column of the work sheet Table 3.4. Our final step is to find the overall level of these square deviations:

$$\text{VAR} = \frac{\sum(x_i - \bar{x})^2}{N - 1}$$

This is just the mean of the squared deviations (except for the $N - 1$ instead of N in the denominator; we use $N - 1$ because, for technical reasons, it is better than N in just about all applications of the variance).

The variance is a very important measure with some good points and some bad points. First the good news. The variance uses all the values in a batch whereas the range and dq use only two; the variance is broadly based. From a mathematician's point of view, the variance uses all the observations in a very simple way; only MAD (the mean absolute deviation) could be simpler, and MAD has unappealing mathematical properties. The variance has more appealing properties that make the construction of confirmatory statistics easier. The variance therefore plays a major role in the most popular confirmatory statistics and we want to know it well.

And now for the bad news: from an exploratory point of view, the variance is terrible: it is not resistant, it is tedious to compute and it is not very intuitive. The variance is even less resistant than the mean because it is even more affected by extremes. Look at Table 3.4 again. The extreme cases like 48 and 4 are farthest from the mean, so their deviations are the largest ones; when these values are squared they become extremely big. The value 48 alone contributes 789.61 to the total of 1846.9 for $\sum (x_1 - \bar{x})^2$: over a third from just one case! Any unusually high or low values can really blow up the variance.

The variance is more work than the range and dq, each of which requires only a subtraction once the batch is ordered. Well, if you must do this by hand, at least we can minimize the computational work by using a fast form of the variance formula:

$$\text{VAR} = \frac{\sum x^2 - (\sum x)^2/N}{N - 1}$$

This is not as forbidding as it may look if you have been away from basic algebra for a while. The numerator of the expression has two parts, each easy to compute:

$\sum x^2$ says: first square each of the x values, then add all the squares up.

$(\sum x)^2/N$ says: first add up all the x values, then square the total, and finally divide the squared total by N.

Finally, we remarked that the variance is low on intuitive appeal as well as on resistance and computational speed. Somehow you can't *see* a variance. With the dq or the range, you can see the spread right in the batch; thus the spread has a direct and obvious meaning. But the variance puts a number of things together (all the N deviations from the mean) in a number of steps (the deviations are squared, then their level is taken) which goes beyond what visual

Table 3.5 Some properties of the standard deviation

A: Lack of resistance

Batch 1	Batch 2	Batch 3	Batch 4	Batch 5

	Batch 1	Batch 2	Batch 3	Batch 4	Batch 5
9					2
8				2	
7			2		
6		2			
5	2				
4	37	37	37	37	37
3	926	926	926	926	926
2	428	428	428	428	428
1	39	39	39	39	39
0	5	5	5	5	5

stem: tens   *leaves:* units

$sd = 14.2$	15.8	17.7	19.9	22.2
$\bar{x} = 30.0$	30.8	31.7	32.5	33.3

Increases

sd	1.6	1.9	2.2	2.3
$\bar{x}$	0.8	0.9	0.8	0.8

Md is 30 and *dq* is 20.5 for all 5 batches

B: Independence from mean
Batch 1 Plus 100

15	2
14	37
13	926
12	428
11	39
10	5

$sd = 14.2$
$\bar{x} = 130.0$

C: Why 'standard' deviation
Batch 1

5	2
4	37
3	926
2	428
1	39
0	5

$\bar{x}$ sd

↑
Includes 24,
28, 32, 36

$sd = 14.2$
$\bar{x} = 30.0$

Batch 1 – all doubled

10	4
9	4
8	8
7	82
6	4
5	6
4	84
3	8
2	6
1	0

sd $\bar{x}$

Includes 48,
56, 64, 72

stems: tens
leaves: units

$sd = 28.4$
$\bar{x} = 60.0$

imagination can handle. Most people never visualize the variance, they just get used to it.

Part of the problem is that the variance can't be readily compared to the numbers it is based on, because the variance is in different units: the data units squared. We can overcome that hurdle easily enough by taking the square root of the variance, thus getting us back to the data units. This slightly more intuitive measure of spread is the *standard deviation*:

$$sd = \sqrt{\text{VAR}},$$

often further abbreviated

$$s = \sqrt{s^2}$$

For the 25–34 batch we know that $\text{VAR} = 131.92$ so sd is the square root of this or 11.5. We can use the standard deviation to talk about the relationship of a value to the rest of a batch.

For now, we will give you a few examples illustrating important aspects of how the standard deviation works. Then we will discuss sd, dq and range for the suicide batches. First consider Table 3.5. In part A we see four batches that are just the same except for one value, the X_U, which increases by equal amounts from batch to batch. The mean increases too, of course; we have seen that the mean is not resistant. But the standard deviation increases faster and faster; it is even more sensitive than the mean. By the way, we have not invented a bizarre example with no practical importance: look at the oldest suicide batch. It is not at all uncommon to find batches with values that look far more unusual than the X_U in batch 5 of Table 3.5A (note that the exploratory tools like Md and dq are not affected at all by X_U's behaviour here).

Let's get a little more feeling for the standard deviation's behaviour by looking at part B of Table 3.5. Here we have just changed the level of batch 1 from part A by adding 100 to everything. The mean increases by 100, but the standard deviation does not change at all. This makes sense; the numbers are no more or less spread out than before, they are merely higher up. Level and spread are separate issues. Finally, part C of Table 3.5 gives some idea of why the sd is called the *standard* deviation. Part C shows batch 1 again and batch 1 with all values doubled. The sd and $\bar{x}$ also double. But the sd continues to do the same job. We have marked the amount of the standard deviation (one sd) around the mean for both batches (e.g. for the original batch 1 the square bracket covers the mean (30), plus and minus half the sd, a range of one sd altogether). The four values in the middle of the batch are those within half a standard deviation of the mean; and this is true whether we use the original figures or the doubled ones. We can think of 'one standard deviation' as a unit of spread that will mean the same thing for any batch. We will develop this idea further in the next chapter when we talk about standardization.

Now let us turn to a comparison of different spread measures in action by looking at the midspread, range and standard deviation for our suicide rate batches. We could try to compare these spread measures' values for one batch, like the 25–34 batch:

$$\text{standard deviation} = 11.5$$
$$\text{range} = 44$$
$$\text{midspread} = 19$$

But a moment's thought shows that we can't compare these numbers the way we compared the levels. All the levels were trying to locate the same thing, the centre of the data, and were easily comparable, but the spreads are doing rather different things; for example, the range can't possibly be smaller than the midspread: it covers more ground. But we can compare the spread measures in action by computing each of them for all five suicide batches and considering the messages each of them sends.

Table 3.6 gives the standard deviations, ranges and midspreads of all five batches of suicide rates. Let's look first at the broad relationships among the spread measures. The range is always the largest. By comparison, the dq and sd are in roughly the same ballpark, with the dq a bit larger. The sd can be larger than the dq; this usually means there are some very atypical values in the batch, as in batch 5 of Table 3.5A, where the sd is larger than the dq and there is one quite unusual-looking upper value.

Now let's see what the three measures tell us about the five suicide batches' behaviour. As we go from the youngest batch to the oldest batch, the *range* increases at every step except from 45–54 to 55–64, increasing faster and faster;

Table 3.6   A comparison of the range, dq and sd for male suicide rates

	25–34	35–44	45–54	55–64	65–74
10					7
9					
8			4	1	
7					
6		5			9
5			2	013	126
4	8	01	116	79	9
3		45	166	4123	57
2	20226889	7259	18	0	4227788
1	06	0139	00158	4678	
0	9784	78			
sd	11.5	15.8	19.9	18.7	23.0
Range	44	58	74	67	85
dq	19	24	26	32	25

the *standard deviation* increases at every step but one, increasing about the same amount each time except for the step from 45–54 to 55–64, where it declines; the *midspread* increases pretty steadily except for the last step, from 55–64 to 65–74, where the dq drops sharply, and the move into the middle group where the increase is slight. In a very broad way, the messages are the same: spread increases as we go from younger to older batches. But the messages are different in details that may be important. First, why are they different? Because of the different characteristics of the different measures, characteristics we pointed out above. The range was said to be unreliable, being based on just two points and those the most extreme. Sure enough, a hard look at the stems and leaves shows that Hungary, the highest value in all the batches, fluctuates rather briskly and pretty much on its own; Hungary does not look like a good guide to the spread of the batches as a whole. For example, when the range suggests that spread declined in the 55–64 batch, it is only that the rate for Hungary declined in that batch. The standard deviation was said to be non-resistant. Again, we see this in the suicide batches: the standard deviation reflects the behaviour of Hungary in rather the same way as the range, although not as strongly because the standard deviation is based on all the observations rather than just the extremes.

Finally, what about the midspread, dq? It reflects the main body of the data quite well; for example, the middle mass of the oldest batch is a little more compact than that of the second oldest batch, largely because the countries with lower rates for 55–64 have similar but higher rates for 65–74, while those already high for 55–64 increase only slightly for 65–74. Perhaps the transition from 55–64 to 65–74 is not an important one for the higher rate countries; for example, perhaps retirement ages are spread out over those 20 years.

The range is easy but not resistant; the variance and standard deviation are a lot of work and not resistant; the midspread is easy and resistant. We think that the dq is giving us the most accurate and resistant picture of batch behaviour, and this together with its ease of computation make it our preferred measure for exploratory work. You should get to know the variance and standard deviation, though, since you will need them soon for confirmatory work.

Numerical Summaries

Now we are in position to give the quick summaries of important batch features that we promised at the start of the chapter. The discussion so far makes it clear that we need to know how many things there are in a batch (N), what the batch level is, what its spread is and what the extreme values are like; all of these have played a role in our computations and discussions. The most economical way of doing these things is to list N, the quartiles, the median (or another level if you prefer) and the extremes. The dq does not have to be written in because you can read it off from the quartiles. It makes sense to list these summary numbers in the same order in which they occur in the batches, that is:

N the count
X_U upper extreme value
q_U upper quartile
Md   median (or substitute other levels)
q_L lower quartile
X_L lower extreme value

Using the Computer

All this information, and more, can be obtained from MINITAB using the DESCRIBE command. If we wanted to DESCRIBE our five sub-batches of male suicide rates, the procedure and output would be as follows:

```
MTB> DESC C13–17
           N     MEAN  MEDIAN  TRMEAN  STDEV  SEMEAN
C13   15    19.86  21.50    18.89   11.49   2.97
C14   15    25.66  25.20    24.07   15.80   4.08
C15   15    31.97  31.10    29.68   19.97   5.16
C16   15    36.43  32.80    34.71   18.81   4.86
C17   15    42.10  35.10    38.65   23.12   5.97

           MIN    MAX    Q1      Q3
C13    4.10   48.20   9.40    27.60
C14    7.00   65.00  10.60    34.60
C15    9.60   84.10  14.60    41.30
C16   14.00   81.30  17.90    50.30
C17   21.70  107.40  26.60    51.80
MTB>
```

Table 3.7 Numerical summaries for all suicide batches

		Batch			
	25–34	35–44	45–54	55–64	65–74
N	15	15	15	15	15
X_U	48	65	84	81	107
q_U	28	35	41	50	52
Md	22	25	31	33	35
q_L	9	11	15	18	27
X_L	4	7	10	14	22

Numerical summaries provided by MINITAB include some statistics not covered in the text, particularly TRMEAN (this is TRIMMED MEAN *not* TRIMEAN) and SEMEAN. These two terms are explained in the MINITAB Manual if you are interested. At the same time, the MINITAB summary excludes some statistics, particularly the MIDMEAN and TRIMEAN, which would be useful to us.

Table 3.7 gives numerical summaries for all five batches of suicide data. We can see the flow of the batch levels from the medians, we can see the extremes and we can read off spreads quickly. We also get the ingredients of trimeans. Comparisons of the major features of the batches are much easier in the condensed form of Table 3.7 than in the densely detailed form of Table 3.2.

Exploratory and Confirmatory

The following terms are more or less standard:

mean   interquartile range
median   range
                       variance
interquartile mean   standard deviation

There are several ways to define quartiles, and you will find that different books define them differently. All, however, give answers that are very close. We will use an example to demonstrate the difference between hand and MINITAB calculations.

We have the following column of numbers:

C1 = 8   9   10   11   12   13   14   15   15   16   17   20
$N = 13$

To calculate the quartiles by hand:

$$\frac{N}{4} = \frac{13}{4} = 3\tfrac{1}{4} \to 4 \qquad \text{Thus } q_{\text{L}} = 11 \text{ and } q_{\text{U}} = 16$$

MINITAB'S calculations:

$$\frac{N+1}{4} = \frac{14}{4} = 3\tfrac{1}{2} \qquad \text{Thus } q_{\text{L}} = 10.5 \text{ and } q_{\text{U}} = 16.5$$

These two sets of values are slightly different, as you can see. This is because the MINITAB computations are more precise while hand calculations are quicker and approximate, but usually close enough for exploration.

We prefer to use midmean for interquartile mean and midspread for interquartile range because these terms are less cumbersome. The only unusual measure we have introduced is the trimean,

$$\text{TRI} = \frac{q_{\text{U}} + q_{\text{L}} + 2\,\text{Md}}{4}$$

What we call level is usually called central tendency, and spread is often called dispersion.

Tukey uses some different terms, such as *hinge* for upper or lower quartile; thus upper hinge for upper quartile, lower hinge for lower quartile, and H-spread for midspread. Tukey also uses a different way to display the numerical summary; in more recent work he prefers a box display like this:

N Md

q_L q_U
X_L X_U

We find this somewhat less easy to read than the display in this chapter, which is similar to Tukey's earlier (1970) suggestion. Finally, Tukey has some additional terms and display methods that we do not cover here.

HOMEWORK

1 Since the main point of this chapter is to learn about two really fundamental features of batches, level and spread, a good idea for homework is trying out the various level and spread measures on several batches to see them at work. We suggest that you find all the level measures and range and midspread for the female suicide rates in Table 2.1. Find variance and standard deviation for one or two of these batches.

It is fastest to go about this in some orderly way. We suggest working in stages like this:

(a) Stem-and-leaf batches.
(b) Find your numerical summaries and jot them down under the stems and leaves they go with.
(c) Find the various levels (mean, median, midmean, trimean) for each batch, note them down in some neat array, and discuss.
(d) Find the ranges and midspreads of each batch and discuss (again, very easy from step b). Also find the variance and standard deviation by hand for two batches – these are time-consuming so do not do too many.
(e) Discuss any remaining aspects of the data which have caught your eye: behaviour of extremes, batch differences or similarities, or whatever.

2 We have often mentioned the importance of resistance as a characteristic of numerical summaries. To see how different levels are affected by extreme values, calculate mean, median, trimean and midmean, range, midspread and variance for the male suicide data, *without* Hungary. How do these compare to the values calculated including Hungary? Describe the changes in the various levels and discuss why these changes happen.

4
Graphs: Seeing and Setting Aside

In Chapter 3 we saw how quick numerical summaries could help us when we had to compare many batches of data, something for which the stem and leaf is poor. Numerical summaries seemed quite good for this, and we will see in the next few chapters that they can be enormously helpful. However, they lack the visual impact of the stem and leaf. In this kind of situation, we will find that graphical displays can help.

All of the things we have done so far with numerical analyses of batches of data can be done with graphs, usually with less effort. We have seen from stems and leaves how quickly and easily a visual presentation can be digested. In the end, we will see that there are things that can be done better with graphs and things that can be done better with numbers. Often we will find that we can do still better with both; there are no hard and fast rules here. Being a good data analyst involves judgement, but personal preferences are not irrelevant: we will usually want to use those tools that we feel most comfortable with. On the other hand, we should want to be comfortable with as many tools as possible.

First of all we will discuss some general points related to the presentation of any kind of graph: the magnification of the graph (like the magnification of a stem and leaf) and the use of a zero point on a graph's scale. Both these procedural points make differences to the ways that graphs are seen. Then we will show you a special kind of visual presentation, the box plot, which we will find very useful. Finally, we show how to remove level and spread from batches once they have been sufficiently examined through numerical summaries and/or box plots.

The Magnification of a Graph

Graphs often make it possible to communicate complex ideas easily but there are many types of graphs and you must be careful to select the right sort for each job. Often there will be several types that will be useful, each telling a different important thing about your data. One feature of graphs is magnification: the more we blow our graphs up, the more easily we can see details and the less we can see overall features. This point was illustrated for stems and leaves in Chapter 2, where we showed the same batches in three kinds of magnification (Tables 2.5, 2.9 and 2.10). The same point holds for graphs: use the magnification that best shows what you want to see, and use several different magnifications if you want to see different things.

Using the Zero Point

When preparing graphs for public viewing, one should always show the zero point as part of the graph because this gives an immediate feeling for where the data are centred (their level). Otherwise one has to look carefully at the numbers on the scale and a careless reader may get the impression that the bottom line is the zero level.

In Figure 4.1 the medians of the five suicide rate batches are plotted without including the zero point. A quick glance (which is all that most readers give to a graph) gives the impression that the elderly are just lined up on bridges and tall buildings waiting to jump off! But in Figure 4.2, which does include the zero point, the rate of increase with age seems more moderate. For publication purposes it is usually more honest and informative to use the Figure 4.2 format rather than that of Figure 4.1 (Huff, *How to Lie with Statistics*, has an excellent and very entertaining discussion of many kinds of misleading graphs).

The format in Figure 4.1 does have advantages over that in Figure 4.2: it shows details more clearly, since it is a kind of close-up, high-magnification graph. Thus it is a bit easier to see that the increases from 45–54 to 55–64 and

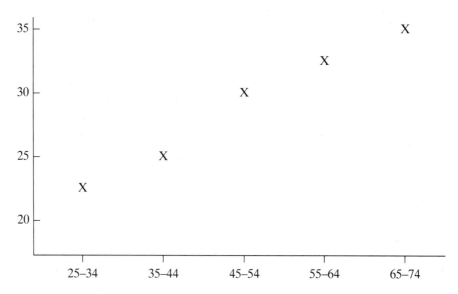

Figure 4.1   Suicide batch medians, no zero point

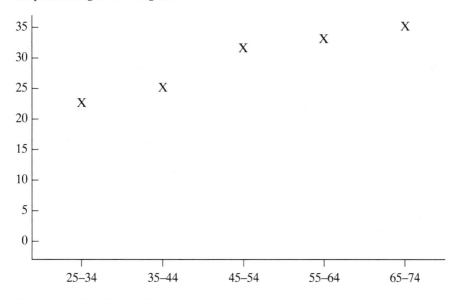

Figure 4.2   Suicide batch medians, zero point included

from 55–64 to 65–74 are the smallest ones while the 35–44 to 45–54 increase is much bigger. With a more complex graph, say one with more points plotted, a close-up would be essential for seeing detail. Often it makes sense to plot with zero point included (so you can see the overall level of the data and their overall pattern, as in Figure 4.2) and also excluded to get a detailed view, as in Figure 4.1. Tukey argues that if we are interested in a detail of a graph, we ought to make a new graph in which this is no longer a detail, but rather is a central feature.

Remember that we are talking here about exploration that is mainly intended for private use. You won't be misled by the detailed graph because you will know how it was constructed and you will already have seen and absorbed the graph with zero point. For public presentation, however, statistics designed to convey information honestly and accurately to a general audience that may be very short of time or expertise are to be preferred. Such an audience may be misled by graphs that focus on particular aspects of data while taking other aspects (like general level) for granted. Exploratory statistics are definitely not intended for these unwary readers but for the analyst committed to probing some set of data deeply. Setting some aspects of the data aside while going deeply into others is the sort of thing an analyst can and must do. When you reach conclusions that should be made public, you switch back to the public mode of presentation. That is not to say that what we are learning here is irrelevant to the public aspect of analysis. Our exploratory skills (like knowing how to find a good magnification and type of display quickly) can be helpful in this public mode too.

The Box Plot

To compare batches quickly, we want graphs that retain important features but leave out unnecessary detail, and we want graphs that can be quickly plotted. The numerical summaries from the previous chapter gave important features of batches in just five numbers, so why not simply plot them? This is the basic idea behind the box and dot plot.

Table 4.1 shows the batch of suicide rates for males 65–74 in a stem and leaf and in a box and dot. As you see, the main trick is putting the important summary numbers (the ends, quartiles and median of the batch) as far apart on the paper as they are in numerical size, which allows us literally to see how far apart they are. To do this we need a scale, off to the left in this case, that is roughly similar to the stem part of the stem and leaf. Now, when we plot the graph, we can use various kinds of marks for different essential features of the batch to display them clearly.

As we have remarked several times, the middle half of the batch is very important: it holds half the data, and the more reliable half. We use a box for

Table 4.1 Plotting the males 65–74 batch

| STEM AND LEAF | BOX AND DOT | BOX PLOT |

this part, called the *midbox*, with lines across the ends of the box marking the upper and lower quartiles and a line in the middle part for the median. Usually it is easiest to draw lines for the median and quartiles and then draw the cross lines to make the box. One advantage of the box is that it makes the size of the midspread very clear: just the length of the box. This takes care of everything but the extremes, which are marked with Xs; the range, of course, is just the distance between the Xs. Thus we can see level and spread at a glance. We can also easily spot upward or downward trends and many sorts of asymmetry. For example, in the box and dot of Table 4.1 the median is not quite in the centre of the midbox; it is closer to the lower quartile than to the upper. This suggests that the data might be trailing off upward, as they are. Of course, all these insights *can* be obtained from the numerical summaries, but they must be looked for, whereas these features in plots *demand* to be seen. Find the point half-way between the ends of the box: half-way between this point and the line for the median is the trimean. It can be done by eye, quickly, which is one reason for defining the trimean the way we do.

All of the required values can be obtained directly from our stem and leaf, needing little computation even with large batches of data. The actual plotting is no trouble, especially if you use tracing paper. You can put some tracing paper over some graph paper, mark off a scale, and then mark off the crucial values. You then remove the graph paper so no guide lines remain to mar the simplicity of the plot. Another trick is simply to lay the tracing paper over the stem and leaf and, using the stem as a *Y* axis, indicate the median, quartiles and extremes directly from the stem and leaf. If we are comparing several batches, we can only use this method if we are using identical stems for each batch. This method also requires stems and leaves with the same stems from top to bottom, evenly spaced. Often we change stems in the middle of a stem and leaf to fit in batch values conveniently; but we almost never do this in a plot. The strength of a plot is its quick visual impact, and the visual impression can be quite misleading if the scale is not consistent throughout the plot.

Can we do better still? Well, we have marked off extreme values, but it would probably also be useful to note those observations straying from the main body of the data, whether or not they are extremes. These strays should be unusual enough to be worth special attention: they should be not only outside the middle half of the data, but well outside it. How far outside? Some rule based on the midspread should be useful, since the midspread tell us how spread out the main body of the data is. Tukey suggests some rules of thumb using the *step*, or one and a half midspreads:

$$\text{step} = 1.5 \, dq$$

Observations of a step or more from the midbox are quite different from most of the batch, while observations of two or more steps from the middle are very different indeed. Hence there are two new terms and some rules of thumb connected with them:

● *Outside observations* are at least one step above the upper quartile, or at

Table 4.2   Checking outliers for oldest batch

Males 65–74

10	7	N	15
9		X_U	107
8		q_U	52
7		Md	35
6	9	q_L	27
5	126	X_L	22
4	9		
3	57		
2	4227788		
1			
0			

$dq = 25$ step = 37.5
outliers: upper threshold = $52 + 37.5 = 89.5$; one upper outlier, 107.
                 lower threshold = $27 - 37.5 = -10.5$; no lower outliers.
far outliers: upper threshold = $52 + 75 = 127$; no upper far outliers.
                 lower threshold = $27 - 75 = -48$; no lower far outliers.

least one step below the lower quartile; we usually call them *outliers* for short.

● *Far outside observations* are at least two steps above the upper quartile or at least two steps below the lower quartile; *far outliers* for short.

Let's work through an example for the 65–74 suicide batch, using the numerical summary and the stem and leaf in Table 4.2. The *dq* is 25, so one step is 1.5(25) or 37.5. An upper outlier must be at least q_U plus a step, or $52 + 37.5 = 89.5$. From the stem and leaf we see there is only one such case, 107 (the rate for Hungary), so there is one upper outlier. Is it 'far out'? Clearly not, but let's check the arithmetic just to be sure; q_U plus two steps is $52 + 2(37.5) = 52 + 75 = 127$, and none of the values in the batch is that big. Thus there is just one upper outlier, which is not 'far out'. How about lower outliers? They would be q_L minus a step or smaller, or at most $27 - 37.5 = -10.5$. Nothing can be that small, since negative suicide rates are impossible, so the batch has no lower outliers and thus no low 'far out' values either.

In practice, this goes very quickly. Table 4.2 shows the kind of work sheet you will probably find handy. The stem and leaf, and the numerical summary along with it, you get routinely. Then comes the essential arithmetic for finding outliers: *dq*, step, q_U + step, and so on. When you have become used to this process you may want to put down even less here, perhaps just which values are outliers or far outliers. Figure 4.3 gives a more pictorial version of finding outliers.

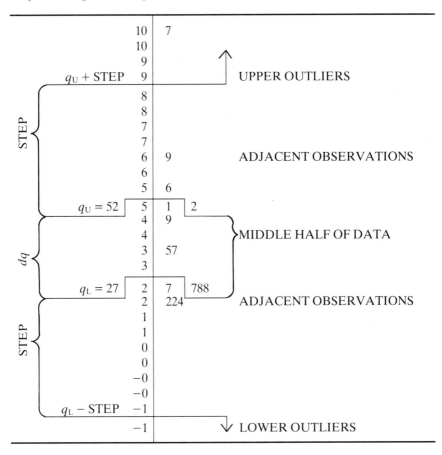

Figure 4.3 Checking for outliers: picture

There is only one other outlier, again upper, for the 45–54 batch (check this). Since outliers should get special attention, we want them to be unusual cases, so it is possible to have a set of several batches with no outliers at all. On the other hand, some batches have several outliers, so don't automatically stop checking as soon as you find one; scan the stem and leaf carefully and make sure you find them all.

Since outliers are uncommon, it pays to look hard at a few more values as well. Let us call those observations that are outside the midbox but not outliers *adjacents*. We may want to identify the largest and smallest of these because they are next to being outliers. In the 65–74 batch we just looked at, the largest adjacent value is 69 and the smallest is 22. Identifying the extreme adjacents in Figure 4.4 helps us to locate Austria and Spain as especially interesting observations.

Both outliers and extreme adjacent values should be clearly identified to make it easier to think about them. This brings us to the *box plot*: a box and dot plot with all outlying and extreme adjacent values marked in, the outlying values labelled in capital letters and the adjacent values in small letters. For example, look at the third part of Table 4.1, a box plot for the batch of rates for males 65–74. It is immediately clear that Hungary is an upper outlier: HUNGARY is in capitals. (Besides, we can see that this value is more than one and a half box-lengths above the upper end of the box, or more than one step above the upper quartile.) We can see that the lower extreme, United Kingdom, is *not* an outlier since its label is in small letters. When we have a far outlier we give it a really eye-catching label, upper case letters with underlining (and maybe a different colour of ink as well, something we cannot show in this text). The labelling system provides an immediate visual summary of the arithmetic we did to find outliers. Moreover, it tells us what the unusual cases *are*, which is often helpful when trying to figure out what makes the cases unusual.

Figure 4.4 gives the box plots of all five suicide batches. For an overall visual comparison of the five batches, the box plot form of Figure 4.4 is clearly a good one. It shows summary values, thus avoiding the too-rich detail of the

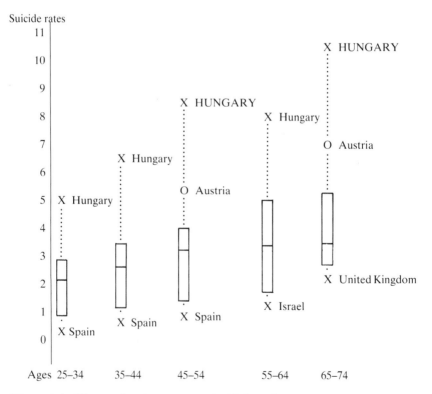

Figure 4.4   Five age batches compared with box plots

stem and leaf; and it shows them in directly visual form, thus avoiding even the little time it takes to interpret a numerical summary.

The schematic plots show the relationship between age and suicide rate level and spread at a glance. They also show the behaviour of the extreme cases, both in raw value and in relation to the rest of the data in their batches. The lower extreme is Spain in the three youngest groups, then Israel and finally the UK, although Spain's rates stay quite low for the latter two groups as well. The lower extreme is never far from the rest of the batch, never an outlier. The upper extreme is always Hungary, whose rates tend to increase with age and to become more unusual (compared to other batch values), the only break in the pattern being the 55–64 age group. Clearly special research on Hungary and perhaps Spain will be needed. Finally, the schematic plots show us shape more easily than other displays. All batches trail up in the extremes, the two oldest batches being the only ones to trail up in the middle, with the other midboxes all trailing down. Perhaps the extremes all trail upwards because the numbers can't go very far down (there is no such thing as a negative suicide rate). A lower limit on a batch's possible values is called a *floor*, and an upper limit a *ceiling*. The presence of floors or ceilings often affects shape.

Schematic plots show off most important batch features very well. But remember that they do not show everything. To be simple enough to show some major features really well, the plot must suppress other features. Probably the most important suppressed feature is clumping. For example, consider Table 4.1 again. The stem-and-leaf version of the 65–74 batch suggests that there may be two clumps, one in the twenties and one higher. The plot only shows that higher rates are, on the whole, more spread out.

Setting Aside Levels

By now we are well equipped with ways to find, look at and interpret two of the main features of batches: level and spread. But there are other features of batches as well, such as shape. These features are usually less striking than level and spread and will not show up too clearly while level and spread differences dominate our batch comparisons. It would be nice to be able to get level and spread differences out of the picture (once we have looked at them thoroughly) in order to see the subtler features more clearly. This order of battle is one that will become very familiar to us:

1 Summarize, display and interpret a big noticeable feature of the data.
2 Get the feature out of the way *once you understand it*.
3 Look for the next most noticeable feature, which will now be easier to see.

In our case the big features so far are levels and spreads. Now, how can we set them aside?

We will illustrate the setting-aside techniques with the suicide batches (but cheer up, we are almost finished with them). First of all, let us think about getting level differences out of the suicide batches. We are not losing the level differences; we have thought about them, and we will keep a note of them. We just don't want to be distracted by them. We can set them aside by literally taking them away: by subtracting them! In more detail, go to the first batch, look up whatever level you want to work with, and subtract that level from every case in the batch. Then go to the second batch, find the same kind of level for it, and subtract it from all the cases. Continue until every batch has had its level taken away.

Now, after subtracting each batch's own level you are left with several new batches of numbers derived from the old ones. What levels do the batches have? All zero! If you start with a batch which has (say) a mean of six, and you subtract six from everything in the batch, you get a new set of numbers whose mean is zero (of course, the median or other levels may not be zero). We now have a set of batches all having the same level. Therefore, contrasting the levels to make inferences about the batches is impossible. Level has been set aside, and we are now free to examine other features of the data.

Remember, if you are going to compare batches you should subtract the same kind of level from all of them. Most often it will be the batch's own level, but sometimes it will be the level of all the batches and sometimes some theoretical level. This last sort of level removal should be familiar to golf fans in particular. Scores in a tournament are often given relative to par, making it easy to compare scores of players who have completed play with others still on the course. Also, this system allows us to see at a glance whether a given score on a hole is good. Four will be a good score, for example, where the par is five,

Table 4.3   Removing a level from male suicide rates, 45–54

Rates	Rates − Md (i.e. 31)				
84	53	8	4	5	3
52	21	7		4	
41	10	6		3	
41	10	5	2	2	1
46	15	4	161	1	005
36	5	3	166	0	550
36	5	2	18	−0	3
31	0	1	01805	−1	036
21	−10	0		−2	110
28	−3				
10	−21		Original data Md = 31 Subtracted		
10	−21				
11	−20				
18	−13				
15	−16				
Md = 31	Md = 0				

meaning a score of minus 1; it will be a poor score where par is three, meaning a score of plus 1. Level removal makes such comparisons possible and easy.

Table 4.3 gives an example using the 45–54 suicide rates. The level subtracted is the median, which is 31. There is a stem and leaf of the original batch, and a stem and leaf of the new batch to show what has changed and what has not. The level has changed: the new median is zero. Has anything else changed? No, nothing else has changed at all. We have put the two stems and leaves side by side to make this really clear, though you have to look closely. The 'before' and 'after' pictures have the same spread, same shape, and in fact are alike in every way except for level. This means that we can take levels out of the picture by subtraction without fearing that we may be taking out something else as well without realizing it. Note a couple of procedural points. The new stem and leaf has been clearly labelled with the level we subtracted: again, we have not lost this level, or thrown it away, just put it aside. Also note that the new stem and leaf has two stems called zero, one positive and one negative. That is because we want stems to cover the same amount throughout a basic

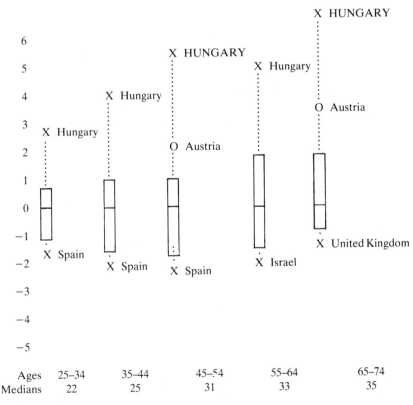

Figure 4.5 Suicide batches with level removed

stem and leaf. In this case the stems cover ten units. Now 0 to 9 is ten units and so is 0 to −9 so we need two zero stems. (Zero itself is a moot case: people usually put it with the plus-zero stem.)

This removal of differences in level by subtraction is easy enough, but since we enjoy being lazy we are pleased to be able to tell you that there is a still easier way to get levels out! Look hard at what we just did with the 45–54 rates and you will see that we simply moved the scale of the stem and leaf until the midpoint was opposite the zero part of the scale. Moving a scale up and down is just like adding and subtracting. This technique works beautifully with box plots and tracing paper: draw a scale on a sheet of tracing paper and draw a faint guideline through the zero level. Lay this paper over a box plot so that the guideline is just over the median line in the box plot. Trace the plot, and there you are: you have the plot for the batch with its median removed. All the other points (upper extreme and so on) are just where they should be. Try it and convince yourself. This approach can be a time-saver when you want to compare several batches after removing levels. You do the same thing for all the batches, remembering to line up each batch's median with the zero-level guide line before tracing.

By the way, the box plot, unlike the stem and leaf, doesn't require two zero entries on the scale. The entry −3 in Table 4.3 would simply be located between 0 and −10 as in any standard plot.

Figure 4.5 shows the results of this subtraction-by-tracing with the five suicide plots of Figure 4.4. The effect is as though we had passed a string through each median and then pulled it taut so that lower batches came up and higher ones went down until all the levels were on a line. Note that the original median of each batch is recorded underneath it. This plot does not make as much difference to the suicide batches as it would to many others, since the medians were quite close to start with, but even so it is now easier to see some things, especially the play of the extremes relative to the median. The pattern of the extremes is not entirely neat, so it could be summarized in various ways. We see a mirror-image pattern: both X_U and X_L first pull away from the batch centre and then come in again. There is one exception, Hungary in the oldest batch. This pattern suggests that intermediate age groups are most spread out. Earlier we saw that the dqs increase with age except for the oldest batch. Why?

We can often get interesting results by reordering the plots according to their original levels. Here, the plots are ordered by level already but often they are not. Ordering by level may show that spread increases with level (as it does for the suicide data up to a point); and sometimes shape is related to level. Sometimes ordering by level shows nothing at all, but it is so easy to do that it is always worth a try.

Standardizing

Spread is another major data feature that, like level, tends to obscure subtler aspects of the data. We have seen that the suicide batches have spreads that increase with age, except for the oldest batch; this pattern is especially clear in Figure 4.5, where the removal of level has lined the boxes up so that they can be very easily compared. Perhaps we were right earlier in suggesting that older men were socialized in periods when the nations were more different. If so, why does the 65–74 batch not fit? Why isn't its dq the largest one instead of being smaller than the dqs for the two next oldest batches? Well, this could be a chance fluctuation; after all, the range fits the pattern of increasing spread with age. Or it could have something to do with retirement; perhaps the difficulties caused by ill health, loss of friends, kin, job, etc. are so severe, and so similar from place to place, that they swamp the cultural differences between older men. In that case it is the extremes that don't quite fit for this batch. We could explore these ideas further, perhaps by seeing whether other rates become more diverse with age and by comparing the services for older people in our 15 countries.

Having obtained some ideas about what the spread might mean, we would like to remove differences in spread, as we did with level, so that we can look more deeply. We cannot do this with subtraction, for we have already seen that increasing or decreasing the numbers in a batch does nothing to the spread. We can equalize spread by simple arithmetic, however: we use division. Specifically, we divide each batch by its own spread (this is parallel to subtracting its own level). We have done this for the 25–34 batch in Table 4.4, removing the midspread ($dq = 19$). The new batch of numbers has a dq of 1.0. This is exactly what will happen with any spread measure using the original data units

Table 4.4   Removing a spread

25–34 batch	Divided by dq = 19
48	2.5
29	1.5
28	1.5
28	1.5
26	1.4
22	1.2
22	1.2
22	1.2
20	1.1
16	0.8
10	0.5
9	0.5
8	0.4
7	0.4
4	0.2
$dq = 28 - 9 = 19$	$dq = 1.5 - 0.5 = 1$
Md = 22	Md = 1.2

(midspread, range or standard deviation, but *not* variance): whatever the spread of the original batch, the new spread will be 1.0 after we divide the data by the old spread. Thus we can equalize the spreads of a number of batches by dividing each by its own value of some chosen spread, getting new batches that all have the same spread: one. If we are doing this by hand, it could get a little tedious, so we usually do not divide every number in every batch, only the summary points and unusual points needed for our schematic plots.

Before leaving Table 4.4 note what does change and what does not. The level is affected; the spread, of course, becomes one; but nothing else is altered. The relative positions of the extreme values, the general shape of the batch and so on are the same. However, unless we have removed differences in level the effects on level can be confusing. For example, in the original data the median for the youngest group (22) is lower than that for the next oldest (25). If we remove the midspread, the median for the youngest group becomes

$$\frac{22}{19} = 1.2 \text{ and the median for the next oldest becomes} \frac{25}{24} = 1,$$

a reversal. We don't want such confusing changes in the order of something as important as level, so we routinely remove differences in spread after level has been set to zero, never differences in spread alone. This treatment of the data is known as *standardization*. Thus, if we want to remove both level and spread, we just find

$$\text{standard score} = \frac{\text{observation} - \text{level}}{\text{spread}}$$

Looking at this simple equation it is easy to show why the standardized data must have zero level and unit spread. Suppose that our level is the mean. If we subtract the mean from everything in the batch we get, in symbols, $x_i - \bar{x}$ and the mean of this is

$$\frac{\sum(x_i - \bar{x})}{N} = \frac{\sum x_i - \sum \bar{x}}{N} = \frac{\sum x_i}{N} - \frac{N\bar{x}}{N}$$
$$= \bar{x} - \bar{x}$$
$$= 0$$

Or suppose that our spread is the midspread. Then after we divide the elements of the batch through by the midspread we get x/dq and the spread of these new values is

$$\text{new } q_U - \text{new } q_L = \frac{\text{old } q_U - \text{old } q_L}{\text{old } dq}$$
$$= \frac{\text{old } dq}{\text{old } dq} = 1$$

The same sort of thing can be done with any type of level and any type of spread. It should be clear, though, that if you standardize using mean and standard deviation you may well get a transformed batch with a median and midspread that are not zero and one, and vice versa. Just in passing: it is possible to get a dq of 0. Should that happen use some other spread measure for standardization, as division by zero is meaningless.

Suppose we use an exploratory kind of standardization on our suicide data. Table 4.5 shows the arithmetic. For example, X_U in the youngest batch the standard score is

$$\frac{48 - 22}{19} = \frac{26}{19} = 1.4$$

Since the arithmetic does take a little time we have standardized only summary numbers plus any additional outliers or adjacent values. The new values do have zero level and unit spread (you may get 1.1 or 0.9 as a spread, but this should just be rounding error).

The standardized summary numbers are plotted in Figure 4.6. Note that the outliers and adjacent values are the same as before. Remember, we have changed level and spread but nothing else, so things other than level and spread are still to be seen and can be seen more easily. This is the best view of shape we have had. We can see that shape fluctuates upward as age increases; the rates for the youngest group trail down in the midbox, the rates for the oldest group trail up. The behaviour of extremes is clarified since we see how extreme they are allowing for batch spread. In this example standardization (in Figure 4.6) reinforces our impressions from the raw data (in Figure 4.4): Hungary becomes more and more unusual as we go from younger to older batches with one

Table 4.5 Standardizing the suicide batches

	25–34	35–44	45–54	55–64	65–74
Numerical summary values					
X_U	48	65	84	81	107
q_U	28	35	41	50	52
Md	22	25	31	33	35
q_L	9	11	15	18	27
X_L	4	7	10	14	22
dq	19	24	26	32	25
adjacent			52		69
Numerical summary values, standardized					
X_U	1.4	1.7	2.0	1.5	2.9
q_U	0.3	0.4	0.4	0.5	0.7
Md	0.0	0.0	0.0	0.0	0.0
q_L	−0.7	−0.6	−0.6	−0.5	−0.3
X_L	−0.9	−0.8	−0.8	−0.6	−0.5
adjacent values			0.8		1.4

exception. The lower extremes are in about the same relative position in all batches.

One often standardizes data sets that were measured by different rulers: heights measured in feet and metres, incomes measured in dollars and pounds, IQ measured by Stanford–Binet or Wexler–Bellevue, etc. This is a way of getting rid of arbitrary features of measurement; for example, choosing a yardstick instead of a metric rule. In our case, though, the level and spread differences of the two batches are not simply accidental by-products of a measurement scale. The difference between suicide rates of 20 or 35 per 100 000 is a very real one. We do not want to get rid of level and spread here, but rather to note it carefully and then to set it aside so other things can be seen. What we can see most vividly, of course, is shape; with more basic things like level and spread out of the picture, shape shows up very clearly.

At first, students often have difficulty seeing how standardization might be useful. This illustration might clarify matters.

Often, the absolute level of a variable is less important than the comparative level; relative deprivation is such a case. In the same way, how well-educated a person is considered to be may depend on more than the simple number of years of schooling accomplished. Thus a man born in the backwoods in 1900 who has earned a high school diploma might be seen to have relatively more education than a man born in New York City in 1950 with two years of university. Standardization provides a way of comparing the educational achievements of these two men controlling for their different backgrounds. Part of this background is the different levels in 1900 and 1950, in the backwoods and in New York City. Another important part is the spread in

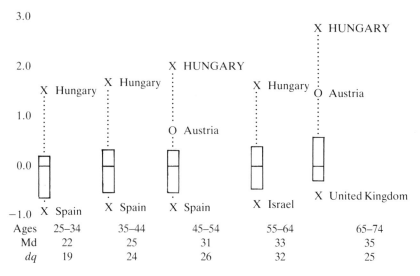

Figure 4.6 Plots of standardized suicide batches

educational achievement in the two settings. Once we have controlled for these two effects by computing 'standard education scores', comparison is more direct and meaningful.

We have described (exploratory) standardization here and discussed some of the insights it offers. More importantly, we have argued that this technique gives us our best view of shape yet, although the suicide batches are really too similar for this to help a great deal here. Being able to see shape clearly can be a real help but the material in the next two chapters on transformation will enable us to work with shape without requiring standardization. The principal benefits of standardization will become evident when we turn to confirmatory analysis, where this technique becomes central.

Fits and Residuals

In passing we have had a very brief and rather trivial introduction to a technique that will be used throughout in exploration and often in confirmation; the separation of an observation into a *fit* part and a *residual* part. At each stage in the analysis, we think carefully about those aspects of the data that are easiest to see; and when we think we understand these, we remove them and set them aside (not throw them away). We do this because obvious features of a body of data may partially obscure subtler things, so removing what is now obvious makes those more subtle components stand out more clearly. This is rather like the steps in a dissection: first study the surface layer, understand it and then cut it away, leaving the next layer as the new surface. That is, one can't clearly see the musculature until the skin is removed, and similarly, the skeleton is obscure until the musculature is removed (after it is 'understood', of course).

Since we go through this process so often it is useful to have basic terms for its steps. In the first step, we find and explain a feature of the data; for example, we found batch levels and tried to come to terms with them by thinking about why suicide levels should increase with age. The data feature is summed up in appropriate numbers (here, the batch medians), which we call a *fit*. In the second step we remove the feature just explained by setting aside the fitted values; for example, we set aside the level fit by subtracting each batch's median from the batch values. When the first layer of fit is found, explained and set aside we get *residuals* from the first fit, or left-over aspects of the data which still need attention. Here, we saw that spread was a notable feature of the residuals from level in Figure 4.5; we tried to explain it too; and in Figure 4.6 we went on to another wave of residuals with two layers of fit (level and spread) removed. There are still other features of the data to see, notably shape, which we will soon learn how to deal with as well. The process continues through fitting, finding residuals, finding new fits for the residuals, and so on until you run out of time or out of ideas for new fits. Each layer of fit is removed in an appropriate way: level fits by subtraction, spread fits by division, and shape fits by transformation (the subject of the next two chapters).

Exploratory and Confirmatory

The magnification of graphs and the use of zero points are things you have to think about whether you are doing exploration or confirmation. When doing exploration, suit yourself; try this and that until something pays off. When doing confirmation you are often also planning to do publication (if only of a limited sort like handing in a paper), so you ought to present the data in whatever way gives the most honest initial picture.

Standardization is a common term and the technique is often used. In most published sources it is taken for granted that standardization is confirmatory standardization: subtracting the mean, dividing by the standard deviation. But, as we have seen, the resistant version can also be useful.

The major business of this chapter, the box plots, have no standard equivalents. But these tools are so useful that it is sometimes worthwhile to use them for public presentation, explaining as necessary, and it is always worthwhile to work with them routinely in exploratory analyses.

The terms 'fit' and 'residual' are used in both exploratory and confirmatory work; the kinds of fits made tend to be different, with exploratory work relying more on fast, resistant, approximate fits.

As before, the reader familiar with Tukey (1977) will note some discrepancies. Most of these are merely terminological; where more or less standard terms exist, we have tended to use them as a way of providing a bridge to the less familiar material.

One thing you might watch for: we denote adjacents and outliers with names in lower and upper case, respectively, the treatment Tukey gives to outliers and far outliers, respectively. Generally, readers familiar with this material from one source should have little difficulty following it in the other.

Detective Work and Critical Thinking

Earlier, we made an analogy between exploratory data analysis and detective work. We argued that for both we need clues, need to think about them, and want to try to construct hypotheses that account for them. This is a good time to stop for a moment and elaborate on these notions. Earl Babbie (1986: 145) in his essay on critical thinking lays out a five-step procedure for what we see as detective work. These steps are:

Observe the way things are;
Ask why they are this way;
Suggest an explanation;
Then ask, if this explanation is true, what else must (or might) be true;
Look to see if it is true.

Thus far, in substantive discussions, most of you have not gone much beyond the first three steps; using careful exploration to illuminate suggestive or provocative data features, framing questions about them (what is there about Hungary that results in such a high suicide rate?) and thinking speculatively about explanations for these data features, at least broadly (Hungary experienced a failed revolution; perhaps people who have gone through such an event are more suicide-prone . . .?). These speculations don't have to be perfect. They just have to be good enough to get you started thinking hard and focusing hard.

The best way to improve your homework and your analytical skills is by trying to incorporate the last two steps into your analyses. We have seen the fourth step in action in the Sherlock Holmes episode quoted in Chapter 2. Several clues had suggested an 'inside job', notably that someone had entered the stable and taken a horse, but the dog had not barked. Further, several clues pointed to Straker. So Holmes reasoned, if Straker had planned to lame the racehorse Silver Blaze, a difficult task, he might have wanted to practise the technique first. He saw the sheep, viewed them as suitable for practising and hypothesized that Straker might have tried the operation out on them. He enquired of the shepherd and found that indeed several of the sheep had gone lame – the fifth step, looking to see if the prediction is true.

How would this work with our analyses? Well, if Hungary's suicide rate is extra high because of its failed popular uprising, then:

(a) suicide rates for Hungary before 1956 would have been substantially lower – you can look for earlier suicide rate data;
(b) other countries that had experienced failed popular revolutions might also have elevated rates – do they?;
(c) it is at least arguable that people who were young, or even unborn, in 1956 would be relatively unaffected by the experience, and if so their cohorts should have lower rates – do they?

There is nothing difficult about this sort of thinking, except getting into the habit of following the five steps carefully. Or if you prefer a less rigid view of the process, George Smiley, John Le Carré's master spy, describes the process as 'learn the facts . . . then try on the stories like clothes'.

Using the Computer

Getting a box plot from MINITAB is easy; you don't need numerical summaries, or anything else. The simple command BOXPLOT is sufficient. The BOXPLOT output for C13, which is males in the 25–34 age group, is reproduced here, (note that MINITAB prints the boxplots from left to right, not up and down, the way we presented our handwork):

MTB> BOXPLOT C13

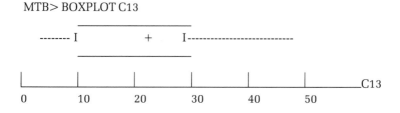

There is not much to interpreting the BOXPLOT diagram shown here. First, the enclosed box is the midbox, which runs from the lower to the upper quartiles. The median is marked with a + and the dotted line runs to the extreme adjacents (the two most extreme values which are not outliers) on each side. Outliers are marked with * and far outliers with a 0. Below the box plot is a line indicating the scale of the plot.

A final note concerning box plots has to do with subcommands. There are a number of subcommands for BOXPLOT command, but one in particular – BY – may be of interest. This subcommand allows you to create a separate box plot for each distinct value in another column. Thus, if you take the original data on suicide for both males and females (Table 2.1) it would be possible to create two box plots – one for each sex – for each age category, using the subcommand BY. The procedure is as follows:

```
MTB> BOXPLOT C3;
SUBC> BY 'SEX'.
SEX
```

```
                    _____
1         _____I         +      I_____
                    _____


2    __I   +    I_
     _____
   |_____|_____|_____|_____|_____|_____ 25–34
   0         10         20         30          40         50
MTB>
```

How to Standardize

The main command here is CENTER, which, in the absence of subcommands, will remove the confirmatory measures, mean and standard deviation. If you want to use exploratory values you must specify them, first getting them by means of the DESCRIBE command. The process for the five male suicide batches is:

```
MTB> CENTER C13 – C17 INTO C18 – C22;
SUBC> LOCATION  21.5   25.2   31.3   32.8   25.1;
SUBC> SCALE     18.2   24     26.7   32.4   25.2.
MTB>
```

You could now PRINT the standardized columns, DESCRIBE and BOX-PLOT them – in each case the median would now equal 0, and the $dq = 1$.

HOMEWORK

1 Using the numerical summaries and stems and leaves you have made for the female suicide rates:

(a) find any outliers and detached values;
(b) make schematic plots and discuss;
(c) make plots with levels removed and discuss.

If you have time left over, pick two batches you would like to compare; standardize, plot, discuss.

5
Transforming Data

So far we have learned how to deal with two of the major features of batches, level and spread. We learned how to summarize these fits and how to remove them so that we could look more deeply at the residuals for further features. The most notable 'further feature' so far has been shape, which turns out to be a very important batch feature indeed. So we would like to be able to summarize and remove shape as well as level or spread. For levels, we subtracted; for spreads, we divided; for shape, we turn to *transformation*.

In this chapter, we will discuss how transformation deals with shape by looking at transformations of a single batch. We will begin by discussing the most important transform, the logarithm. The logarithm is worth special attention because it is the most frequently used transform and because it may be a little less familiar to many readers than some of the other commonly used transforms. Next, we will look at shape more generally and see how the various transforms that we want in our tool box affect shape and also how we can sensibly decide between them. In the next chapter, we will go through a similar procedure for finding good transforms for several related batches.

A Simple Application

Let's begin with an unusually simple example in which logging works well for easily understandable reasons. Consider Table 5.1, which gives population sizes for Canada for 12 consecutive censuses. Clearly population grew dramatically in this period. We can get a more detailed picture of how population grew by looking at the column headed 'growth', which gives the difference between each census and the one before. For example, between 1851 and 1861 the Canadian population count grew by 0.79 million. Clearly, the amount of growth is larger for later years than for earlier ones. To see some further important features of the data, let's look at the schematic plot in Figure 5.1. The batch clearly trails upwards: the upper extreme is further from the midbox than the lower extreme is, and the upper quartile is further from the

Table 5.1   Canadian population (in millions) 1851–1961

		Growth, since previous census*
1851	2.44	
1861	3.23	0.79
1871	3.69	0.46
1881	4.32	0.63
1891	4.83	0.51
1901	5.37	0.54
1911	7.21	1.84
1921	8.79	1.58
1931	10.38	1.59
1941	11.51	1.13
1951	14.01	2.50
1961	18.24	4.23

Source: Statistics Canada (1973).
* Growth between adjacent censuses is defined as the difference between the populations they show.

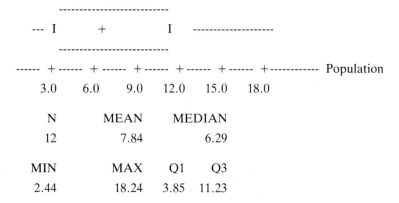

Figure 5.1   Box plot of raw population data for Canada

median than the lower quartile is. That is, within the batch we find that higher values are more spread out than lower ones.

At first glance this may seem like quite a bundle of data features, but one simple idea will explain most of them. Populations gain by births and immigration, and lose by deaths and emigration. If these four factors operate at roughly constant rates, or their net effect simply remains about the same, then

Table 5.2 Ratios of adjacent censal years

Canada

1861/1851	1.32
1871/1861	1.14
1881/1871	1.17
1891/1881	1.11
1901/1891	1.11
1911/1901	1.34
1921/1911	1.21
1931/1921	1.18
1941/1931	1.10
1951/1941	1.21
1961/1951	1.30

Stem and leaf of rates
1.3   240
1.2   11
1.1   471180
1.0

Md   1.18

stem = units and tenths; *leaf* = hundredths

population changes by a roughly constant *rate*. Does that seem to be happening here? Let's look at Table 5.2, which gives the ratio of each population figure to that from the preceding census. Table 5.2 shows us a kind of growth *rate*, while Table 5.1 showed us growth amounts. The ratios look rather similar from census to census, which suggests that Canada has indeed generally had fairly constant rates of growth. Since the 1850s death rates have declined a lot but so have birth rates, so it is reasonable that population growth has been roughly steady.

A constant rate of growth explains a lot about the data. First, we can now see why the amounts of growth in Table 5.1 are larger for later years: later years have larger populations, so the same growth *rate* means bigger growth *amounts*. This is precisely like getting compound interest on a fixed amount of savings. To illustrate with a very simple and probably familiar example, imagine £100 in an account earning 10 per cent interest compounded annually. At the end of the first year, the account contains £110, a gain of £10, while at the end of the second year, the account is at £121, a gain of £11. But the *rate* of increase is unchanged; the two ratios,

$$\frac{110}{100} \text{ and } \frac{121}{110}, \text{ are equal } \left(\frac{11}{10}\right)$$

as they should be. Secondly, we can see why the batch trails off upward. If the

Table 5.3 Logarithms of population sizes and differences

	Canada	Growth
1851	6.39	
1861	6.51	0.12
1871	6.57	0.06
1881	6.64	0.07
1891	6.68	0.04
1901	6.73	0.05
1911	6.86	0.13
1921	6.94	0.08
1931	7.02	0.08
1941	7.06	0.04
1951	7.15	0.09
1961	7.26	0.11

Logged population

7.2	6
7.1	5
7.0	26
6.9	4
6.8	6
6.7	3
6.6	48
6.5	17
6.4	
6.3	9

stem: units and tenths   *leaves:* hundredths

larger figures (populations in later years) are growing by larger amounts, then they are more different from each other and more spread out.

Now we know what we are dealing with; but we are not dealing with it very effectively. Using ratios is good in some ways – it is easy, familiar, and clearly brings out the rate of growth idea – but it has two annoying problems. First, taking ratios involves simple but somewhat time-consuming arithmetic. Secondly, once you find ratios you can't get back to your original numbers. Consider a ratio of 1.21. What pair of population sizes does that ratio go with? There are infinitely many possibilities. In our example we have two: the 1921/1911 values and the 1951/1941 values. We can't tell which from the ratio. And in general, it is hard to analyse the ratios much further.

Thus, what we are seeking is a transformation that controls for the

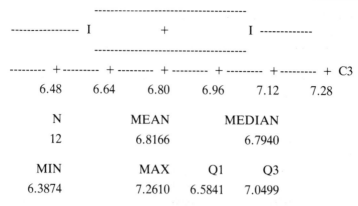

Figure 5.2   Logged population figures

compound interest effect, that is painless to compute and still leaves the original numbers recoverable. Taking logarithms is such a transformation. Results for our example are shown in Table 5.3, and the corresponding plot in Figure 5.2. For the moment, let us not worry about where these logs come from or how they were calculated; let's see whether the logs are coping with the data as we would like them to.

First, we would like to see that the compound interest effect is removed: that differences from census to census are no longer greater for later periods with larger populations. To check this, we found growth figures for logged data in Table 5.3 as we found growth for raw figures in Table 5.1. Growth in logs does seem pretty even, not noticeably higher for earlier or later years. Secondly, if logging captures the constant rate of growth idea then the batch should not trail upward after logging. If we look at the stem and leaf for logged population in Table 5.3, or the box plot in Figure 5.2, it is clear that the upward trailing we found in the raw data is indeed gone. The batch is quite neat, with both the extremes and the quartiles well balanced around the median.

Logging sets aside most of the data features that caught our eyes at first; does it also help us to understand them? Certainly. Table 5.3 showed us that the logged population figures grow by a roughly constant amount from one census to the next. We will see that addition in logs is like multiplication in raw numbers, and subtraction in logs is like division in raw numbers. So the roughly constant differences from census to census in logs are the same thing as the roughly constant ratios from census to census in raw data. The logs, like the ratios, indicate a roughly constant rate of population growth. Logs can do all that ratios do, and more: it is easy to see further with logs, to set the constant growth pattern aside, thus illuminating detailed deviations.

Before going on to details, let's go over what logs are and how they can be found quickly. Every statistical package and many hand-held calculators can calculate logs effortlessly. Let's focus on logarithms to the base 10 ($\log_{10}$). It makes no difference to your analysis which type of log you choose, but most people find $\log_{10}$ easier to make sense of at the start. Formally, a log of a particular number is the power the base must be raised to to give that number. So if your number is 100 and your base is 10, then $10^2 = 100$ and $\log_{10}(100) = 2$. Similarly, $\log_{10}(10) = 1$ and $\log_{10}(1000) = 3$. Thus, with a very little practice, it is possible to look at a $\log_{10}$ and 'guestimate' the real value and vice versa. However, $\log_{10}(0)$ is undefined and negative numbers are a problem to log.

Some Uses of Logging

We hope this example has convinced you that logging is easy, often makes clear sense and is very much worthwhile. We saw that logging was a good *fit* for a *process* of steady growth rates. It was good numerically, in that it neatly removed the compound interest effect. It was good analytically, in that we could easily understand why logging worked numerically: addition in logs is like multiplication in raw numbers. Best of all, logging helped us to sort out what belonged to the overall constant growth pattern and what did not. After logging, it is easy to examine the residuals from a constant growth process and see the things that don't fit such a process and hence have to be explained with other factors (like changing patterns of immigration). We have stressed the intercensal growth figures, but logging sheds light on other facets of the data as well. For example, in the raw data the upper extreme looks a bit unusual, though it is not an outlier. After logging, we see that the population figure is not especially high (see Figure 5.2). That means this value is in line with what we expected given a constant rate of growth; it is pretty big in raw numbers, but only because the growth rate has been applied to a large base figure (the population in the previous census).

It Is Seldom So Simple

Our first example, though simple, illustrated several important points very well. We hope that these points are now clear enough, so that we can move on to a kind of analysis that is both more common and more complex. Analogous issues will come up, although we will not always be able to resolve them in as straightforward a way.

The main uses of transformation are fitting shape and removing shape to allow us to see more. Let's begin, then, with a discussion of what we mean by shape.

What We Mean by Shape

Figure 5.3 offers some simple examples of what we mean by shape. In the first example the batch 'straggles upward': the small values are clumped relatively close together, while the larger values trail off. Conversely, the data in the third

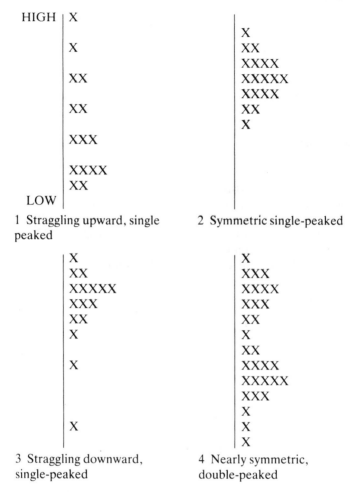

Figure 5.3   Different shapes

example 'straggle down': here it is the high values which are bunched and the lower ones which are more spread out. In the second example, the batch is symmetric: most of the observations are in the middle, with the higher and lower values both trailing off at the same rate. Scores of all North American eight-year-olds on a standard IQ test would look like this. All the first three batches are basically single-peaked, unlike the fourth which has two peaks.

All our procedures for summarizing and removing shape are designed for single-peaked data. Transformations that can cope with data having many peaks do exist but we ignore them here. They are not useful all that often, they are less easy and you can usually avoid them. If you do get a batch with many

Table 5.4   Municipal election turn-out: Vancouver 1970

A: Original batches

East or West End   % of eligible voters

W	6	7
W W	6	40
W W	5	77
E	5	1
E W E E	4	8597
W E W E E E E E W	4	333424233
W W	3	66
E	3	1
E E	2	88
	2	

                    stem: tens   *leaf:* area or units

B: Sub-batched

West End   East End

7	6	
04	6	
77	5	
	5	1
9	4	857
323	4	334243
66	3	1
	3	
	2	88
	2	

                    stem: tens   *leaf:* units

Source: Ewing (1972).

peaks, like the fourth one in Figure 5.3 it is often because two or more different batches with different levels (and/or spreads and shapes) have been mixed together. You can remove the many-peakedness and avoid fancy transforms by breaking the batch down into sub-batches, which is probably the better, as well as the more convenient thing to do. For example, consider Table 5.4. Part A gives a stem and leaf for 24 districts in Vancouver, Canada: on the right is the rate of turn-out in the 1970 municipal election and on the left either W (if the district is part of the generally wealthier West end) or E (for East end). The plot may look roughly single-peaked and symmetric overall but a close look shows some clumping at both the top and bottom, with Ws at the top and Es at the bottom. So we go to Part B, separate plots for West and East rates. Clearly this is a difference worth knowing about; for example, the East end rates are lower and less spread out. Some further sub-batching might be useful here since the two new batches (especially the West end batch) still show clumping.

Finally, note that the importance of peaking as part of shape underlines the importance of the stem and leaf in judging shape. Box plots show symmetry or asymmetry very well but do not clearly reveal whether the data are single-peaked. Remember, in Chapter 4 we pointed out that box plots do not show everything: they do not show clumping. It is best to use both box plots and stems and leaves when working with shape.

The Standard Shape: Symmetric and Single-Peaked

What do we do about single-peaked shapes? Before, for levels and spreads, we set aside batch features by making them standard, getting levels to be zero and/or getting spreads to be one. In a similar spirit we remove shape by trying to get a batch into a standard shape: symmetric. Why a standard shape? To make batch comparisons easier and to avoid arbitrary fiddling with shape. Batch comparison is easier if all or nearly all the batches are in the same standard form, because differences in shape can get in the way of seeing and interpreting finer aspects of the data. A standard shape also gives a clear-cut goal for transformations, which saves time and cuts down on arbitrary transformation. If a standard shape, why the symmetric? Well, it is the most 'neutral' shape. Batches usually straggle up or down for a reason and we try to figure out what the reason is; but a symmetric batch doesn't call out for shape explanation in the same way. Further, symmetry is the standard goal for compelling practical reasons: the confirmatory statistics we will soon be turning to assume *normally distributed* data. A single-peaked symmetric batch may not be quite normal but it is usually close enough, so confirmatory tools that assume normality can be used safely. We will have more to say about this issue from Chapter 7 on.

Most of the batches we will meet begin with some straggle (most frequently upward straggle) and become roughly symmetric after a suitable transformation. The suitable transformation is very often logging, which is one reason why we spend so much time here on this transformation. Some batches are so 'ugly' that no transform can make them roughly standard. Even the Canadian census data don't end up perfectly standard. The figures are quite symmetric, but they are not single-peaked; instead they tend to be nearly evenly spread over their stems, close to what is sometimes called a 'uniform' distribution in which all the stems have the same number of cases.

Finding the Best Transformation

So far in this chapter, we have discussed one very important transform, the log, not only for its own sake (considerable) but also to help illustrate how transformation works and how it can help. But as we have seen, batches can

a Stem and leaf and box plot of hypothetical batch

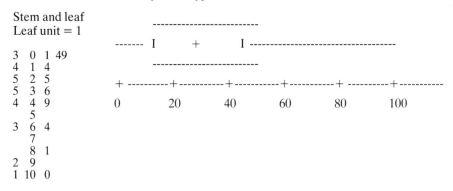

Stem and leaf
Leaf unit = 1

```
3   0   1 49
4   1   4
5   2   5
5   3   6
4   4   9
    5
3   6   4
    7
    8   1
2   9
1  10   0
```

b Box plot of logged hypothetical batch

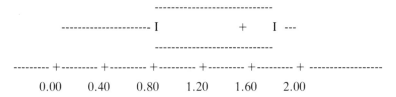

c Box plot of square-rooted hypothetical batch

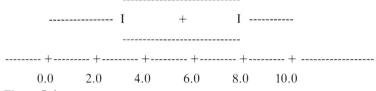

Figure 5.4

have different shapes and logging won't even work for all batches that trail up. So we need to know several kinds of transforms and how to choose the best one quickly and easily.

Relax: we are not about to dazzle you with a mass of weird and unfamiliar functions. Almost all the shapes you will run into can be handled quite adequately with logs or one of a very few familiar alternatives. Consider the hypothetical batch in Figure 5.4a; both the stem and leaf and box plot indicate upward trailing. If we log the batch and examine the new box plot, it trails down! Logging is too strong a transform; it overcorrects (Figure 5.4b). Let's try a square root transform, weaker than logging. The box plot is perfect (no surprise – the data were constructed for this purpose) (Figure 5.4c). Now, suppose that we had tried logs and the transformed data still straggled upward, suggesting the need for a stronger transform. One that is fairly commonly used is the negative reciprocal – negative to keep the order of the numbers the same; 2 is greater than 1, and 1/2 is less than 1/1 but −1/2 is bigger (less negative) than −1. Data can also straggle down, though this is less common in social science applications.

What do you do if a batch straggles down? You want to spread out the higher values and pull the lower ones together to make the batch symmetric. This is easy to do by trying powers of the batch numbers: x^2, x^3, x^4, or whatever it takes. This is pretty simple so we have not bothered to work out examples for you. The antilog transformation corrects for downward straggle too (being the opposite of logs) but is awkward if the data are large numbers; the antilogs can really get enormous. Consequently this transform will rarely be used as a way of handling shape, though it is used in getting results from log transforms back to the original data units. For most data that straggle down, finding squares or cubes is likely to be adequate. You should feel free to try powers or roots or negative reciprocals or any other simple function of the data that will make them amenable, so become familiar with enough options to be flexible.

Choosing an Appropriate Transformation

By now you have seen, and can easily work with, several kinds of transformation. Different transformations have different effects on data; some spread the data out where values are high and condense them where values are low, some do the opposite. In addition some change spread a lot more than others. How do you decide which to use?

When working with a single batch you want to get it as close as possible to standard form: single-peaked, symmetric and falling off smoothly on both sides. This is particularly important and, other things being equal, we choose that transform which symmetrizes the middle. Thus, we chose a log transform for the Canadian population data (Figure 5.2). But if we have two transforms that are pretty good for the middle we can choose between them by looking at how they handle the observations beyond the quartiles.

Now we want to show how you can quickly choose symmetrizing transformations for whatever batches come your way. We want a better choice procedure than hit or miss, trial and error, because that takes time and wastes energy. The first step is to get an orderly idea of what transformations do what kind of things. In Figure 5.4 we saw that square roots, logs and negative reciprocals all correct for upward straggle to varying extents; the square root transform is weaker in its effect than logging, which is in turn weaker than negative reciprocals. We can also see with a little thought that powers of x correct for downward straggle and do so to varying extents. Consider a little example: the numbers 5, 6, 7. If we transform these by squaring we get 25, 36 and 49. The smaller pair are one unit apart in the original form and are 11 apart in the squared form. The larger pair are again one unit apart in raw form, but are further apart than the smaller pair after squaring: 13. And these are numbers that are not very different in the first place. Now suppose we try x^3, getting 125, 216 and 343. Now the smaller pair are 91 units apart and the larger pair are 127 apart. Again the larger numbers have been spread out relatively more, with a higher power of x exaggerating the effect. In general, the higher the power of x the more the larger numbers are stretched compared to the smaller ones (or the more the smaller ones are squeezed together compared to the larger ones).

We can sum up this useful information by what Tukey calls the *ladder of transformation*:

$$-\frac{1}{x^2} \quad -\frac{1}{x} \quad \log x \sqrt{x} \quad x \quad x^2 \quad x^3 \quad \text{antilog} \, x$$

STRONGER	MILD	NO SHAPE CHANGE	MILD	STRONGER

Correct upward straggle   Correct downward straggle

Moving to the right spreads out larger x values and clumps the smaller ones; moving to the left spreads out smaller values and clumps the larger ones.

Table 5.5 US population (in 000 000)

1850	23.2
1860	31.4
1870	39.8
1880	50.2
1890	62.9
1900	76.0
1910	92.0
1920	105.7
1930	122.8
1940	131.7
1950	150.7
1960	178.5

Source: Statistical Abstract of the United States, 92nd edn, 1971.

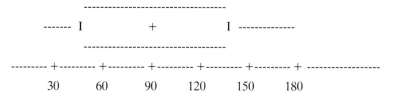

Figure 5.5 Box plot of US population

Table 5.6 US population figures and transforms for upward trailing

	N	Mean	Median	
X	12	88.7	84.0	
Square root X	12	9.044	9.155	
$Log_{10} X$	12	1.8724	1.9223	
$-1/X$	12	-0.01645	-0.01201	

	Min	Max	Q_1	Q_3
	23.2	178.5	42.4	129.5
	4.817	13.360	6.503	11.377
	1.3655	2.2516	1.6251	2.1120
	-0.04310	-0.00560	-0.02382	-0.00773

```
                            --------------------------------
            -------------- I        +              I ----------------

   --------- + --------- + --------- + --------- + --------- + --------- + -------------   √x
       4.8        6.4        8.0        9.6       11.2       12.8


                            -------------------------------
   ------------------------ I            +        I ----------------
                            -------------------------------

   --------- + --------- + --------- + --------- + --------- + -------------   log₁₀ X
     1.40       1.60       1.80       2.00       2.20


                                  ---------------------------------
   ------------------------------------------- I            +    I -----------
                                  ---------------------------------

   --------- + --------- + --------- + --------- + --------- + --------- + -------------   0.1/X
   -0.0420   -0.0350   -0.0280   -0.0210   -0.0140   -0.0070
```

Figure 5.6 Box plots of US population figures after transforms

Suppose you start with original data that straggle down. You might try x^3 and, alas, this straggles up. Try x^2 then, of course. One or two stabs are usually enough to identify a good transformation.

To get a sense of how we might go about selecting an appropriate transform for a batch of data and the sorts of judgements involved, let us look at the set of US census data in Table 5.5, which is comparable to the Canadian data in Table 5.1. Its easy to see that this batch, like the Canadian batch, trails up strongly. This is even easier to see in a box plot (Figure 5.5). The box plot of the raw data sends a somewhat mixed message; balance within the midbox and upward trailing outside it. Such mixed messages are pretty common and resolving them can require judgement. Since the batch trails up, we want to move to the left on the ladder of transforms. Here we consider the three commonest transforms for upward trailing; square root, log and negative reciprocal. The summaries are shown in Table 5.6 and the box plots in Figure 5.6.

Quite clearly, the negative reciprocal overcorrects substantially. Between the log and square root, the square root looks better; the median is closer to the middle of the midbox and the extremes are better balanced. If we were to make a decision about this batch in isolation, the choice would be clear. However, there are two other issues that could be important. First, the log transform is a 'natural' for population growth so it makes sense to try to use it and think hard about where and why it doesn't quite fit. Secondly, if our analysis of these data is in a context that includes other population data, we would want to use the same transform on all of them – it may be of interest to compare US and Canadian population growth during this time period. We have seen that logging removes the compound interest effect of an approximately steady growth rate. Logging is therefore a fit for the process of growth at a constant rate: when we log, the effects of that process are removed from the data. Like any fit, logging leaves *residuals* or details that do not fit the overall pattern and hence call for special attention. In our example, residuals are given in Table 5.7. First we found the median growth amount in logs: in both countries, one census figure tends to be 0.08 greater than the previous one. (Remember, this

Table 5.7 Growth of logged population figures

Canada		USA
X	0.13	X
X	0.12	
X	0.11	
	0.10	XXX
X	0.09	
XX	0.08	XX
X	0.07	XX
X	0.06	XX
X	0.05	
XX	0.04	
	0.03	X
Md = 0.08		Md = 0.08

Table 5.8   Growth of logged population with level
(0.08) removed

Canada		USA	
To:		To:	
1861	0.04	1860	0.05
1871	−0.02	1870	0.02
1881	−0.01	1880	0.02
1891	−0.04	1890	0.02
1901	−0.03	1900	0.00
1911	0.05	1910	0.00
1921	0.00	1920	−0.02
1931	0.00	1930	−0.01
1941	−0.04	1940	−0.05
1951	0.01	1950	−0.02
1961	0.03	1960	−0.01
Md = 0.08		Md = 0.08	

corresponds to the roughly constant ratio of 1.2 between adjacent census figures in the raw data. In fact, 0.08 is the log of 1.2, as it should be.) Then we subtracted 0.08 from each of the intercensal differences in logs (found in Table 5.7 under Growth). If population really did grow quite constantly, we would have only zero residuals but in fact we have many that are non-zero because the population sometimes grew by more than 0.08 (positive residuals) and sometimes grew by less (negative residuals) (Table 5.8).

Getting these residuals is one of the main benefits of transformation: now we can see beyond the overall pattern of roughly constant growth rate to less obvious details, the interesting discrepancies that prevent growth rates from being perfectly constant. We could have looked at these details in the raw data, but only with a lot of trouble; and in practice it is so much trouble that we are not likely to get around to it. So let's go back to the residuals in Table 5.8.

The picture for the USA data seems simplest: relatively rapid growth before 1890 in the heyday of expansion and immigration, followed by slower growth after immigration was restricted and particularly slow growth in the depression decade. In Canada there were similar influences, though in a less neat pattern of years: immigration booms for confederation, whole provinces added in later years (Saskatchewan and Alberta entered in 1905, Newfoundland in 1949), the settlement of the wheatlands, slower growth in economically slow decades.

The growth picture may also have been affected by changes in birth and death rates. Death rates have declined fairly steadily over this period, but birth rates have declined more erratically (they went down during the depression, producing lower than usual figures in 1940 or 1941, and rose again after the

Second World War, producing the 'baby boom', which shows up in higher figures for later years). You could pursue any of these points further, or ask yourself why the Canadian figures have more extremes of large or small increases than the USA figures do.

Some General Remarks about Transformation

Transformation lets us work with shape as we work with level and spread. We define a standard shape (symmetric and single-peaked) as we defined standard level (0) and standard spread (1). We can fit almost any single-peaked batch shape by finding the transformation that puts the batch most nearly into standard form; this transformation is a fit for the shape that summarizes and removes it. We try to explain the fit and then go beyond it by looking hard at the transformation data.

It is important to note that our transformations are made on the raw data, and not, for example, on standardized data. It often happens that transformation does most or all of the standardization for you. Besides, it is easier to understand and interpret transformations if they are as simple as possible, and transformation of raw data is simpler and more easily communicated. Furthermore, standardizing makes some transformations effectively impossible; we can't take logs of zero or negative numbers, for example. So if you want to get some level or spread differences out of some batches after transformation, go ahead and do it in the usual way on the transformed batches. Batches with transformed numbers in them are still batches and can be batch analysed like any other numbers.

In particular, they can be examined for outliers. After transformation many things can happen to outliers; outliers in the raw data may stop being outliers ('false outliers') or persist, or new outliers may be revealed ('hidden outliers'). Take the transformed version of what is or is not an outlier more seriously; when a batch is symmetrized, upper and lower ends of the batch are treated more even-handedly in defining outliers, and the overall pattern of the batch is allowed for.

Of course, a foolish or unscrupulous person could use transformations to create or destroy outliers to suit himself; for example, logging often gives new lower outliers and eliminates upper outliers, and never the opposite (why?), while the reverse may occur for some other kinds of transformation. This is one reason why we argued that having a standard form is useful in part to avoid arbitrary transformation: if the goal of the transform is clear then the choice of transform is restricted.

Exploratory and Confirmatory

As we remarked at the start of this chapter, transformation is also very useful in confirmatory work since the most widely used confirmatory tools are meant for data with a special kind of standard shape. If your data do not have this shape, they can often be transformed so that they do have it.

We have spoken here of 'single-peaked' and 'multi-peaked' data. In standard language it is more usual to speak of unimodal and multimodal data. The *mode* of a batch is the most frequent value, the value which occurs most often. If two values occur equally often and more often than any others, the batch is bimodal; if several values are tied for first place, the batch is multimodal. In Figure 5.3, where several kinds of shape are illustrated, the first three batches are all unimodal. The fourth batch is double-peaked, but not (as it may at first seem) bimodal: one stem has five cases and no other stem has as many, so this batch is unimodal too. This example should be enough to show why we have not used the 'mode' language very much: batch 4 in Figure 5.3 very clearly has two clusters, but the mode language does not capture this. Like all confirmatory measures, the mode is very exactly defined and can sometimes be misleading.

Using the Computer

The basic transformations described in this chapter are all pretty painless with MINITAB. If your raw data are in C1 (when transforming, it is best to work with raw data) then:
To obtain logs

    MTB> LOGTEN C1 INTO C2

For square roots

    MTB> SQRT C1 INTO C2

For negative reciprocals

    MTB> LET C2 = $-(1/C1)$

To square the values in column one

    MTB> LET C2 = C1 * C1

Similarly, to cube the values

    LET C2 = C1 * C1 * C1, etc.

You can then stem-and-leaf and box plot C2 in the usual way.

HOMEWORK

1 Return to the data on homicide victim rates for males and females (Chapter 2, problem 3):

(a) Describe the shape of each batch of raw data.
(b) Select a transformation for each batch. How good a job does it do?
(c) Has your interpretation of each of these batches been affected by transforming? How?

2 Table 5.9 contains abortion rates (per 1000 women aged 15–44) for 11 countries in 1987 (the US figures are for 1985).

(a) Describe and briefly discuss the raw data.
(b) Select the best transform for these data. Comment on how well this transform works for this batch.
(c) How has your interpretation of the data been changed by transforming?

Table 5.9   Abortion rate per 1000 aged 15–44

Country	
Canada	10.2
New Zealand	11.4
England and Wales	14.2
Italy	15.3
Israel	16.2
Australia	16.3
Japan	18.6
Sweden	19.8
United States	28.2
Hungary	38.2
Soviet Union	111.9

Source: Toronto *Globe and Mail*, 20 February 1991.

6
Choosing a Transformation for Several Related Batches

In the previous chapter, we learned how to use transformations to fit shape for a single batch. The idea of a standard shape was introduced and we saw how differing initial shapes called for different transforms. We also saw that a single batch can send a mixed message: trailing one way in the midbox and the other way in the extremes. This problem can be even more complex when working with several related batches where subsets of batches can behave in quite different ways from the rest. In short, the criteria for the successful transformation of a single batch are no longer adequate when we consider several batches.

Balancing Batches

For one batch we try to even up within-batch spread, so that the upper and lower halves of the batch straggle about the same amount. For several related batches we try to even up spread within each batch and between batches as well. This is not as difficult as it sounds. If the same process underlies all or most of the batches, then at least some of the special differences within and between batches will have been a consequence of that process. So both problems should be improved by a transform that accounts for that process. The ideal multi-batch transformation will result in all the batches having medians that are well centred between both the quartiles, with the extremes equally far from the quartiles and each of the batches having similar spreads even if their levels differ. How often do you get a set of batches that can be transformed so neatly? Well, let's get back to the real world.

It can be tricky to decide what the best overall transformation for a set of batches is. The best overall may be the one that makes all the batches balanced, or at least makes most of them balanced. This is just our single-batch criterion expanded to several related batches. Consider the five related batches in Table 6.1. Each batch is defined by a 'stage' of economic growth, with the stages defined by levels of gross national product (GNP) per capita for about 1957. The batch entries are the number of students enrolled in higher education per

Table 6.1 Enrolment in higher education at different levels of economic growth

Country	Higher ed. per 100 000	Country	Higher ed. per 100 000	Country	Higher ed. per 100 000
Stage 1 GNPC 45–64		**Stage III GNPC 108–239**		**Stage IV GNPC 262–794**	
Nepal	56	Iran	90	Mexico	258
Afghanistan	12	Paraguay	188	Colombia	296
Laos	4	Ceylon	56	Yugoslavia	524
Ethiopia	5	Indonesia	62	Hong Kong	176
Burma	63	Rhodesia and		Brazil	132
Libya	49	Nyasaland	3	Spain	258
Sudan	34	Egypt	399	Japan	750
Tanganyika	9	Morocco	40	Jamaica	42
Uganda	14	Surinam	109	Panama	371
		South Korea	397	Greece	320
		Iraq	173	Malaya	475
		Nicaragua	110	Costa Rica	326
		Taiwan	329	Romania	226
		Saudi Arabia	6	Lebanon	345
		Ghana	29	Bulgaria	456
Stage II GNPC 70–105		Syria	223	Malta	142
		Tunisia	64	Chile	257
Pakistan	165	Albania	145	South Africa	189
China		Algeria	70	Singapore	437
(Mainland)	69	Peru	253	Trinidad and	
India	220	Ecuador	193	Tobago	61
South Vietnam	83	Guatemala	135	Cyprus	78
Nigeria	4	Honduras	78	Poland	351
Kenya	5	Barbados	24	Uruguay	541
Madagascar	21	El Salvador	89	Argentina	827
Congo		Philippines	976	Hungary	258
(Leopoldville)	4	Turkey	255	Italy	362
Thailand	251	Portugal	272	Ireland	362
Bolivia	166	Mauritius	14	Puerto Rico	1192
Cambodia	18	British Guiana	27	Iceland	445
Haiti	29	Dominican		USSR	539
		Republic	149	Venezuela	355
Stage V GNPC 836–2577				Austria	546
				Czechoslovakia	398
Netherlands	923	New Zealand	839	Israel	668
West Germany	528	Australia	856	Finland	529
France	667	Sweden	401		
Denmark	570	Luxembourg	36		
Norway	258	Switzerland	398		
United Kingdom	460	Canada	645		
Belgium	536	United States	1983		

GNPC = gross national product per capita, US dollar equivalent, circa 1957.
Higher Ed. per 100 000 = number of students enrolled in higher education per 100 000 of total population; primary and secondary schools, adult education and technical training excluded.
Source: Russett *et al.* (1964: 294–8)

Table 6.2 Numerical summaries for data in Table 6.1

Stage 1 *stems:* tens *leaves:* units	*Stage 2* *stems:* hundreds, tens *leaves:* tens and units	*Stage 3* *stems:* hundreds, tens *leaves:* tens and units; units	*Stage 4* *stems:* hundreds	*Stage 5* *stems:* hundreds *leaves:* rounded tens
N = 9	N = 12	N = 30	N = 36	N = 14
X_U 63	X_U 251	X_U 976	X_U 1190	X_U 1980
q_U 49	q_U 166	q_U 223	q_U 500	q_U 840
Md 14	Md 49	Md 110	Md 360	Md 555
q_L 9	q_L 12	q_L 56	q_L 260	q_L 400
X_L 4	X_L 4	X_L 3	X_L 42	X_L 36
dq = 40	dq = 154	dq = 167	dq = 240	dq = 440

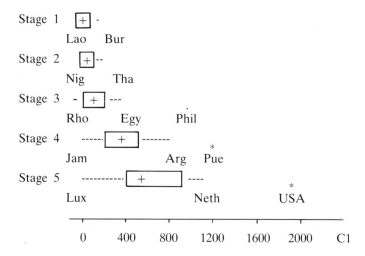

Figure 6.1 Box plots for data in Table 6.1

100 000 population, for about 1960. (The exact values of these figures would be different now, no doubt higher on the whole, but the patterns would probably be similar.) Table 6.2 gives the numerical summaries for these batches, and Figure 6.1 gives the box plots.

What transformation might make all, or nearly all, of these batches balanced? Clearly some correction for upward straggle is called for. Why not start by logging, since it often works out well? The logs are given in Table 6.3 and plotted in Figure 6.2. How well do logs work? The most important part of the data is the middle: we look first at the midboxes. Batches II to V look pretty balanced, while batch I still straggles up. This is pretty good; we will rarely find

Table 6.3   Logged numerical summaries from Table 6.1

	I	II	III	IV	V
X_U	1.80	2.40	2.99	3.08	3.30
q_U	1.69	2.22	2.35	2.70	2.92
Md	1.15	1.69	2.04	2.56	2.74
Q_L	0.95	1.08	1.75	2.42	2.60
X_L	0.60	0.60	0.48	1.60	1.60

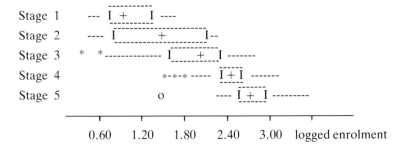

Figure 6.2   Logged box plots from Table 6.1

all the batches balanced. Next we check the extremes, less important than the midboxes (because more likely to fluctuate erratically) but still worth looking at. Here, logging does not seem to do so well: each lower extreme is further from its batch's lower quartile than the upper extreme is from the upper quartile. We would not worry about one or two unbalanced extremes, probably, but this is a pattern of imbalance. The extremes straggle down for every batch, and some of the lower extremes are outliers. Logging may have overcorrected; let's try square roots. Table 6.4 reports the square roots of the summary numbers. Compare the plot in Figure 6.3 to that for logs in Figure 6.2.

Table 6.4   Numerical summaries of square-rooted data from Table 6.1

	I	II	III	IV	V
X_U	8.0	15.9	31.2	34.5	44.5
q_U	7.0	12.9	14.9	22.4	29.0
Md	3.7	7.0	10.5	19.0	23.6
Q_L	3.0	3.5	7.5	16.1	20.0
X_L	2.0	2.0	1.7	6.3	6.3

```
                      --------
Stage 1 Laos   ---I +   I -  Bur
                      --------


                ------------------
Stage 2 Nig   ----I    +     I - Tha
        Con     ------------------


                     -----------
Stage 3 Rho  ------------- I  +   I---Egy        *Phil
                     -----------


                         -----------
Stage 4         Jam*Trin -------I   +   I ------Arg   *Pue
                         -----------


                          ---------
Stage 5         Lux*             Por----I  +  I-- Neth        *USA
                          ---------

          _____C4
          0.0        8.0      16.0    24.0    32.0     40.0
```

Figure 6.3   Box plots of square-rooted data from Table 6.1

The square-rooted batches straggle up a bit in the midboxes (to be expected, since logging balances the midboxes) but the straggle is not severe; and the extremes are well balanced for all the square-rooted batches whereas they are quite off-balance for the logged version. It also looks as if the square root version will have fewer outliers, with some above and some below the midbox. Overall, square roots seem to do a better job balancing the batches, although the decision is close.

A further point in favour of the square-rooted batches relates to two features of the spreads; they are more nearly equal than in the raw or logged form, and the covariation of level and spread that is evident in the box plots of Figure 6.1 has completely disappeared. This reflects our second criterion for a good multi-batch transform.

Equalizing Spreads

Instead of trying to make spread even within batches, so that upper and lower halves straggle similar amounts, we would like to try to make spread even between batches, so that each batch midspread is about the same. As we said earlier, we would like to do both these things, but cannot always do so. Tukey recommends another tool that can be very much the fastest way to choose a transformation when you have a large number of related batches.

To equalize the spreads, we need to know how they are related to level. If the spreads tend to increase as levels do, then square roots or logs or one of the negative inverses will help: they will make the spreads of the higher-level batches smaller, just what we need. On the other hand, if the spreads tend to get smaller as levels get bigger then we need some power of the observations (a positive power greater than one); this will draw the lower batch values together and spread out the higher ones, relatively speaking. Here is a rule of thumb that suggests a transform for the former case (by far the more common one) by looking at ratios summing up how much spread changes as level changes. We will not try to justify exactly how the procedure works in detail; pragmatically, the important thing is that this rule of thumb does the job much of the time.

The procedure is illustrated in Table 6.5 and Figure 6.4, using the five higher education batches in raw form again (Table 6.1). First, find the Md and dq of each batch from the numerical summary. Next, find the logs of these levels and spreads. For example, for batch I the Md and dq are 14 and 40, respectively, in the raw data; log (14) = 1.15 and log (40) = 1.60 are entered in Table 6.5 (by the way, we want the log of the raw dq, not the dq of logged data). To see how spread is related to level overall, we plot the logged dq on the Y-axis and the logged Md on the X-axis as shown in Figure 6.4. There seems to be a fairly steady increase of spread with level, so some transformation that corrects for upward straggle is called for. Which one? First we sum up just how much log dq increases as log Md does. Wiggle a piece of string or a ruler around a bit on the plot until you find a line that looks pretty close to most of the points and passes through two of them. The dashed line in the plot shows the line we like

Table 6.5   Logged spread and level

Logged	I	II	III	IV	V
Md	1.15	1.69	2.04	2.56	2.74
dq	1.60	2.19	2.22	2.38	2.64

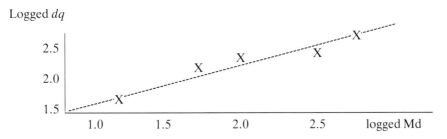

Figure 6.4   Plot of logged spread and level

the looks of. (Don't worry too much about finding such a line for your own data. If it looks right, it is probably close enough; if you have a terrible time deciding, that probably means that spread is not increasing very regularly with level and transformation is not going to even up the spreads very well whatever you do.)

Having found two points we ask how much the log spread increases as the log level does:

$$\frac{\text{log spread for higher point} - \text{log spread for lower}}{\text{log level for higher point} - \text{log level for lower}}$$

(This is just a slope: more on this in Chapter 11.) For our example, the higher point is that for batch V and the lower is that for batch I, so the ratio is:

$$\frac{2.64 - 1.60}{2.74 - 1.15} = \frac{1.04}{1.59} = 0.65$$

Now turn to the chart below that tells you what transformation is likely to work given the ratio from the log spread/log level plot:

Ratio is about:	Transform to try:
1/2	$\sqrt{x}$
1	$\log x$
3/2	$-\dfrac{1}{x}$
2	$-\dfrac{1}{x^2}$

Our ratio is 0.65, between one-half and one; so square roots or logs should help to even up the batch dqs. The ratio is nearer to one-half, so square roots should do a better job than logs. Let's go back to our plots (Figures 6.2 and 6.3) to see. Clearly square-rooting does produce more nearly equal midspreads; logging overcorrects, so that the dq actually declines as level increases. Logging comes close to making the ranges equal, but ranges are unreliable and much less important than the dq, which looks awful in logs.

The procedure does work, and not only for midspreads and medians. You can use this for any level and spread combination that makes sense to you. For example, you often want to have equal batch spreads in confirmatory work. But the spreads you want to equalize are standard deviations and the levels you work with are means. No problem: just follow the same procedure as above, using sds and means instead of dqs and Mds.

If you have many related batches to work with, this procedure is certainly the place to start, since it is far faster (given a lot of batches) than the informal trial-and-error we began with. As we noted earlier, the transformation that evens up the spreads best often balances the batches best, as square-rooting does in our higher education example. This is handy: we want our ideal transformation to do both things. We would rather not have to decide between a transform good for one goal and another transform good for the other goal.

Close Choices

So far, things seem pretty easy: we can often get a good multi-batch transformation with either of the approaches described above. But is it always so simple? What if the choice of transformation is close? What if some of the batches don't respond as well to the chosen transform as others do? Such problems do come up. For the higher education batches we think that square roots look clearly better than logs overall, but there are some things that logs handle better, and the choice can be much closer. In such cases, it comes down to judgement once again. Sometimes your judgement is helped along because you know that equal spreads are more important, or balanced batches are, for some reason; but most of the time you use your eyes and experience and make a choice.

Sometimes there is a sensible interpretation for one of the possible transforms. The choice becomes easier. For example, we found logging irresistible for over-time population figures because logging fitted so well with a sensible baseline hypothesis of constant growth. In similar ways, logging also works well for income data, GNPs, etc. If a good interpretation is available, from theory or from your own thinking about the data, by all means try the transformation involved. Even if the theoretical transform fails to fit everything perfectly, it will still be useful. Those failures of fit will be worth discussion, like the dog not barking in the night: why did the expected not happen? For example, in the US and Canadian population example we found that the US batch straggled down a bit after logging, perhaps a reflection of declining immigration in the USA.

On the other hand, if your choice of transformation is based on the data then you will want to try to come up with an interpretation of your choice. For example, why do square roots work well for the higher education batches? Perhaps a look at the box plot (Figure 6.3) is in order. Clearly enrolment in higher education is related to levels of economic development, or levels of GNP per capita. This in itself should not surprise you; the wealthier the country, the more highly educated people it needs (to run a more sophisticated economy) and the more it can afford to train. Perhaps the process generating the enrolment figures is, quite simply, wealth and its consequences; then enrolment and wealth will have much the same shape. GNP per capita figures are available to check this out. In any case, it is clear that wealth is not the whole explanation of higher enrolment rates (although it is a large part of the explanation). Within each batch in Table 6.1, the countries are ordered from poorest to richest; and some of our outliers are not unusually poor or rich. For example, Luxembourg is a lower outlier among the most wealthy nations as far as enrolment goes but Table 6.1 shows that it is on the wealthy side in that group if anything. Perhaps Luxembourg's size is important. Luxembourg may be too small to support many institutions of higher education, so that people go outside the country to one of the many institutions in neighbouring nations and are not counted in Luxembourg's figures. Some of the other lower cases are on the small side too. Size, like GNP per capita, straggles up, which again may contribute to the shape of our batches. The country's age may matter too.

We are used to thinking about cases like Luxembourg as outliers from batches, as cases that cry out for special attention and explanation. We should also get used to thinking of batches as outliers (loosely speaking) when they are very different from the set of batches to which they belong. For example, just as Luxembourg looks very different from the bulk of the batch V countries, batch I looks very different from the rest of the batches: its shape is different, much more markedly upward straggling. From Figure 6.2 we see that logging does not balance this batch; something stronger, perhaps the negative inverse, would be needed. That implies quite a difference in shape, since we can get a rough feel for shape differences by seeing how far apart shape fits are on the ladder of transformations. Probably this shape difference is just a simple floor effect. The enrolment figures for the lower half of this batch are very low indeed and could hardly get much smaller. We probably should not make too much of this batch's unusual shape since the batch size is small ($N = 9$) and the figures may not be very accurate; accurate statistics are expensive and the poorer countries like those in batches I and II often cannot afford them. In many ways the shape difference between the US and Canadian population batches in Chapter 5 was more impressive. That shape difference was much smaller (the same transform worked tolerably for both batches, though the US batch looks a bit better in square roots than in logs) but the small difference in shape was based on very good data and a good idea of what the processes underlying the shape might be.

By this stage you can do transformations of various kinds, can decide which to do, and can see many of the varied uses of transformation. You will get both more practice and more knowledge of these uses as we go along, for there will be case after case in which we cannot do without transformations.

Summary

Let us briefly recap what we have learned about transformations in Chapters 5 and 6. First, we have seen that transformations can be used as summaries of the shapes of batches. With summaries of shape, level and spread we have three pieces of information that tell us a great deal about a batch. This powerful three-part summary is a kind of 'troika' in which all three pieces are important. Indeed, sometimes knowing shape is even more important than knowing level or spread: for example, consider income distributions. Some students of revolution and conflict argue that the wealth of a country (level) is not very important by itself because people define themselves as rich or poor in relative terms; further, even the distance between wealth and poverty (spread) is not necessarily important since there are usually persuasive ideologies to justify inequality; what may really provide potential for unrest is heavy concentration of much of the wealth in a very few hands (an extreme straggling upward) or a sudden change in the shape of wealth so that substantial portions of the population gain and lose a lot in relative position. This is one example of ways in which the shape of a batch may have important effects; we have already given an example of ways in which the shape may be an effect of something else (that is, the shape of population batches was traced to a fairly steady growth rate).

When we have a shape and understand it, we can make use of it. For example, if population increases exponentially (as in our example in Chapter 5) then we can extrapolate future population figures by assuming that this kind of growth will continue. Extrapolation will work if we have found the shape correctly (our data might be inadequate and mislead us) and if the mechanisms underlying the shape continue to work in the same way (e.g. if birth and death rates do not change too much). But it is much better if you understand the mechanisms because you feel much more confident about the projections. You can keep an eye on the mechanisms and adjust your predictions as the mechanisms change. Then you will not be like the chicken that ran to the farmhouse door every day at the sound of the bell to be fed – until the day it ran at the sound of the bell to have its head chopped off.

Once a shape is found, and understood as well as possible at the time, the next step is to remove it. This step provides many conveniences for further analysis. For example, it will then be possible to see more: often details of clumping are clearer, and very often the role of outliers is clarified. Apparent outliers may turn out to be just a reflection of the shape of the batch; or outliers may remain outliers after transformation; or extremes that did not look like outliers originally may become so after the batch has been transformed to the standard shape.

Transformation may also underline batch differences in shape. Often no transformation will do a good job for all the batches. If you find that your data are like this, note that what you do *not* do is find the best transformation for each batch considered independently. If these are related batches we want to compare them; and if they have been transformed in varying ways they will be no longer comparable. Instead, try to get some mileage out of looking at these aberrant batches as outliers from shape. Remember that the data in the batches are often imperfect, so that slight variations in shape may be nothing but chance fluctuations or errors of some sort. Only rather striking shape differences should really 'grab' you.

Finally, there is another use of transformation that is very important indeed. We will soon see that many of the confirmatory statistics, especially the most common and most useful ones, are designed for normally distributed data and will work less well or not at all when the data have very different shapes. Therefore, when we have a confirmatory question to ask of single-peaked but asymmetric data, we make the data more nearly symmetric by transforming. How much simpler it is to make distributions more nearly normal than to make new statistics for every distribution.

We have stressed symmetry and the use of box plots in these chapters because these tend to be the most important issue and the most useful tool. But do not forget that the standard shape has just one major peak as well as symmetry, and the number of peaks in a batch is not easily detected in a box plot alone. If your raw data look clumped, it is best to transform the whole batch and look at its stem and leaf after transformation; then if the data are clearly multi-peaked you can think about sub-batching. We have one other technical reminder; it is often awkward or impossible to transform batches with zero or negative values (for example, zero has no log). If your data include such values, add some number to all that data, where the number is large enough to remove all zero and negative values. For example, if the lowest value is −50 you could add +51 to every value. This will move all the levels up by the same amount but usually won't seriously affect anything else and will make transformation much more feasible and appropriate.

Some of these uses of transformation are more sophisticated than others and take longer to get used to, but all of them are important and all will become clear to you as you work with data and get to know more about them. So we urge you, for these reasons, to think about shapes and try to understand them. It takes a lot of experience to do this really well, so start soon.

Exploratory and Confirmatory

We have used the picturesque term 'straggle' for a trailing off of the data. It is more conventionally called *skewness*. 'Shape' is closest to the standard term *distribution*. Transformation is used in confirmatory as well as exploratory work, but in confirmatory work the criteria for 'good' transformation may be modified a bit. For example, if you want to transform several related batches before using a confirmatory test like analysis of variance (Chapter 10) then you often want batch spreads to be roughly equal, as suggested here; but the spreads you equalize are standard deviations, not midspreads. This is just a difference in emphasis; basically, the procedures and purposes of transformation stay much the same.

Using the Computer

In Figure 6.4 we showed how to plot log spread against log level and to find the slope by hand. This slope can then be used to give a first guess in finding a spread equalizing transform for a set of batches. MINITAB can help in a variety of ways here.

1 To obtain levels and spreads use the DESCRIBE command which gives the median and both quartiles: Q3-Q1 gives the midspread.
2 You can input these data into a column of medians and a column of midspreads; make sure you keep them in the same order – this is important.
3 Say your batch of medians is in C1 and the midspreads are in C2. The logged values can be found by:

MTB> LOGTEN C1 INTO C3
MTB> LOGTEN C2 INTO C4

4 To get your log level – log spread plot:

MTB> PLOT C4 vs C2

5 If you have *six or more* batches, you can usually find the slope easily by:

MTB> RLINE C4 C3

This will give you more output than you will need here, but the first entry in the first line is the slope. This won't work with fewer than six batches though.

Table 6.6 National populations, 1970 (estimated) in thousands

Africa		Americas (Excluding USA, Canada)		Europe Plus USA and Canada	
Algeria	14 330	Argentina	23 748	Albania	2 136
Burundi	3 544	Barbados	238	Austria	7 391
Congo	1 191	Bolivia	4 931	Belgium	9 656
Equatorial Guinea	285	Brazil	93 319	Bulgaria	8 490
Guinea	3 921	Chile	9 369	Canada	21 324
Kenya	11 225	Colombia	21 118	Finland	4 606
Lesotho	931	Costa Rica	1 727	France	50 768
Liberia	1 523	Cuba	8 472	German Democratic	
Madagascar	6 750	Dominican Rep.	4 062	Republic	17 058
Mali	5 047	Ecuador	6 093	Greece	8 793
Niger	4 024	El Salvador	3 534	Hungary	10 338
Nigeria	55 073	Guatemala	5 097	Iceland	204
Rwanda	3 679	Guyana	709	Italy	53 661
Somalia	2 789	Haiti	4 235	Liechtenstein	21
South Africa	22 469	Honduras	2 509	Monaco	23
Swaziland	422	Jamaica	1 869	Netherlands	13 032
Togo	1 960	Mexico	50 695	Norway	3 877
Uganda	9 806	Nicaragua	1 833	Portugal	8 663
Tanzania	13 273	Panama	1 434	Romania	20 253
Upper Volta	5 380	Paraguay	2 386	Spain	33 779
		Peru	13 586	Sweden	8 043
		Trinidad-Tobago	1 027	Switzerland	6 187
		Uruguay	2 886	United States	204 875
		Venezuela	10 275		

Source: United Nations (1976); reproduced by permission.

HOMEWORK

1 Consider the data in Table 6.6, which provides estimates of the populations of nations in about 1970, in three batches: Africa, the Americas and Europe. Only nations that were independent by 1970 were included. Canada and the USA are included in the Europe batch because they are more similar to the batch demographically and technically. Use trial-and-error to find a satisfactory transform for the set of three batches. Note any false or hidden outliers and discuss.

2 Use the plot of logged *dq* by logged median to suggest a transformation for the female suicide rates and for the male suicide rates.

FIRST REVIEW
Batch Analysis

In this section we have brought together several sets of batch data. Each of them is complex enough and interesting enough (we hope) to make them suitable for reviewing most of the things you've learned about batches. Select any one of these sets and explore it thoroughly. Since these data come from standard sources, you should expect to find yourselves turning to these sources for additional relevant data where you are led to interesting speculations that need checking out, or generally where it is necessary for pushing an analysis further.

In assignments of this sort, there is a strong tendency for students to try to do some of everything to show that they know how. Such assignments tend to have a very disorganized, helter-skelter sense to them, and are generally not very good as data analyses. Much better is the organic analysis, where the paper is organized around a few initial questions or speculations, which may have been suggested by initial exploration of the data, and which are pursued in depth. Such an analysis uses those techniques that are called for by the situation. In short, we suggest that you treat this like a data analysis rather than like a test: write an essay based on the data and the ideas you get from thinking about and playing with them. If you feel obliged to show that you can, for example, compute a variance though your analysis didn't require it, put it in an appendix.

The order of your work and the organization of your write-up are your business, but we will make a few suggestions that many students find helpful. First, try to order your analysis 'organically' as suggested above. This often means not doing things in the order used in the chapters. The chapters moved (of course!) from easy things to harder things, which may not be a meaningful order for your analysis. For example, often the initial plotting of the batches suggests you should transform before getting deeply into level, spread or outliers. Secondly, the order of your work does not have to be linear or tidy. Since you are exploring, you may change your mind as you go; or you may not be able to foresee later steps before earlier ones are done, and this can lead to dead ends, backtracking, missed insights that occur to you in the supermarket checkout queue, and so on. That is the nature of the enterprise. With regard to writing up, we strongly urge you to write as you go: the resulting essay will backtrack as your work does, and hence may be a poor piece of composition but a good report of an actual exploration. You can keep things sufficiently clear and organized by having summaries of major ideas from time to time and at the end. If you try to write after all the numerical work and thinking is over (an option people find peculiarly tempting) you will probably find it difficult. Ideas may be forgotten, so analyses must be re-thought; ideas from different parts of the analysis are hard to sort out. Anyway, it is boring to do the same thing for a long time (first just numbers, then just writing).

We have just one final comment on batching. So far, we have batched for you, but you may want to do your own batching, perhaps even in this review work. For example, suppose you work on Example 2, infant mortality rates. We have divided up the countries in this table by level of wealth and development. This makes sense if you think that these are the critical variables. You may prefer to look at batching by region, politics or any other variable you think is crucial. In short, you should feel free to make this *your* analysis.

Example 1 Socialization and Fear of People

Many personality theorists look at experience in childhood for explanations of numerous maladaptive adult behaviours. In the opinion of these theorists an experience like weaning, common to children in every society, involves discomfort and anxiety which may have long-term effects. Whiting and Child (1962) look at weaning, toilet training, independence training, sexual behaviour training and socialization of aggression, all of them universal and all with the potential for producing long-term anxiety. What Whiting and Child looked at especially was the severity of socialization, arguing that the greater the parental severity, the greater likelihood of anxiety in the children. We use a summary measure of all the areas, called 'average socialization anxiety', for our batching. Societies with anxiety scores of 13 or more are placed in the high batch, those with anxiety scores of 11 or 12 in the moderate batch, and the rest in the low batch in Table R1.1.

One major way in which long-term effects of socialization anxiety might manifest themselves in adults would be the inability to deal satisfactorily with others. The authors also provide ratings of the various societies on fear of human beings, the higher the rating the greater the fear. Table R1.1 gives 'fear of human beings' scores for 48 societies plus the society names in case you want to learn more about them. Whiting and Child (1962) provide additional information about these societies and more still is available in the Human Relations Area Files, as indeed are additional ethnographies.

Example 2 Infant Mortality Rates by Levels of Development

The next table reports the number of infants who die before reaching one year of age, per thousand live births, mostly for 1978. These data are batched by

Table R1.1   Socialization anxiety and fear of human beings

High socialization anxiety		Moderate anxiety		Low anxiety	
Alorese	5	Ainu	6	Bena	7
Ashanti	5	Arapesh	10	Chenchu	2
Azande	10	Baiga	10	Comanche	5
Chagga	9	Balinese	4	Marquesans	7
Chamorro	6	Hopi	8	Siriono	2
Chiricahua	9	Kurtatchi	9	Tikopia	5
Dahomeans	6	Kwakiutl	10	Yagua	11
Dobuans	8	Lakher	7	Yakut	6
Kutenai	6	Lepcha	7		
Kwoma	10	Lesu	9		
Navaho	7	Manus	4		
Paiute	11	Maori	9		
Rwala	7	Ontong-Javanese	6		
Sanpoil	9	Papago	4		
Tanala	7	Pukapukans	6		
Tenino	8	Samoans	5		
Thonga	7	Slave	8		
Western Apache	8	Teton	0		
		Trobrianders	10		
		Venda	9		
		Wogeo	10		

Source: Whiting and Child (1962).

level of development. A long look at Table R1.2 will clearly indicate that infant mortality is related to industrial development and wealth. But thoughtful exploration will suggest a variety of fruitful avenues for pursuing the analysis further.

Example 3   Male and Female Education in Developing Countries

These data (Table R1.3), randomly selected from the three levels of developing economies, are taken from *The World Development Report*, 1986. There are numerous ways of approaching these data. You can look for example at each batch as a combination of development and gender, or alternatively examine the three batches of differences. Further education can be viewed as a consequence of development, or the reverse.

Table R1.2   Infant mortality rates per 1000 live births

Low income developing

Bangladesh	139	Madagascar	69
Rwanda	127	Haiti	112
Tanzania	185	Upper Volta (Burkina Faso)	208
Afghanistan	237	Mali	152
Chad	146	Niger	143
Ethiopia	145		
Nepal	148		
Sri Lanka	43		
Togo	107		

Middle income developing

Egypt	108	Guatemala	77
Honduras	118	Tunisia	123
Thailand	68	Malaysia	31
Bolivia	158	Jamaica	20
Philippines	65	South Korea	37
El Salvador	60		
Nicaragua	37		
Colombia	98		
Ecuador	66		
Dominican Republic	37		

Higher income developing

Turkey	118	Taiwan	25
Panama	47	Greece	19
Chile	55	Singapore	12
Costa Rica	78	Spain	16
Brazil	92	Israel	15
Uruguay	46		
Portugal	39		
Hong Kong	12		

Centrally planned economies

Cuba	25	Poland	22
Romania	31	North Korea	33
Yugoslavia	34	Czechoslovakia	19
Bulgaria	22	East Germany	13
Hungary	24	China	71

Industrialized countries

Ireland	16	Belgium	12
Italy	18	Canada	12
UK	14	Norway	9
Finland	9	West Germany	15
Austria	15	USA	14
Japan	10	Denmark	9
France	11	Sweden	8
Netherlands	10	Switzerland	10

Source: World Development Report, 1980.

Table R1.3 Male and female education* in developing countries

	Male	Female
Low income		
Mali	30	18
Nepal	100	43
Niger	34	19
Uganda	65	49
India	100	68
Benin	92	43
Kenya	104	97
Guinea	49	23
Sudan	59	42
Senegal	63	42
Laos	94	80
Vietnam	120	105
Middle income		
Bolivia	94	81
Philippines	115	113
Egypt	101	76
Thailand	101	97
Ecuador	117	114
Turkey	116	107
Jordan	101	98
Mongolia	105	107
Upper middle income		
Brazil	106	99
Malaysia	100	98
Uruguay	110	107
South Korea	104	102
Argentina	107	107
Algeria	106	82
Greece	105	105
Hong Kong	107	104
Singapore	115	111
Iraq	113	99

* Number enrolled in primary school as percentage of age group

Section II
From Exploration to Confirmation

You have now acquired a good variety of exploratory techniques for studying batches. You can fit, remove, and discuss major batch features; level, shape, and spread. You can look hard at outliers and at exceptions to overall patterns in sets of related batches. Many ideas can be generated in the process. Now we move to the different, but related and equally important matter of testing ideas after they have been generated. The next four chapters introduce some basic confirmatory tools like random sampling and hypothesis testing, and show how these can be applied to the problem of testing possible differences in levels. You should reread the first chapter soon to remind yourself of the major differences between exploratory and confirmatory approaches.

7
The Random Sample

In previous chapters we used recent statistics from 15 countries to develop a number of ideas about suicide. Will those ideas hold for these countries at other times, or for the hundred or more other countries in the world? A little thought suggests that we would be rash to assume so. On the one hand, the patterns we found may have been flukes based on a set of countries that happen, by chance, to be unusual (we will talk more about this kind of possibility in the next chapter). On the other hand, the patterns may be misleading because they are usual, but usual only for some kinds of countries. Here the difficulty is that our 15 countries are obviously not a typical cross-section of the world's nations. Instead, they are countries that were selected for particular reasons, one of which is that their suicide statistics are considered fairly reliable (according to WHO); this in turn suggests that they are wealthier and more developed than most. The patterns we saw may not hold at all for poorer countries or for countries from different regions (say Africa) with different cultures and social structures. If we want to make a well-founded guess about patterns for all countries by looking at some countries, we would do better if we had a more representative set to work with. Choosing representative sets brings us to sampling, which is the topic of this chapter.

More formally, *sampling* consists of selecting elements from some *universe* with the intention of making inferences about that universe. The universe can be any collection of objects of interest: all the countries in the world, all the females in London, all the manufacturing companies with fewer than 5000 employees, all protest movements in the nineteenth century or whatever. Basically, the universe is the set of things you want to know about. So the sample you pick from the universe should be chosen in a way that will give as accurate a picture as possible. A lot of this chapter will be spent describing a method of choosing known as random sampling, and showing how accuracy is related to sample size.

Why Sample?

Clearly it is the universe, the full slice of reality, that we want to know about. So why, you might ask, don't we just go and look at it? Sometimes we do; the modern census is the most familiar example of this. A decision is made that the population of a given country is the universe you want to know about, you decide what you want to know, and then you go and ask everyone about the things you want to know. (Some writers use the term 'population' where we have used 'universe'. We avoid it here because of the easy confusion with 'population' meaning 'the total number of people living in a given area'.)

Looking at the universe seems like a good idea, and often it is; but there are problems that prevent us from studying complete universes all the time. One problem is expense; it should be clear that complete enumerations of large universes can be very costly in both time and money. Another problem is that of 'reality', the possibility that what we are studying can be changed or even destroyed by observing or measuring it. In order to 'measure' the taste of a cake you must eat at least a part; to measure the life of a light bulb you must burn it out; when you have a blood test, the doctor takes a sample of your blood (do you want her to take it all?); even measuring a respondent's opinions can significantly alter these opinions. In cases like these, if we study a whole universe then we change or even destroy that universe so that the results we get are no longer true. This is not desirable scientifically and it may be undesirable ethically as well. Further, a complete enumeration may take so long that from the time the survey begins to the time it ends the universe may have changed greatly. Finally, we may not want to study the universe itself because we can get a more accurate picture by studying a sample of it. This may sound paradoxical but there are simple and solid reasons for it. Most importantly, it is feasible to do a very high-quality job of data collection and analysis on a sample and often not feasible to be as careful with a census. In the case of the recent Canadian censuses, the requirement that there be a complete enumeration made it necessary to use mailed questionnaires or many poorly trained interviewers, or to spend far more time and money than was budgeted for. Statistics Canada chose the first option, knowing they were letting themselves in for some error thereby. Similarly, analysis of very large amounts of data cannot economically be done as accurately or thoroughly as with smaller amounts of data. It is interesting to note that in the USA, for example, the census is *corrected* on the basis of the Current Population Survey, based on a sample of less than one per cent of the population!

Thus we often want to study a universe through studying a sample of it. This is a more familiar procedure than you may realize at first, since 'home-grown' sampling is done a lot outside of science. A manufacturer will often try out a new product on a sample of consumers or communities, intending to go into full production should the try-out be a success; this would be a case of generalizing from sample results (the try-out went well) to a universe (the product should sell well in general). Similarly, governments will often try out a new policy suggestion before deciding whether to implement it across the board; for example, the Canadian and US governments have tried out income supplement plans in selected communities. Everyone samples in small ways: we look at the sky to see if we need to take an umbrella (sample the weather to predict whether it will rain that day), we eat a meal at a new restaurant to see if 'the food is good there' or we read the synopsis on the back cover of a murder mystery and decide that we will or won't like the book.

Casual sampling is generally better than no data gathering at all, but clearly it presents problems. What if we hit the restaurant on a bad night or order one of the poorer dishes? What if sample communities are chosen because they are handy, and they turn out not to be typical? Without some careful effort to get a sample that reflects the universe adequately, we could easily be misled. Ann Landers asked her readers, 'If you had to do it over again, would you have children?' Almost 70 per cent of nearly 10 000 respondents said that they wouldn't. Subsequently, the newspaper *Newsday* commissioned a national random sample of fewer than 1400 parents, more than 90 per cent of whom said that they *would* have children again. Which result do you believe? Even though Ann Landers had far more responses, a little thought should convince you that we should be very cautious about interpreting her results. After all, who writes to Ann Landers? Often, it is people with problems, writing when their problems are severe. In short, her respondents were a self-selected group perhaps mostly of unhappy parents. The professional poll, on the other hand, was selected without bias, so while there were certainly some unhappy parents in their sample, there were also far more for whom parenting had at least some pleasures.

We would like a good sample to be unbiased, to reflect the universe accurately. Then we would be a great deal more confident that the sample results were a good guide to the general universe pattern. The key to getting an unbiased, representative sample is selecting the sample in the right way: selecting it *randomly*. Randomness is the best guarantee that the sample will have no *systematic biases* in it. What would a systematic bias be like? Imagine sampling, say, every tenth person leaving the men's changing room at a gym – funny, very few women in our sample. Far-fetched, you say. Perhaps, but samples have been collected on weekday mornings at shopping centres and the researchers have been astonished to find so few employed adult males represented. When Dr Spock, a famous pediatrician was being tried in the USA for his anti-war activities, there were no women on the jury! This was despite the fact that both men and women were equally eligible. Several more or less deliberate steps had resulted in the complete absence of those persons who would be most likely to be favourable to the defendant (Zeisel and Kalven, 1972). Other sorts of biases can be found even when the initial target sample is a good one. If you mail out questionnaires, who will respond? Typically, it is those who are more involved, have more to gain from your enquiry, etc.

What do we mean by 'random'? Well, we do not mean haphazard or hit-and-miss. Quite the opposite in fact; we mean a sampling procedure with a clearly defined property, ordinarily that each element of the universe we are interested in has an equal chance of being selected for the sample. Such a procedure gives the best chance of getting a representative cross-section of the universe. (We say 'best chance' because sampling is, after all, a chance procedure. You could take a random sample and get something very atypical while someone else collected oddments haphazardly and got better results; but although this is conceivable, it is not very likely.) We will soon show you how random sampling can be done very easily.

Suppose we have a random sample; what can we expect of it? Let's get more specific and ask about levels, since levels are of basic importance. We have used levels a lot in exploration and they will be the main focus of the first confirmatory tests we meet. What can we learn about the universe level (which is what we would like to know) from the sample level (which is what we will have)? You can see right away that the sample mean is not likely to be exactly the same as the universe mean; the sample mean will probably be close to the universe mean (after all, the sample mean is supposed to reflect the universe); and the sample mean may sometimes be far off the universe value (accidents can happen). Obviously we need to get some idea of how misleading a sample is likely to be. So our next step will be to get some samples and examine their relationship to the universe. This will show you how simple random sampling is done as well as illustrating how random samples behave.

Random Samples and Ghosts

The first step in learning about random samples is to get a nice small universe so that it can easily be compared with samples from it. We have chosen data from Whiting and Child (1962) on 'fear of others'; specifically, on the extent to which human illness is thought to be caused by others. Agents sometimes thought responsible for illness included other people, both living and dead, as well as non-human spirits. Ethnographies of 75 societies were examined and rated by each of two judges on the extent to which illness was attributed to each of the agents. The scores range from 0, a very low degree of attribution to the agent, to 12, a very high degree of attribution. Table 7.1 contains scores for three agents: ghosts (dead people), other human beings (sorcerers, etc.) and spirits (supernatural beings) (see Whiting and Child, 1962, for further descriptions). We will sample from the 'ghost' scores, leaving the other two as homework for you.

Just in passing, we should make it clear that these 75 societies are only our small universe for the purpose of this chapter. They are not the universe of all societies, nor are they all 'primitive' societies or any other easily described universe, nor a random sample of any of these. Whiting and Child used these 75 societies because, at time of writing, they were the only cases for which appropriate data had been recorded to the extent that Whiting and Child needed. We will treat these 75 cases as a universe in themselves, and try not to think of them as representative of a larger universe – they probably are not.

Table 7.2 presents the 'fear of ghosts' universe in tally form. The shape is

Table 7.1   Ratings on fear of ghosts, human beings and spirits
for 75 primitive societies

		Ghosts	Humans	Spirits
	Abipone	3	9	3
	Ainu	5	6	10
	Alorese	9	5	9
	Andamanese	10	4	10
5	Arapesh	8	10	8
	Ashanti	5	5	8
	Azande	0	10	5
	Baiga	7	10	8
	Balinese	3	4	9
10	Bena	7	7	8
	Chagga	9	9	9
	Chamorro	4	6	10
	Chenchu	8	2	8
	Chewa	8	8	9
15	Chiricahua	8	9	10
	Comanche	2	5	8
	Copper Eskimo	8	7	8
	Dahomeans	7	6	7
	Dobuans	0	8	9
20	Dusun	8	0	9
	Flathead	0	0	4
	Hopi	0	8	9
	Ifugao	8	8	10
	Jivaro	4	10	9
25	Kazak	0	0	8
	Kiwai	4	9	9
	Kurtatchi	4	9	6
	Kutenai	0	6	0
	Kwakiutl	8	10	8
30	Kwoma	4	10	4
	Lakher	0	7	9
	Lamba	9	4	10
	Lapp	8	10	9
	Lepcha	3	7	5
35	Lesu	3	9	3
	Malekula	7	10	7
	Manus	11	4	11
	Maori	9	9	10

Table 7.1—continued

		Ghosts	Humans	Spirits
	Marquesans	8	7	10
40	Marshallese	9	7	9
	Masai	1	6	3
	Murngin	7	10	7
	Nauru	8	9	8
	Navaho	9	7	10
45	Omaha	7	10	7
	Ontong-Javanese	10	6	10
	Paiute	8	11	10
	Palaung	0	8	10
	Papago	8	4	9
50	Pukapukans	8	6	8
	Riffians	0	9	10
	Rwala	0	7	8
	Samoans	8	5	8
	Sanpoil	3	9	9
55	Siriono	3	2	10
	Slave	0	8	4
	Tanala	9	7	9
	Taos	0	10	8
	Tenino	0	8	8
60	Teton	0	0	10
	Thonga	3	7	7
	Tikopia	6	5	8
	Tiv	0	9	10
	Trobrianders	0	10	9
65	Venda	7	9	7
	Wapisiana	0	10	9
	Warrau	0	3	8
	Western Apache	4	8	9
	Witoto	7	10	9
70	Wogeo	6	10	6
	Yagua	0	11	1
	Yakut	5	6	10
	Yukaghir	3	4	10
	Yungar	0	10	8
75	Zuni	4	10	4
	Mean		$\mu = 7.17$	$\mu = 7.95$
	Standard deviation		$\sigma = 2.81$	$\sigma = 2.28$

Source: Whiting and Child (1962: 344–6)

Table 7.2   The 'fear of ghosts' universe

Rating	Distribution
11	1
10	11
9	~~1111~~ 11
8	~~1111~~ ~~1111~~ ~~1111~~
7	~~1111~~ 111
6	11
5	111
4	~~1111~~ 11
3	~~1111~~ 111
2	1
1	1
0	~~1111~~ ~~1111~~ ~~1111~~ ~~1111~~

Mean $= \mu = 4.7$
Standard deviation $= \sigma = 3.5$

not much like the 'standard' one we have been stressing, the bell-shaped 'normal distribution' we will meet so often in the confirmatory work to come. Single-peaked? Hardly. The distribution is at least double-peaked (clumping around 0 and at 8) and maybe triple-peaked (some lesser clumping around 3 and 4). Symmetric? Not that either. Trailing off smoothly to either side of the centre? Not with all those zeroes. The ugliness of this bumpy shape is a welcome sight because the distributions that we study often *are* ugly (though not often as far from standard shape as this); and it is important for us to know how samples behave even when they are taken from less-than-perfectly-normal universes. Table 7.2 also reports the mean and standard deviation of the universe.

How will we go about sampling from the mini-universe of societies and their scores on fear of ghosts? The procedure used is similar to one that would be used in sampling on a large universe, and the patterns we will find illustrate things true of sampling generally. Drawing samples would be quite a chore if we tried to do it by flipping coins, worthless if we tried to do it by guess work. Fortunately there is an effective and easy way: use a set of random numbers already worked out by somebody else (or something else – computers do the actual work). Table A.1 (p. 367), consisting of 2500 random digits, is a small example. The great advantage of a random number table is that the numbers in it are random in very strict senses: in this table, each digit is equally likely to appear at any given place, as is each pair of numbers, each triplet, etc. If we pull out a chunk of a random number table we get a random selection of numbers. So if we want a random selection from a population we can just link each item in the universe with an index number, pull a set of random numbers from the table, and let the universe items with the associated index numbers be our sample.

Let's try this technique out by drawing a random sample from our mini-universe. First we must link each item in the universe with a number; as you can see in Table 7.1, each item has an index number from 01 to 75 (we have just noted the 'fives'). Thus, the society with index number 2 is the Ainu, which has a score of 5 on fear of ghosts; don't confuse the 5 which is the datum with the 2 which is its 'house number'. Now we can use Table A.1, because every pair of digits in this table corresponds to an index number of one unique member of our universe. Seventy-six to ninety-nine, and 00 (the number corresponding to 100), are simply dropped from our sample; there are no elements in the mini-universe that correspond to them). Next, we take as many pairs of random digits from Table A.1 as we need. They can be taken in any way as long as you decide before looking at the table. We decided to start at the upper left and read from left to right along the rows this time; next time we will have to start somewhere else, or go in a different direction. Otherwise we would get the identical sample each time. We will choose ten samples of size two – the 'ghost' scores from ten pairs of societies. Reading across Table A.1 we get 15, 77 (we drop this one), 01, 64, 69, 69, etc. These correspond to scores of 8, 3, 0, 7, 7, etc.; so our first sample of size two is (8,3) and the mean of this sample is 5.5. Table 7.3 gives the samples of size two, their means and the grand mean of sample means, $\bar{x}$. The mini-sample means vary a lot from 0 to 7, though the grand mean is pretty close to the true mean of 4.7.

This is an easy method and it works. The digits in the random number table are random, so any row or column or diagonal we read off is random, giving us a random selection of identification numbers, and a random sample.

Table 7.3   Random samples of size two, fear of ghosts

Sample number	Index numbers selected from random number table	Data corresponding to index numbers selected	Means
1	15, 01	8, 3	5.5
2	64, 69	0, 7	3.5
3	69, 58	7, 0	3.5
4	40, 16	9, 2	5.5
5	60, 20	0, 8	4.0
6	22, 28	0, 0	0.0
7	26, 46	4, 10	7.0
8	66, 36	0, 7	3.5
9	66, 17	0, 8	4.0
10	34, 40	3, 9	6.0
			$\bar{x} = 4.25$

There is one last problem about drawing simple random samples: sometimes one or more index numbers will come up more than once in a single sample. This didn't happen in any of the samples of size two, but did in the larger samples. This happens less often when sampling from very large universes, but even so it does happen. What do we do? There are two sampling strategies here: sampling with, and without, replacement. When sampling without replacement, a data point can be used only once in any particular sample; if its index number is drawn again the second (or third or nth) drawing is ignored. When sampling with replacement (what we did here), if a data point is drawn several times in the sample, it is included that many times just as if it were an entirely new point. Sampling without replacement is similar to playing a hand of poker: once one person draws the ace of clubs, say, it cannot be dealt again. Sampling with replacement is more like roulette: if 17 comes up on one spin, nothing prevents it from coming up again on the very next spin.

We use 'sampling with replacement' because the results are a bit simpler. In practice, most researchers sample universes far larger than the sample size so that there is little practical difference between 'with' and 'without'.

Table 7.4 Means and standard deviations for samples of size 5, 10 and 20 from 'fear of ghosts'

N = 5		N = 10		N = 20	
6.2	3.56	6.4	3.03	5.30	3.827
2.2	3.49	5.4	3.41	3.40	3.604
8.0	1.00	5.5	3.34	5.30	3.466
4.0	4.00	5.2	3.22	4.40	3.885
4.8	4.44	3.9	3.84	4.35	3.787
5.8	3.35	5.5	3.31	2.85	3.468
6.6	3.78	5.1	3.21	5.40	3.691
2.8	3.27	4.2	3.12	4.85	4.043
2.4	3.91	3.5	4.09	5.35	3.631
2.6	2.61	4.4	2.95	4.10	3.370
3.0	3.32	4.0	3.68	3.70	3.197
5.0	3.16	3.6	4.35	5.35	3.133
5.0	3.61	4.3	3.20	5.10	3.684
5.0	4.58	2.7	3.80	4.60	3.604
5.4	2.88	6.0	3.68	4.90	3.597
5.6	1.82	5.6	3.53	5.25	4.025
2.6	3.44	3.7	3.56	4.20	3.473
6.8	2.95	5.2	3.36	5.10	3.493
5.6	3.44	3.5	4.12	3.65	3.731
4.6	3.78	4.6	3.53	4.65	3.631

How Samples Behave

Now we have seen one way to get random samples and we are ready to consider the question raised earlier: how accurately will the sample mean reflect the universe mean? To help explore this question, we have taken 20 samples of size 5, 10 and 20 and put the sample means and standard deviations in Table 7.4.

We see that the means of sample means (4.71, 4.62, 4.59) tend to be close to the mean of the universe (4.69). They are not dead on, but then we can't expect them to be. Sometimes a sample or set of samples will be too high or sometimes too low just by chance. This is inevitable, and we must be prepared to live with it, but we would like to know how serious it is likely to be – how far off a sample mean is likely to be from the mean of the universe. We can get insight into this problem by looking at a feature of the batch displays of Table 7.5: the spread. The eye is struck by a strong 'funnelling' in the batches: as the count grows from 5 to 20, the spread of the sample means narrows strongly. The sds of the means and dq show this pattern clearly. Means of samples of size 5 often are far away from their batch centre, means of samples of size 20 are usually closer. In general, the larger the sample, the closer an individual sample mean tends to be to the true value in the universe. This is an illustration of the *law of large numbers*, and of the most important features of random sampling, because it guarantees that, *in general*, larger samples give us greater accuracy

Table 7.5   Behaviour of sample means by size of sample

Stem and leaf N = 5 Leaf unit = 0.10			Stem and leaf N = 10 Leaf unit = 0.10			Stem and leaf N = 20 Leaf unit = 0.10		
2	2	24	1	2	7	1	2	8
5	2	668	1	3		2	3	4
6	3	0	6	3	55679	4	3	67
6	3		10	4	0234	8	4	1234
7	4	0	10	4	6	(4)	4	6689
9	4	88	9	5	1224	8	5	11233334
(4)	5	0004	5	5	556			
.7	5	668	2	6	04			
4	6	2						
3	6	68						
1	7							
1	7							
1	8	0						
$\bar{x} = 4.71$			$\bar{x} = 4.62$			$\bar{x} = 4.59$		
$sd = 1.66$			$sd = 0.98$			$sd = 0.75$		
$dq = 2.9$			$dq = 1.725$			$dq = 1.162$		

(though sometimes, by chance, smaller samples outperform larger ones – as here).

The Standard Error

The previous points are new enough and important enough to reiterate: if you take a lot of random samples, the sample means have a distribution (they are a batch); this distribution of the means has a mean of its own, which tends towards the mean of the universe; finally, this distribution of the means has a spread of its own, which gets smaller as the sample size gets bigger.

We can go further than this and tell you exactly how the spread in the batch of sample means is related to the sample size in the long run. In the long run, if you have an enormous number of samples, it can be shown that the batch of sample means has, as its standard deviation, the standard deviation of the universe divided by the square root of the number of cases in the *sample* (here 5, 10 and 20). This quantity is important enough to have a name of its own: the *standard error* (SE). We will not prove this for you, but we will appeal to your intuition. Look at what the formula says: the sample means will be less spread out as the samples get larger (the denominator increases with N), and they will be more spread out if the universe is more spread out (the numerator is the *sd* of the universe). Both these points are pretty reasonable ones. The samples are supposed to reflect the universe, so if the universe has a big spread, the samples should too. And we expect that big samples are more reliable than smaller ones, so larger Ns should produce samples that tend to have means closer to the true mean (the mean of the universe).

This general rule is meant to apply to the long run, to very large sets of samples; again, we can't expect it to work perfectly for just a few samples because of the sampling fluctuation. But still, if we look at our examples we find that the rule is not far off. The theory says that samples of sizes 5, 10 and 20 should have means whose SEs are 1.57, 1.11 and 0.79 because the standard deviation of the 75 fear-of-ghost scores is 3.5, and $3.5/\sqrt{5} = 1.57$ etc. In our examples the *sd*s of 1.66, 0.98 and 0.75 are really quite close to the theoretical values. We would get much closer if we took more samples, because then we would have bigger samples of the samples themselves!

The Central Limit Theorem

We have several related levels here, so it is handy to distinguish them with special terms to avoid confusion. At the most basic level, we have the universe and its mean and standard deviation (4.7 and 3.5 in our example). We set off universe parameters by giving them Greek letters, so the mean is symbolized by μ (pronounced 'mew'), the Greek equivalent of 'm', and the standard deviation is symbolized by σ (pronounced 'sigma'), the Greek equivalent of 's'.

The usage is standard: Greek letters, in statistics, tend to stand for characteristics of a universe.

At the other extreme we have a particular single sample, and it has a mean and a standard deviation too; we label these $\bar{x}$ and sd_x or s_x (standard deviation of x, the variable we are looking at).

This single sample is one of many that could be drawn. If we draw more than one (it is rare for a research plan to require more than one random sample), the sample mean will have a distribution that we call the 'sampling distribution of the mean', which we know will have a mean of μ and a standard deviation of $\sigma/\sqrt{N}$ (the standard error) in the long run. We know the level and spread of the sampling distribution of the mean; what about its shape? This can't be guessed at from our results in Table 7.5 as easily as the level and spread can be. It would take more samples to get a good look at shape, because shape is a more complex thing than level or spread. But if we had a lot of samples, with the samples of fairly large size, we would find the batch of sample means to be standard in its shape even though the universe is not. The bumps and lumps in the universe get 'averaged out' when sample means are taken, if the samples are reasonably large and plentiful. This will turn out to be another very important result; in statistics this is referred to as the *central limit theorem*. This theorem assures us that almost irrespective of the shape of the universe, as the size of the sample increases, the distribution of *means* becomes closer and closer to standard, with parameters μ and $\sigma/\sqrt{N}$. Thus a mean should not only reflect the level of the universe, it should also become more accurate (smaller spread) as N gets large.

It Isn't Only Means

We have only looked at sampling distribution of the mean because that will occupy our attention for several more chapters, but you could look at the sampling distribution of anything else and again you would find that the sample values tend to zero in on the universe value more and more closely as the sample size gets bigger.

We will not illustrate this pattern for other features in the detail that we used for the mean, since the basic idea is the same and the number of extra tables required would be excessive. Take a quick look at Table 7.6, which gives the tallies and standard deviations for five samples of size 20. Note that these are standard deviations for the samples; so far we have only seen standard deviations for the universe and for the three batches of means. Here, we see that the standard deviations of the samples tend to be like the standard deviation of the universe: the values 3.8, 3.6, 3.5, 3.8 and 3.9 are quite near the universe value 3.5. The larger the sample, the nearer its standard deviation is likely to be to the universe value (another instance of the law of large numbers).

The shapes of the five samples of size 20 tend to look rather like the universe shape too. The larger the sample, the closer the resemblance of its

Table 7.6 Distribution of five samples of size 20

1 Leaf unit = 0.10			2 Leaf unit = 0.10			3 Leaf unit = 0.10			4 Leaf unit = 0.10			5 Leaf unit = 0.10		
5	0	00000	9	0	000000000	4	0	0000	7	0	0000000	7	0	0000000
5	1		9	1		4	1		8	1	0	7	1	
6	2	0	9	2		4	2		8	2		7	2	
7	3	0	(3)	3	000	7	3	000	8	3		10	3	000
9	4	00	8	4	0	9	4	00	9	4	0	10	4	0
9	5		7	5		9	5		(2)	5	00	9	5	
9	6		7	6		9	6		9	6	0	9	6	
10	7	0	7	7	00	(4)	7	0000	8	7	0	9	7	0
10	8	000000	5	8	0000	7	8	000	7	8	0000	8	8	00000
4	9	00	1	9	0	4	9	000	3	9	000	3	9	00
												1	10	0

$\bar{x} = 5.3$ $s = 3.83$ $\bar{x} = 3.4$ $s = 3.60$ $\bar{x} = 5.3$ $s = 3.47$ $\bar{x} = 4.35$ $s = 3.79$ $\bar{x} = 4.4$ $s = 3.89$

shape to the universe; and so on for all of the many batch features one could calculate.

Different Kinds of Samples

We have just illustrated simple random sampling (often abbreviated to SRS), in which each element of the universe has an equal chance of ending up in the sample. This is the kind of sampling we assume in all the rest of the book; other kinds of random samples also 'work' but they introduce minor complications that we would prefer to ignore here. However, it is important to know that there are other important kinds of samples that are useful and often used.

We may not always want the basic type of sample in which all elements have an equal probability of inclusion. Sometimes it is less expensive or more useful just to have a *known* probability for each element. For example, a comparison of religious groups might require a greater probability of inclusion for members of smaller groups (Jews, Jehovah's Witnesses, etc.) so that one can get a reasonable number of them without getting far more of the majority of mainstream Christians than are needed. Samples with known (but unequal) probabilities of inclusion for various groups (called *strata*) are known as stratified random samples.

Another sort of problem, and solution, arises where travel costs become more important in the collection of data. Suppose, for example, you are doing a survey of Newfoundlanders, many of whom live in virtually inaccessible outports. If your sample has, say, 100 outporters in perhaps 50 outports, the costs of just getting interviewers in and out would be immense. It would be much more economical to define your sample in two stages: first, randomly sample the outports (perhaps five of these) and then sample residents within each outport (perhaps 20 in each), thus cutting 90 per cent off travel costs. This sort of two-stage procedure is called a cluster sample. Most large studies use combinations of cluster and stratified samples called multistage samples. Be aware, though, that should you be working with a sample more complex than SRS some formulae may require modification. Consult either a statistician or a book on sampling.

So far we have been talking as if it were easy to obtain perfectly random samples. All too often, however, we just can't avoid working with biased data. For example, it is very difficult and expensive to get much more than 80 per cent of the people randomly selected for a survey actually to take part. Among typical non-respondents are people on the move, people with fewer years of school, people uninterested in the research area, etc. Thus the effective sample, the people you get data for, tends to be biased towards residential stability, higher education, concern about the research, etc. Biased data can still be useful as long as we know about how large the bias is so we can allow for it. Kish (1965) provides a very useful discussion of the consequences of non-randomness, different kinds of sampling, and other important topics (see also Sudman, 1976).

Sample Size

If you are doing a study, how big a sample do you need? It depends on what you are looking for. If the patterns you expect to find are very strong (like big differences between batch means) then a relatively small sample may do; if you are looking for a subtle effect, a larger N will be needed. If you know roughly what kinds of data patterns and what kind of statistics you will work with, you can calculate the necessary N; we will give a small example later.

Sample size also depends on how expensive each data point is and how many things you plan to look at; for example, if you want to examine the relationship among many variables at once then more cases are needed than if you were looking at just a few variables. Another critical issue is how serious an incorrect decision will be – the costlier an error, the more data you should collect.

The necessary N can be a lot smaller than you might expect. National surveys, in which many variables are examined and many of the patterns are weak, can be done quite comfortably with two thousand cases or fewer. To get more would actually be a waste for most purposes: the bigger the sample, the less rapidly $\sqrt{N}$ grows and the less we gain by adding another case. If we have samples with $N = 1600$, the standard error is

$$\frac{\sigma}{\sqrt{N}} = \frac{\sigma}{40}; \text{ if } N = 6400, \text{ SE} = \frac{\sigma}{80}$$

Because we use the square root of sample size, we must quadruple the sample (and expense and trouble) to cut the standard error in half. It is a problem of diminishing returns. Researchers very rarely get samples of more than a few thousand, even if they can afford to, unless they have a very compelling reason, such as interest in a special group that can't be easily identified in advance. (If it could be listed in advance the researcher could just opt for stratified sampling, getting as many cases from the special group as needed without getting an overdose of the rest of the universe.)

Combining and Dividing Samples

A random sample can be subdivided into smaller random samples – just break it up randomly. This simple property turns out to be very useful indeed. If you have a large sample, it is often desirable to take a small subsample, explore it, then test your ideas with the rest of the original sample, which is a perfectly good random sample itself. Or you can take a small part for open-ended exploring to get broad ideas, then take a somewhat bigger part to polish these ideas into precision, and test the precise predictions on the remainder. Each of the subsamples is a random sample and reflects the universe as far as its N allows; each is an independent sample, and you can do whatever you like to one and be free to do what you like to another.

On the other hand it can be useful to know that two random samples of the same universe can be combined, making one larger but still random sample. This is handy if several comparable samples are available and none is big enough for the job at hand. Even if the samples are not exactly alike, a little artfulness can often succeed in merging them effectively. This is one of the principles underlying *meta-analysis*, a technique by which the results of many studies can be combined.

Overview

The relationship between a sample and its universe depends on two things: how you select the sample and how big it is. If the sample is chosen non-randomly then the sample is likely to be a biased picture of the universe and it is wise to be careful, correcting for the bias as far as possible and being cautious in drawing conclusions. If the sample is probably badly biased but you don't know enough about the bias to correct it, you are safest sticking to exploration. In the long run, this may help you get a fix on the size and kind of bias.

If your sample is selected randomly then you are in the much happier position of knowing what its relationship to the universe is like: the larger the sample, the closer any of its statistics is likely to be to the value for the universe, although, as we have seen, samples fluctuate and a small sample may turn out to be more accurate than a larger one just by chance. You now know exactly how this works for one very important statistic, the mean. If a very large number of samples of size N are drawn and their means calculated, the sample means have the same mean, μ, as the universe and they have standard deviation $\sigma/(\sqrt{N})$ (also called standard error).

Bigger samples are more accurate. Bigger samples can also be used more flexibly; for example, one can afford to use part of a large sample for exploration. But there always comes a point (varying with the research goals) when a larger N is not worthwhile. Finally, samples can be randomly subdivided or, if comparable, they can be merged, and the results are random samples too.

Using the Computer

Taking a random sample is easy using MINITAB. If you want four samples of size ten from a mini-universe stored in C1, then:

```
MTB> SAMPLE 10 C1 put into C4
MTB> SAMPLE 10 C1 C5
MTB> SAMPLE 10 C1 C6
MTB> SAMPLE 10 C1 C7.
```

These samples can be stem-and-leafed, box-plotted and described in the usual way.

If you want a set of random numbers (say, 100) to apply to a universe of, say, 15 000 that is not stored in memory (the more typical case):

```
MTB> RANDOM 100 C1;
SUBC> INTEGER a = 1 b = 15 000
```

where a and b represent the smallest and largest permissible index numbers respectively. Unless otherwise specified, sampling is without replacement.

HOMEWORK

1 Table 7.1 presents data on fear of humans and of spirits in Whiting and Childs's 75 societies. For either one of these, select ten random samples of size four and ten samples of size ten. Discuss what you find, remembering to bring in:

● universe mean and standard deviation (see Table 7.1);
● how you drew your sample, e.g. where you started in Table A.1, which direction you went in etc.;
● the means of each of the samples, standard deviation of the two batches of sample means and standard errors.

The sampling procedure is easy but a little dull; working with a friend is suggested.

We will be using means, variances and standard deviations a lot in this set of chapters. This might be a good time to review Chapter 3.

8
Confirmatory Statistics

In this chapter we continue our search for ways to generalize the ideas gained from exploratory work. In Chapter 7 we learned about the random sample, on which all confirmatory work is based. In this chapter we begin to show how such samples are used to make decisions about patterns in the universe as a whole. We will discuss the procedure in general and will describe one very simple case in particular.

Confirmatory work begins with a random sample and ends with conclusions about the universe from which the sample has come. The conclusions can be wrong; for example, we have seen that a sample mean can, by chance, be far from the mean of the universe, and hence can be really misleading. But the golden thing about random samples is that we know *how likely* it is that a sample result has seriously misled us; individual samples can be very unpredictable, but the samples in the long run behave very predictably. Here we discuss how our knowledge about sample means can be used to test a simple hypothesis. First we will consider a hypothetical example using very little in the way of new ideas; then we will discuss some of the new issues and concepts raised.

An Example

Suppose we are interested in a new teaching method which its designers claim will increase IQ in children. Further, let us say that we selected, randomly, 100 children for our test, testing them only after they had gone through the process, at which time they were found to have a mean IQ of 107. (We preferred not to test them beforehand because that alone could raise their later IQ scores by giving them practice.) IQ is a much-studied variable, so we know what the universe is like: for this IQ test and children of the age studied, the universe of test scores has a mean of 100 and standard deviation of 14, and the shape is normal. The children exposed to the new method do score higher than the mean for all children (107 is bigger than 100). But that *could* be an accident. We saw in Chapter 7 how much samples fluctuate. The problem is: can we conclude that the process has increased the IQ scores, or is it reasonable to attribute this difference of seven points between the sample and the universe simply to chance – to the undoubted fluctuation of samples.

First things first: we note that the children were randomly sampled. So we are not observing higher scores just because of some bias (as would happen if, say, the test had been done on good students or if the students had been pre-tested). The students were originally selected to be representative of the universe, not to be a smarter part of it. But the random selection, as we know now, does not guarantee perfect representation. As we saw from the samples in Chapter 7, a sample will almost never have a mean that is exactly μ, and thus a mean greater than μ would be expected about half the time just by chance. Hence, we have as yet no reason to conclude that the higher IQs were because of the new teaching method. This brings us to our *null hypothesis*, abbreviated H_0, that the teaching method really had no effect. If so, the random sample from the original universe and the apparent gain of seven IQ points can simply be attributed to an accident of random sampling. Now this is always possible: a random sample of this universe could have a mean of 107, or 50, or 200 or whatever. But some of these possibilities are pretty unlikely. What about our result: could it be just a fluke?

To answer that, we first need to know what means of random samples from this universe are like. That is easy after Chapter 7. Our $N = 100$, $\mu = 100$, $\sigma = 14$. The distribution of means from a random sample of 100 is known, from the central limit theorem, to be approximately normal in shape and to have a standard error of:

$$SE = \sigma/\sqrt{N} = 14/\sqrt{100} = 1.4$$

Furthermore, a batch of means from this universe would have a level that is close to the true universe mean of 100 (the law of large numbers). Of course, this batch is in some sense hypothetical; we rarely select more than one random sample for such a study. But even though this batch exists only hypothetically, we know what it looks like, its level, spread and shape. Our null hypothesis holds that our sample mean is a not too atypical member of this batch. Looking at it from an exploratory point of view, this observation would clearly be an outlier. It is five spread units, here standard errors, above the mean ($7/1.4 = 5$, and the sample mean is seven points above μ), where outliers 'begin' at 1.5 spread units beyond the quartiles (two spreads beyond the level since this batch is symmetric), so this observation is far outside.

In fact, it is so unusual that it does not look like a member of this batch/universe at all. While we must remember that it always could be, it seems much more plausible to say that the teaching method actually raises IQs and the sample is typical of the samples that are likely to be drawn from a universe in which IQs are elevated. Essentially, we are choosing between two options: the null hypothesis, H_0 – it could be true but if it is, the evidence (the mean) is pretty exotic; and the alternative hypothesis, H_1 – if the treatment does raise IQs then this is the sort of outcome we would expect. From an informal, exploratory point of view, we are likely to reject H_0 in favour of H_1, that the

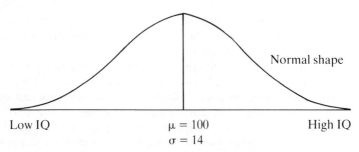

Figure 8.1   IQ scores for all untreated children

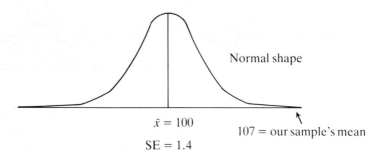

Figure 8.2 H_0 distribution of sample means, $N = 100$

programme actually does work, at least tentatively. We entertain the alternative hypothesis tentatively, rather than dramatically claiming to have proven it, because H_0 still may be true; and even if H_0 is false, the difference may be due to something other than the teaching method.

Again (as in Chapter 7) we have several related layers to keep straight. Perhaps a few diagrams will help. H_0 asserts that our 100 children are a sample from the universe shown in Figure 8.1. (This diagram is like a stem and leaf turned on its side.) If so, then the sample mean belongs to the sampling distribution of means of all samples of size 100 that could be taken from this universe (Figure 8.2). If H_0 is true, our sample mean fits in about where the arrow points – and it looks pretty odd. (We will show no diagrams of the sample itself. For the purposes of this chapter, we only need to know $\bar{x}$ and N; everything else about the sample is irrelevant.)

Thus, hypothesis testing is a lot like looking for outliers in exploratory work. Begin by assuming that the variables you are interested in are not related (in this case, that the teaching method doesn't raise IQ). Then figure out what things would be like if this null hypothesis, H_0, were true (e.g. if the teaching method does not raise or lower IQ, the children exposed to it should be like a random sample from the universe; specifically, their mean IQ will be a fairly typical member of the batch of means from samples of size 100). If the results look plausible assuming the H_0 situation, then you can't reasonably reject H_0; but if your results are very unusual, an outlying value, you can reject H_0 as unlikely.

This broad sketch is not enough. We have been using phrases like 'very unusual case', loose impressionistic phrases. That's fine for exploration, where rules of thumb and intuitive interpretations are routine and useful. It won't do for confirmatory, where we want to know exactly where we stand; we need more precise results usable for conclusions (not insights) and public (not private) communications. For this reason it is necessary to know exactly how unusual a case we have. Happily, as we will see later in this chapter, this is not very hard.

Before considering this let's try to look systematically at the elements of hypothesis testing.

The Logic of Testing

To help illustrate some of the basic steps in the hypothesis-testing strategy, an analogy to the courtroom may be useful. Consider that in both confirmatory work and the courtroom we want to compare some strongly held hypothesis to suitable evidence in an appropriate way and come to a reasonable conclusion about whether the hypothesis is acceptable or not. Now it is time to look a little harder at what this goal implies. How do we make reasonable conclusions, what do we make them about, what is 'reasonable', what sort of evidence do we need to work with? Let us examine some of the basic and familiar elements of criminal courtroom procedure and then compare this procedure with the process of confirmation in data analysis.

1 The charge must be carefully specified. Before the trial even begins, the defendant must be indicted; that is, there is a specific accusation that the defendant committed an act or acts at a specific time or times. Thus the defendant is not required to defend himself against an amorphous charge. If it is often difficult to find an alibi for a single specific time and place, imagine the problems of the defendant if the crime, time and place are not even specified!

2 A major element in our legal system is the presumption of innocence; the legal version of H_0 is that the defendant is presumed innocent until proven guilty, even though the prosecution clearly believes the defendant to be guilty. After all, there are large monetary costs in any trial, large social costs in glutted court calendars and large professional costs to the prosecutor who tries too many cases that result in acquittals. The burden of proof rests with the prosecution and if, after the trial, the result is ambiguous, the defendant is found 'not guilty'. There is no verdict of 'innocent'; rather, the verdict just states that the defendant was not demonstrated to be guilty.

3 The criminal trial is based on the adversary system; competition between

defence and prosecution together with rules of evidence. In this way, it is hoped, only proper, unbiased evidence will result.

4 In order to convict, the evidence should be conclusive 'beyond a reasonable doubt'. The value to society of this requirement is that more harm accrues from convicting an innocent person than from failing to convict a guilty person. Indeed, a familiar rule of thumb is 'better a hundred guilty men go free than one innocent man be convicted'. It is expected that we will make some mistakes (no decision is without some risk of error); and we see here that one sort of error, finding a guilty person not guilty, is strongly preferred to the other sort of error, convicting the innocent. You might have encountered the expression 'unshackling the police', expressed by politicians and the media. What is implied is a modification of this priority – convicting more of the guilty, presumably at the cost of more frequently convicting the innocent.

We can see this line of thought in Figure 8.3. This sets out the possible decisions: the court may decide that a man is guilty when he really is, or is not, and may decide that he is innocent when he really is, or is not. If the verdict and truth correspond, the process of justice has worked as it was supposed to and an appropriate decision has been made. But unfortunately errors do happen. In one type of error (type I error or α error) the accused is innocent but is found guilty; in the other (type II error or β error) the accused is guilty but found not guilty. One way to restate the rule of thumb mentioned earlier is 'try to have 100 type II errors for every type I'. If you decide on a verdict of 'guilty' you risk the first kind of mistake, and if you choose a verdict of 'not guilty' you risk the second kind of mistake; there is no choice you can make that avoids mistakes entirely. There is always some risk in decision, and you can't even escape the risk of error by making no decision because non-decision (here a 'hung jury') is itself a kind of decision with risks and costs of its own. If the person is guilty, then he has been set free incorrectly; if the person is innocent, the trial has failed to clear him, and the social costs may be immense.

		Verdict	
		Not guilty	Guilty
Real state of affairs	Innocent	Justice	Error type I or α
	Guilty	Error type II, or β	Justice

Figure 8.3   The possible courtroom decisions

In short, then, the familiar courtroom procedure has four important attributes. These are: an explicit accusation before the trial, assumption of the opposite state of affairs from that which the prosecution believes, the reliance on unbiased evidence through the adversary system, and the necessity that guilt (the prosecution's cherished belief) be demonstrated beyond a reasonable doubt. With minor variations the process of testing hypotheses with confirmatory statistics can be seen to possess these same four attributes.

In the same way that an explicit accusation is made before the trial, for example, the researcher is obliged to make a careful and explicit prediction before looking at the test data, usually before collecting them. Unlike the indictment, however, the hypothesis can vary in degree of specificity. Consider predictions involving means, for example. When little is known about the effects of a treatment, the hypothesis may simply be that two (or more) universes have different means for some attribute under consideration: perhaps children from urban areas are less able to resist pressure to conform than children from rural areas, perhaps the reverse. We expect a difference, but it's not clear which way the difference will go. This form of test is known as 'two-tailed'. If more is known, the direction of the relation may be specifiable: for example, on the basis of theory and other data first-born children can be predicted to have higher IQs than later-borns. This is a 'directional hypothesis', which is tested by a one-tailed test.

The assumption of innocence, too, has a direct analogue in hypothesis testing. Here, the researcher formulates each problem in terms of a null hypothesis (H_0) which specifies that there is no difference between the various populations or treatments; like the presumption of innocence, this is clearly not what the researcher believes. This null hypothesis is held until it is disproven in favour of our preferred expectation, the alternative hypothesis (H_1). Again as in the court, failure to disprove H_0 is not the same as proving H_0.

The research process, however, does not make use of an adversary system to obtain unbiased evidence; instead, we depend for unbiased data on an element of our methodology, the random sample. We have just learned about many of its important properties. The adversary system also attempts to prevent unwarranted deductions from the evidence; in social sciences research, journal editors and readers serve this function.

Finally, while we prefer not to make any errors, we are particularly averse to type I errors, again like the court (see Figure 8.4). We do not want to make type I errors too easily because they affect our actions more; if an alternative hypothesis is accepted, it may often be assumed in subsequent research. If it has been accepted because of a type I error, that error will be compounded in the subsequent research and decisions. However, if we make a type II error we just sigh deeply and go on looking. After all, in research as in the courts and in life generally, there is no way to avoid these risks; once again, making no decision is a decision too. If we refuse to say whether a null hypothesis is rejected or not then we may in effect have made a decision to do nothing, which is sometimes the most costly error of all.

So in both cases, the courtroom trial and the statistical test, we put most of

Decision on null hypothesis

Accept   Reject

		Accept	Reject
In reality, null hypothesis is:	True	Correct decision	Type I (α) error
	False	Type II (β) error	Correct decision

Figure 8.4 The possible test decisions

our effort into minimizing errors of type I; but you should be aware that there are other orientations towards error preferences that are fairly familiar. For example, medical screening tests, like the cervical smear, give priority to avoiding false negatives. Such tests spread a 'net' that, ideally, identifies *every* instance of the disease at an early stage. There is a cost, however, in that there are many, many false positives, patients who need additional, more exact (and expensive) tests before they can be cleared and who presumably suffer substantial anxiety in the process. The ideal is, of course, to make as few errors of either sort as possible. How can we avoid both kinds of errors and get as much justice or accurate knowledge as possible? We can collect more data, and we can use evidence-evaluation procedures that get the most out of the evidence, that let us make better and better decisions on the basis of the same amount of data. For example, consider the use of more and more powerful forensic techniques in the courts. Faced with a hand print, Sherlock Holmes had to make do with broad measures like hand size in showing who was at the scene of the crime, and errors were quite likely; many people have size eight hands, so a size eight hand print might or might not have been left at the scene by the (size eight) suspect. Nowadays much more exact devices such as fingerprinting and blood typing can be used. When the techniques are more exact the decisions are less risky. In particular, we can keep the risk of convicting an innocent person low (i.e. avoid type I errors) while at the same time reducing the risk of acquitting the guilty (i.e. bringing down the rate of type II errors).

A similar pattern is found in statistics: some statistical tests are able to make finer distinctions than others, some can reduce the risk of rejecting the null hypothesis erroneously while not increasing the risk of erroneously failing to reject it. We speak of these tests as having greater *power* compared to other tests. To put this more exactly:

α is the chance that we will reject H_0 when H_0 is true;
β is the chance that we will not reject H_0 when it is false;
$1 - \beta$ is the *power of the test* (that is, its power to reject correctly the null hypothesis).

Various confirmatory tests differ in power and we can usually choose the highest power test. (The tests we emphasize in this book are quite powerful, which is one reason for their popularity.)

More powerful tests are often based on more stringent assumptions about the batches of data tested: the spreads should be similar, the shapes symmetric, the counts (nearly) equal, and so on. Fortunately the tests we examined in this volume are quite *robust*; in statistics, this means that the data being examined do not need to satisfy these assumptions totally. For each of the tests we examine we will consider, at least briefly, its theoretical assumptions as well as the extent to which they may be violated. Finally, we can almost always increase power by increasing sample size. By the way, this approach to hypothesis testing is called the *classical model*. It is perhaps the commonest approach, but there are other equally valid models.

Before going further, let's sum up the major steps in hypothesis testing as we have them so far:

1 A null hypothesis, H_0, is constructed which we expect and hope to reject in favour of the alternative hypothesis H_1. H_1 may be quite loose. For a comparison of two means, H_1 may just assert that there is some difference (two-tailed test); H_1 may also specify a direction, in which case we have a one-tailed test.
2 A statistical test is chosen, keeping its assumptions and robustness in mind. Naturally you pick the most powerful one appropriate to the data, thus minimizing type II error.
3 The decision is whether or not to reject H_0. To do this, compute the test statistic for your data. Then find out how likely it is that you could get such a statistic (or one even more extreme) if H_0 were true. This likelihood (or probability) is found in the statistical table that goes with the particular test used.

Most of this is pretty simple once you get over the initial shock of having to disprove the null hypothesis rather than proving H_1, the one you probably believe in. However, some of the process has not been discussed very much so far, step 3 in particular.

Much of step 3 goes beyond this chapter and into all the other confirmatory chapters in this book, for all the other confirmatory chapters boil down to figuring out how probable the observed data are, if H_0 is really true. Different kinds of data and hypotheses require different tests so there are many ways to do the computations. The basic logic is usually the same, though. You might find it useful to read this general discussion of testing again after a few more chapters, when you know more tests and can see how the basic logic is used repeatedly. For now, let's return to our example and see how to do a test on it.

Children's IQs Continued

Now we can return to our original example of testing a process that purported

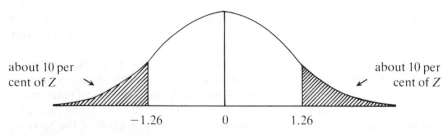

about 10 per
cent of Z   ↘

about 10 per
↙   cent of Z

-1.26 0   1.26

Figure 8.5   The standard normal distribution

to raise IQs in children. You will recall that the mean IQ of children taught in the new way is five SEs above the mean of the means of all samples of that size. How likely is it that our batch mean would be so far away from this grand mean if the null hypothesis were actually true? We may ask this question in a different way: if H_0 is true what proportion of the sample means would be as high as our batch mean or even higher? If it is a very small fraction, then this is an unusual case. The probability of getting a sample with a given property (e.g. a sample five or more SEs above the mean) is just the proportion of all samples that have that property. Again, we often got a rough feel for probability in exploratory work; where a stem and leaf had just a few cases (usually at the extremes), cases were viewed as unusual, while where the cases were thick (usually the middle) they were seen as quite typical.

Now for a normal distribution we can get at the same sort of idea in a much more formal way. The exact proportion of cases in any part of a normally distributed batch has been worked out to as many decimal points as you are ever going to need. Table A.2 (pp. 368–9) gives these values for the 'standard normal distribution', called Z for short, which is a hypothetical batch with infinitely many cases, perfect normal shape, mean of zero and standard deviation of one. This table is invaluable, so let's spend a minute learning how to read it. The numbers down the left hand side give the values of Z to one decimal place, and the numbers across the top give the second decimal place. Thus where the row labelled 1.2 and the column labelled .06 intersect, we find information about a Z of 1.26. That information is the proportion of Z cases as far away from the mean as 1.26 or farther, that is, the *probability* of getting a Z-value as big as 1.26 or bigger, and that value is 0.1038, about one-tenth. Normal distributions are perfectly symmetrical, so this table is fine for both halves of Z; the half above the mean (zero) and the half below. For example, the probability of a Z value as small as -1.26 or smaller is also 0.1038. (See Figure 8.5.)

What good is Z to us? We are thinking about an example where the H_0 distribution of sample means is normal but its mean is 100 and its *sd* is 1.4. No problem at all: just think back to standardization. If we remove level and spread from a batch, as follows,

$$\frac{\text{observation} - \text{level}}{\text{spread}}$$

we get a new batch with new level of zero and new spread of one but nothing else changed; the shape is the same, so the probabilities are the same too. So we can standardize our H_0 distribution (in confirmatory terms, of course) by finding

$$\frac{\text{observation} - 100}{1.4}$$

which has a mean 0 and *sd* 1, just like Z; and it will still be normal. In fact, it is Z! That's why Z is called the *standard* normal distribution. Any normal distribution becomes Z when standardized. So the Z table is the only normal table that we need (very handy).

   Back to our example. We want to know how likely it is that we would get a sample of 100 with mean 107 or more if H_0 is true. We know the sampling distribution of the mean is normal, with mean 100 and SE 1.4, if H_0 is true. So let's standardize and turn to the Z table. Thus

$$Z = \frac{107 - 100}{1.4}$$

$$= 5.00$$

as we noted before. The probability of a value as big as this or bigger is about 0.0000003, which is pretty small! This means that the probability of our result or one more extreme if H_0 is true is about three in ten million. This is so small that we just can't believe H_0 is true: it's too unlikely, and hence the decision is to reject H_0. We say that the mean IQ of the specially trained sample of children is *significantly* greater than 100, the μ under the null hypothesis; that is, H_0 still could be true but it's too unlikely for us to hold to. This is our version of 'beyond a reasonable doubt'.

The Basic Z-test Procedure

We have discussed this example at length, with a discussion of hypothesis testing in general thrown in; of course, this is not what you usually have to go through to do a simple Z-test! So let's review the process step by step as it would routinely be done.

   First, what do we need for a Z-test? We must be interested in some variable x that is measured numerically (in order that means and so on can be found). We must know the universe mean and the standard deviation of x, that is, μ and σ. We must assume that the shape of this universe is normal, or we must have a fairly large sample, at least 30 or 40 cases; the normality assumption can be violated fairly freely for large samples. This robustness with respect to normality has been proven empirically by looking at samples drawn from non-normal universes. We also need a random sample, size N, for which x has been measured to give us the sample mean, $\bar{x}$.

How do we treat these components? Our basic question is, how different are $\bar{x}$ and μ? So our two hypotheses are:

$H_0 : \bar{x} = \mu$

$H_1 : \bar{x} \neq \mu$ if the test is two-tailed,

or $\bar{x} > \mu$ if the test is one-tailed and we expect that $\bar{x}$ will be bigger than μ

or $\bar{x} < \mu$ if the test is one-tailed and we expect that $\bar{x}$ will be smaller than μ.

We must decide whether H_1 will be one-tailed or two-tailed before doing the rest of the test. We must also decide beforehand on an α-level, or how unlikely our sample results must seem before we decide we can't accept H_0. Usually people use $\alpha = 0.05$, or $\alpha = 0.01$ if they want to be very careful. Decisions about α, and about whether the test is one- or two-tailed, are made in advance to avoid temptation; if you have strong feelings about a topic it is hard to avoid bending the confirmatory rules in the direction of the results you would prefer.

Then we are ready to compute a Z score.

$$Z = \frac{\bar{x} - \mu}{\sigma/\sqrt{N}}$$

That is, we compare the observed difference of the means $(\bar{x} - \mu)$ to how variable this difference is expected to be if H_0 is true $(\sigma/\sqrt{N})$. We can then look up Z in our normal Table A.2. As we argued before, as Z gets more extreme we are more sure that the difference $\bar{x} - \mu$ is no accident. The Z-table tells us just how sure we can be, because this table gives the probability of getting a Z of a given size or one even more extreme. Finally, if this probability is α or less, we decide to reject H_0. If this probability is greater than α, we decide we can't reject H_0.

Hypothesis testing can give us very precise information, but at a price. To get precise results you have first to make precise assumptions (here we assumed a normal distribution for IQ scores with a mean of 100 and sd of 14). Then you have to use mathematically tractable measures (here, mean and standard deviation) which sacrifice a great deal of resistance. Finally, you have to feed in suitable data (a good random sample). These are much stronger demands than exploratory analysis called for, but they produce results that are needed.

Using the Z-table: An Easier Way

Many people are initially turned off by the Z-table: it's too full of numbers, far more than we are likely to need. If this bothers you, take a look at Table 8.1. To use this table, just decide on an α-level, and whether the test is one- or two-tailed. Look up the appropriate row and column in Table 8.1 to find the *critical value*, or the least extreme Z-value needed to make H_0 unacceptable. For example, consider a one-tailed test with $\alpha = 0.05$. Let's say we expect $\bar{x}$ will be smaller than μ ($H_1 : \bar{x} < \mu$). The big Z-table (Table A.2) tells that 5 per cent

Table 8.1 Critical values for the Z-test

	α-levels			
	0.05	*0.01*	*0.005*	*0.001*
One tail	1.645	2.326	2.576	3.090
Two tails	±1.960	±2.576	±2.805	±3.291

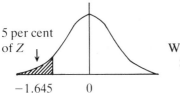

5 per cent
of Z

If α = 0.05
White area: can't reject H_0
Shaded area: reject H_0

−1.645   0

Figure 8.6 H_0 distribution

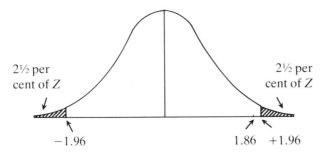

2½ per
cent of Z

2½ per
cent of Z

−1.96   1.86   +1.96

Figure 8.7

of the Z-values are less than or equal to −1.645 if H_0 is true (Figure 8.6). So if our Z works out to −1.645 or less, we will reject H_0. Thus −1.645 is the *critical value* of Z here: we reject H_0 for any Z this far from zero or farther. Knowing this *CV* (critical value) we don't need the large Table A.2.

The tables you will see for other tests are more like Table 8.1 than Table A.2: they just provide critical values for selected significance levels. They tell you how extreme your statistic must be in order to be the kind of thing that happens only (say) 5 per cent of the time if H_0 is true (α = 0.05).

Another Example

Consider the following hypothetical problem. A social psychologist is doing research on conformity, using a measure that has been validated on urban males and found to have a μ of 3.1 and σ of 4.8. The researcher next turns to a random sample of 500 rural males and finds that they have a mean $\bar{x}$ of 3.5. What should she conclude? We can simply do the Z-test step by step as before. The first part is just like the previous example: we know μ, σ, $\bar{x}$, N. We do not know whether the population is normal but the N is so large that this almost certainly won't matter. The sample is random. Fine: we have all we need for the Z-test.

Next we set up H_0 and H_1. Here there is an important change from the previous example. Was there any reasonable way that we could have very confidently predicted that rural males would score higher on this test? Not as far as we know. Therefore, we must use a two-tailed test because we could not confidently have predicted the direction of the difference; it was, of course, easy once we had seen the results, but the decision should be made ahead of time and on compelling grounds. For a two-tailed test we have the following hypotheses:

$H_0 : \bar{x} = \mu$
$H_1 : \bar{x} \neq \mu$.

Let's use $\alpha = 0.05$. For a two-tailed Z-test at the 5 per cent level, the critical values are ± 1.96. Now we can compute the observed Z:

$$Z = \frac{\bar{x} - \mu}{\sigma / \sqrt{N}}$$

$$= \frac{3.5 - 3.1}{4.8 / \sqrt{500}} = \frac{0.4}{4.8/22.36} = \frac{0.4}{0.215}$$

$$= 1.86$$

In diagram form again, if H_0 is true then $\dfrac{\bar{x} - \mu}{\sigma / \sqrt{N}} = Z$ is part of the Z-distribution (Figure 8.7).

Our observed Z does not look like an especially unusual member of this batch; it is between the two critical values, so we know we could get a value like 1.86 more than 5 per cent of the time just by chance when H_0 is true. In other words, the observed value of Z is less extreme than either critical value. Therefore, we can't reject H_0: we are unable to conclude, at this level of significance, that rural males differ from urban males as regards conformity. The results are, however, suggestive and would appear to be worth further research. We don't reject H_0 but we do keep thinking about conformity, urban and rural.

Another Use For the Z-Table

To a large extent, easy access to computers has made the traditional statistical tables like the Z-table redundant for most purposes. Nevertheless, there are good reasons for learning enough about such tables to be able to set up and solve standard problems. For one thing, without such 'hands on' experience the logic of testing is likely to be harder to understand.

We have illustrated one principal use of the Z-table in the text: we have a sample mean and want to know if it is plausible that it comes from a null hypothesis distribution with parameters μ and σ. We learned that standardizing using the mean and the standard error gives us a Z score that translates into a probability, the type I error. But there are other important uses of the Z-table as well.

Consider this question: some educators argue that for someone to be university-educable, an IQ of 120 or more is needed. Let's not worry about whether this is true or not, but ask instead, if this is true, what proportion of the population would be university-educable? This kind of question turns out to be the easiest Z-table question to answer – just standardize. And it's even easier than testing. Because we are looking at the universe and not a sample, we use σ rather than the standard error in the denominator. Thus, if μ = 100 and σ = 15 (different tests have different sigmas) we get (120 − 100)/15 = 1.33. Now we need only to use the Z-table to turn this into a probability, 0.09176, so approximately one person in every eleven would qualify.

So far, we have been using the Z-table 'from the outside in'. Let's consider a different question. Imagine that you are on a school board of a city with 100 000 adolescents, and you have just enough funds for 50 gifted students in a special enriched programme. Assuming that IQ is the appropriate way to determine who is gifted (it isn't, but it's convenient to assume it, just like it's convenient to put you on the school board) we would want to know the minimum score such that there are 50 students with that IQ or higher. How do we do this? We don't have the score (if we did the problem would be a familiar one) but to compensate, we have the proportion that qualify, a probability of 50/100 000 = 0.0005. To make use of this, look *inside* the Z-table for this probability and obtain the corresponding Z score, which turns out to be 3.29. So we want an IQ score such that it is 3.29 spread units above the mean μ (which is known to be 100). If σ for this (hypothetical) IQ test is 15 then

$$3.29 = (X - 100)/15$$

Solving for X gives a score of 149.35, which rounds to 150. This is a very common sort of application for the Z-table, requiring only simple algebra and an understanding of what the table means.

Sample Size

In Chapter 7, in discussing how large a sample should be, we left the answer rather vague. We are now in a position to tighten this up a bit. In order to estimate minimum sample size for a Z-test problem we must know one thing about the universe, its standard deviation, σ. And we must make two decisions: the smallest difference you would be interested in, that is ($\bar{x} - μ$); and the significance level at which you wish to detect this difference. For example, suppose in our IQ example we wanted to be able to detect an IQ gain of five points, at the 0.01 level (one-tailed, as it is only a gain we are interested in – why would we want a programme that reduced IQ?).

$$Z = \frac{\bar{x} - \mu}{\sigma/\sqrt{N}} \text{ gives us for } \alpha = 0.01$$

$$\bar{x} - \mu = 5$$

$$\sigma = 14$$

So Z must be at least 2.326 (see Table 8.1).

$$2.326 = \frac{5}{14/\sqrt{N}} \text{ and we just solve for } N$$

$$\frac{32.564}{\sqrt{N}} = 5$$

$$32.564 = 5\sqrt{N}$$

$$\sqrt{N} = 6.513$$

$$N \simeq 43$$

Here our omnibus formula plus a little algebra gives pretty strong results. The same idea can be applied to other tests.

Using the Computer

To use the Z-test in MINITAB, we need a column of data, a value for μ, a value for σ and an α-level, and as well we must 'tell' MINITAB if the test is one- or two-tailed.

As an example, we generated ten observations of children exposed to a new teaching method and we want to find out if the teaching method has any effect on IQ scores. Therefore, our null hypothesis for a two-tailed test is that the sample comes from the universe or that $\bar{x}$ is consistent with μ. The alternative hypothesis is the opposite, that the mean of x is not equal to μ. The (fictitious) data are stored in C1. Let us assume that we know the universe mean to be 100 with a standard deviation of 1.4. Inserting these values into the Z-test command we will have a command that looks like this:

ZTEST $\mu = 100\ \sigma = 1.4$ C1.

However, before we do the Z-test we have to determine the direction of the test and the α-level. Since we have decided to carry out a two-tailed test, we only have to decide now what α-level to use. As $\alpha = 0.05$ is conventionally used we will use it here as well. The purpose of determining the α-level is to establish a limit for rejecting the null hypothesis. This limit is called the critical value. In our test the critical value for $\alpha = 0.05$ is ± 1.96.

The output of the Z-test using the generated sample of ten is reproduced here.

```
MTB> PRINT C1
      90   100   120   108   106   102   103   100   99   106
MTB> ZTEST μ = 100 σ = 1.4 C1
TEST OF μ = 100 vs μ N.E. 100
THE ASSUMED σ = 1.40
        N         MEAN      STDEV     SE MEAN   Z          P VALUE
C4      10        103.40    7.71      0.44      7.68       0.0000
                                                (larger than (smaller
                                                1.96)       than .05)
```

If you want a one-tailed test, use the subcommand ALTERNATIVE = 1 or −1. That is:

```
MTB> ZTEST μ = 100 σ = 1.4 C1;
SUBC> ALTERNATIVE = 1.
```

This test is one-tailed in the positive direction and will reject H_0 only if the mean is significantly larger than μ.

By the way, you don't have to specify α here, just look at the *P*-value. If it is equal to or smaller than your preferred α, reject. If it is larger, then you cannot reject.

HOMEWORK

1 In a normal distribution, what proportion of the cases are:

(a) More than 1.8 standard deviations beyond the mean?
(b) Less than 0.72 *sds* beyond the mean?
(c) More than 0.44 *sd above* the mean?
(d) Between 0.17 and 2.29 *sds below* the mean?

(Hint: for these sorts or problems, always draw a picture.)
2 We administer a French language skills test to a group of first-year pupils. For this group on this (hypothetical) test, $\mu = 85$ and $\sigma = 13.2$. What score is required to be in:

(a) The top 1 per cent?
(b) The top 25 per cent?
(c) The bottom 40 per cent?

3 A test of reading achievement is scored so that the universe mean and standard deviation are 50 and 10, respectively. What proportion of the students score:

(a) Less than 43? More than 47?

(b) Between 56 and 62? Between 48 and 81?

4 On a standard test of mathematical skills, the mean score is 100 with a standard deviation of 10. A teacher tries out a new teaching method with a class of 30 randomly selected students and finds their mean performance is 103.

(a) Can he conclude that the new method is more effective than usual methods?

(b) How large a sample of students would we need to detect reliably a difference of this size (103 versus 100) at the 0.02 significance level? the 0.001 level?

5 Identify the types of hypothesis specified in each of the following statements:

(a) Vitamin C has no effect on susceptibility to colds.

(b) Lengthy prison sentences are an effective weapon against crime.

(c) Men and women differ in their attitudes about justice.

6 If the research results are inconsistent with H_0, why would we reject the H_0 rather than accept the H_1?

7 What is meant by an α-level of 0.01, 0.05, or 0.10?

8 Identify whether a type I or a type II error may have been made in each of the following:

(a) Dr Linus Pauling reports that mega doses of vitamin C are effective against colds. Other researchers have been unable to replicate this.

(b) Several controlled studies have determined the 'scared stiff' approach to have no value for treating delinquency. People associated with the programme are convinced of its effectiveness, however.

9 A headteacher had just received the test scores of 75 sixth-formers on a new achievement test. The mean test score of the seniors was 104.3 and the mean of the achievement test for all students who took it was 100 with a standard deviation of 30. The headteacher felt very proud. Was she justified? Did the students in her high school score significantly higher than the mean of all students who took the test? In making this assessment, formulate the null and alternative hypothesis and specify if the H_0 can be rejected. If the school had a class of only 25 sixth-formers, would this fact have changed the conclusion?

9
When σ Is Not Known

Chapter 8 (we hope!) made hypothesis testing look fairly easy. It does mean getting used to a new way of thinking, but that's mainly a matter of practice. The procedural details are simple and straightforward. If we know the universe mean and standard deviation, μ and σ, we can always tell how likely we would be to obtain a sample mean at least as extreme as a given $\bar{x}$ if sampling that universe. If the mean is an outlier from the theoretical batch of possible means, then the probability associated with a mean as or more extreme than this *when H_0 is true* is small, and we would reject the null hypothesis ($\bar{x} = \mu$) in favour of the alternative ($\bar{x} \neq \mu$ if two-tailed; $\bar{x} > \mu$ or $\bar{x} < \mu$ if one-tailed). If the probability is not small, then we tentatively retain the null hypothesis. To find the probabilities, all we need to do is compute the ratio:

$$Z = \frac{\bar{x} - \mu}{\sigma/\sqrt{N}}$$

and look it up in a Z-table; this turns Z scores directly into probabilities.

Unfortunately, like many problems that are easy to solve, this situation rarely occurs in the real world because we only rarely know the true variance of a universe. Our knowledge of a universe is not often so complete. Therefore, we must decide what to do in the more typical situation, which is like the Z-test but with one piece of information missing: there is an $\bar{x}$, and a μ to compare it to, but we do not know σ. Now we have already suggested in Chapter 7 that sample values tend to reflect universe values, and this is true for standard deviations as well as for means (although we discussed means more thoroughly). So why not use the sample standard deviation to estimate the universe value, σ? This is in fact just what we do. In symbols,

$$\hat{\sigma} = sd = \sqrt{\frac{\sqrt{\sum(x_i - \bar{x})^2}}{N - 1}}$$

This says that the estimated standard deviation of the universe, $\hat{\sigma}$, equals the standard deviation of the sample. (Statisticians often use ˆ, called a 'hat', to denote an estimate.)

The test created in this way is called the t-test, and the formula for calculating t-values looks nearly identical to the formula for calculating Z-values:

$$t_{N-1} = \frac{\bar{x} - \mu}{\hat{\sigma}/\sqrt{N}} \text{ compared to } Z = \frac{\bar{x} - \mu}{\sigma/\sqrt{N}}$$

Comparing the t-formula to the Z-formula shows that the basic idea is the same: the size of a difference (the top part) is compared to the size of sampling fluctuations one can expect if H_0 is true (the bottom part). Still, there is a difference between the statistics that should be explained.

A feature in the t-formula but not in the Z-formula is the subscript $N - 1$ appended to the t. This refers to the number of *degrees of freedom* or df, which is $N - 1$ here. Why is there this extra complexity? Well, we have a less simple problem now because we have less certainty in our formula. In the Z-test only *one* thing was an estimate: $\bar{x}$, which is an estimate of μ when the null hypothesis is correct. All of the uncertainty in the case of the Z-test arose from the sampling variability of the $\bar{x}$ estimate. But things are different now: we have an estimate not only in the numerator ($\bar{x}$), but also in the denominator ($\hat{\sigma}$) and this too is subject to great sampling variability. This extra element of uncertainty has to be accommodated somehow, and we do so by using different tables for different df; since df are equal to the count minus one, this amounts to having different tables for different sample sizes.

To get a feeling for what is happening, consider the following two hypothetical batches:

A		B	
10		9	11
$sd_A = 1.41$		9	11
12		9	12 $sd_B = 1.43$
		10	12
		10	13

Which batch gives us the more secure feeling, the feeling that our estimates of mean and standard deviation are more soundly based? Clearly batch B, not batch A, even though batch A has the smaller standard deviation. The difference in the size of the two batches seems to matter to our intuition, and intuition and mathematics are in agreement here. Thus, if we calculate a t-value for a small batch like A and one for a larger batch like B, we would want to be a good deal more cautious about the t-value from the smaller batch. In other words, we want to see a much bigger discrepancy between $\bar{x}$ and μ before rejecting the null hypothesis; that is, we want to have a larger (more extreme) critical value.

Have a look at Table A.3 (p. 370), a table of critical values for t, and you will see that this is happening. The first column of figures on the far left gives degrees of freedom, or $N - 1$. The double line of figures at the top gives α-levels, either one-tailed (upper row) or two-tailed (lower row). If you look from left to right across any row, the critical values increase in size. This is familiar from working with Z: to reduce α, or the risk of wrongly rejecting H_0, we have to use a more extreme critical value so we have less chance of a type I error. (By the way, t is symmetric, like Z, so these values do for either positive or negative t.) The novelty here is what happens within any column, that is for a fixed α but differing degrees of freedom. As $N - 1$ gets larger and larger, increasing our confidence in the estimate of universe standard deviation, the entries in the table get smaller and smaller. H_0 can be rejected more and more easily because the accuracy of our estimate of σ increases as $N - 1$ does. At some point we get very accurate estimates indeed, so accurate that we might as well assume that our estimate is the same as σ. What then? Why, we can go right back to the Z-test! Look at the last row of the t-table, where the dfs are infinitely large, so our estimate of σ should be perfect: the values for t are exactly the same as the values for Z! They have to be, because the only real difference between t and Z, the uncertainty about σ, has disappeared. When $N = 30$ (or 40 or 50, depending on how conservative you wish to be), the Z-values and t-values are 'close enough' that the Z-table may be used rather than the t-table. It is sometimes convenient and the error introduced is small.

There is one other parallel to Z-testing that should be remembered: the t-test is appropriate for *normal* data. If the sample size is small, say, fewer than 20, it is wise to stem and leaf the batch to see whether it looks roughly normal; if it doesn't, transform it. But if the sample size is large, then you don't have to worry (remember, if N is large then $\bar{x}$ will tend to be distributed normally even if the individual observations aren't).

Let's try an example – an artificial one so that we can keep things simple, but not an unrealistic one. As the university external examiner is reviewing the lists of final grades, she comes to Professor Aardvark's grade list, and remembers that last year Aardvark's grades were much higher than those of his colleagues. At that time she didn't know whether Aardvark graded more 'tenderly' or had a better group, so she planned then to test this year's grades against a mean (μ) of 65 per cent, the theoretical 'average'. If this year's grades are also very high, she may decide to have a few words with Professor Aardvark.

To turn this vignette into a statistical example, we first identify the components. We know μ, which is 65 or the mean grade for students in general. We don't know σ (presumably because no one has bothered to calculate it), so we can't do a Z-test. Our sample is Aardvark's ten students, whose grades are stem-and-leafed below:

9	4	$N = 10$
8	63	$\bar{x} = 72$
7	15	$sd_x = 12.36$
6	249	
5	88	

stem: tens   *leaf:* units

Now we have all the components we need for a t-test. Before doing one, is it appropriate to do so? Do the data meet the assumptions that should be met for a t-test to be appropriate? First, we look for normality: the sample is small, just ten, so we should examine the data. The stem and leaf looks all right; it's not perfectly symmetric and bell-shaped but it doesn't diverge wildly and there is no serious straggling or clumping or straying values. Checking for random sampling, our second assumption, is trickier, since it depends on how students were chosen for the group and we don't really know. Let's tentatively assume students choose courses at random (not an entirely false assumption!) and go on, remembering that this assumption may need to be checked. We set up our hypotheses:

H_0: $\bar{x} = \mu = 65$
H_1: $\bar{x} > \mu = 65$

Note that our alternative hypothesis is one-tailed; the examiner had predicted on the basis of last year's grades that these would be higher than average. Next we compute t for our data:

$$t_{N-1} = \frac{\bar{x} - \mu}{sd_x/\sqrt{N}} = \frac{72 - 65}{12.36/\sqrt{10}}$$

$$t_9 = 1.79$$

From our t-table we see that a one-tailed test for nine degrees of freedom and $\alpha = 0.05$ has a critical value of $t = 1.833$. Our value is not quite extreme enough to reject H_0 (i.e. to have words with Aardvark), but the examiner will probably keep her eye on him carefully.

In summary, then, when we are faced with a Z-type problem but don't know the true universe variance, we can test our hypotheses by means of the t-statistic. The t-statistic looks very much like the Z but uses the sample standard deviation in the denominator instead of the (unknown) standard deviation of the universe. Since the accuracy of the substitution depends in large part upon the number of observations we have, we take this number into account via the degrees of freedom of our sample. The greater the df the more *powerful* the test will be, i.e. the more likely we are to decide correctly when H_1, the alternative hypothesis, is true.

How Can You Find Out What μ Is?

The one-sample t-test is pretty simple, and so are the complications we are about to consider. First, while we must always have a value for μ in order to do the test, there are a number of different ways of finding it. Sometimes μ is known from extensive previous evidence: mean IQ is known to be 100 for many tests. Sometimes μ is a standard that is fixed arbitrarily; for example, in some schools 65 is defined as the proper mean grade and instructors are responsible for making their means as close to that as possible, and spot-checked to see that they are not straying too far from $\bar{x} = 65$ ('grading on a curve' is a more elaborate version of this). Often μ is known even though σ is not; many common sources of data publish means but not variances (for example, censuses often give means only; and the distributions given are usually not detailed enough to allow accurate calculation of variances). Finally, there are times when you can reason out a meaningful μ, as in the next example.

Working with Two Matched Samples

The simple *t*-formula above was described for one sample, whose mean $\bar{x}$ is compared to μ. The formula can also be used for two samples at once if the samples are *matched*. Consider Table 9.1. Its author, Robert Zajonc, discusses the relationship between familiarity with things and liking them, using a variety of data. To gather the data in Table 9.1, Zajonc and colleagues gave a list of antonym pairs to 100 students and asked them to judge which member of each pair had the more pleasant meaning. All the students thought 'able' to be more pleasant than 'unable', while 52 per cent preferred 'play' to 'work', with the other preferences in between. Table 9.1 also includes frequencies of usage for each word; the frequencies were taken from a standard reference. Now if frequency and favourable meaning are linked, the preferred halves of the antonym pairs should be more frequent. So if we find the difference between

Table 9.1 Preference and frequency of antonym pairs

Preference	Word	Frequency	Preference	Antonym	Frequency	(More preferred −Less)
100	Able	930	0	Unable	239	691
100	Better	2354	0	Worse	450	1904
99	Peace	472	1	War	1118	−646
99	Responsible	267	1	Irresponsible	30	237
99	Smile	2143	1	Frown	216	1927
98	Friend	2553	2	Enemy	883	1670
98	Moral	272	2	Immoral	19	253
97	Important	1130	3	Unimportant	40	1090
97	Profitable	57	3	Unprofitable	12	45
96	Live	4307	4	Die	1079	3228
96	Superior	166	4	Inferior	40	126
93	First	5154	7	Last	3517	1637
91	Always	3285	9	Never	5715	−2430
90	Agree	729	10	Disagree	38	691
78	Long	5362	22	Short	887	4475
67	Infinite	71	33	Finite	2	69
52	Play	2606	48	Work	2720	−114

Source: Zajonc (1968); reprinted by permission.

Table 9.2   Checking normality of differences of word frequencies

4	5	X_U	4500		X
4					⋮
3					⋮
3	2				⋮
2					⋮
2					⋮
1	9976	q_U	1700		
1	1				
0	717	Md	700	$\bar{D} = 874$	
0	23010	q_L	0		
−0	1				⋮
−0	6				⋮
−1					⋮
−1					⋮
−2	4	X_L	−2400		X

stems: thousands   *leaves:* hundreds

the frequencies of each pair of antonyms, subtracting the frequency of the less preferred word from that of the more preferred, these differences should, on the whole, be greater than zero. Because we have two sets of matched data, we can reduce them to one set of differences and do a *t*-test.

Before doing this we consider whether the data satisfy the assumptions that must hold if the *t*-test is to be appropriate. Are the 17 word pairs in Table 9.1 a random sample? Our source is not clear on this point, so we will have to hope for the best and make a mental note to be cautious. We can see that these pairs are not a sample of all words, since many words do not have opposites. Does that matter? Are the 17 differences in frequency roughly normally distributed? We have to give this careful attention since an *N* of 17 is not large enough to allow much leeway here. Note that *N* is 17 and not 34; we will do our test on 17 differences, not 34 separate words. Similarly, we check normality for the differences, not the original frequencies. For the raw data the differences are found in Table 9.1, and stem-and-leafed and box-plotted in Table 9.2. The plot alone does not look terrible, although there is upward straggle in both the midbox and the extremes, suggesting that transformation is worth trying. The stem and leaf looks worse than the plot, for the stem and leaf shows two peaks (rather than the desired single peak) and a lack of symmetry. There is no big problem; we can just transform the data. It is best to transform the original frequencies rather than the differences of frequencies (among other things, the differences have negative values). The logs of the original frequencies are found in Table 9.3, and the differences of logged frequencies are found in Table 9.3 and stemmed-and-leafed and plotted in Table 9.4. The plot does not look much improved after logging; the midbox still straggles up in the same way and

Table 9.3 Analysis of logged frequencies

Logged frequency

Preferred	Opposite	$(P - O) = D$	D^2
2.97	2.38	0.59	0.3481
3.37	2.65	0.72	0.5184
2.67	3.05	−0.38	0.1444
2.43	1.48	0.95	0.9025
3.33	2.33	1.00	1.0000
3.41	2.95	0.46	0.2116
2.43	1.28	1.15	1.3225
3.05	1.60	1.45	2.1025
1.76	1.08	0.68	0.4624
3.63	3.03	0.60	0.3600
2.22	1.60	0.62	0.3844
3.71	3.55	0.16	0.0256
3.52	3.76	−0.24	0.0576
2.86	1.58	1.28	1.6384
3.73	2.95	0.78	0.6084
1.85	.30	1.55	2.4025
3.42	3.43	−0.01	0.0001
		$\sum D = 11.36$	$\sum D^2 = 12.4894$
		$\bar{D} = 0.67$	

$$\text{VAR}(D) = \frac{12.4894 - 7.5912}{16}$$
$$= 0.3061$$
$$sd_D = 0.5533$$

Table 9.4 Checking normality for differences of logged word frequencies

14:	15	5:5	$X_U = 1.55$		X
12:	13	8:			⋮
10:	11	0:5	$q_U = 1.00$		⋮
8:	9	:5			
6:	7	028:28	$Md = 0.68$	$\bar{D} = 0.67$	
4:	5	6:9	$q_L = 0.46$		
2:	3				⋮
0:	1	:6			⋮
−1:	−0	:1			⋮
−3:	−2	8:4	$X_L = -0.38$		X

the upper outlier has been replaced by a lower outlier. But perhaps the overall symmetry is better, in that we have no systematic straggling. As a final check of overall symmetry we considered the mean versus the median. For the logged data, Md = 0.68 and $\bar{D}$ = 0.67; for the raw data, Md = 700 and $\bar{D}$ = 874; the median is clearly much nearer to the mean for the logged data. In the stem and leaf we see a very clear advantage for the logged version: it comes much closer to being single-peaked. All in all, logging seems preferable. The results are not quite ideal, but they do not have to be since rough normality is sufficient for a t-test. We will proceed to do a t-test on the differences of logged word frequencies.

If being preferred or not preferred makes no difference to word frequencies, then the differences should be zero overall; so our H_0 is that the true mean of the differences, μ, is zero (note that μ does not come from data, but from the nature of H_0). On the other hand our H_1 is based on the argument that liking and familiarity go together; this is a well documented assertion, so a one-tailed test is reasonable. Thus our hypotheses are:

H_0: $\bar{D} = \mu = 0$ (where $\bar{D}$ is found by subtracting the log of the frequency of the opposite from the log of the frequency of the preferred word).

H_1: $\bar{D} > 0$

Our last decision is which α to use; let's try 0.01 for a change.

With assumptions checked out and the basic decisions about H_1 and α made, we are finally ready to compute. From table 9.3 we find:

$$df = N - 1 = 16$$
$$\bar{D} = 0.67$$
$$sd_D = 0.5533$$

From Table A.3 we find that the critical value of 16 dfs and $\alpha = 0.01$ (one-tailed) is 2.583. Finally we do the test, still using the basic t procedure applied to differences:

$$t_{16} = \frac{\bar{D} - \mu}{sd_D/\sqrt{N}} = \frac{0.67 - 0}{0.5533/\sqrt{N}} = 4.99$$

so we can easily reject H_0.

There are two things worth discussing: why are the more likeable words more frequent in general, and why are there exceptions to this rule? Zajonc argues that it is familiarity that leads to liking, perhaps because lack of familiarity produces mild discomfort from uncertainty as to know how to respond. We have tested for the opposite causal possibility: liking leading to frequency of use. This is also plausible since people probably enjoy writing and reading about pleasant things. The discrepancies are three cases for which the less preferred word is more frequent: war versus peace, never versus always, and work versus play. The work versus play case is not striking; work is only a little more frequent and only a little less popular. We confess to puzzlement over 'never': why should it be more frequent than 'always'? Pessimism, perhaps? ('Mark my words, it'll never fly!') The greater frequency of war than of peace is sadly easy to understand: war is more newsworthy, peace less so.

Matching is often appropriate when one has scores before and after some treatment, when one has subjects identical on all salient variables but one, and so on; and matching lends itself to powerful statistical tests. The process does have some problems (for example, you can't always get close matches for all the cases you would like to use).

Comparing Two Batches

Thus far, we have looked at a variety of applications of the t-test, but all of them testing the mean of a single batch against some theoretical expectation μ. You may feel that the word frequencies example is an exception, since it has two samples. But because cases were matched, we turned each pair into a single case by taking differences and worked with the mean and standard deviation of the batch of differences (very tricky). However, for many applications, you may have samples from two universes that you would like to compare, but you cannot readily match your cases. For instance, you might be interested in comparing random samples of children from intact and broken families on academic performance. But since these children are likely to differ greatly on a variety of potentially important variables, adequate matches might be difficult or impossible for much of your sample. If the counts and spreads of the two batches are not too different, a two sample t-test can be used. The (very ugly) equation in this instance is:

$$t_{(N_1 + N_2 - 2)} = (\bar{x}_1 - \bar{x}_2)/\hat{\sigma}_{\bar{x}_1 - \bar{x}_2}, \text{ where } \sigma_{\bar{x}_1 - \bar{x}_2} = \sqrt{\frac{N_1 s_1^2 + N_2 s_1^2}{N_1 + N_2 - 2}} \sqrt{\frac{N_1 + N_2}{N_1 N_2}}$$

Generally, the H_0 will be that the means of the two universes are the same (e.g. $\mu_1 - \mu_2 = 0$), although different null hypotheses can be used where warranted. We don't go into greater detail on this because the topic in the next chapter, analysis of variance, permits us to compare the levels of any number of batches, with two batches as the simplest case.

Ordinal Versus Numeric Data

So far, we have not considered the issue of the quality of the data we analyse. We usually assume that when we have scores of 3, 4 and 5, say, the '5' is higher on what is being measured than the '4' (i.e. the data have order properties). Furthermore, we usually assume that the difference between a 5 and a 4 is about the same as that between a 4 and a 3 (the 'interval' property). Data with both properties are called interval or numeric and most statistics are designed for such data. Data with order properties but not interval properties are called ordinal, and such data are often considered not good enough for classic confirmatory procedures like the t-test.

This is a serious restriction, as data of this sort occur frequently.

Fortunately pragmatic investigations have shown that ordinal data can be treated like interval data pretty safely if the data have a fairly smooth distribution, N is fairly large and the test is robust. Well, the t-test is certainly robust, and if the stem and leaf looks good, 30 or more cases would probably be enough to let you proceed.

Estimating μ

So far in this chapter, and the previous one, we have been looking at means from the testing perspective: is an observed mean so different from some hypothetical value (the null hypothesis) that it is unreasonable to believe it could have happened by chance (sampling variation)? This is an important question, but there are other issues that are at least as important. One of these is a question that sounds like one that we were concerned with in exploratory analysis – what do we know about the level in the universe?

In one sense, this is a trivial question that is answered easily by finding the level of our sample or batch. But while this is known to be our best guess, we also know that it may not be a very good one. Even if we have managed to collect a perfectly random sample, the mean we get from it is very unlikely to be dead on and in fact, owing to sample fluctuations, it could be very wrong. In Chapter 3, we introduced middle means. Part of the 'message' of the trimean, for example, is that while the median is a best guess about where the middle is, we are much more confident that it is somewhere between the quartiles (and even this could be wrong).

We can hear echoes of this insight from exploration in reports of election and opinion polls. A typical report might read: 'of decided voters, 57 per cent are in favour of Party A and 43 per cent in favour of Party B. This result is accurate to within 3 percentage points 95 times in 100'. This statement is intended to convey that (a) our best guess about the level of support for Party A is 57 per cent and (b) nearly always (95 per cent of the time) the true level of support for Party A in the universe is between 54 and 60 per cent. This is the confirmatory analogue of a box plot, but one where the 'midbox' contains not half the observations but rather 95 per cent of them. The remaining 5 per cent of the time we will get a sample that is 'wacky', that will give us an interval that not only doesn't include the true level in the universe but may even be far off it. Unfortunately, we never know which of our estimates are being based on one of these wacky samples (exactly like α errors in hypothesis testing). But we do know that if we follow 'the rules' (random sampling, no non-response, etc.) our guesses, which are quite accurate even with modestly sized samples, will be wrong only one time in twenty. If this doesn't impress you, consider how difficult it is to be correct about non-trivial predictions (e.g. the weather) much more than half the time.

It should be apparent that there is a lot of similarity between finding such intervals and testing hypotheses. In fact, it will turn out that these intervals, usually called confidence intervals (CI), are obtained essentially by turning hypothesis testing upside down. Consider a two-tailed Z-test at the 0.05 level. We use the Z-test here because it is the least complicated example – the procedure works in exactly the same way for the t and other tests. For this test, we reject H_0 if the difference between the sample mean and μ is more than 1.96 standard errors, our version of 'beyond a reasonable doubt'. That, then, is our region of rejection for H_0. If we turn this on its head, we have a region of 'non-rejection', which is the entire area that is not extreme enough to reject the null hypothesis, an area that, in a sense, is consistent with H_0. Symbolically, that region is:

$$-1.96\,\sigma/\sqrt{N} < \bar{x} - \mu < 1.96\,\sigma/\sqrt{N}$$

A very little algebra (subtracting $\bar{x}$ from each part and multiplying by -1) gives us our confidence interval, the region that we believe contains μ as well as the likelihood that we are wrong about this.

$$\bar{x} + 1.96\,\sigma/\sqrt{N} > \mu > \bar{x} - 1.96\,\sigma/\sqrt{N}$$

If you have calculated the test statistic by hand, you will have all the information needed to calculate your confidence interval. If the computer has done the testing for you, it can also calculate your CI.

By the way, we have chosen to use an α of 0.05 for this example, but only to keep the illustration as simple and familiar as possible. You can construct CIs at any α-level that your research concerns dictate. For example, if your interests are more nearly exploratory, you might prefer a narrower, more precise interval, but at the cost of being wrong more often (using an α of 10, 15 or even 25 per cent or more). On the other hand, if you can't afford many mistakes (that is, to specify an interval that doesn't include μ) you might prefer an α of 0.01, 0.001 or even less, but at the cost of a wider, less informative interval.

One Last Wrinkle: Proportions

So far in our treatment of statistics, we have looked at counts, at rates and at scores. One important omission has been proportions. There are many important questions where the answers involve percentages: what proportion of eligible voters would support which party in an election; what proportion of males never marry? The most familiar instance of this is the public opinion poll, although this is perhaps not the best example since it rarely uses truly random samples. Still, it will do for an illustration.

Suppose Parliament is faced with a free vote on the decriminalization of marijuana. Many of the Members of Parliament without strong personal views may wish to go along with the majorities in their constituencies, if they can find out what the majorities want. Clark Kent MP (Metropolis) decides to hire Truth Ltd to sample his constituency and report back to him. If there is clear evidence of a majority for or against, Kent plans to vote with the majority. If there isn't clear evidence of a majority either way, if it is 'too close to call', Kent plans to come down with a 24-hour virus on voting day rather than decide which half of his voters to offend. Truth Ltd interviews 800 voters and reports 52 per cent opposed and 48 per cent in favour (the issue had been so hotly debated that no one is undecided). Now what?

Some of the testing is easy enough. We can see that Kent wants to do a two-tailed test. If it looks like μ really is 0.50, he does not want to make a decision at all; he will dodge. But if there is a detectable majority either way, he wants to go with it; if more than 50 per cent oppose it he will too; if less than 50 per cent oppose, he will vote for it. Thus

H_0: $\mu = 0.50$ (decision: get ill)
H_1: either $\mu < 0.50$ (decision: vote against decriminalization)
   or $\mu > 0.50$ (decision: vote for decriminalization)

We can also set a reasonable α-value: since a politician must get off the fence more readily than a scientist (the former is expected to decide whenever he can, the latter to decide only when she is pretty sure about things), we select $\alpha = 0.10$ or a somewhat looser standard than usual in research situations. Now Kent does a test.

Are you thinking that he doesn't have the information to do a test? He doesn't know σ and doesn't have the information to compute $\hat{\sigma}$? Well, there is a very handy fact about proportions and percentages: if you know the universe mean, you know σ (not $\hat{\sigma}$!) as well. If your universe consists of people in one of two categories, for example those who favour or are opposed to decriminalization, then you have two proportions, p and q (where $p + q = 1.0$). A little algebra shows that the variance here is just pq. So under the H_0: $\mu = p$, $\sigma^2 = pq$ and we can do a simple Z-test. Turning to Table 8.1, we find a $CV = 1.645$. Thus:

$$H_0: \mu = 0.50$$
$$H_1: \mu \neq 0.50$$
$$\bar{x} = 0.52$$
$$\mu = 0.50 \quad \sigma^2 = 0.25$$
$$N = 800$$
$$CV = \pm1.645$$

$$Z = \frac{0.52 - 0.50}{\sqrt{0.25/800}} = \frac{0.02}{0.0177} = 1.130$$

The Z score is between the critical values, meaning that we can't reject H_0. Poor Kent is likely to be very sick when the bill comes to a vote.

Several general cautions apply to reading poll results as you usually see them, very briefly reported in newspapers. First, remember that commercial firms have to keep costs down; they use cluster sampling at best, and their results can't always be relied on to the last decimal place. Some polls are more carefully accurate than others but it is hard to tell about this from brief reports. Moreover, most large polls give results accurate to within, say, 3 or 4 per cent for the whole sample. If the results are given for subsamples (e.g. the percentage approval for men, or Jews, or urban Glasgow), then the N is reduced, and so is the accuracy of the results. Finally, you should be especially careful in reading polls for forecasting, for example pre-election polls. Everyone has seen examples of embarrassing failures with all the big pollsters reporting an edge for party X up to the eve of the election, which is won by party Y. Usually the thing to watch for is either a trend (for example, one party is behind but increasing its share of the vote in successive polls, with greater increases occurring in more recent polls), or a large proportion of undecided voters (who often swing elections with last-minute decisions). The relationship between pre-election polls and election results is pretty complicated, so either learn a lot about it, or take the poll indications as little more than a very broad guide (see Gallup, 1972; Link, 1972).

Using the Computer

The command structure for the t-test is much like that for the Z-test. If the data are in C1:

```
MTB> TTEST MU = 65 C1;     (main command H₀: μ = 65)
SUBC> ALTERNATIVE = 1.     (subcommand H₁: μ > 65)
TEST of μ = 65.0 vs μ G.T. 65.0
          N        MEAN     STDEV    SE MEAN   the T-test   P VALUE
C1        10       72.0     12.0     3.9       1.79         0.054
MTB> STOP
```

To use the t-test to compare the means of two batches, the appropriate command is:

TWOSAMPLE.

To obtain a confidence interval, the commands TINTERVAL or ZIN-TERVAL can be used. To obtain a 90 per cent CI for data in column 1, use the command:

MTB> TINTERVAL 90 C1.

HOMEWORK

1 In our society, children are almost uniformly toilet-trained substantially later than they are weaned. Such an ordering seems 'natural' to us. You might be interested in looking at the timing of these two stages in a number of primitive societies as recorded in Table 9.5 (all societies in Whiting and Child (1962) for which stable estimates of ages at the start of weaning and toilet training are provided). These data can be used in a t-test; lay the problem out as a t-test, making sure you discuss all important assumptions.

2 A study was conducted on the possible effects of marijuana: Weil *et al.*

Table 9.5   Weaning and toilet training

Society	Age at weaning	Age at toilet training	Society	Age at weaning	Age at toilet training
Alorese	2.3	1.8	Marquesans	0.5	1.0
Balinese	2.7	3.0	Navaho	2.0	2.2
Bena	1.8	4.7	Ontong-Javanese	3.0	1.2
Chagga	2.7	0.8	Papago	2.3	1.9
Comanche	1.5	1.2	Pukapukans	1.5	1.7
Dahomeans	2.5	2.0	Siriono	2.3	2.8
Hopi	2.0	1.5	Slave	2.0	1.7
Kwakiutl	2.0	1.5	Tanala	1.7	0.3
Kwoma	2.5	3.0	Tenino	2.0	2.2
Lepcha	2.8	2.2	Teton	2.7	2.2
Lesu	2.2	2.0	Western Apache	1.3	2.7
Manus	2.5	1.2	Wogeo	2.8	2.0
Maori	1.3	2.2			

Source: Whiting and Child (1962)

Table 9.6   Increases in score on digit symbol substitution test after smoking (negative values indicate the score decreased)

Subject	1	2	3	4	5	6	7	8	9
No marijuana	−3	+10	−3	+3	+4	−3	+2	−1	−1
With marijuana	+5	−17	−7	−3	−7	−9	−6	+1	−3

(1968). Nine male volunteers smoked a cigarette containing marijuana on one day; on the other day they smoked a cigarette containing no marijuana (but flavoured so they couldn't tell the difference). On each day tests of alertness were given before smoking and 15 minutes after smoking, and the authors report the change (after − before), which is shown in Table 9.6.

Lay the problem out as a *t*-test. In addition to the *t*-test, find confidence intervals for $\alpha = 0.01$.

3 In the same study the authors also used a third option – a cigarette with a small amount of marijuana. In Table 9.7 are differences (before − after) on another alertness test.

Here, H_0: $\mu = 0$. Set up and run a *t*-test and calculate confidence intervals for $\alpha = 0.25$.

Table 9.7   Differences on an alertness test

Subject	1	2	3	4	5	6	7	8	9
Change score	−1.04	−1.43	−0.60	−0.11	0.39	−0.32	0.48	−0.39	−1.94

10
Comparing Several Batch Levels

Our experience so far with hypothesis testing about levels has been peculiar. First, we spent a fair amount of time learning to deal with the Z-test only to find out that the Z-test is rarely useful because we're very unlikely to know σ. Consequently, we found we needed to learn the *t*-test. Now we know how to test a single mean against a theoretical expectation, and how to compare the means of two batches. Ironically, although we have begun to understand hypothesis-testing logic we really haven't gotten far in terms of widely useful tests. Most of the interesting questions involving batch levels deal with several differences: the effects of half a dozen different teaching methods on reading skills, the effects of being in different age cohorts on propensity to commit suicide, the effects of different work situations on union involvement, the effects of living in various neighbourhoods on delinquency rates, and so on.

In each of these examples, we have one variable, such as reading skill, suicide rates, etc., that we want to explain. This is the *dependent variable*. And we have another variable, like teaching methods, age group, etc., which we believe affects the first: for example, teaching method may have an effect on reading skill. This is the *independent variable*. We will learn how to work with various kinds of independent and dependent variables. For now we are interested in cases where the independent variable is categorical and the dependent variable is numeric. A categorical variable (or nominal variable) is a batching variable, a set of related categories into which cases can be sorted. Preferably the sorting is unambiguous: each case belongs in one and only one category. The world regions used in Review example 2 (following Chapter 6) are one example of a categorical variable. The age groups used in the suicide rates example (Chapters 2 to 4) are another. But the age groups have something the world regions do not have: an order (from youngest to oldest). In batch analysis, or in confirmatory equivalents, the batching variable can be categorical or ordinal. The dependent variable is numeric. Sometimes cases are borderline; for example, the 'fear of ghosts' could be seen as ordinal or as numeric. In Chapter 9 we said that the distinction matters because theoretically, at least, ordinal variables should not be analysed with tools that take more than order into account; but a number of pragmatic investigations have shown that you will not be misled if you define 'numeric' pretty freely.

Let's return to our current problem: categorical independent variable, numeric dependent variable. To see the effect (if any) of the independent on the dependent variable, we see whether the level of the dependent variable is different from batch to batch depending on the 'value' of the independent variable. For example, in the suicide data we found that suicide rates were different by age group (with older groups having higher levels of suicide) so we concluded that age has an effect on suicide; if the levels had been pretty much the same for all age categories we would have concluded that age is unrelated to suicide.

For such examples, there are more than two batches so the t-test will not do. On the one hand, we cannot boil the multiple batch differences down to one difference and compare it to the t-distribution. On the other hand, if we look at every pair of batches we can use a form of the test; but it costs too much to do so, since it takes a lot of time and wastes a lot of statistical power. We need a new approach. Fortunately, we will find that our new approach will turn out to be far simpler than the direct approach used in both the Z-test and t-test.

In the t- and Z-tests we used the same basic idea: to decide whether two means ($\bar{x}$ and μ) are different, compute the observed difference and compare it to a measure of how large such differences are likely to be when the two means are 'really' the same, when they appear different just because of sampling fluctuations. We compared observed and chance differences in a ratio:

$$\frac{\text{difference of means}}{\text{'chance' difference}} = \frac{\bar{x} - \mu}{\text{SE of } \bar{x} \text{ if } H_0 \text{ true}}$$

$$= \frac{\bar{x} - \mu}{\sigma/\sqrt{N}} \text{ for } Z$$

$$\text{or} = \frac{\bar{x} - \mu}{sd_x/\sqrt{N}} \text{ for } t$$

If H_0 is true and $\bar{x}$ differs from μ only because of sampling fluctuations then the ratio probably will not be very large (positive or negative); if H_0 is false and the means really are different, the ratio is quite likely to be large.

Now we can adopt the same basic idea for comparisons between several means (not just $\bar{x}$ and μ). Again we use a ratio, but now the top part should tell us how different the several means are from each other. Well, we know how to sum that up: the variance of the category means tells us how different they are, how spread out they are as a batch. For the bottom of the ratio we need a measure of how big the top will be if H_0 is true and the category means differ because of sampling fluctuations alone. This turns out to be easy too: it's based on the variance within the categories, just as the denominator for the one-sample t-ratio is based on the variance in the sample. This technique is called *analysis of variance* or 'anova'. Let's see how this works for a simple hypothetical example to convince ourselves that it makes sense, and then go through a real example in detail.

Anova Thinking

Suppose we are attempting to treat the disease pellagra, and we have two experimental drugs we want to test, 'curit' and 'stopit'. We want to compare the effects of these drugs on untreated sufferers, but since some people recover simply as a result of thinking they've been treated, we have a *placebo*, perhaps a sugar pill, that we give to our untreated group. So we take a random sample of sufferers that we divide into three random subsamples: a curit group (c), a stopit group (s) and a placebo group (p) (naturally the doctors, patients and experimenters must not know which people are getting which until the data have been collected). How can we compare the three treatments, which form the three categories of our independent variable 'type of treatment'? Let us consider how the three batches are related. In the first place all three groups were selected randomly from the same original sample of patients. Some of them have mild cases, some severe; some respond well to treatment, some poorly. In short, the sample of pellagra sufferers, like the universe from which it comes, has a level of 'curability' and a spread (variance) about that level.

Let us suppose that the distribution looks like the one in Figure 10.1. (We are assuming a normal distribution.) Now each of the three subsamples will have a distribution too, with mean and variance of its own. What will the three distributions look like? This has to depend in part on the effects (or lack of effects) of the three treatments. For example, suppose that all three treatments are ineffective; then the three distributions of relief will tend to look like

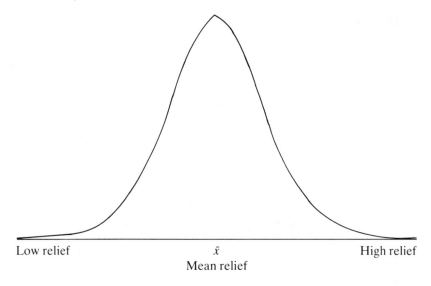

Low relief $\bar{x}$ High relief
                              Mean relief

Figure 10.1 The original sample of pellagra sufferers: distribution of relief

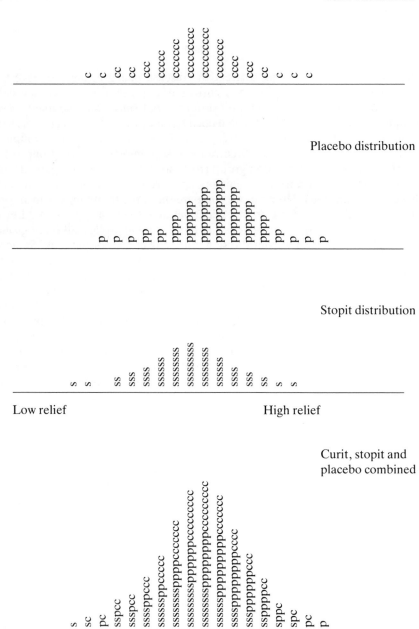

Figure 10.2   Typical results for ineffectual treatments

Curit distribution

Placebo distribution

Stopit distribution

Low relief   High relief

Curit, stopit and
placebo combined

Low relief $\bar{x}$ High relief

Figure 10.3   Possible results for an effective 'curit'

smaller versions of Figure 10.1 because they will just be three random samples from the original sample portrayed in Figure 10.1. We would not expect the groups to look identical because there will usually be some random fluctuations, but they will be close most of the time, so we expect something like the top of Figure 10.2. The curit, stopit and placebo distributions are shown one underneath another to allow comparison. Each distribution is roughly normal and has roughly the same spread; the means will vary a little bit (the placebo mean relief being highest here) but essentially the three treatment groups look the same. If we combine them, as at the bottom of Figure 10.2, we get a combined distribution just like the three separate ones (similar level, spread and shape) with the only difference being a larger number of cases. This combined distribution looks like the original sample's distribution in Figure 10.1. In short, the three treatments do not differ so the differences between them are no more than one would expect from the random allocation of sufferers to the groups.

Now let us see what happens when the treatments do have different effects. We will get something like Figure 10.3 perhaps, where the mean relief from curit is clearly greater than the mean relief from stopit or placebo. Again, we show the three groups pooled together in the bottom of Figure 10.3. Now one striking thing about this comparison is that the variance around $\bar{x}$ (bottom picture) is large compared to the variance around subsample means (top picture). This is quite different from Figure 10.2, where the pooled distribution has about the same variance as the three subsamples. Where does the 'extra' variance in Figure 10.3 come from? Clearly from the separation of the means of the subsamples. The stopit and placebo samples have lower means than the curit sample, so overall the observations are quite spread out compared to spread within subsamples. When the three samples had closer means (as in Figure 10.2) the variance around the grand mean was a lot smaller. To generalize this, we can say that overall (or total) variance will be great compared to subsample variance if the subsample means are far apart.

We can make this insight more precise because a useful and easily proven relationship exists among the variances. The total variance can be broken down into two components, one describing the 'average' variance within the subsamples (the 'within groups' term) and the second describing the variances of subsample means around the grand mean (the 'between groups' term). A simple proof of this relationship can be found in Appendix A at the end of the book. Now the 'between groups' term tells us how different the batch means are. What about the 'within groups' term? Since this is approximately the average variance within treatment groups (the average of the variance of cs only, p's only, s's only) it does not depend on differences between treatments; it tells us what variability to expect if H_0 is true and the treatments do not differ in effectiveness. But this brings us right back to the ratio idea in the introduction:

$$\frac{\text{difference of means}}{\text{'chance' difference}} = \frac{\text{'between' term}}{\text{'within' term}} \simeq \frac{\text{observed variance}}{\text{variance if } H_0 \text{ true}}$$

If this ratio is very large then the means are more different than one could reasonably expect, given H_0. So if the ratio is big enough, we'll reject H_0 and decide that the independent variable probably does have an effect. Again, we'll find out what 'big enough' means by looking at a table of critical values. We are asking the same kind of question as for t- or Z-tests, and asking it in the same way. However, with our new approach we can now ask this question of as many means as we wish. We are still looking at differences between means, because as the means become more different, the 'between' component must increase, but one test makes all of our comparisons simultaneously.

There is one difference from the t or Z case: we don't have to worry about one- or two-tailed tests here. We only reject H_0 when we get significantly large ratios. Negative ratios are impossible (the top and bottom parts must both be positive, being like variances, i.e. sums of squares, SS). Thus we have a kind of omnibus test for any kind of difference between the means, because any substantial differences between them will make their variance big.

Now that you have seen what we are after, let's go through the formulae used to compute the ratio. You will rarely be called upon to use these formulae; after all, computers do these things more quickly, more easily and more accurately. But if you're like many people, looking at computer output doesn't help you to understand what the test really does. So we will show you how to read the computer output, but we also go through the same problem by hand in detail.

Computations for the Analysis of Variance Ratio

We need two variance analogues for our ratio: 'between groups' and 'within groups'. What should they look like? Well, that familiar quantity, the simple variance of a batch, is:

$$\text{variance} = \frac{\sum(x - \bar{x})^2}{N - 1} = \frac{\text{sum of squares}}{\text{degrees of freedom}}$$

Or, in computation form, we have

$$\text{variance} = \frac{\sum x^2 - (\sum x)^2/N}{N - 1}$$

The 'between' and 'within' parts of our ratio are very similar:

for 'between', we have $\dfrac{\text{between sum of squares}}{\text{between } df}$

and for 'within' $\dfrac{\text{within sum of squares}}{\text{within } df}$

These are called 'mean squares' or MS for short. Then our test ratio will be

$$\frac{\text{mean square between}}{\text{mean square within}} \text{ or } \frac{\text{MS}_\text{B}}{\text{MS}_\text{W}}$$

So we need sums of squares and degrees of freedom for top and bottom, between and within. The total variance is also computed from sums of squares and degrees of freedom, and it gives us a useful arithmetic check since these pieces must add up:

Total sum of squares = between SS + within SS.
Total df = between df + within df.

Let's work out the degrees of freedom first. We have N observations in all (N items in all the groups together), so the total df is equal to $N - 1$ (just as for any simple variance). The df for the between groups 'variance' is very similar: the number of groups (K) minus 1. And if we have $N - 1$ dfs altogether, with $K - 1$ for between groups, then we must have $N - K$ for the within group df since $(K - 1) + (N - K) = N - 1$.

To get sums of squares we need convenient computing formulae (as we did even for the simple one-batch variance). We get the least wear and tear if we do three computations (A, B and C) which serve as efficient building blocks: they are fast and easy, and fit together to make the within group and between group estimates we want. We give both formulae and verbal descriptions for each one. First, a term reflecting the behaviour of the individual observations:

$$A = \sum x_{ij}^2$$

where i indexes the groups and j indexes the observations within the groups. The formula says: take every observation in every group, square each one, then add them all together. Next, a term that reflects the grand mean:

$$B = \frac{(\sum x_{ij})^2}{N}$$

That is, take the sum of all the observations, square it, then divide by the count, N. Last, a term reflecting the various treatments:

$$C = \sum_i \frac{(\sum_j x_{ij})^2}{N_i}$$

To get C, take the sum in each separate group, $\sum_j x_{ij}$, square each sum, and divide by the count in that group, $N_i (\sum N_i = N)$. Then add up these group figures. Now we are in business.

A and B should look familiar: they are the same sums we use in the computational form of the variance. The total sum of squares is $A - B$,

Total SS = $A - B$

which is just the numerator in the formula for the variance. The other two sums of squares are just as easy:

between SS = $C - B$
within   SS = $A - C$

All three of these sums of squares must be positive; if they are not, you have made an error! They must also add up: $(C - B) + (A - C) = A - B$.

Table 10.1   Analysis of variance summary table

Source of variance	df	Sum of squares	Mean squares	F-ratio
Between groups (factor)	$K - 1$	$C - B$	$SS/df = MS_B$	$\dfrac{MS_B}{MS_W}$
Within groups (error)	$N - K$	$A - C$	$SS/df = MS_W$	
Total	$N - 1$	$A - B$		

This gives us all we need for the two mean squares we need as variance analogues for our ratio:

$$\frac{\text{between}}{\text{within}} = \frac{\text{between SS/between } df}{\text{within SS/within } df} = \frac{\text{between MS}}{\text{within MS}}$$

This ratio is called the F-ratio. None of this is hard, but there's a certain amount of detail to keep straight so we use an analysis of variance summary table (Table 10.1). First we use it to summarize the computations using A, B and C.

The F-ratio contains two variance estimates, unlike the t-test where there was only one, and thus two df figures instead of one. For each pair of dfs we could generate an entire table similar to the Z-table of Table 8.1, but ordinarily F-tables just provide CVs for popular levels of significance. Table A.4 gives CVs for $\alpha = 0.05$. To use Table A.4, find the column with the df for the numerator (between) and the row with the denominator (within) df: the CV is at the intersection of that row and column. For $\alpha = 0.05$ the critical value for $F_{4,10}$ is 3.48; that is, we would get an F-ratio as large or larger than 3.48 5 per cent of the time if H_0 is true and we reject H_0 at the 0.05 level if we get such a value. In short, the F-table, like the t-table, gives us a critical value; we simply compute our ratio and compare it to the CV. If our ratio exceeds or equals the CV we reject H_0. If not, we don't.

Now we're ready for a real example. First we apply the formulae just given; later we will go briefly into the assumptions made in doing an analysis of variance and finally we will provide the output from the MINITAB sub-routine 'AOVONEWAY' together with annotations. Please note that, in practice, you check the assumptions first! If the data do not meet them, the test is likely to be misleading.

A Worked Example

An observer sat in a primary school classroom observing and coding interactions between the teacher and the pupils. Among the types of interaction observed was the mean frequency of criticism of each pupil by the teacher per session. We have sorted the students into three categories by IQ: low (IQ less than 90), medium (IQ from 90 to 110), and high (IQ over 110). Our

Table 10.2   Criticism by IQ

Low IQ (under 90)	Medium IQ (90–110)	High IQ (over 110)
2.3	3.8	0
4.4	1.6	1.8
4.9	3.5	0
2.0	2.1	2.3
4.7	4.9	1.8
2.2	2.0	2.9
1.2	3.4	1.2
5.5	2.4	1.6
0	4.8	5.4
1.5	1.2	0
0	4.9	0
1.6	2.0	1.2
3.7	2.6	0
	4.2	2.8
	0	
	5.4	
	2.0	
	1.7	
Group 1:	Group 2:	Group 3:
$N_1 = 13$	$N_2 = 18$	$N_3 = 14$
$\sum X = 34$	$\sum X = 52.5$	$\sum X = 21$
$\sum X^2 = 129.78$	$\sum X^2 = 191.93$	$\sum X^2 = 62.62$

Source: Data from an unpublished study by Sally Luce; transformed by taking square roots.

observations in each IQ group are the mean number of times that each student in the group was given a 'shot'. The data are presented in Table 10.2, in the form of square roots of the original observations (we will return to why we used square roots after we have gone through the example). Does a child's IQ have any effect on how likely the teacher is to criticize? According to H_0, no; the rate of criticism is the same for each of the three IQ categories in general:

$$H_0: \mu_{low} = \mu_{medium} = \mu_{high}$$

The sample means may differ a bit because of sampling fluctuations. H_1 is more complicated since it includes any inequality among the means. Perhaps all three are different, perhaps one is quite different from the other two; we do not usually write it down explicitly.

Let's compute A, B and C. We have made a start in Table 10.2 by adding up x and x^2 values for each of the three groups. So A, the sum of the squared values, is just

$$A = 129.78 + 191.93 + 62.62 = 384.33$$

For B we sum all the values, square the sum, and divide by N, or

$$B = \frac{(34.0 + 52.5 + 21.0)^2}{45}$$

$$= \frac{11556.25}{45} = 256.81$$

For C we first square each group's total and divide the squared total by the group's size, getting

$$\frac{(34)^2}{13}, \frac{(52.5)^2}{18} \text{ and } \frac{(21)^2}{14}$$

(Note that each group's squared total is divided by its own count.) Then C is the sum of these values:

$$C = 88.92 + 153.13 + 31.5 = 273.55$$

All we need now to construct a summary table and do our test is the degrees of freedom. The total count is 45, so total $df = 44$. The number of groups is $K = 3$ so the between df is $K - 1 = 2$, and $N - K = 45 - 3 = 42$, is the within df. This gives Table 10.3.

For example, the values in the between row were found by plugging our values in the formulae given earlier:

$$\text{between SS} = C - B = 273.55 - 256.81 = 16.74$$

$$\text{between MS} = \frac{\text{between SS}}{\text{between } df} = \frac{16.74}{2} = 8.37$$

Having found all the SS and df values separately we can check our arithmetic easily:

$$16.74 + 110.78 = 127.52$$
$$2 + 42 = 44$$

So we finally have an F-ratio for our example: 3.17. We look at our $\alpha = 0.05$ table of F-values, Table A.4, and find that the critical value for 2 and

Table 10.3

Source of variance	df	Sum of squares	Mean squares	F-ratio
Between IQ groups	2	16.74	8.37	3.17
Within IQ groups	42	110.78	2.64	
Total	44	127.52		

42 *dfs* is 3.23 (or thereabouts). Our value 3.17 is not quite as extreme as this so we can't reject H_0; the observed differences among the group means are almost but not quite large enough compared to chance differences one could reasonably expect if H_0 is true. But the F is so close to significance at the standard 5 per cent level that we can't help wondering if perhaps H_0 is wrong and there is some connection between child's IQ and criticism received. We don't reject H_0 but we do go back to exploratory thinking to see if we should study this problem further.

We can start by exploring the batches we have. The values in Table 10.2 are box-plotted in Figure 10.4. In the middle of each box, the horizontal line is the median and the X is the trimean. Both levels suggest that the children with high IQs get less criticism, perhaps because they are more academically successful and hence more likely to please the teacher. The low and medium IQ children get about the same amount of criticism on the whole. Perhaps the low IQ children get a bit less; this is not strongly indicated, but if it is true then maybe the teacher does not expect as much of the least bright children and ignores more than criticizes their failings. Well, this all makes sense but we weren't able to support it: why not? Figure 10.4 makes one possibility clear; there is a near upper outlier in the high IQ groups. This value probably pulled up the non-resistant mean, making the group means more alike. With the very high value (5.4) dropped, the mean for the high IQ batch goes from 1.5 to 1.3. Furthermore, the variance goes from 2.39 to 1.23. Thus this one case makes the group means more alike and makes the 'within' value larger. Well, if the high IQ mean has been distorted by this one value, is there some reason for it to be so unusual? We looked back at our data source and found this child had an IQ of 112; very near the boundary line between the medium IQ and high IQ groups, and may perhaps be more similar to students in the medium group.

All in all, our failure to get a significant result may be a result of one slightly misclassified case; we almost got a significant result, and the pattern we found in exploration made sense. So we conclude that we should collect more data to clarify the possible link between IQ and criticism.

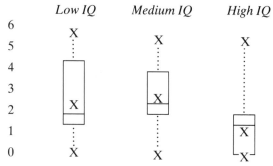

Figure 10.4   Box plots of 'criticism' data

Table 10.4 The untransformed criticism batches

Low IQ		Medium IQ		High IQ	
3		3		3	
3	1	3		3	
2		2	59	2	9
2	42	2	34	2	
1	9	1	58	1	
1	3	1	22	1	
0	55	0	67	0	588
0	410203	0	34414043	0	0303130010

stems: tens   *leaves:* units   (rounded data)

Analysis of Variance Assumptions

The analysis of variance, like all confirmatory tests, is based on some assumptions about the nature of the data. There are three assumptions, the first of which is a familiar one.

Assumption 1: Normality. Each group's values should be drawn from a normally distributed universe. Of course, we don't have the universes at hand, so we check whether this assumption is met by looking at the shapes of our batches. In our example, the original values did not look normal. The original values are stemmed-and-leaved in Table 10.4 and plotted in Figure 10.5, which show a lot of upward straggle. We coped quite easily by taking square roots, which produced the tolerably normal batches plotted in Figure 10.4. The shapes aren't perfect but they are single-peaked and quite symmetric around the trimean, which is usually good enough.

Analysis of variance is robust with respect to the normality assumption: the data don't have to meet it exactly, or even very closely if the data are plentiful, with many cases in each group. We transformed our data because the group sizes were not all that large. It is hard to give exact rules here, because

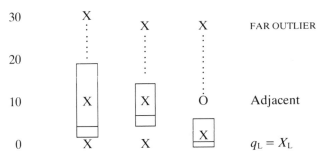

Figure 10.5

the amount of non-normality you can safely work with depends on group sizes and both can vary a lot. In many cases you can correct non-normal data by transformation. If you are unsure whether to proceed or not, consult an expert.

Assumption 2: Equal variances. Each of the groups should be drawn from populations with equal variances; again, in practice we check out the batches we have. There isn't much need for concern if the groups are approximately equal in size: if they are, the variances can be moderately unequal without messing up the anova test. But if the group Ns are substantially unequal, then unequal variances can produce misleading results. We had slightly unequal group Ns in our example so we will check out the group variances. Note, by the way, that we check variances for square-rooted data since we just decided to use square roots to help satisfy the normality assumption. From low to high IQ the variances are: 3.405, 2.282, 2.394. This isn't too bad; in this case the variances would have to differ by a multiplicative factor of about three or more before the difference would begin to make itself felt. Again, there is no simple rule for how much difference you can tolerate; so as before, when in doubt, consult an expert. On the whole though, your own eyes are a good guide; for example, we only have to look at Figure 10.4 to see that our batches are roughly normal and roughly alike in spread.

If you have unequal groups with clearly unequal variances, transformation can help again. Think back to the rule of thumb, described in Chapter 6, for picking a good transformation for several batches, log spread plotted against log level. That procedure often suggested a transform that would equalize batch spreads (and with luck even up spread inside batches too, leading to symmetry). Surely we can use it here for the same purpose. Log of standard deviation versus log of mean would be most appropriate. As long as the batch spreads rise or fall fairly regularly with batch levels, this is likely to work.

Assumption 3: Independent observations. Roughly, this implies that each value is a separate piece of information, not affected by the others. Randomly sampling cases and randomly assigning them to treatment groups guarantees this; indeed, this is one reason why analysis of variance is so popular with experimentalists, who can and do randomly assign people to groups. Non-experimental studies have to sample randomly within groups defined naturally (like our IQ groups, over which we have no control) and hope for the best. This assumption applies to how the data were gathered (were the respondents discussing the questions as they filled out the questionnaire?) and can't be checked by looking at the data, as the other two assumptions can. A more detailed discussion of it really belongs in a course on research design.

In summary, there are three assumptions that must be considered in doing an analysis of variance. If they are not met, the analysis can be very misleading. Fortunately anova is robust with respect to the first two assumptions, which need not be met exactly and can be somewhat bent safely if conditions are right.

Normality tends not to matter much if the group Ns are large. If they are small, transform the data to roughly normal shape. If this can't be done (e.g. if some groups straggle up and some down) be very cautious; treat anova results as merely suggestive and do exploratory work to find out why the shapes differ.

Equal variance tends not to matter much if the group sizes are equal. If group sizes and group variances are both clearly unequal, transformation may help; if it doesn't, be very cautious. If the largest variance is less than three times the smallest and the group sizes are nearly equal, relax.

Independence is hard to get around. Think ahead when gathering the data to be sure this assumption is met.

If you collect your own data you can clearly avoid possible future grief by a few simple precautions: make the observations independent, randomly sample a roughly equal number of cases for each group or category of the independent variable, and get as many cases for each group as you can afford. Then you will not have to worry about anova assumptions. These precautions are easy to take if you are doing an experiment. We have stressed that confirmatory statistics are relatively rigid, requiring standard procedures and assumptions that must be taken seriously. Here we see that the analysis of variance assumptions are indeed important, but not paralysing: mild violations of them are tolerable. The test is quite robust, which is one of the reasons for its usefulness.

Summary

You can use analysis of variance if you want to look at the effect of one variable (the 'independent' variable) on another (the 'dependent') and the variables have the right levels of measurement. The dependent variable has to be numeric (otherwise how can you compute means?) and the independent variable has to be a set of categories or something that can be sensibly turned into a set of categories (otherwise how do you get your batches?).

The test is appropriate if the data meet the three basic assumptions, which, as we just saw, are not very restrictive in practice. You can't use anova blindly, since you often need to adjust your data by transformation beforehand, but you can use it a great deal. Very few problems are hopelessly unsuitable.

The basic idea behind the test is simple and familiar; even the mathematics (in Appendix A) is simple if you know a bit of algebra; and certainly the computations are simple; in fact, you end up doing no more work than you would do for a *t*-test. Analysis of variance has a reputation for difficulty that it does not deserve, and a reputation as a high-powered technique that *is* deserved. A few simple modifications give the basic approach remarkable flexibility. If you wish to learn more, or to find just the right version for a particular problem, there are many good standard sources, such as Winer (1962).

Exploratory and Confirmatory

This chapter is a particularly good example of the interdependence of the two statistical approaches. Exploratory techniques are useful in making sure that the confirmatory anova can be safely used; exploratory methods also help in adjusting the data (usually by transformation) if necessary. After an anova analysis is finished, exploration starts again. If the test was not significant (as in our example), why? If the test was significant, then what happened, that is, which group means are higher or lower and why? (The anova only tells us that there is some significant difference, not what the difference is.) On the other hand, the anova is often done to test ideas that came from previous exploration of other data in the first place.

Our batch explorations suggested that level, spread, shape and outliers are all important. Anova as described here deals only with level, though interpreting results may involve shape, spread and outliers. There are confirmatory tests for differences of variance and shape as well. You should not be too surprised to hear that the F-test can be adapted as a test for differences of batch variances (the Cochran 'C-test' is one such adaptation) and there are tests for differences of shape. We don't propose to go into these in this book, but we do want you to know that tests are available if you need them.

Using the Computer

The MINITAB command for ANOVA is AOVONEWAY or more simply AOVO. For data stored in columns, 1, 3 and 5,

    MTB> AOVO C1 C3 C5

    ANALYSIS OF VARIANCE

SOURCE	DF	SS	MS	F	← (the F-ratio – compare to the CV
FACTOR	2	16.74	8.37	3.17	in the F-table)
ERROR	42	110.78	2.64		
TOTAL	44	127.52			

                                    INDIVIDUAL 95 PCT CI'S FOR MEAN
                                    BASED ON POOLED STDEV

LEVEL	N	MEAN	STDEV	--------- + ----------- + ----------- + ----------- +
C1	13	2.615	1.845	(--------------*--------------)
C3	18	2.917	1.511	(--------------*--------------)
C5	14	1.500	1.547	(---------------*---------------)

                                    --------- + ----------- + ----------- + ----------- +
    POOLED STDEV = 1.624   1.0   2.0   3.0   4.0

    MTB> STOP

The confidence intervals tell a story similar to the one told by the box plots. It is easy to see that the high IQ group gets less criticism than the other two and, were the spread slightly smaller, the intervals would not overlap, which would signify a statistically significant difference.

HOMEWORK

The data in Table 10.5 come from a study by Atkinson and Polivy (1976) on the effects of unprovoked verbal attack. Randomly selected subjects first filled out a large number of items, some of which were self-reports of hostility (scores increase as hostility increases). After a long wait, the experimenter came to collect their responses, while behaving in a very abusive manner. The experimenter said, among other things, that they should do it again and *this* time do it properly! The data here are the hostility scores before and after this treatment. Do they differ? And do males and females differ? These questions can be approached in various ways. Clearly describe your reasons for setting up the problems as you do.

Table 10.5   Hostility before and after being insulted

Female subjects		Male subjects	
Before	*After insult*	*Before*	*After insult*
51	58	86	82
54	65	28	37
61	86	45	51
54	77	59	56
49	74	49	53
54	59	56	90
46	46	69	80
47	50	51	71
43	37	74	88
		42	43

Source: These data appear in another form in Atkinson and Polivy (1976). © The American Psychological Association; reprinted by permission.

SECOND REVIEW
Confirmatory Comparison of Levels

It is now time for you to review your new tools: confirmatory techniques to test differences between levels. As you come to each problem, do not forget to go through the necessary steps in the right order. First, decide what kind of test is suitable: *t*-test, analysis of variance, or another. Secondly, check to see if the test assumptions are met (and if they aren't, do something about that). Third, do the test (don't forget to specify α, H_0 and H_1 in advance). Finally, discuss the results, using exploratory tools and thinking as seems appropriate. You do *not* have to use every exploratory or confirmatory tool you have learned; use what you need.

Example 1

Here we examine some possible effects of child abuse. The data in Table R2.1 are from Marion Cuddy's PhD dissertation (1989). The data (self-reports on a screening questionnaire) look at both depression levels and nightmare frequency for three groups of women; those reporting sexual abuse in childhood, those reporting physical abuse and those reporting no abuse. Analyse either the depression scores or the nightmare frequency data. What information would you like to have about your interesting cases?

1 Beck Depression Inventory; higher scores suggest greater depression.
2 Nightmare frequency ranges from
       0 = no nightmares in the past year
       1 = one or two in the past year
       2 = up to once a month
       3 = up to once a week
       4 = once a week or more.

Example 2

In Table 10.5 we described one part of the Atkinson and Polivy study for males

Table R2.1   Child abuse, depression and nightmare frequency

Group 1 Physical abuse		Group 2 Sexual abuse		Group 3 No reported abuse	
BDI	Nightmares	BDI	Nightmares	BDI	Nightmares
5	2	20	2	5	3
19	2	16	2	13	1
5	2	7	3	3	0
19	3	24	2	13	2
10	2	5	2	5	0
15	0	19	3	13	2
14	1	25	3	14	0
9	2	7	1	3	1
4	1	6	1	13	2
3	1	21	2	13	0
23	2	23	2	5	2
6	1	18	1	13	1
18	3	18	2	3	2
15	3	8	1	13	1
14	3	13	2	13	2
10	2	14	2	7	2
9	1	14	3	13	0
9	0	19	2	13	2
0	3	21	2	14	0
8	2	24	2	5	3
5	1	7	2	13	1
11	2	5	2	13	1
14	2	11	1	15	1
10	2	5	2	13	0
11	2	12	2	13	1
14	2	23	3	13	1
1	1	27	3	3	1
11	2	8	2	3	2
7	0	11	3	13	1
7	1	8	2	15	1

Source: Cuddy (1989).

and females; here we describe another part of the study, giving data only for the male subjects in Table R2.2. In the first part, subjects were just insulted as described above; so the data in column 1 of Table R2.2 are the same data as in column 4 of Table 10.5. In the second part, other subjects weren't insulted but after the long wait were given an apology and an explanation for the experimenter's behaviour (an explanation meant to arouse empathy with the experimenter). In the third part, subjects were insulted and then given a chance to retaliate against the experimenter by recommending a bad grade for her. In the fourth part, delay was followed by both an apology and a chance to retaliate. Subjects were randomly assigned to the four treatments, so they should start off without any significant differences in level of hostility. Do they differ after these different treatments? If so, in what way and why? If not, why?

A brief sketch of the theory behind the experiment may be helpful. Apology with an empathy-arousing explanation is supposed to reduce hostility by making the insult understandable and making the subject feel closer to the experimenter. A chance to retaliate is also supposed to reduce hostility, but by a different mechanism: catharsis rather than empathy. Getting a chance for revenge might help people to 'work it off' so they end up less hostile.

These two problems probably appear quite similar, but they differ greatly in at least one important way, randomization. In the Atkinson and Polivy study, the subjects are randomly allocated to the various treatments, while in the Cuddy study they aren't (and couldn't be!). Comment on some of the implications of this difference for your analysis.

Table R2.2   Male hostility after delay

Insult, no retaliation	Apology, no retaliation	Insult, retaliation	Apology, retaliation
82	53	69	80
37	67	51	55
51	38	77	54
56	68	30	42
53	99	89	41
90	49	76	58
80	33	55	60
71	47	57	50
88	32	55	67
43	50	52	59

Source: Atkinson and Polivy (1976). © The American Psychological Association; reprinted by permission.

SECTION III
Y by X Analysis

The first sections of this book have dealt with batches. We've learned quick and easy ways of analysing and comparing batches, ways of noting and removing batch features, and most importantly, learning to go further by trying to understand the nature of the process that produced the batches. We've also learned how to test some of our insights by means of confirmatory procedures. But everything we've learned is set up to treat the simplest collections of numbers, those with no influence on one another, with no connection beyond their common origin in the process being investigated.

Now we move to a new form of data: numbers that are somehow linked together. Usually, the numbers are linked because they relate to the same unit; for example, one person (one kind of unit) has an age, an income, a political preference and so on. Thus age, income, and politics are numbers linked person by person.

Let's clarify this rather abstract distinction by looking at some numbers. One nice thing about the mental illness figures of Table 11.5 (p. 202) is that they can be looked at as batch data *or* as linked data (also known as *Y* by *X* data), thus giving a chance to compare the two. These male and female mental illness rates come from a study by Gove and Tudor (1973) which argued that women are more likely to be mentally ill than men because female roles in modern industrial societies are more frustrating and less rewarding than male roles. Each row in Table 11.5 gives the results of one post-World War II community survey (using interviews) for men and for women. Here we see one kind of batch idea; the sets of survey results were divided into two batches (one male, one female) and a batch summary (percentage ill) was computed. In analysing these data, one familiar approach involves looking at the whole table as a set of two batches: one batch is the female rates, one batch the male rates. Briefly, it is easy to see that the level for the female batch is well above the level for the male batch (you could follow this up with schematic plots). Looking at batch levels alone can take us a fair way with this set of numbers. It also seems natural to make use of the fact that each community studied gives both a male and a female rate; that is, we can compare the male and female rates and see at a glance that the rate of mental illness is higher among women in every study.

This is consistent with Gove and Tudor's argument: the level of mental illness for women is higher than the level for men in many different studies. Some process (they say sex role experience) is acting differently on men than on women and yielding different rates.

But we can ask a new, more sophisticated question that is possible because the male and female rates are paired. This means we can ask about relationships between male and female rates: not only, 'Is one batch higher overall?' but, 'Is each observation related to its mate? Do they vary together?' A longer look at Table 11.5 suggests that female and male rates do in fact rise and fall together: where one is low, the other is, and where one is high the other is. Maybe the higher rates come from studies done in more stressful places (inner cities?) or perhaps from studies with a more inclusive definition of mental illness. If we follow up ideas like these we may learn some things about illness rates that go beyond the Gove and Tudor argument.

To follow this new line of attack we need new approaches, called Y by X techniques, which the next set of chapters outlines. As usual, the exploratory version comes first and the analogous confirmatory technique follows. In addition to the Y by X techniques, another tool useful for working with two categorical variables will be described in this section (the chi-square test) as part of an introduction to tabular analysis in Chapter 14.

11
Y by X and Straight Lines

This chapter begins with a very simple example; one where the simplest Y by X technique works in the simplest way. After the technique has been described and illustrated we will discuss it broadly.

Seeing a Y by X Pattern

Consider the data in Table 11.1, which give the winning times in seconds for the men's 1500 metre run in each Olympic Games from 1900 to 1984. Clearly these are Y by X data because the value for each winning time is linked to a specific Olympics. As you may have noticed, several of the years are missing (you can probably think why). We want to use year to predict the winning time, making year X, the independent or predictor variable, and time Y, the dependent variable. This doesn't mean that year 'causes' time, although there are a variety of things associated with year that are likely to affect runners' speed. Some of these would be improvements in tracks, equipment (especially shoes), training, nutrition, etc.

Our next step is to plot X against Y so that we can look at the way they are related. Note that in Figure 11.1 the X-axis, year, is horizontal and the Y-axis, time, is vertical – this is conventional. Without any statistical help at all, just using your eyes, you can easily see quite a lot. Something is going on here; these points aren't randomly scattered about – they form a pattern. Broadly, they sweep from higher on the left to lower on the right; generally people are running faster – taking fewer seconds, over time. A straight line from upper left to lower right would do quite a good job of capturing the pattern. Try it: wiggle a piece of black thread or a pencil or (better) a transparent ruler around on the plot until it looks right. Then compare your intuitive try to the line in Figure 11.3, found by the technique we will describe shortly. Chances are these lines are quite close, and they should be: the technique just gives a precise numerical summary of a trend that you can often see plainly.

A linear pattern (like the one in Figure 11.1) is the simplest pattern one can find in Y by X data, and also one of the commonest. The rest of the chapter

Table 11.1   Winning times for the men's 1500
metre run for each Olympiad from 1900 to 1984

Year	Time (seconds)
1900	246
1904	245
1908	243
1912	237
1920	242
1924	234
1928	233
1932	231
1936	228
1948	230
1952	225
1956	221
1960	216
1964	218
1968	215
1972	216
1976	219
1980	218
1984	213

Source: Information Please (1988).

will show how to find resistant summaries of such patterns easily, and how to go
beyond the summaries by looking at residuals from them. Just as a mean or
trimean is a numerical summary of level, a straight line equation is the
numerical summary of a linear pattern.

The equation of a straight line looks like this:

$$Y = bX + a$$

where Y is the dependent variable, the variable you want to predict or explain;
X is the independent or predictor variable (sometimes but not always the
'cause' of Y); b is the slope, the number of units Y changes for every unit
change in X; a is the intercept or constant, the value of Y when X is 0.

In our example, we want to find values for b and a that will do a good job of
summarizing the time–year relationship, i.e.

time $= b$(year) $+ a$

Finding a line would be easy if we had only two points – just connect them. But

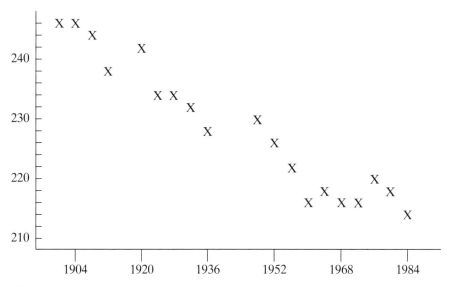

Figure 11.1   Year by time

we have 19 points in our example and often have many more. A convenient first step is to find summary points that sum up the main pattern of the data; then we use the summary points to find the line equation.

Finding Three Summary Points

We want a few points that sum up the general trend of the data, points that reflect most of the cases while not being deflected by the atypical ones: *resistant* summary points. If we base our line on resistant summary points, the line will give a resistant fit. Tukey suggests that we break up our data into thirds on X, giving us three batches of points that can be summarized with the familiar batch tool, level. Since only two points are needed to define a straight line, you may feel that breaking the data into two parts and summarizing each half would be a more natural thing to do. But the middle third turns out to be useful in a number of ways, one of these being that it gives us an easy way to find the intercept a. Some other uses for the middle third will be demonstrated in later chapters.

   The first step is to break the data into thirds. If we are doing this by hand, we begin by ordering the points on X from lowest to highest (or the reverse – it doesn't much matter), being careful to keep each Y value together with its associated X. As it happens, Table 11.1 has come to us ordered on X, year. In this table, we can just draw two lines, marking off the thirds clearly and easily. This has been done in Table 11.1: the first six Olympiads from 1900 to 1924

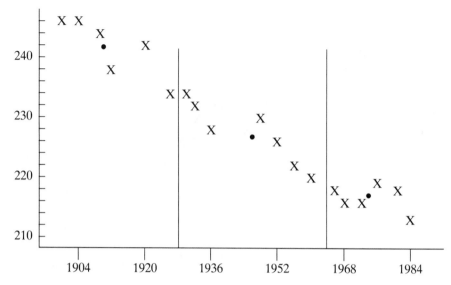

Figure 11.2   Constructing the line

make up the lowest third on X, the middle third consists of the next seven, from 1928 to 1960, and so on.

Having found the thirds, we need to summarize them, to find 'typical' X and Y values for each third. In Table 11.1, the low third on X, for example, is just a batch of six values that is summarized by finding the resistant level – the median or trimean, etc. Using trimeans for our example, we get:

X_L = 1911 Y_L = 241.75
X_M = 1946 Y_M = 227
X_H = 1974 Y_H = 216.75

Figure 11.2 shows the thirds marked off with vertical lines and summary points indicated by filled-in circles. You can see there that the summary points don't correspond to any real points (though they can); they are right in the middle of each third on both X and Y. These points, then, are resistant summaries for the batches where X is high, medium or low, which provide a good picture without drowning us in detail.

Finding thirds is not usually this easy. Much of the time, as we noted earlier, the points will have to be ordered on X before beginning. In addition, there are several potential traps to watch for. It is preferable to split the points into batches that are as nearly equal as possible, and further, where they can't be equal, to have the greatest number of cases in the middle third. Thus, in our race example with 19 observations, each third ideally would contain six or seven cases, with the middle third having seven, other things being equal.

If there are several observations with identical X values, it is very important that they all be in the same third. This may conflict with our ideal of (nearly) equal thirds. All you can do in such a case is to choose the least disruptive way to split the points – in short, cope. Finally, problems can be created where either X or Y (or both) trails excessively, or where a few points are extreme outliers. We will look at these problems in the next chapter.

So far we have done nothing elaborate; we have just divided the data on X and summarized X and Y for each part with a basic batch tool, level. But there are several common errors to watch out for:

1 Do not find the highest and lowest thirds for Y by ordering the Y values on Y itself; keep them together with their associated Xs.
2 Once you have found the thirds, the X and Y values within each third are summarized separately. Don't just take the Y paired with the summary X (if there is one).
3 Y_M should lie between Y_H and Y_L: if it doesn't, a linear fit will usually do a poor job of summarizing the data.

Finding a Line From the Summary Points

Now we are ready to find a line equation using the summary points. First b is found, then a. As we noted earlier you can find the slope of a line from any two points on the line: call them (X_1, Y_1), and (X_2, Y_2). We just find the 'rise over the run' or the amount Y changes, $(Y_2 - Y_1)$, divided by the amount X changes, $(X_2 - X_1)$. Here the two points are the high and low summary points:

$$b = (Y_H - Y_L)/(X_H - X_L) = (216.75 - 241.74)/(1974 - 1911)$$
$$= -25/63 = -0.4$$

which is just the slope of the line that connects the high and low summary points (we use the two end-points to find the slope because these points give the best estimate of the slope). There are several easy ways to find the intercept a, but one of the easiest is to use our three summary points; find $Y - bX$ for each of the three summary points and take the mean of those three values. For our example,

$$a_L = Y_L - bX_L = 241.75 - (-0.4)\, 1911 = 1006.15$$
$$a_M = Y_M - bX_M = 227 - (-0.4)\, 1946 = 1005.4$$
$$a_H = Y_H - bX_H = 216.75 - (-0.4)\, 1974 = 1006.35$$

The mean of these is 1005.9, which we could round to 1006, or 1010 or even 1000 if we were doing this by hand, depending on what happened to be most convenient for us. Let's take 1006, giving us the equation:

$$Y = -0.4X + 1006$$

Now that we have the line equation, we can obtain residuals. Table 11.2 shows a handy kind of worksheet for Y by X analysis. Column 4 shows the residuals $Y' = Y - (bX + a)$.

To plot the line, you can either draw it by eye using the summary points (a

Table 11.2 Basic work sheet

X	Y	bX	Y − (bX + a)
1900	246	−760	0.0
1904	245	−761.6	0.6
1908	243	−763.2	0.2
1912	237	−764.8	−4.2
1920	242	−768	4.0
1924	234	−769.6	−2.4
1928	233	−722.2	−1.8
1932	231	−772.8	−2.2
1936	228	−774.4	−3.6
1948	230	−779.2	3.2
1952	225	−780.8	−0.2
1956	221	−782.4	−2.6
1960	216	−784	−6.0
1964	218	−785.6	−2.4
1968	215	−787.2	−3.8
1972	216	−788.8	−1.2
1976	219	−790.4	3.4
1980	218	−792	4.0
1984	213	−793.6	0.6

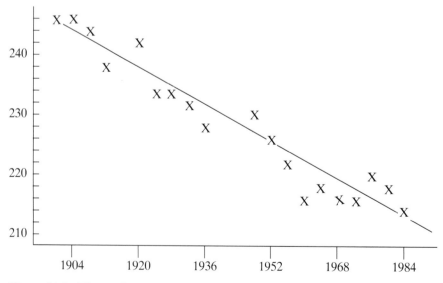

Figure 11.3 The exploratory line

rough method but usually good enough once you have become used to line fitting) or you can solve the line equation for two convenient values of X. These should be well separated; where you can, choose X values like 0, 1, 10, 100 etc. For our data set, these numbers make no sense, but we can use $X = 1900$ and, say, $X = 1950$ (we can choose values that aren't part of the data set), giving

$$Y = -0.4\,(1900) + 1006 = 246$$
$$Y = -0.4\,(1950) + 1006 = 226$$

So our two points would be (1900, 246) and (1950, 226) which, when connected, give the line in Figure 11.3.

Interpreting a and b

Earlier, we defined b as the change in Y for every unit change in X and defined a as the value of Y when X equals 0. These statements are certainly true but they don't convey much to a lot of readers. This is particularly true for the intercept – it is hard to see how the number 1006 has anything to do with the data. Some insights may come out of looking at our race example in a slightly different way.

Table 11.3   Winning times (C2) by year (C1), Olympiad number (C4) and year -1900 (C3)

C1	C2	C3	C4
1900	246	0	1
1904	245	4	2
1908	243	8	3
1912	237	12	4
1920	242	20	6
1924	234	24	7
1928	233	28	8
1932	231	32	9
1936	228	36	10
1948	230	48	13
1952	225	52	14
1956	221	56	15
1960	216	60	16
1964	218	64	17
1968	215	68	18
1972	216	72	19
1976	219	76	20
1980	218	80	21
1984	213	84	22

Instead of using year as a predictor, let's recode to create two different-looking but equivalent predictors (year − 1900) and Olympiad number, in columns 3 and 4 of Table 11.3 (columns 1 and 2 from Table 11.1 are repeated for convenience). A little reflection should convince you that our new predictors must have the same relationship to winning times as year does and should give us exactly the same line. Let's try it, but using Minitab this time to avoid rounding errors (and a fair amount of work!). Using the RLINE command we get:

Time = 1015 − 0.405   (year)
Time =   245 − 0.405   (year−1900)
Time =   247 − 1.62   (Olympiad number)

Why aren't the three equations the same?

Let's look first at the bs; the first two equations have the same b, −0.405 (within rounding of the value obtained by hand). This indicates that on average the winner's time improved by about four-tenths of a second from one year to the next. The third equation uses Olympiad number rather than year, so going from one Olympiad to the next involves a change of four years rather than one, and −1.62 is precisely four times −0.405.

How about the values for a? Each one is different (and none is the same as the one we got by hand). Consider the second equation; here a is 245, a reasonable predicted value for Y when X is 0 (here 1900). The third equation has $a = 247$; since we have taken $X = 1$ for the 1900 games, X would be equal to 0 four years earlier, which means that the predicted winning time for that year would be 1.62 seconds slower, which rounds to two seconds. The strangest looking a is the first one, 1015 (close to the value obtained by hand, but different because we have a more exact value for b). This says that projecting (actually retrojecting) the line back to AD 0 (whatever that means), we estimate that it would have taken almost 17 minutes to run 1500 metres! If that's as fast as people could move in those days, it's amazing that the Wise Men arrived in Bethlehem while Jesus was still an infant!

This illustrates a very important point about Y by X analysis: the line we obtain is the best linear description of the data we have entered. We can reasonably use it to estimate what the winning time might have been for, say, the cancelled games in 1916, or perhaps try to predict the winning time for 1996. But when we move too far away from the range of the data we're using, we are likely to get silly results. If you're hard to convince on this, use the line equation to project the winning time for the 157th Olympiad (now that's speedy).

Uses of the Line Fit

The three main uses of the exploratory line fit are summarizing, predicting, and removing.

Summarizing. This is a simple use of lines but a very important one; don't underestimate it. For example, we summed up part of Figure 11.1 with this brief description of the line from Figure 11.3:

$$Y = -0.4X + 1006$$

or

$$time = -0.4 \, (year) + 1006$$

This says that in year AD 0 time is projected to be 1006 seconds; it also says that each year, on average, the winning time drops by 0.4 seconds. Note how economical the line is: two numbers, a and b, say everything that the line says and much of what the data say. This economy is especially useful if we want to make a lot of comparisons: they could be summed up very compactly with several sets of as and bs. (This is like using numerical summaries to compare several batches.)

Predicting. Our line gives us a way (maybe imperfect) of predicting Y from X. So if we know an X value but not a Y value we can make an educated guess of what Y should be like. You are probably most familiar with projections based on past performance or trends, like population projections: one finds a line summing up the relationship of population to time so far and predicts what is likely to happen next.

Removing. Once we have a numerical summary of the linear relationship between X and Y we can remove this linear fit from Y:

$$Y' = Y - bX - a = Y - (bX + a)$$

These residuals are used for two important things: evaluating the line fit and going beyond it. These uses are so important that we will move now to a separate section on residuals from lines to clarify what such residuals are and how they are used.

Residuals from a Linear Fit

We have already seen what residuals from a linear fit are numerically: $Y - (bX + a)$. But it is easier to understand the residuals when they are shown graphically. Let's have a look at the points in the high half on X as shown in Figure 11.4 (we show just one half to avoid unnecessary complication of the picture). This plot is like the previous ones except that residuals are shown numerically and graphically. Beside each point is its numeric residual, taken from the work sheet in Table 11.2. Graphically, each residual is the vertical distance between the point and the line, shown as dotted vertical lines. One point is right on the line and hence has virtually zero residual (-0.2); one point is well above the line and has a large positive residual (4.0); one point is well below the line and has a large negative residual (-3.8). The plotted point is the observed value and the line gives the predicted or fitted value for the same X, so the point-to-line distance is the same as 'observation − fit' or the residual.

The only trick here is that your eyes may not be quite used to it. When

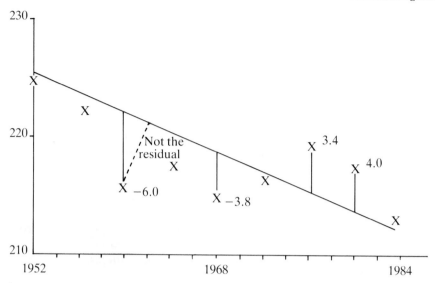

Figure 11.4   A close-up view of some residuals

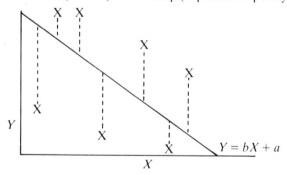

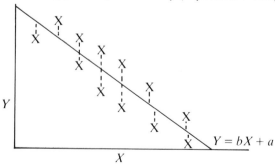

Figure 11.5   Relationships and residuals

starting, it is awfully tempting to think that the residual is the distance from the point to the line by the shortest route, like the dotted line shown for the point with residual −6.0. The dotted line is not the residual: it connects with our fitted line at a point with an X value different from the one we are interested in.

With the line fit, $Y = bX + a$, we can find numeric residuals easily; with the residuals we can evaluate the line fit. Evaluating the line fit means finding out how good a fit is, how closely it predicts Y. If X and Y are weakly related we get something like the top plot in Figure 11.5: the points are widely scattered and don't fall into a clear linear pattern, so the residuals from a line fit are big. For most of the points, the observed and predicted Y are far apart. On the other hand if X and Y are strongly related in a linear way then their values fall into a tidy pattern like that in the bottom plot of Figure 11.5: the points are close to the fitted line and the residuals are small. In general, the greater the spread of the residuals, the worse the fit is: the more poorly the line predicts Y, and the more variation in Y there is left to explain. But spread alone won't be useful for evaluating fit because of problems of scale; the data could be big or small to begin with. For example, residuals for a population Y in the millions will be larger than those for a mobility index Y in the tens even if the population Y is much better predicted. We compensate for the scale factor, the original spread of Y, by using

$$\frac{dq \text{ residuals}}{dq \text{ original } Y}$$

as our general guide to how good a fit is. In our example, from the data in Table 11.2, we find:

$$\frac{dq \text{ residuals}}{dq \text{ original } Y} = \frac{3.5}{19} = 0.18$$

This is close to the best possible fit (where Y is predicted almost exactly, residuals are mainly zero and the ratio is zero). In contrast, the worst fit, one where X doesn't help at all in predicting Y, can give a ratio of 1 (or even more if you have really bad luck).

Another way of looking at the ratio is to focus on one major question: why is one Y value higher or lower than another? We hope our line will explain part of this variation, and if it does then the amount of variation should decrease when the effects of year (X) are removed.

So removing the line gives residuals useful in evaluating the line. If the line isn't a perfect fit for Y (and it hardly ever is) we want to go further and attempt to explain some of the still unexplained part of Y. But that just means explaining the residuals. The equation for the line is an economical summary statement of what we 'know' about the relationship between the variables X and Y; the residuals are the part we don't yet know, so having 'cleared away the underbrush' we can now look hard at what still needs to be explained without being distracted. New variables can be suggested. Since these residuals have had an 'X effect' subtracted, we sometimes say we have 'controlled' for X; the residuals indicate activity in Y that has nothing to do with X (nothing we can get

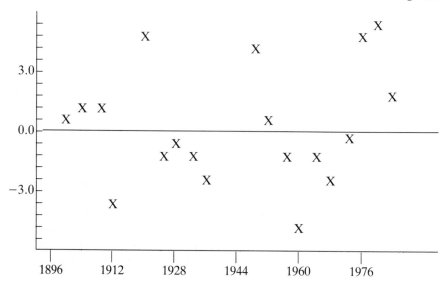

Figure 11.6   Residuals (Y') versus X

at with a straight line, anyway). In the race example we could start by looking hard at the $Y - bX - a$ residuals in Table 11.2.

It is always a good idea to make the data patterns as visually clear as possible. We have two general strategies for this. First, the residuals are a batch and can be analysed using familiar batch tools. It is often useful to note outliers (none in our example) and compare them with adjacents and 'inliers' (residuals inside the midbox).

We can also take advantage of the Y by X character of the data a bit more by plotting the residuals: make another Y by X plot, but this time use $Y - (bX + a)$ instead of the original Y. The residuals can also be seen graphically in a plot like the one in Figure 11.2, where the points can be compared to the line fit, but many people find this a bit hard at first; your eyes may not be used to comparing the points to the line vertically, as in Figure 11.6. Plotting the residuals against X avoids possible confusion. You can make the residuals plot even clearer by labelling the larger residuals with any information that may help explain them. Finally, the residuals plot often shows a pattern of some sort that demands a better fit. For example, if the residual plot has some slope or level in it then the line fit probably needs to be improved; or the residuals plot may show a curve more clearly than the original Y by X plot did.

These residuals are small, rarely more than four seconds away from the predicted values, and as we've seen from the dq ratio, the fit is very strong. In short, the straight line does a very good job of summarizing almost a century of trending. But even so, there is more juice that can be squeezed from these data. Consider that in a field of world-class runners, three seconds may be the difference between winning and finishing last, and for nearly half of the races our predictions are off by three or more seconds. Are there any patterns in the residuals that can help us to discover more about the kinds of things that affect runners' speed?

One of the easiest ways to see patterns in the residuals is to look at a plot like the one in Figure 11.6. If we look at the large positive residuals, we quickly see that two of the largest, 1920 and 1948, immediately follow missing games. This suggests that something about world wars may adversely affect runners' performances. What might this be? Several possibilities suggest themselves. In the ordinary way, athletes train intensively over a long period of time for these most important games – this level of individual and societal commitment is likely to be impossible during wartime. More tragically, many of those who might have competed in peacetime become the victims in wartime.

If these speculations are true, what else might be true? Well, the 1952 games took place during the more limited Korean War. That residual, while not as extreme as the 1920 and 1948 values, is still positive. Further, the American involvement in Vietnam was near its peak in 1972, another large positive residual. A further point of interest here is the last three residuals – all are positive and each corresponds to an Olympic Games that was boycotted by a significant number of countries. Taken together, these observations suggest that speeds are likely to continue improving (though probably not at the current rate) as technology continues to improve, as long as the field of eligible athletes and support for their training continues to grow.

This is just a brief example of how examination of residuals can help to push an analysis further. And we've only looked at the large positive residuals here. A good analysis would take in the large negative ones, and perhaps some small ones also, to search for additional factors and conditions.

Residuals versus Original Y

You may have noticed something surprising about the set of residuals in our race example. They can behave in unpredictable ways, often opposite to the behaviour of the original data. The winning time for 1984 was 213 seconds while for 1912 it was 237 seconds, much slower. Yet the residual for 1912 is -3.6 while that for 1984 is $+1.2$, so the earlier time, while slow, was faster than predicted (hence the residual is negative), and the later time is slower than predicted (hence a positive residual). Thus, controlling for a variable, as we did here with year, can dramatically change the data.

Since Y' is a very different affair from Y, we need different ways of talking about Y'. If you've been reading carefully, you'll have noticed that we used several ways of describing the residuals from a fit, with all the phrases meaning much the same thing. Here we list some of the commoner ones. Y' is:

● the set of residuals from a fit of Y to X;
● the part of Y not explained by X;
● Y with effects of X removed;

- Y with X controlled (or held constant);
- the difference between Y and what we predict it is, given X.

Use whatever phrasing you find most comfortable. You will find all of these, and variations on them, in the literature.

What We Have Learned So Far

With the help of the race data we have learned how to fit an exploratory straight line. Divide the data into thirds on X; summarize each third with a resistant level; then use the two end thirds to find the slope, and subsequently make use of all three to find a. This produces a simple linear summary of the relationship between X and Y. By finding residuals $(Y - bX - a)$ we can evaluate the straight line fit and try to add new ideas to it.

The Y by X numerical summary of a relationship (a line) has the same properties as exploratory numerical summaries for batches. The exploratory straight line is quickly found and resistant, and it conforms with what your eyes tell you. Fits and residuals crop up again, and indeed these concepts are especially important and clear for Y by X data. The residuals from the linear fit, $Y - (bX + a)$, deserve detailed attention because they are the potential source of new insights beyond the line.

A straight line is the simplest line, and a straight line fit is easily made. Finding a and b is mostly a matter of using familiar tools like medians and trifling arithmetic like subtraction. Once you have your line you have a very powerful gadget indeed. It summarizes, it predicts, it can be removed easily to leave interesting residuals.

Exploratory and Confirmatory

In standard confirmatory statistics, fitting a straight line is called 'linear regression'. The general strategy is the same: fit a line, evaluate the fit, find residuals, try to explain them. Plots (usually called 'scatterplots') are used in the same way as well. The main difference is that a more rigorous, less resistant technique for finding the line is used. We will say no more about this here since confirmatory regression has a chapter of its own, and we will point out the parallels to exploration there.

Using the Computer

If the variable X is stored in C1 and Y in C2 then

    RLINE C2 C1 C3 C4

provides the full set of output from this subroutine, with the fitted values in C4 and residuals in C3. For our example, slope $= -0.405$, level $= 1015$.

MINITAB uses medians rather than trimeans for calculating summary points. You may find that the slope which MINITAB calculates is somewhat different from that calculated by hand. This is most often the result of a process known as 'polishing the data', in which the computer refines the data. The discrepancy between the two methods is usually quite small and is therefore not too important.

'Level' is the value of a (the intercept), i.e. the value of Y when $X = 0$ (in other words, the value of Y when the line intersects the X axis). The half-slope ratio is calculated by taking the ratio of the slope for the top half of the data (the right half-slope $(Y_H - Y_M)/(X_H - X_M)$ to the slope for the lower half (the left half-slope $(Y_M - M_L)/(X_M - X_L)$. This is a measure of non-linearity in our data and will be used in the next chapter.

HOMEWORK

Table 11.4 Winning speeds at the Indianapolis 500 auto race for 1961–1970

Year	Winning speed
1960	138.767
1961	139.130
1962	140.293
1963	143.137
1964	147.350
1965	151.388
1966	144.317
1967	151.207
1968	153.882
1969	156.867
1970	155.749
1971	157.735
1972	162.962

Source: Information Please (1988: 933).

1 Plot speed (Y) versus year (X).
2 Find the equation for the line.
3 Calculate the residuals and discuss. (You might be able to go to a newspaper file for 1966 to find out what happened.)
4 In 1979, the winning speed was 158.899 m.p.h. How does this compare to the estimate you get from your line? What estimate does your line give for 1950?

Table 11.5   Sex and mental illness

Mentally ill (percentage)

Male	Female
13.1	26.3
14.9	34.2
14.9	33.3
15.6	22.9
18.2	25.3
18.4	38.0
20.3	38.9
21.0	34.0
21.2	35.5
22.0	43.0
22.0	40.0
31.0	54.0

Source: Adapted from Table 1 (p. 819) of Gove and Tudor (1973). © University of Chicago; reprinted with permission. This table includes all studies from part A of the original table for which exact percentages for both sexes are given.

1 Plot female rates (Y) against male rates (X).
2 Find the equation for the line.
3 Find the residuals, plot against X and discuss.
4 Evaluate the fit.

12
Unbending

Data Can Be 'Curvy'

Many of you may have been thinking, as you were reading and working through the last chapter, that this was all a 'put-up job'. Our straight line fits worked reasonably well only because the data were quite linear. You might also wonder how often we actually have linear data to work with; the answer to this is, surprisingly often. There are, however, many familiar processes that generate curvy data. Consider the relationship between age and average earnings for people in the labour force, for example. Generally, income will increase with age/experience. But for many occupations, income peaks and then declines years before retirement; training can become out-dated, health problems may necessitate a reduction in hours worked or even a change to a less demanding, less highly paid job, etc. Thus, when income is plotted against age, such a line will initially increase, then level off and perhaps decline, yielding a curve. However, even when our data are substantially non-linear, we can often cope easily by using transformations. Let us return to some simple data we first looked at in Chapter 5, Canadian population from 1851 to 1961, in Table 12.1.

This time, we will treat these data as Y by X data where X is time and Y is population. To keep the arithmetic easy we use census number in place of census year: or 1, 2, 3, etc. in place of 1851, 1861, 1871, etc. The relationship is plotted along with the summary points in Figure 12.1. The plot clearly shows that there is a strong relationship between time and population size; equally clearly, the relationship is not linear. The middle summary point is below the line between the other two. It doesn't look like much, but we will soon see that this departure from linearity is pretty important.

Population does not grow steadily with time, growing by the same amount for every time interval; instead, it grows faster and faster as time goes by. Since the data are curved, no straight line fit can do them justice and we will have to do something new.

Let's try transforming the population values. In Chapter 5, we saw that logging is a natural choice because logging will make population batch data

Table 12.1 Canadian population, 1851–1961 (in millions)

Census number	Census year	Population (millions)
1	1851	2.44
2	1861	3.23
3	1871	3.69
4	1881	4.32
5	1891	4.83
6	1901	5.37
7	1911	7.21
8	1921	8.79
9	1931	10.38
10	1941	11.51
11	1951	14.01
12	1961	18.24

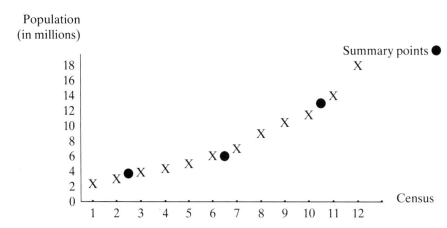

Figure 12.1 Canadian population by census, 1851–1961

symmetric when the rate of net growth is constant; perhaps logging will help with our Y by X problem too. The logged population figures are found as part of Table 12.2 and they are plotted in Figure 12.2. The three summary points are almost perfectly in line: that's more like a straight line! Therefore, we can use our familiar line-fitting technique for straight lines after all, once transformation has straightened the data out. Table 12.2 also gives the residuals:

$$Y = bX + a$$
logged population = 0.074 (census number) +6.34

From the plot in Figure 12.2 or from the dq ratio in Table 12.2 (dq ratio = 0.08) we can see that the fit is very good indeed. This is slightly misleading as several

Table 12.2 Worksheet for equation $Y = 0.074X + 6.34$

X	0.074X	Y	$Y' = Y - 0.074X - 6.34$
1	0.074	6.39	−0.03
2	0.148	6.51	0.02
3	0.222	6.57	0.00
4	0.296	6.64	0.00
5	0.370	6.68	−0.03
6	0.444	6.73	−0.06
7	0.518	6.86	0.00
8	0.591	6.94	0.01
9	0.666	7.02	0.01
10	0.740	7.06	−0.02
11	0.814	7.15	−0.01
12	0.888	7.26	0.03
		$dq = 0.47$	$dq = 0.036$

$$dq \ \text{ratio} = \frac{0.036}{0.47} = 0.08$$

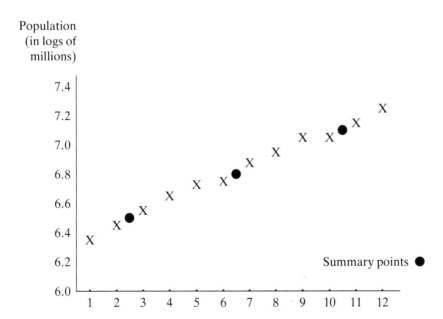

Figure 12.2 Population (in logs of millions)

of the estimates are 'off' by 10 per cent or more when we translate from logs back to populations (an error of about 2½ million in 1961), though how much of this is 'translation error' that we could reduce by using more accurate log tables is difficult to say without trying. Even so, the fit is very good.

What does the fit mean? Well, the population grows by a constant amount in logs: it grows by about 0.074 from census to census (a figure quite close to the 0.08 growth in logs that we found in Chapter 5 using a different approach to the data). Adding logs corresponds to multiplying raw numbers, so on average the population grows by a constant proportion in raw numbers. As we've argued before, this makes a great deal of sense. We could push the interpretation further by looking at the larger residuals. For example, why was the population smaller than predicted in the sixth census, that for 1901? Why was it larger than predicted in the twelfth census, for 1961? Economic conditions and migration patterns might help to explain these slight departures from a simple basic pattern of steady growth rates.

When to Unbend

We have just seen that it can be very easy to handle a curve by transformation. Now we need to know some useful practical details like: when should you make a curve fit instead of a straight one, and how do you decide which transformation to use?

First, how much curvature do we tolerate before we decide that the linear fit won't do and transforming should be tried? This really depends on many things: how many points there are, how close the points are to the best-fitting line, etc. As a result, we can only provide some very loose rules of thumb that, when used with careful visual examination, can be a useful judgement aid. One rule emphasizes the amount of curvature in the summary points. To see how this works, consider the three summary points for the untransformed population data:

$$X_L \quad 2.5 \qquad Y_L \quad 3.46$$
$$X_M \quad 6.5 \qquad Y_M \quad 6.29$$
$$X_H \quad 10.5 \qquad Y_H \quad 12.76$$

Now instead of computing one slope, compute two: from the low summary point to the middle, and from the middle point to the high. The two slopes are:

$$b_{LM} = \frac{6.29 - 3.46}{6.5 - 2.5} = 0.71; \qquad b_{MH} = \frac{12.76 - 6.29}{10.5 - 6.5} = 1.62$$

These two slopes tell us the same thing as the plot in Figure 12.1: the second part of the curve is increasing faster than the first. If the line were straight then b_{LM} and b_{MH} would be roughly the same. The advantage of looking at the two slopes instead of just at the plot is that we can use the slopes to give us a simple numerical summary of how curvy the line is, *if* b_{LM} and b_{MH} have the same sign. The easiest way to do this is a ratio: b_{LM}/b_{MH}. In our example, this means

$$\frac{0.71}{1.62} = 0.44$$

If this half-slope ratio is one or very nearly one, then the two slopes are about equal and a straight line will do; if the ratio is much different from one, then the slopes are unequal and perhaps fitting a curve should be tried. Here is one crude judgement aid:

If the ratio is	*You should*
0.8 to 1.25	leave the data alone and make a linear fit
0.5 to 0.8 or 1.25 to 2.0	consider a curve fit, depending on the situation (see below)
under 0.5 or more than 2.0	transform *X* or *Y* or both to straighten the data out; this is too much curve to ignore

(Use only if the half-slope ratio is *positive*.)

Where the slope ratio is in the discretionary range you have to use your judgement. Several issues may be important in the decision:

1 The number of data points: the more points you have, the more fits – including curve fits – you should be willing to try.
2 The strength of the relationship: if you look at the plot of *X* and *Y* and find that the data are all over the place, with a very weak relationship between *X* and *Y*, you usually go for a simple linear fit instead of a more complicated curve fit. But if the relationship is very strong, it is worthwhile to fit it as closely as you can by transforming as required.
3 The amount of sense a transformation makes. If there is a natural explanation for transforming, if the slight curve in the data seems to be there for a reason you understand, then treat it more seriously than something that may be just an accident as far as you can tell.

In the population example, the case for transformation is very clear-cut: the half-slope ratio of 0.44 is less than 0.5, the plot in Figure 12.1 makes it clear that the relationship is strong, and the curve makes very good sense. The number of data points is a bit small but this poses no problem with such clear-cut data.

We cannot overemphasize the importance of plotting and judgement here. The half-slope ratio is just a rule of thumb: it is often helpful, especially when you are just getting started, but it is not foolproof and should not be used automatically. Always make a plot like Figure 12.1, showing data points and summary points; often the plot is the clearest guide to whether unbending will be worthwhile or not.

Choosing Transformations

The choice of transformation will not always be as obvious as it was for the familiar population data. Faced with a curve we know less well, how do we decide which transformation to use? Tukey suggests a table like Table 12.3, which shows four basic curves, gives verbal descriptions of them, and indicates which side of the ladder of transformations should be used for X and/or for Y to straighten out that curve. For example, the population data have $b_{LM} < b_{MH}$, with both positive; and we saw that logging Y worked out nicely. Taking some power of X would have worked too, but would have been rather silly in this particular case.

Still using the population data, a little thought will show you why transformations can unbend a curve. The population curve involves a more rapid growth of high Y values than of low Y values; that is, the higher two Y summary values differ more than the lower two. Some correction for upward straggle in Y will even this up so that Y grows evenly with X. Alternatively, we could think about X. The three summary points would be straighter if the middle point were more to the left; that is, if the lower X values were squeezed together and the higher ones spread out. This suggests a correction for downward straggle, or some power of X, which is just what Table 12.3 chart indicates.

You can use Table 12.3 to suggest the correct side of the ladder for straightening by transforming X; for transforming Y; or for straightening by transforming both X and Y. You don't often transform both X and Y because that is more work and harder to interpret; but sometimes you may feel it is worthwhile because transforming both variables improves the fit. For example, you might find that log X undercorrects and the negative reciprocal of X overcorrects but log X along with the square root of Y is just right. As always, feel free to follow your judgement.

Table 12.3   Appropriate transforms for various curves

Curve	Verbal Description	X transform	Y transform
	X trails up; Y trails down $b_{LM} > b_{MH}$, both positive	$\sqrt{X}$, log X, $-1/X$, etc.	Y^2, Y^3, etc.
	both X and Y trail up $b_{LM} > b_{MH}$, both negative	$\sqrt{X}$, log X, etc.	$\sqrt{Y}$, log Y, etc.
	X trails down, Y trails up $b_{LM} < b_{MH}$, both positive	X^2, X^3, etc.	$\sqrt{Y}$, log Y, etc.
	both X and Y trail down $b_{LM} < b_{MH}$, both negative	X^2, etc.	Y^2, etc.

Source: Tukey (1970).

When Are the Data Unbent?

How do you know when you have pretty well straightened out the line? How do you know which transformation to use? Using the computer, you can try a few transforms and look at the plots. If you are doing the work by hand, we suggest that you make life easy for yourself by deciding on the basis of the summary points; there are only three of them, so how long can this take? Try a transform on the summary points, find the new b_{LM} and b_{MH}, and go ahead with the transform when you get two slopes that are nearly equal.

Suppose we are trying this with our population figures. We would start from the raw data summary points, then log the Y summary values:

Raw X		Raw Y		Log Y
X_L	2.5	Y_L	3.46	6.54
X_M	6.5	Y_M	6.29	6.79
X_H	10.5	Y_H	12.76	7.11

(These logged Y values are not exactly the same as those we used earlier, which were medians of the logged Y rather than logs of Y medians. It is more accurate to transform first and then find the summary values, but you don't want to bother transforming all the values until you are sure the transform is pretty good.)

Next we check the two slopes:

$$b_{LM} = \frac{6.79 - 6.54}{6.5 - 2.5} = 0.063 \qquad b_{MH} = \frac{7.11 - 6.79}{10.5 - 6.5} = 0.080$$

$$\text{ratio} = \frac{0.063}{0.080} = 0.79$$

The two slopes are not equal, but neither are they dramatically unequal; they are in our discretionary range. On the one hand, we might like to try to fit the curve a bit more exactly: when logs are used the curve still has b_{LM} a little lower than b_{MH}, so perhaps the curve is undercorrected and negative reciprocals would work better. On the other hand, the log transformation is so natural and so easily interpreted for these data that we would rather use it even if it does not flatten out the curve perfectly.

Another Example: Wealth and Literacy

Unbending with transformation is pretty easy, with no new major tools, but it does involve some unfamiliar rules of thumb; so we will go through another simple example that happens to illustrate a slightly different use of logging. Table 12.4 presents gross national product (GNP) per capita and adult literacy rates (per cent) for 22 countries or areas. The data are taken from the *World Handbook of Political and Social Indicators* (we have used every fifth case from their Table B2). Remember, we have suggested that sampling a small number

Table 12.4 Wealth and literacy

Country	GNP per capita	Adult literacy rate (%)	Log (GNP per capita)
Nepal	45	5.0	1.65
Burma	57	47.5	1.76
Uganda	64	27.5	1.81
South Vietnam	76	17.5	1.88
Thailand	96	68.0	1.98
Haiti	105	10.5	2.02
Indonesia	131	17.5	2.12
South Korea	144	77.0	2.16
Ghana	172	22.5	2.24
Peru	179	47.5	2.25
El Salvador	219	39.4	2.34
British Guiana	235	74.0	2.37
Hong Kong	272	57.5	2.43
Panama	329	65.7	2.52
Lebanon	362	47.5	2.56
Singapore	400	50.0	2.60
Argentina	490	86.4	2.69
Iceland	572	98.5	2.76
Czechoslovakia	680	97.5	2.83
France	943	96.4	2.97
New Zealand	1310	98.5	3.12
Canada	1947	97.5	3.29
(USA, not part of sample:	2577	98)	

Source: Russett *et al.* (1964: 294–8); used by permission.

of cases to explore makes a lot of sense; you can get useful ideas without investing too much time.

The raw data are plotted in Figure 12.3. It is easy to see two things here; the *X* values, per capita GNP, trail up strongly and, perhaps because of this, the plot is sharply curved. Alternatively, instead of viewing this as a single curve we may prefer to treat it as two very different patterns, one for developed countries with literacy rates close to 100 per cent and another one for underdeveloped countries with lower and more variable rates, and begin the analysis by sub-batching. Both of these approaches to the data make sense and, if we have the time and interest, we might choose to try both. For our present purposes, we will operate on the assumption that there is a single process linking wealth and literacy at all levels of development and just use transformation.

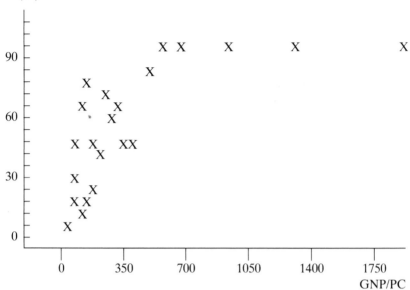

Figure 12.3   Wealth and literacy, raw data plot

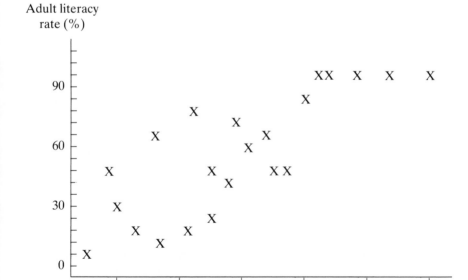

Figure 12.4   Literacy and logged wealth

Variables like GNP (and per capita GNP) often respond well to logging and since this is one of the suggested transforms for a curve of this sort, we'll try that first. We have included log GNP/PC in Table 12.4 and it is easy to see that the X values are now better balanced. But it is hard to tell from looking at Figure 12.4 whether the curve has been unbent. The resistant line equation is:

$$Y = 69.2 \,(\log \text{GNP/PC}) - 109.4$$

with a half-slope ratio of 1.281. This is in the discretionary range – should we try to improve on it? Well, the relationship isn't strong enough to make it worthwhile to search for a more nearly perfect fit, and logging makes a great deal of sense in this connection. Consequently our judgement is to work with the data in this functional form.

In interpreting the curve that we just fitted by logging X, we have to remember that logging is used differently from the use in the population example. For one thing, X was logged, not Y; so there is no use trying to think of steady rates of growth here. The per cent adult literacy grows very rapidly as GNP per capita does, then less rapidly, and less rapidly still until the rate of growth seems to stop for the most highly developed countries. A ceiling effect comes to mind immediately: no matter how wealthy a country is, it cannot have more than 100 per cent adult literacy. In fact, it cannot have more than 98 or 99 per cent literacy, since a small fraction of any population is incapable of reading for one reason or another. This ceiling effect certainly helps to explain the Canadian point, which is well below its predicted value (a large negative residual): here the regression equation predicts a value of about 125 per cent! You may wonder about a floor effect here: after all, no matter how poor a country is it cannot have less than 0 per cent literate. Such a floor effect might well have shown up if there were more countries near the floor: more countries like Nepal, with very low rates of literacy. Although this does not happen here, it is possible for floor and ceiling effects to happen together, producing a sort of S-shaped curve, which requires a transformation slightly harder than those we use in this book ('logit' transforms often help with data bounded both above and below).

We don't feel happy with the ceiling effect as an explanation of the whole curve, since there is a curve even for countries well below the ceiling. Why? Perhaps it is easier to increase the literacy rate when the rate is low. Suppose the rate is 10 per cent and goes to 20 per cent; the additional 10 per cent of the population is probably an elite in many ways: wealthier, more highly motivated and educated (after all, literacy is a rare thing). On the other hand suppose that the rate is 80 per cent and goes to 90 per cent. Surely that 10 per cent increase takes much more effort: the people involved are likely to be less advantaged. This implies that raising the rate the same amount takes more effort (more expense) when the rate is higher to start with, so that it takes massive increases in GNP per capita to raise literacy 10 per cent for wealthy nations where the rate is high but takes less of an increase in GNP per capita to raise the rate 10 per cent for poorer nations where the rate is low.

Residuals

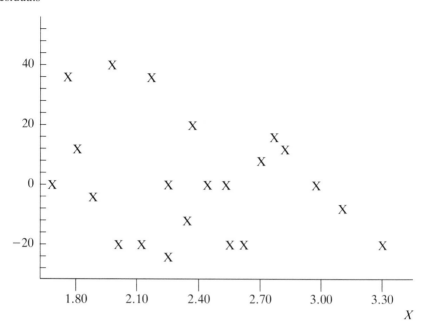

Figure 12.5   Residuals plotted against X

Some Final Remarks

Coping with curviness via transformation has many advantages. First, it uses tools we already know how to work with: transforms and the basic straight line fit. Secondly, it is very flexible: we can transform X or Y or both, allowing us to cope with a great variety of simple curves. Thirdly, we can work with it quite quickly by: (a) using the chart to see roughly what kind of transforms are in order and (b) checking out exactly which transforms work best by trying them on the three summary points. Fourthly, it is often a great time-saver. Suppose we are getting curviness here and there in a data set because one or two of the variables straggle a lot: if we transform these variables early on, we often find that everything is nice and straight and easy. (This is not always the case, but things often work out as suggested.)

On the other hand, there are problems as well. Perhaps the most important problem is that transformation does not always work. First, our transformations can straighten out only the curves shown in the chart, curves which have only one bend and which either increase or decrease all the way. Transformations are not much help with curves that look like a U or a J; these have just one bend but Y increases with X in one part of the curve and decreases with X in the other part. For curves like these, one can use a more complex kind of equation:

$$Y = cX^2 + bX + a$$

There are both exploratory and confirmatory ways to make such fits, although we will not go into them here (see Chapter 20 for the confirmatory approach). Occasionally you see Y by X data with several bends; these more complicated curves take more complicated fits, either more complex transformations than we use here or more complex equations using X^3 or X^4, or even higher powers. Fortunately, such complex curves are quite rare in sociology. You will be able to cope quite nicely with nearly all of the data you are likely to see with the simple transformations used in this chapter. This chapter's approach should work as long as b_{LM} and b_{MH} both have the same sign and neither one is zero. (If they have different signs then the curve must be something like a J or a U.)

Secondly, it sometimes happens that the transformation needed to handle extreme trailing in X conflicts awkwardly with transformations suggested to unbend a curve. If this comes up, use your judgement. Is the curve strong enough to worry about? Can you cope by transforming X (for the trailing) and Y (for the curve)? If things seem unmanageable, you may decide to fit a curved line with a cX^2 term. Things rarely are really unmanageable.

Finally, which variable should you transform, X or Y? Often this is up to you: do what you think is most convenient or makes most sense. Some possible grounds for decision are:

- the simpler transformation is preferable, e.g. log X is usually better than the fifteenth power of Y;
- if one of the variables is symmetric and the other has straggle, the straggling one should be transformed. Often the curve and the straggle have the same sources and both will respond to the same transformation (as is true in this chapter's population example).

Using the Computer

There is little that is new for this chapter. We already know how to calculate a resistant line in MINITAB (RLINE) and how to transform. But RLINE provides a half-slope ratio on the first line of the RLINE output, defined just as in the text.

HOMEWORK

Keep a copy of your homework results; you will need it for the next chapter. Choose one of the two following examples. Decide whether a curve fit is needed. If one is needed, choose a transformation; then make a line fit for the

Table 12.5   Socialist rule and pension quality

Country	Socialist rule	Pension quality
Sweden	24	186
Norway	20	158
Finland	9	168
The Netherlands	6	147
Austria	10	145
Belgium	9	124
Denmark	16	144
New Zealand	7	136
United Kingdom	12	111
Canada	0	134
France	4	131
United States	0	120
Switzerland	0	118
Germany	3	115
Australia	5	79

Source: Adapted from Table 4.2 in Myles (1984).

Table 12.6   Medical care and life expectancy

Country	LE	PPP
Belgium	75	380
Canada	76	510
Czechoslovakia	70	350
France	77	460
India	56	2 610
Iran	61	2 630
Italy	77	750
Japan	77	740
Nepal	47	30 060
Netherlands	77	480
Nigeria	50	10 540
Philippines	63	2 150
Poland	71	550
Sweden	77	410
Thailand	64	6 770
Turkey	64	1 500
UK	74	680
USA	76	500

Source: World Development Report (1986).

transformed data. Do not forget to discuss both the overall relationship (for example, if it was curved originally why was it curved?) and the more striking residuals.

1 Socialist rule and pension quality (Table 12.5). The dependent variable here is pension quality in 1975 (the higher the index the better the pension). The predictor variable, socialist rule, is the number of years between 1945 and 1970 in which the government executive branch was controlled by left-wing parties (or for coalition governments, the proportion of parliamentary seats held by such parties).

2 Medical care and life expectancy (Table 12.6). The data in Table 12.6 are life expectancy (LE) and number of people per physician (PPP), for 18 countries. What LE would you predict for a hypothetical country with a PPP of 1000; of 5000?

13
Linear Regression

The standard confirmatory approach to fitting a straight line for Y by X data is called linear regression. In many ways this approach is analogous to the exploratory techniques developed in Chapters 11 and 12. The confirmatory line is useful in the same ways that the exploratory line is useful: the confirmatory line summarizes a relationship, can be used to make projections, and so on. The line is fitted rather differently in a way that makes it less resistant than the exploratory line. However, confirmatory residuals are found in exactly the same way and can also be used in very similar ways to evaluate the fit and to go beyond it. Besides these parallel uses and procedures, the confirmatory techniques let us do one important thing we could not do before: we can ask whether a linear relationship is statistically significant, whether there is likely to be a relationship in general and not just in our sample data.

Linear Fits: Two Sets of Goals

A confirmatory linear fit has goals somewhat different from those of an exploratory fit and is thus made somewhat differently. Both fits summarize an Y by X pattern, but the exploratory fit emphasizes speed and resistance whereas the confirmatory fit emphasizes mathematically useful procedures based on all the data. In exploratory work we have seen that a straight line can be fitted to a set of points simply and resistantly by breaking the points up into three parts and finding a resistant summary point for each. The confirmatory approach, on the other hand, uses all the points (however unusual some of them may be); this alone loses resistance. Further, this line is the one that makes the sum of the squared residuals as small as possible. For this reason these are often referred to as 'least-square measures'. Using squared residuals has handy mathematical properties but as we saw with the variance, resistance is lost. In particular, unusual values become even more extreme when squared, so that one or two odd values can really affect the results.

Consider the little plots in Figure 13.1. Figure 13.1a shows a tidy direct relationship with some scatter (not a perfect relationship) but no really unusual

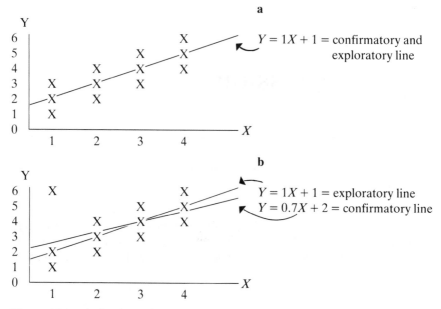

Figure 13.1   A simple exploratory–confirmatory comparison

values that stand out from the rest. Here, the exploratory and the confirmatory procedures give exactly the same line: $Y = X + 1$. (You can fit the exploratory line by eye, and you can fit the confirmatory one as a very easy warm-up for the confirmatory procedure described below if you wish.) Figure 13.1**b** is just like **a** except that one point has been moved: (1,3) has become (1,6). The exploratory line is not affected, it is still $Y = X + 1$. But the confirmatory line is affected. The line moves clockwise to reduce that one very large residual. The residuals for most of the other points are increased in the process, but the average squared residual is made as small as possible. Thus the confirmatory line is based on all the data points, at the cost of decreased resistance to unusual points.

The two approaches to linear fitting have different strengths and weaknesses. The confirmatory fit is better if you want to go on to make a statistical test, or if you want the data summarized in a form suitable for publication (everyone should know linear regression; not everyone knows the corresponding exploratory technique yet). The exploratory way is best if you are working hastily and/or working with erratic data, looking for the main message of most of the data. Does this sound familiar? Of course: the differences here are very like those between the mean and the median, or between the standard deviation and the midspread.

Finding the Line

It can be shown that the following formulae for b and a produce a line that minimizes squared residuals:

$$b = \frac{N\sum X_i Y_i - (\sum Y_i)(\sum X_i)}{N\sum X_i^2 - (\sum X_i)^2}$$

$$a = \bar{Y} - b\bar{X}$$

The formula for a is very easy, but the one for b is a bit more complex so let's go over it:

Top part
$N\sum X_i Y_i$:   multiply each X value by the Y value it is paired with; next, add up these cross-products; then multiply the total by N, the number of pairs (X, Y).

$(\sum Y_i)(\sum X_i)$:   find the total of the X values, find the total of the Y values, and multiply the two totals.

Bottom part
$N\sum X_i^2$:   square all the X values, then add up these squares, then multiply by N.

$(\sum X_i)^2$:   add up all the X values and then square the total.

These are computing formulae, designed for speedy work rather than for intuitive appeal. Let's see the formulae in action by computing the confirmatory linear fit for the 1500 metre race data; then we can compare this fit to the exploratory one already made in Chapter 11. For simplicity we use Olympiad number for X.

A Worked Example: the Race Data

Table 13.1 illustrates a useful kind of basic work sheet for getting the sums and sums of squares needed for confirmatory work. You have done this sort of thing for analysis of variance; it can be tedious but is easy enough (especially with a calculator and a little help from your friends). The only rather new thing is the column of XY or 'cross-product' figures. Each cross-product is the product of a paired X and Y; for example, for the first point the cross-product is 1×246 (see the first line of the work sheet). Once the basic figures have been found in such a work sheet, they are just plugged into the formulae above.

$$N = 19$$
$$\sum X = 225$$
$$\sum Y = 4330$$
$$\sum Y^2 = 988984$$
$$\sum X^2 = 3505$$
$$(\sum X)(\sum Y) = 974250$$
$$(\sum X)^2 = 50625$$
$$\sum XY = 49961$$
$$b = \frac{N\sum XY - (\sum X)(\sum Y)}{N\sum X^2 - (\sum X)^2} = \frac{19(49961) - 974250}{66595 - 50625} = -1.56$$
$$a = \bar{Y} - b\bar{X} = 227.89 - (-1.56)(11.84) = 246$$

Note that we hang on to extra decimal places until the end, rounding only when

Table 13.1 Confirmatory Y by X worksheet, race data basic regression worksheet

X	Y	XY	X^2	Y^2	$Y' = Y - (-1.56X + 246)$
1	246	246	1	60516	1.14
2	245	490	4	60025	1.70
3	243	729	9	59049	1.27
4	237	948	16	56169	−3.17
6	242	1452	36	58564	4.96
7	234	1638	49	54756	−1.47
8	233	1864	64	54289	−0.91
9	231	2079	81	53361	−1.34
10	228	2280	100	51984	−2.78
13	230	2990	169	52900	3.92
14	225	3150	196	50625	0.48
15	221	3318	225	48841	−1.95
16	216	3456	256	46656	−5.39
17	218	3706	289	47524	−1.82
18	215	3870	324	46225	−3.26
19	216	4104	361	46656	−0.69
20	219	4380	400	47961	3.87
21	218	4578	441	47524	4.44
22	213	4686	484	45369	1.00
Totals 225	4330	49961	3505	988984	0

we have the final figures for b and a. Confirmatory work involves so much arithmetic that small rounding errors can have a big cumulative effect, so we can't be quite as quick and approximate as we are in exploratory work. Note also that we have in fact used every data point in finding both b and a by linear regression. There are no summary points in this procedure, no way to cope with stray or flukey values.

Now let's compare the two fits for these data. The confirmatory fit is:

$$Y = -1.56X + 246$$

and the exploratory fit found in Chapter 11 was:

$$Y = -1.62X + 247$$

The equations are virtually identical, so much so that we couldn't draw the lines on to the plot carefully enough to see any difference. This is likely to happen where the data are linear, well behaved and tightly bound to the line.

Evaluating the Fit

We can and should find residuals from the confirmatory fit as we found them earlier from the exploratory fit: we find $Y - (bX + a) = Y'$, although now, of

Table 13.2   Exploratory and confirmatory residuals

	Residuals from:	
	Confirmatory: $Y = -1.56X + 246$	Exploratory: $Y = -1.62X + 245$
dq	3.65	3.5
Range	10.35	10.11
Variance	8.42	8.57
$\dfrac{dqY'}{dqY}$	0.19	0.18
$\dfrac{\text{Var } Y'}{\text{Var } Y}$	0.069	0.070
$\Sigma(Y')^2$	151.5	154.3

course, the b and a are those found by linear regression. The residuals from the confirmatory fit are shown in the last column of Table 13.1.

We have contrasted the exploratory and confirmatory fits; Table 13.2 contrasts the residuals in various ways. These again mainly serve to emphasize their similarity.

Once again the residuals from the fit serve to evaluate the strength of the fit. The more the spread of Y is reduced by the fit, the less there is of Y unexplained. So the spread of the Y residuals is compared to the spread of the original Y. Now, however, we make the comparison in confirmatory terms by using variances instead of dqs:

$$\text{proportion of } Y \text{ unexplained by regression} = \frac{\text{variance } Y'}{\text{variance } Y}$$

In Table 13.2 we see that this works out to 0.069 for the confirmatory fit; so the linear regression leaves 6.9 per cent of the variance in Y unexplained, that is to say, 6.9 per cent of the variance in time is not explained by a linear fit to Olympiad. On the other hand, it follows that 93.1 per cent is explained, which is very high.

We have now broken the original variance of Y into two parts: the proportion explained by the regression and the proportion not explained. The proportion explained is symbolized by

$$r^2 = \frac{\text{amount explained by regression}}{\text{variance of original } Y}$$

The proportion not explained by the confirmatory line is

$$1 - r^2 = \frac{\text{Variance of residuals}}{\text{Variance of original } Y} = \frac{\text{amount not explained}}{\text{total } Y \text{ variance}}$$

The second term $(1 - r^2)$ is the confirmatory parallel to the dq ratio we have used in exploration since both sum up the amount the line does not account for. The first term, r^2, is a bit more familiar in confirmatory write-ups. The square root of r^2, or r, is the very familiar product–moment correlation coefficient or, more simply, the correlation between X and Y. The correlation has the same sign as the slope b. So in the race example the correlation is

$$- \sqrt{0.93} = -0.965 \text{ (negative because } b \text{ is).}$$

The sign of the correlation tells you the direction of the relationship: r is negative for an inverse relationship like that between year and time, positive for a direct relationship. The correlation also indicates the strength of the relationship, although r^2 has a more natural interpretation: the proportion of the variance of Y explained by the fit. r^2 goes from a minimum of 0 (the fit explains none of Y) to 1.0 (the fit predicts Y perfectly). The correlation, r, goes from -1.0 (perfect inverse relationship) through 0 (no linear relationship at all) to $+1.0$ (perfect direct relationship).

Since the correlation is so useful, it is worthwhile to have a fast computing form for it:

$$r = \frac{N\sum XY - (\sum X)\,(\sum Y)}{\sqrt{[N\sum X^2 - (\sum X)^2]\,[N\sum Y^2 - (\sum Y)^2]}}$$

All of the components can be found easily in a work sheet like Table 13.1, most of them having already been found for the slope calculation anyway.

The correlation is a popular measure with a clear interpretation. However, it can be misleading if you do not watch out for a few common traps. First, the correlation tells you how much of Y is explained by a *linear* fit to X. Some other fit, like a curve, may work much better. It is even possible to have a correlation of 0 when X and Y are perfectly related, but related in a perfect curve rather than in a straight line form (see Figure 13.2a). A second trap is lack of resistance. The correlation uses variances, and it sums up the strength of a confirmatory fit, so it is not very resistant and this can give various kinds of misleading results. One of the best known is the 'one-point correlation'. Figure 13.2b gives an extreme example: there are 16 points showing absolutely no relationship between X and Y, and one point off by itself. Common sense (and exploratory analysis) suggests that X and Y are unrelated and there is something odd about the discrepant point; it may well be an error of some kind. But linear regression produces a line with a fairly strong r^2 value of 0.46 – quite high for social science data. The fit looks great if we only look at r^2.

The moral of this story is clear: always plot the data! A possible curve or misleading fits overly influenced by a few odd points can be seen immediately in plots, and not in the line equation or the r^2 value. A plot of Y by X is indispensable and a plot of Y' by X is also a good idea just as before, especially if the residuals are labelled.

Let us just stress once again that r depends on the strength of a confirmatory, linear fit; and that fit is the straight line which minimizes the sum of the squared residuals over all points. For example, if we look at Table 13.2 again briefly we see that the sum of the squared residuals, $(Y')^2$, is smaller for

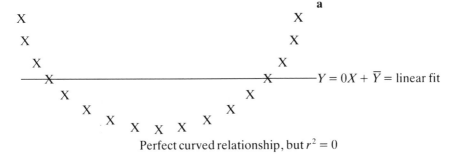

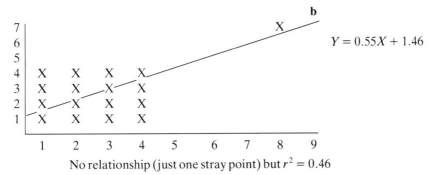

Figure 13.2 Examples of misleading correlations

the confirmatory fit than for the exploratory one (151.5 versus 154.3). No other straight line will make the sum of the $(Y')^2$ smaller than the confirmatory line does. As a result, the proportion of Y left unexplained,

$$1 - r^2 = \frac{\text{variance } (Y')}{\text{variance } (Y)}$$

will be smaller for the confirmatory line than for the exploratory line or for any other possible line. That's the job the linear regression is designed to do. In doing it, resistance is lost, so that the confirmatory line is often poorer than the exploratory line in exploratory terms, which is to say that residuals are more often moderate and less often extreme. Generally the dq ratio is better for the exploratory residuals, as is true here, although there are many exceptions.

Another Version of the Confirmatory Slope

The formula we gave above for b is the best one for computation, but it does not say very much to most people. Here is another version with more familiar components:

$$b = r \frac{sd_Y}{sd_X}.$$

If you plug in the formulae for r, s_X, and s_Y and do lots of algebra you can get back to exactly the same computing formula we saw earlier. Now, what does this version suggest?

We see that r is part of b. That means that b and r should have the same sign, as we said earlier. The stronger the relationship the more different b is from zero (because the more different r is from zero). In fact, b is r if X and Y happen to have equal spreads ($s_X = s_Y$). However, this is not very likely unless we have standardized both X and Y (standardizing in confirmatory terms, of course, using sd, and the mean). If we have, our regression equation becomes very simple indeed:

$$Y = rX$$

We have no great use for this fact now but it will be handy in later chapters. In the meantime, be careful: b translates units of X into units of Y, so it also includes s_X and s_Y, which are not usually the same and may not even be similar, so you can't tell how strong a linear fit is just by looking at the size of b (as beginners are often tempted to do).

Hypothesis Tests for the Linear Regression

We have seen how to make a confirmatory linear fit that minimizes squared residuals from the line, and we have seen how to evaluate the strength of the fit by finding r^2, the proportion of the variance of Y explained by the fit. The confirmatory line tends to be similar to the exploratory one, unless there are some unusual points to which the less resistant confirmatory line is sensitive. We have also seen that the proportion of Y not explained by the regression ($1 - r^2$) is parallel to the dq ratio used in exploratory work: both are ratios of Y' spread to Y spread, or

$$1 - r^2 = \frac{Y' \text{ variance}}{Y \text{ variance}} \qquad dq \text{ ratio} = \frac{Y' \text{ midspread}}{Y \text{ midspread}}$$

Now we want to go beyond the confirmatory–exploratory parallels to what confirmatory alone can do: a test of significance for the fit. Can we conclude that there is a linear relationship in general in the universe, beyond a reasonable doubt?

This question could be stated in many ways; for example, we can ask whether b is significantly different from zero or we can ask whether r^2 is significantly different from zero. These are equivalent questions, so we might as well focus on the one with the easiest test procedure; thus we will look at r^2. Our null hypothesis becomes:

H_0: $r^2 = 0$ in the universe

If this is true then X does not explain any of Y, at least not in a linear way. Our alternative hypothesis is:

H_1: $r^2 > 0$ in the universe

If this is true then knowing X does help to predict Y to some extent (we don't usually specify just how big r^2 is). This may look like a one-tailed test, but it's really two-tailed; r^2 cannot be negative, although its square root, the correlation, can be. In any example, we will probably find that r^2 is not exactly zero: even if H_0 is true, we will almost always get a little pattern in our sample data by chance alone. But as r^2 gets big, H_0 gets harder and harder to believe. It is also easier to reject H_0 if the sample size N is larger so that we feel more confidence in the sample estimate of r^2. This should sound rather like previous tests, in which more striking differences among means and larger N meant easier rejection of H_0. It is not too surprising to find that the test statistic looks like this:

$$F_{1,N-2} = \frac{r^2(N-2)}{1-r^2}$$

Even the fact that the F-table comes into play again may not seem too surprising if we remind ourselves of what r^2 and $1 - r^2$ mean:

$$F_{1,N-2} = \frac{(\text{variance explained}) \, (N-2)}{\text{variance of residuals}}$$

$$= \frac{(\text{variance explained by regression})/1}{(\text{error variance})/(N-2)}$$

This closely resembles

$$\frac{(\text{between SS})/df}{(\text{within SS})/df}$$

Regression and analysis of variance are very similar indeed, although a demonstration of that similarity takes more mathematics than we want to get into.

Computing the value of F for the sample is easy. As before, the critical value for F is found from the F-table and depends on the degrees of freedom and on the α-level chosen. We will show an example of an F-test for linear regression below, using the wealth and literacy example from the previous chapter, but we will not do so until the data have been checked to see whether they satisfy the assumptions that must be met for the test to be appropriate.

One assumption must be met very strictly: the sample should be a random sample of points independently observed. Proper data collection will meet this requirement. The data should also have an appropriate form. Odd as it may seem, this does not mean that X and Y must be normally distributed (which is probably what you're expecting): this assumption applies to the residuals! This assumption can be phrased very technically in ways that are difficult to understand or to check, but in practice it boils down to making sure that the X by Y plot looks reasonable. The points should form a fairly regular oval without badly straying values or large variations in the oval's thickness. (The oval as a whole may be thin or thick, depending on the strength of the relationship: the stronger the relationship the more nearly all the points come to falling on a straight line.) This assumption does not have to be met perfectly, since linear regression is robust (like analysis of variance), especially if N is large.

In concluding this section on testing for linear regression in the universe, let us remind you that significance and strength of a regression are related but not the same. They are related because, as you have seen, it is easier to get significant results for stronger relationships: the bigger r^2 the bigger F. But F is also related to the sample size N. It is possible to get a non-significant result even when the correlation is large, where N is very small; and if N is large enough then almost any weed of a relationship will turn up as significant. r^2 tells you how strongly X and Y are linearly related on the sample; the F-test tells you whether there is likely to be a linear relationship of some degree of strength in the universe.

The Significance Test for Wealth and Literacy

For an example of the regression test procedure we turn to the data on gross national product per capita and adult literacy rates from Chapter 12. First, are the test assumptions met? The 22 cases in Table 12.4 were a very rough sample (every fifth case) but we can't think of any biases in that sampling procedure so we will go ahead. A trickier point is the form of the data: does the X by Y plot look like a rough oval? In raw data, as in Figure 12.3, certainly not! This looks more like a hockey stick than an oval. But if GNP per capita is logged, as in

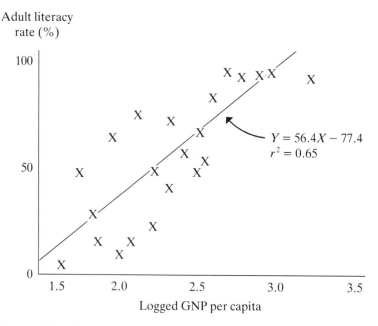

Figure 13.3   Linear regression for literacy and logged wealth

Figure 12.4, the plot does look roughly regular. Perhaps the oval's thickness varies a bit, with countries lower in wealth having more spread in literacy rates, but it is hard to say with only 22 points, and the variation does not look great. Remember, regression is robust so the plot does not have to be absolutely neat, just approximately oval like logged wealth and literacy (but not like raw wealth and literacy, which is too far from oval).

We can proceed with a significance test. The first step is to make a confirmatory fit and find r^2:

$$Y = 56.4X - 77.4 \qquad r^2 = 0.65$$

We omit the details of the calculations (again, you might like to try the calculations to check your understanding of the formulae). The fit is plotted in Figure 13.3; it looks reasonable, very similar to our earlier exploratory fit. Our null and alternate hypotheses are:

$H_o: r^2 = 0$
$H_1: r^2 > 0$

We might as well use the commonest significance level, $\alpha = 0.05$, and N is 22; our F-table tells us that the 5 per cent critical value for 1 and 20 degrees of freedom is 4.35. What F do we get for our sample?

$$F_{1,20} = \frac{r^2(N-2)}{1-r^2}$$

$$= \frac{0.65(20)}{0.35}$$

$$= 37.1$$

The null hypothesis looks quite unlikely. Our F is clearly significant, well beyond the 0.05 level. It seems very likely that literacy rates and logs of GNP per capita are linearly related in general, not just in our sample. (If you check the data for all available countries, given in the *World Handbook*, you find that these variables are indeed related.)

Unbending, Transformation and Regression

We have just seen that transformations can be useful in satisfying the assumptions one must make before doing a test for the linear regression. Transformations can also help to avoid one-point correlation problems; if X or Y or both has a lot of straggle, the few highest or lowest points may have a disproportionate effect on the fit and on r^2. Transformation can help by pulling the unusual values into the main body of the data. Finally, transformation can be used just as we used it in Chapter 12: to unbend curved data so that our simple linear fitting procedure will work better. The same general points apply in confirmatory work as in exploratory work, so we will not go over the procedure in much detail. First, the basic transformations used in this text will only unbend some curves: curves with just one bend which are either always increasing or always decreasing. More complex curves can also be handled, and easily, but they are beyond the scope of the book. Secondly, the chart in Table 12.3 tells what kind of transforms to try, although getting the best choice may involve some trial and error. This is a good place to mix in some exploratory technique because this will often give a transformation choice that works well for confirmatory regression too, although there is no guarantee. Once the data are transformed, the rest is routine: just do basic linear regression on the transformed data.

We have just seen that logging GNP per capita helps satisfy confirmatory assumptions. Take a look at the plot in Figure 12.3 again to remind yourself of the problems posed by the raw data. The data are strongly curved, so a linear regression on the raw data will not be a good fit. Some of the points (those for the wealthiest countries) look out of pattern and may pull the confirmatory line off. Figure 13.4 shows what happens if we go ahead and fit the linear regression line anyway (done only for illustration, and not recommended). The r^2 of 0.48 is quite healthy, so if we only looked at the arithmetic we might conclude that we had a strong linear fit accounting for almost half of the variance in Y. But this is not the case, as the plot makes very clear: the pattern of points is not linear so the line summarizes it poorly. As we saw a moment ago, we get a much better fit if we remove the curve by logging X: r^2 goes from 0.48 to 0.65. For confirmatory as well as for exploratory fitting, the transformation has really

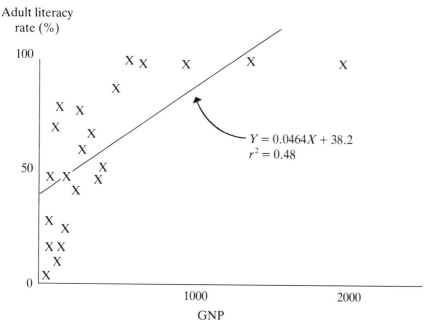

Figure 13.4 Linear regression for raw wealth and literacy

helped. The plot in Figure 13.3 also looks much better than that in Figure 13.4: the fit seems to make visual sense, following the main pattern of the data. (It is also very similar to the exploratory fit in Figure 12.4, although the rather unusual value for Canada has swung the confirmatory line clockwise just a shade.)

Quick Estimates of Strength of Relationship: The Garden of Data

We have been looking at various statistical measures of relationship strength: r^2, the correlation, dq ratio, etc. These are extremely valuable, but so too is the ability to make a crude estimate of strength on the basis of a quick glance at the X by Y plot. This skill, like most others, is best developed by experience, but we can help this along by providing an easy and useful language for describing plots plus some examples.

Broadly speaking, the strength of a relationship can be expressed by the ratio of the 'thickness' of the points along the line to the length of the line, that is, the range of X. We find it helpful to describe the original plots as data fruits or vegetables that provide familiar referents. For example, the race data in Figure 11.1 are very tightly bound to the line and an oval drawn around nearly all the points would resemble a stringbean, very strong. We've seen in Table 13.2 that the plot gives a dq ratio of 0.18 and an r^2 of 0.93. In Figure 13.5 we show a moderate relationship, 'the cucumber', and a weak one, 'the watermelon', together with statistical measures of strength.

Conclusions

There are parallels between exploratory and confirmatory techniques in every part of this book; for Y by X techniques the parallels are especially strong. Both approaches are first and foremost designed to find a straight line that 'well summarizes' a set of Y by X data; the line is useful in the same way whether it is exploratory or confirmatory; residuals are found in the same way; and the line's success in summarizing the data is evaluated in the same general way, by a ratio of the spread of the residuals to the original Y spread. The lines are fitted somewhat differently because 'summarizing well' can mean different things. In confirmatory work there is a unique best line, the one that minimizes squared residuals for all points. This line has useful mathematical properties and keeping residuals small makes sense; but squaring all the points leads to a lack of resistance. On the other hand, in exploratory work there may be several good lines, with different fits coming from different judgements by the analyst, as long as the line summarizes the bulk of the data. An exploratory line is resistant and easy, but cannot be quite as easily communicated as the more standard confirmatory fit.

Being so strongly parallel, the two approaches give very similar results, as long as the data are well-behaved. Some data irregularities, like curvature or

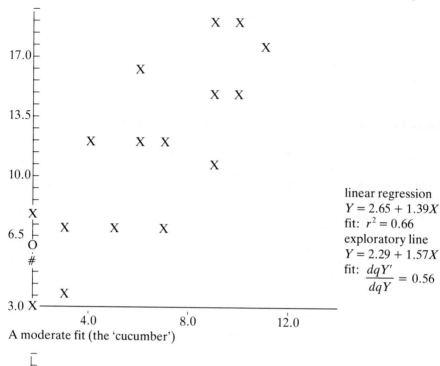

linear regression
$Y = 2.65 + 1.39X$
fit: $r^2 = 0.66$
exploratory line
$Y = 2.29 + 1.57X$
fit: $\dfrac{dqY'}{dqY} = 0.56$

A moderate fit (the 'cucumber')

linear regression
$Y = 8.19 + 0.57X$
fit: $r^2 = 0.09$
exploratory line
$Y = 6.75 + 0.63X$
fit: $\dfrac{dqY'}{dqY} = 0.99$

A weak fit (the 'watermelon')

Figure 13.5

straggling points, can be corrected through transformation. If irregularities cannot be fixed, as might for example happen if one or two points stray widely from the rest, then the more resistant exploratory fit will usually make much more sense. People sometimes try to adapt confirmatory procedures a bit to handle such situations better; for example, you may have seen reports in which a linear regression is given with and without an awkward point included. Dropping the awkward point is roughly similar to basing a fit on resistant summary points, which are not affected by one or two stray values. If regression is modified in this way the analyst should make the modification clear in the report and should not do a significance test: once you start dropping out points you don't like, you no longer have a random sample.

The significance test for a linear regression has no exploratory parallel. With this test, and with suitable data that meet the test's requirements, we can decide whether X predicts Y by a linear rule in general, not only in our sample. The bigger r^2 and the bigger N, the more likely it is that we'll decide that X and Y are really related. As always, making the decision involves risks: we may reject H_0 when X and Y are not linearly related but only happen to seem so in our sample, or we may fail to reject H_0 because of poor sample results when X is in fact linearly related to Y in the universe.

We have encountered one new and very important measure in this chapter: the correlation, which indicates how strongly X and Y are related. If the correlation is squared (r^2) we get the proportion of Y's variance explained by a linear fit to X, a simple interpretation. The correlation can be seen as one particular example of a general group of statistics called measures of association, statistics which indicate how strongly two variables are related. In the next chapter we will look at several measures of association for two categorical variables. There are a great many such measures, designed for different data and different purposes.

As we have hinted in this chapter, exploratory and confirmatory Y by X techniques are especially powerful when used in combination. For example, exploration can help in finding transformations that unbend the data or make them more regular, thus making the data suitable for linear regression and significance tests. Exploratory thinking is useful in pursuing the residuals from a fit whether the fit is exploratory or confirmatory. On the other hand, confirmatory procedures allow tests of ideas generated in exploration. We have shown exploratory and confirmatory techniques on the same data so the techniques could be compared, but the best combination (if you have ample data) is to subdivide your data randomly, explore part and test the exploration-generated ideas on the remaining part.

Using the Computer

While there are few conceptual differences between the resistant line and confirmatory line output, the computer commands look very different.

MTB> REGR C1 1 C2 C3 C4 (main command)
(note: Y in C1, X in C2)
THE REGRESSION EQUATION IS[1]
$Y = -77.38 + 56.4X$

Predictor	Coef[2]	Stdev	t-ratio[3]	P[4]
Constant	-77.38	22.59	-3.43	0.003
C2	56.384	9.337	6.04	0.000

$s = 19.15$ R-sq = 64.6%[5]   R-sq (adj) = 62.8%

Analysis of Variance[6]

SOURCE	DF	SS	MS	F	P
Regression	1	13371	13371	36.47	0.000
Error	20	7333	367		
Total	21	20703			

Unusual observations if present are noted here.[7]

Interpreting the Output of Linear Regression

1 The equation is:

$$Y = -77.4 + 56.4X$$

(in REGR, a is given first, then b).
2 Intercept a (or constant) is -77.38 and the slope, b, is 56.384, rounded to two decimal places.
3 The t-ratio or t-value allows us to evaluate whether each of the independent variables is contributing significantly to the regression. The critical value for the t-value must first be determined by specifying the degrees of freedom (in this case $df = 20$), level of significance (we will use 0.05) and direction of the test (two-tailed). According to Table A.3 (p. 370) the CV for this t-value is 2.086. The actual t-value for C2 is 6.04, so the null hypothesis that X has no effect on Y is rejected at $p = 0.05$.
4 This column provides (nearly) exact probabilities for the t-values in note 3 above. Here we see that H_0 can be rejected not only at 0.05, but at beyond 0.001.
5 r^2 is also called the coefficient of determination. Here r^2 is 64.6 per cent which means 64.6 per cent of Y is explained by knowing X. Generally the higher the r^2 the stronger the relationship.
6 This documents the source of variance in the corresponding columns. There are two sources: REGRESSION and ERROR.
7 In this section of the output, two kinds of unusual observations are identified if present. Those labelled 'R' are outliers from the batch of residuals. Cases labelled with an 'X' are high influence points of one sort or another.

Below is an example of the CORRELATION command. The correlation measures the strength of the linear relationship between X and Y. The data in C1 and C2 are the same as in the regression example above. For a perfect inverse relationship the r score equals -1, for no relationship r equals 0, and for perfect relationship between X and Y, r equals 1. In this output, $r = .804$ and this shows a direct relationship. You will notice that if you square .804 you will get .646 or the R-squared value in the linear regression example above.

MTB> CORR C1 C2 (command)   * * * * * * * * * *

                                                  correlation

                                             * * * * * * * * * *

     CORRELATION OF C1 AND C2 $= -.804$
MTB> LET K1 = .804 * .804   (square of r is r^2 or the co-
                                             efficient of determination)

MTB> PRINT K1
K1 0.646

HOMEWORK

Return to the two homework problems in Chapter 12.
1 Calculate confirmatory a, b and r for both examples.
2 Do a significance test for both regressions and discuss the appropriateness of the test for each regression.
3 For the problem you did as homework in Chapter 12, compare the two sets of results (exploratory and confirmatory) and discuss.

14
Analysing Tables: Two- and Three-variable Percentage Tables

Here we introduce techniques for working with two or more categorical variables. As usual, we begin by treating the data in a more exploratory fashion and follow this up by examining the logic and method of hypothesis testing for such data. We will start with the basics: how to read, construct and interpret the two-variable, or bivariate table. From there we move to multivariate analysis, the introduction of one or more additional variables (test factors) for the purpose of explicating or elaborating the bivariate relationship. Elaboration is particularly useful for understanding causal relationships.

Male Initiation Rites and Mother Bonds

A good way to start is with an interesting question that generates an appropriate but simple set of data. Anthropologists have noted that some societies are characterized by intense male initiation rites while, in others, such rites are mild or absent. Whiting *et al.* (1958) used psychoanalytic theory to argue that such rites would be more probable in societies where typical child-rearing practices might result in children too strongly bonding with the mother, thus inhibiting the development of gender identity for males. They looked for practices involving lengthy and exclusive mother–son relationships. Two stood out for them: lengthy post-partum sexual taboos and extended mother–child sleeping arrangements (they don't claim that these practices invariably have such consequences, nor that these are the only practices with such an effect). Consequently, where such practices exist, something potent would be required in order for boys to develop a male identity.

In searching through the Human Relations Area Files (HRAF), the researchers identified four initiation rites that met their criteria for severity: circumcision in adolescence, hazing, seclusion from women and tests of manliness. Societies with any one of these were classified as possessing intense rites, while those with none were classified as lacking such rites (as with mother-bonding, these rites may not always have the predicted effect and, as well, there may be other rites or social mechanisms with similar effects not considered). Thus, each society for which we have data is cross-classified on these two dimensions – for simplicity, let's call them rites–no rites and mother bonds–no mother bonds. At the time of writing, the researchers had found 54 societies that could be classified on both dimensions. These divided up into societies with:

mother bonds and rites	18
mother bonds and no rites	12
no mother bonds and rites	2
no mother bonds and no rites	22
Total	54

Thus far, we've raised a question, speculated about an answer, operationally defined the variables and collected data, which are the number of societies with the appropriate characteristics. Data in this form, however, are difficult to look at even here, where there are only four cross-classifications; imagine the difficulty if we had 30 or more. Arraying such data in tabular form is both conventional and easier to look at.

The Bivariate Table

The results are shown in the top part of Table 14.1, a form of table that you have probably seen many times before. In general such tables are called cross-tabulations (or cross-tabs or ×-tabs), cross-classifications or contingency tables. The essential thing is that they are tables of counts; for example, the entry 18 in the upper left means that 18 societies had both mother bonds and rites, as defined above. To make it easier to talk about such tables, each part of the table has a name as indicated in the bottom part of Table 14.1. The number 18 just mentioned is a *cell entry*, or the number of societies (or other units of analysis) that belong in the cell. Each cell is formed by combining a category from one variable with a category of the other (e.g. 'mother bonds' combined with 'rites'). Each *marginal* is the total number of societies in one category of one of the variables, just the row or column total; for example, 34 is the total number of societies lacking rites. The total N is the total number of societies reported on in this table; the total N is equal to the sum of the row marginals, or the sum of the column marginals, and also to the sum of all the cell entries, as you can easily check from the top part of Table 14.1.

We want to examine such tables for possible relationships between the row and column variables. For this particular example it is natural to ask: 'Does the absence or presence of rites covary with the absence or presence of mother bonds?' or, framing this question at the data level, 'Where there are mother bonds do most societies have rites, and where rites are absent, are mother bonds likely to be also absent?' The question looks and is easy, but we will need a new set of tools to answer it.

Table 14.1   A simple cross-tabulation

	Rites	*No rites*	
Mother bonds	18	12	30
No mother bonds	2	22	24
	20	34	54

Names of parts of the table   Column variable

		Rites	*No rites*	
Row variable	mother bonds	cell entry	cell entry	row marginal
	no bonds	cell entry	cell entry	marginal
		column marginal	marginal	total N

Analysis

The exploratory analysis of bivariate tables is generally pretty simple, usually little more than percentaging, summarizing the main trends in the percentaged table, and interpreting the results. In almost every way, this table is simpler than most cross-tabs – mainly because it's so small; in fact, a bivariate table can't get any smaller than 2×2.

Why percentage? Data in the form of cross-tabs are so straightforward that there is usually only one problem to deal with: unequal marginals. If we want to compare, say, the first row with the second (this is precisely what we will do here – more on why later), the fact that there are more cases in the first row than the second complicates the comparison. It is obvious, for example, that 22 is greater than 12, but it's less obvious whether it's slightly greater or much greater or what. And these marginals aren't even very different; most tables that you will meet will be far harder to interpret at a glance. Percentaging transforms such a table into one where each row has exactly 100 cases (within rounding error), so comparisons become easy. Table 14.2 shows the data after percentaging.

We noted above that the appropriate comparisons are between rows, the direction in which the table has been percentaged. But deciding on the direction to percentage can be a problem. There are several rules for deciding this (see, for example, Zeisel, 1968) but the single most important one is percentage in the direction of causality; that is, calculate percentages for each category of the causal variable. Here both the hypothesis and the ordering of events suggest that mother bonds should be viewed as the 'cause' and rites as

Table 14.2   The mother bonds/rites relationship in percentage form

	Rites	No rites	
Mother bonds	60	40	100%
	(18)	(12)	(30)
No mother bonds	8	92	100%
	(2)	(22)	(24)
(N)	(20)	(34)	(54)

the 'effect'; in particular, it is easier to see an event that occurs early in life (here, bonds formed in infancy) as impacting on later life events (here, rites, which generally occur in adolescence) than the reverse. This is the criterion of temporal priority for determining causality – we will return to this shortly.

Summarizing the table involves computing a simple statistic that can serve to give the reader a quick sense of the strength of the relationship in the table. One of the easiest and commonest statistics is the percentage difference (%diff). Since we want to compare rows, this is done simply by subtracting the second row from the first. This gives a %diff of $60 - 8 = 52$ per cent, or looking at the second column, $40 - 92 = 52$ per cent (for a 2×2 table, the two %diffs are identical). This measure can range from 0 to 100 per cent, and 52 per cent is a very impressive difference. Many people are more comfortable with a verbal interpretation of the %diff. Here is a very crude rule of thumb:

0–9 per cent:	generally not too important
10–19 per cent:	of moderate importance
20–40 per cent:	of substantial importance
over 40 per cent:	a major difference.

If your table has more than two columns but still only two rows, there are more ways to compute a %diff, but it is still easy. Suppose you want to summarize male/female differences on a hypothetical Likert-scaled item that ranges from 'strongly agree' = 1 to 'strongly disagree' = 5. Your table might look like this:

	1	2	3	4	5
Males	25	15	15	20	25
Females	35	25	10	15	5

There are a variety of ways of calculating the %diff now and you first need to decide what comparison meets your needs. You may want to compare men and women on a particular response category of interest. It could be 'strongly agree' versus others – here the %diff is 10 (females more positive, more likely to agree strongly, just the same as a 2×2 table). Or you might want to compare combinations of categories, perhaps those who agree (category 1 plus category

2) versus disagreers (4 plus 5). This gives, for agree, $(25 + 15) - (35 + 25) =$ -20 (e.g. women are substantially more likely to agree) and $(20 + 25) -$ $(15 + 15) = 15$ (men moderately more likely to disagree). Here, unlike in the 2×2 table, the $+$ diff is not equal to the $-$ diff, because there are different proportions of men and women in the neutral category. Or, if your question required such information, you might even create a category 'extreme responders' (combining 1 and 5), which would work out to be $(25 + 25) -$ $(35 + 15) = 0$. These combinations of categories work because we have combined in the same direction as we percentaged, so adding percentages is legitimate.

When there are more than two rows, a %diff is easy to calculate between any two rows, as with the case above. However, if you wish to combine rows, e.g. compare upper class and middle class against working class, there can be problems. Unless the row marginals are the same, percentages can't meaningfully be added, so calculating such %diffs requires recoding and repercentaging. An example is given in the Appendix at the end of this chapter.

Interpreting Percentage Tables

Unless your table is large, interpreting it is fairly straightforward. Generally this involves carefully describing what you see and making sense of it. A useful metaphor is to view the table as a plot line for a story and the interpretation as the story itself. The most important 'plot element' is the row-to-row or the column-to-column comparison, the direction reflecting causal differences (where these exist). In Table 14.2, it is clear that societies with rites are far more likely to have had bonding practices, while societies without rites are highly likely to lack such practices. The %diff indicates that this is a very important difference. This appears to support the hypothesis that post-partum practices leading to high levels of mother–child bonding 'cause' intense male initiation rites. Can we really conclude this from Table 14.2? Before we can begin to answer this question, we need to know more about the concept of cause and ways of inquiring into it.

Causal Analysis

Most readers probably have a reasonably clear and consistent intuition about causation. It might surprise these readers to learn that, among academics, causality is viewed either as extremely complex or as virtually meaningless. Here, we will treat the concept in a simple and pragmatic fashion, one generally consistent with most readers' intuitive understandings. Within this very simple framework, there are three necessary conditions for one variable X to have causal impact on another variable Y:

1 X and Y are related – in the language of this chapter, this would generally mean that there is a non-negligible %diff in the $X–Y$ table.

2 Temporal priority – X comes before Y in time. This appears natural and sensible but there are some complications here. For one thing, the only causal relationships that we can easily handle are asymmetric ones. This excludes mutual causation, like the marriage in which one spouse nags and the other ignores, with each action reinforcing/causing the other. For another, the timing criterion is not infallible. Rosenberg (1968: 11) observes that 'if someone is born both Negro and poor, and remains that way throughout his life, neither variable has temporal priority. Yet there is no doubt whatever that race is the determining variable. It is not that race came first, in the temporal sense, but that race is not subject to change, whereas income is'.

3 X and Y are not related spuriously. It may be that X and Y are associated, but not because X is the cause of Y. Rather, some temporally prior third variable (or even several) may have caused both. This was our reason for withholding judgement about whether mother bonds caused male initiation rites. Did you know, for example, that reading speed and thumb length are related, and strongly? You would have to be pretty gullible to believe that injecting silicone into your thumbs would be an effective way to improve poor reading skills, or that a speed reading course would make your thumbs grow. Rather, many of the people with small thumbs are children and children generally read more slowly than adults. Thus, because age is prior in time to either of the variables, the thumb length–reading speed relationship is a spurious one.

One further point about causality: you should have some sense of agency between the variables; that is, you should be able to see some sort of process linking your variables, at least in a general and sensible way.

The first two points are pretty straightforward for most readers, even with all the ifs, ands and buts. So too is the idea of spuriousness, but how do we put the idea into practice? Consider the following data provided by Eric Single in personal communication associated with the American study *Consumers in*

Table 14.3 Harassment

	Harassed	Not harassed	Total
6000 or less	525	194	719
Over 6000	313	168	481

Here we treat income as the row variable because if there is a causal relation here, it must be from income to harassment, not the reverse. Percentaging over rows gives the following.

	Harassed	Not harassed	Total
6000 or less	73	27	719
Over 6000	65	35	481

Trouble by Caplovitz (1974). Table 14.3 relates debtors' income (over or under $6000 per year) and whether or not the debtor claims to have been harassed by debt collectors.

The %diff here is 8, modest but still rather interesting. If this relationship is spurious, then there is at least one other variable that is prior in time to both of these and that makes causal sense. Consider the debtor's race: race and income are known to be related, race and harassment are likely to be related (this can be checked), and race is prior in time to both. In diagram form, we are suggesting that the relationship may look like this:

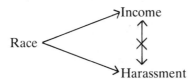

(where → means that the variable at the arrow's tail is the cause and the one at the head is the effect. The symbol ←×→ means that the two variables are spuriously related). How can we tell if the data are consistent with this diagram? We need to control for the third factor (called the *test factor*), race. To control for race, we generate subtables, one for each level of the test factor. Here, this means that we will need two tables, one for white respondents, one for black respondents. These are also called 'first-order tables', tables with one variable controlled. If race really causes both other variables, then within race, there will be (virtually) no income–harassment relationship/%diff. Let's look (Table 14.4).

We conclude from this that the apparent relationship between income and harassment is spurious, and whatever causal force is present here (not much – recall the modest %diff in the zero order table) is due to race. To recap, then, we begin with a bivariate table that is consistent with a causal relationship

Table 14.4 Harassment by income by race

	Black		White	
	Harassed	Not harassed	Harassed	Not harassed
Under 6000	451	119	74	75
Over 6000	197	53	116	115
In percentage form				
Under 6000	79	21	50	50
Over 6000	79	21	50	50
		(%diff = 0)		(%diff = 0)

between the two variables. Testing for spuriousness involves finding a test factor (there may be many possible ones) with the following properties:

(a) the test factor, T, is prior in time to the two variables being investigated;
(b) T is associated with both X and Y;
(c) the relationship between T and X and T and Y makes sense, that is, can be fitted into some process;
(d) after controlling for T by holding it constant, the X–Y relationship (virtually) disappears.

We happened on a reasonable and effective test factor on our first try (at least it appears to be our first try). It doesn't often work like this though. Some researchers faced with a possibly spurious relationship and a variety of other measured variables seem to panic. They try one variable after another without much reason, hoping for the vanishing %diff. It is far better to begin by thinking hard. First, work out the time order and the implications of a possible argument – it needn't be in detail. Only then should you start checking out the appropriate two- and three-variable tables.

Checking for spuriousness is one of the most basic applications of multivariate analysis. But the technique of test factors, often referred to as *elaboration*, lends itself to the examination of a variety of causal models. One very useful type of elaboration involves testing for *intervening variables*, variables that link other variables in a causal chain. In symbols, using Z as the intervening variables:

$$X \rightarrow Z \rightarrow Y.$$

Intervening variables can help us to understand how a causal relationship 'works'. It might operate through a third variable (getting tutoring might increase a student's self-confidence, because tutoring might increase academic success experiences, which in turn would impact on self-confidence). In a similar way, where the independent variable is complex and many-dimensional, like age, race, class, gender, etc., it can be important to determine which of the many dimensions is affecting the dependent variable. For example, a classic finding in delinquency research is that children of working mothers are more likely to be delinquent than those of non-working mothers (Maccoby, 1960). However, after controlling for degree of parental supervision, the children of working mothers turn out to be slightly less likely to be delinquent. The causal argument is now much clearer: non-working mothers are more easily able to supervise their children than working mothers, and supervised children are less likely to get into trouble. But where children of working and non-working mothers have the same level of supervision, that is where supervision is held constant, children of working mothers are a little less likely to get into trouble. We could go further and enquire into what sorts of supervision are effective, whether other sorts of supervisors can take up the slack, etc., with precisely the same technique.

Let's return to the race–income–harassment example to show how this is done. The relationship between race and harassment, while modest, has already been documented. Let's stipulate that the relationship is causal, that one or more things associated with race in the society leads to/increases the likelihood of harassment. What might these 'things' be; or putting this another way, what might the process linking race and harassment look like? Perhaps (these analyses usually begin with a speculation) poor people get harassed irrespective of race, but black people are more likely to be poor. This speculation generates the following causal chain:

Race → Income → Harassment

Note that, unlike in our spuriousness example, we are not suggesting that race doesn't cause harassment, but rather, that if black people were not more likely to be poor, there would be no race/harassment relationship. How do we test this? By controlling for/subtabling on the test factor I. If R is related to H *only* through I, then holding I constant will break the connection, leaving R and H unrelated. Thus, we create race–harassment tables for each level of income, giving Table 14.5.

If the model was correct, then the race–harassment %diff would have disappeared. But rather than vanishing, the %diff has actually become larger. We conclude from this that the intervening variable model we outlined has to be rejected.

We have looked at two different models or ways of organizing the same three variables, both of them intuitively attractive. One, the spuriousness model, asserts that race causes both income and harassment and since these two variables are both related to race they appear to be related to each other. This model, where race was controlled, was supported – the appropriate %diff vanished. The other model asserts that race and harassment are related through income, that black people are more likely to be poor and the poor are more likely to be harassed. This model, where income was controlled, was not supported.

Elaboration can be useful for testing models other than the two we have considered here. For example, most of the interesting dependent variables

Table 14.5 Harassment by race by income

	Income up to 6000		Income over 6000	
	Harassed	Not harassed	Harassed	Not harassed
Black	451	119	197	53
White	74	75	116	115

Percentaging across rows for each subtable gives:

	79%	21%	79%	21%
	50%	50%	50%	50%
	(%diff = 29%)		(%diff = 29%)	

Table 14.6   Willingness to lend money by need by relationship

Need	Friends Willing to loan		Strangers Willing to loan	
	yes	no	yes	no
High	50%	50%	5%	95%
Medium	30%	70%	5%	95%
Low	10%	90%	5%	95%

have many causes and the way they combine can be of real theoretical and practical importance. Consider: women generally earn less than men and recent immigrants generally earn less than native borns. How about the combination: recent immigrant women? Elaboration can help to answer this.

Another way in which a third variable can help to clarify a bivariate relationship is when the relationship is *conditional*, where the X–Y relation is different under differing conditions of the third variable Z. Suppose that X is a person's financial need and Y is your willingness to lend that person £100; then the relationship of X to Y may vary depending on the needful person's relationship with you. We might get tables like the hypothetical ones in Table 14.6.

We could sum this up in a new, more complex kind of diagram:

Z = friend $X \rightarrow Y$

Z = stranger X Y unrelated

When the nature of the relationship between two variables depends on the value of a third, we say the three variables *interact*. Interactions can be of many kinds. Above, X is related to Y for one value of Z and unrelated for another. Sometimes X is related to Y for all values of Z but more strongly related for some Z values than for others. Sometimes X is related to Y in two opposite ways for different Z. Interaction includes *any* way in which the X–Y relationship differs with differences in Z.

Tabular Analysis and Regression

It is far from obvious, but tabular analysis is a form of Y by X analysis with numerous important similarities to regression. For example, when we use a test factor to generate subtables, the process is described as 'the relationship between X and Y, holding Z constant' or 'controlling for Z' – which is the way residuals in a Y by X analysis are described. This is not an accident; these are residuals, though not the familiar sort. The point is that although control tables appear unfamiliar, they can be used in the same way as any other residuals, to be scrutinized carefully as a source of new ideas and insights.

We have not yet used a third variable in regression to obtain causal information about a bivariate relation. It will soon be clear that regression permits the same sorts of inferences in the same (conceptual) way, although the technology looks very different.

Along with these similarities, there are also differences between these two general strategies. One important difference concerns the nature of control: in regression, control is 'fine-grained', while tabular analysis controls much more crudely. To clarify, consider the income–harassment bivariate relationship. Income takes only two values, high/low (divided at $6000), and harassment is coded yes/no. Regression could use fairly exact measures of income and perhaps frequency or intensity of harassment, providing much finer controls. Since survey data are usually collected using fairly crude categories for much of the data, tabular analysis is often the necessary mode of analysis. Surveys also tend to be collected on large samples, often in the thousands, which are necessary for multivariate tabular analysis. On the other hand, we have seen that regression can be used effectively with quite small samples, often less than 30, depending on the number and type of variables. In short, the nature of the data and the number of cases are important in determining the type of analysis you choose.

Confirmatory Tabular Analysis: The Chi-Square Test and Measures of Association

We now move from the more exploratory style of analysing percentage tables to hypothesis testing. The focus here is on the chi-square test, a straightforward and popular way to work in a confirmatory way with bivariate and multivariate tables. We begin with a very simple example, go through the chi-square procedure in detail, describe the assumptions that apply to the chi-square test and then consider a more complex example. Finally, we develop the idea of measures of association and present several of the measures in current use.

Female Response to Success by Men and Women

Levine and Crumrine (1975) examined the attitude of males and females to the success of another person, male or female. Introductory sociology students were given a sentence and asked to make up stories about it. About half the students, both male and female, were asked to write in response to the sentence: 'After first-term exams, Anne finds herself at the top of her medical school class.' The other half of the students were asked to write about exactly the same sentence except that the name 'John' replaced the name 'Anne' (and the pronouns changed too!). The stories were then analysed in several ways. Parts of the results appear in Table 14.7. For the moment, we will consider only the female students' stories. For those stories, we will investigate the possible relationship of two categorical variables. The first variable is the sex of the

Table 14.7   Response to success (female subjects)

Person written about	Negative sentences			Percentage negative sentences		
	High	Low	Total	High	Low	Total
John	35	93	128	27	73	100
Anne	21	96	117	18	82	100
Total	56	189	245			

successful person the female students were asked to write about ('Anne' stories versus 'John' stories). Obviously this is a variable with two categories, male and female. The other variable, extent of negative response to success, was a bit more complex. For each story, the percentage of negative sentences was found. For example, one sentence showing a negative response to success was: 'Anne's roommate kills herself in a fit of jealous anger.' Then the stories were categorized as either high or low in negative sentences ('high' meaning that 60 per cent or more of the sentences in the story had negative connotations). This variable began as numeric but was collapsed into the two categories high and low negative. We have pointed out before that a variable can be categoric to start with (like sex of person written about, or John versus Anne) or it can be formed by breaking up a numerical variable into categories (percentage of negative sentences becomes high or low negative sentences).

We want to examine such tables for possible relationships between the row and column variables. For this particular example it is natural to ask: 'Does the percentage of negative sentences depend on the sex of the person whose success is written about? Do the female subjects respond more negatively to the success of a male or to the success of a female or is there no difference?' This question assumes that the row variable (John or Anne) is the independent variable and the column variable is the dependent variable, which makes sense in this case. But sometimes it is not really clear which variable is the X and which the Y; it may be uncertain, or it may seem that the two variables influence each other. The chi-square technique introduced below does not make any assumptions about which variable is independent (an assumption that does have to be made in linear fits).

The relationship between negative response to success and sex of the successful person is not dramatically obvious in Table 14.7. There is a slight tendency for women to be more negative about John's success, perhaps because they are more likely to empathize with and enjoy success by someone like themselves (i.e. of the same sex). But is this tendency marked enough to suggest a general pattern of responding more favourably to same-sex success? This sounds like the usual confirmatory question: is a sample result striking enough to suggest that a pattern exists in the universe? But we are raising this old question for a rather new form of data and it would be helpful to have some sense of what the tables showing the strongest possible relationship would look like and how they are generated.

Table 14.8   Response to success, female subjects

Person written about	High	Low	Row totals
John			128
Anne			117
	56	189	245

Hypothetical tables such as these begin with the marginals as given. This provides a numerical basis for the calculations while leaving open the question of whether the row and column variables are related. To see this, look at the marginals alone in Table 14.8. What can we tell from this? We can see that the female subjects were fairly evenly divided between those writing about John and those writing about Anne (128 versus 117); and we can see that most of the stories were not very negative (189 out of 245 had a low percentage of negative sentences). But we cannot see how the two variables connect. We know how many females wrote about John, but not how negative those stories were; this information would be in the cell entries. We know how many females wrote stories with a high percentage of negative sentences, but not whether they were more likely to be negative about John or about Anne; again this information would be in the cell entries. To get at the relationship we must be able to look inside the table.

What does a no-relationship table look like? As noted earlier, the marginals are the same as the original table, but the cell entries are modified in such a way as to give a 0 %diff. That's easy; 128 cases out of the total of 245 were written about John, that's 52.2 per cent. For there to be 0 %diff, we will want 52.2 per cent in each column of the John row, or 99 in the second column $(0.522 \times 189 = 98.7$, which rounds to 99), and 29 in the first column. In the same way, we get 90 and 27 for the Anne values, 47.8 per cent of the sample. Thus, each row of the no-relation section of Table 14.9 has exactly (within

Table 14.9   Hypothetical responses to success

	Strongest possible relationship, 'John' stories more negative			No relationship		
	High	Low	Total	High	Low	Total
John	56	72	128	29	99	128
Anne	0	117	117	27	90	117
	56	189	245	56	189	245
	(%diff = 44)			(%diff = 0)		

rounding error) the same proportional distribution, and consequently the desired 0 %diff.

We use the reverse procedure to get a table with the strongest possible relationship, the one with the maximum %diff, given the marginals. For a 2×2 table like this one, the easiest way to maximize the %diff is to set one of the smaller cells equal to zero. Since the marginals are fixed, all of the other cell values are then determined. Here, we set the Anne high cell to zero, forcing Anne low to be 117, etc. What results is the strongest John negative table possible, with a %diff = 44 per cent.

A comparison of the actual results in Table 14.8 with the two hypothetical tables in Table 14.9 shows the actual results to be somewhere in between these two extremes. Should we conclude that there is really no relationship between the variables, and that the tendency Table 14.7 may show is just a sampling accident? Or should we conclude that there is a relationship in the universe? This must depend on how far the actual cell entries get away from the 'no-relationship' entries in Table 14.9. The more different they are from that flat pattern, the harder it is to believe that the two variables are unrelated. This is the general strategy of the chi-square test.

Analysing Response to Success with Chi-Square

We want to see how far our results get from the no-relationship pattern, so our first step is to make a more exact calculation of such a pattern. The version in Table 14.9 was rounded to whole numbers so that it would look like a possible sample result, but for our test we want more accuracy. Now if the two variables are unrelated, knowing something about one of them tells us nothing new about the other one. For example, in the hypothetical no-relationship table in Table 14.9 we saw that the percentage of negative sentences was the same whether we looked at all the stories (ignoring the John–Anne distinction) or whether we knew that the story had been written about a male or a female. But

Table 14.10 Finding chi-square for female response to success

A: Expected values				C: $(O - E)^2$	
	High	Low			
John	29.26	98.74	128	32.95	32.95
Anne	26.74	90.26	117	32.95	32.95
	56	189	245		
B: $O - E$				D: $(O - E)^2/E$	
	5.74	−5.74	0	1.126	0.334
	−5.74	5.74	0	1.232	0.365
	0	0	0		

in the perfect relationship table, knowing the value of the column variable tells us a lot about the percentage of negative sentences: none of the Anne stories have a lot of negative sentences, while 56/128 = 44 per cent of the John stories do. To generalize this, if the row and column variables are not related, then the proportions inside the table will be similar to those in the marginals; but if the variables are related, then the proportions vary from row to row and from column to column.

More formally, suppose H_0 is true:

H_0: the row and column variables are not related

Then the number of cases in each cell just depends on how many cases there are in the row and column the cell belongs to. It is easy to calculate the number of cases we would expect:

$$\text{Expected values if } H_0 \text{ true} = \frac{(\text{row marginal}) (\text{column marginal})}{\text{table total}}$$

The results are given to two decimal places in part A of Table 14.10; rounding these values gets back to the no-relationship table in Table 14.9. For example, the cell entry for women writing negative stories about Anne is

$$\frac{56 \times 117}{245} = 26.74, \text{ which rounds to } 27$$

Of course, any real cell entries will be a little bit different from the expected values; for one thing, they'll be whole numbers. More importantly, the cell entries may be a bit higher or lower than expected just from sampling fluctuations even when the two variables are really unrelated in the universe. But if the actual cell entries get far enough from the H_0 expectations, we'll find H_0 too unlikely to be acceptable and we'll tentatively move to the alternative hypothesis:

H_1: the row and column variables are related in the universe

H_1 does not say how the variables are related; any extensive departure from the H_0 values is of interest, whatever the pattern of departure is. So our next step is to find out how different the observed cell values are from those expected if H_0 is true:

observed value − expected value = $O - E$

These figures are reported in part B of Table 14.10. As an arithmetic check, note that the rows and columns must add up to zero. We see that there's some difference between the observed and expected values but it is hard to say whether the difference is important or something that could easily happen by chance. To help decide this familiar confirmatory question we will put all the differences in the $(O - E)$ table together to get an overall measure of how large they are. First we have to handle a couple of problems with the differences: some are positive and some negative, and they are not all equally impressive.

First we dispose of the minus signs by squaring all the values to get

$$(O - E)^2$$

as in part C of Table 14.10. (You may have noticed that statisticians usually prefer squaring things to get rid of minus signs; once again squaring turns out to have useful mathematical properties.) Next we allow for the fact that the $(O - E)^2$ values are not all equally impressive even though they all happen to be the same number here. This may be easiest to think about if we turn back to the $(O - E)$ values in part B briefly, comparing them to the expected values in part A. Somehow the difference of 5.74 in the lower left hand corner, where we expect about 27 cases, looks more impressive than the difference of 5.74 in the upper right hand corner, where we expect about 99 cases. The lower left difference is a proportionally bigger departure from what we expect if H_0 is true. To get the departures in proportion to the expected values, we can just divide by the expected values. This brings us to

$$\frac{(O - E)^2}{E}$$

as in part D of Table 14.10. For example, the value in the John low cell is

$$\frac{(-5.74)^2}{98.74} = 0.334$$

Now chi-square, our overall measure of the difference between the observed data and the null expected, is just the total of the entries in part D:

$$\text{chi-square} = \chi_1^2 = \Sigma \, \frac{(O - E)^2}{E}$$

$$= 0.334 + 0.365 + 1.126 + 1.232$$

$$= 3.057$$

This value can be compared to a critical value from Table A.5 (page 372). To use Table A.5 we need to know (a) what level of significance we want to use, and (b) how many degrees of freedom we have. As with anova we don't usually predict direction, so the test is ordinarily two-tailed. Let's use a 5 per cent level of significance. The degrees of freedom for a chi-square test are found by multiplying the number of rows in the tables less one $(R - 1)$ by the number of columns less one $(C - 1)$:

$$df = (R - 1)(C - 1)$$

In our example, $df = (2 - 1)(2 - 1) = 1$. Note that the degrees of freedom have nothing to do with the sample size, N, which has been crucial in all the other tests we've looked at. More on this later. Table A.5 tells us that the CV for one degree of freedom, 5 per cent level, is 3.841. Our chi-square value is not that large, so we cannot reject H_0; the relationship between the sex of the person written about and the number of negative sentences is not significant at the 0.05

level. By this measure, at any rate, female response to success is not reliably affected by the gender of the successful person.

Finding a non-significant result was of considerable interest, since an important previous study had suggested that women may fear success and react more negatively to a woman's success than to a man's. Failure to replicate, and/or failure to find significant relationships where they are expected, are always interesting and can often be far more productive than getting the predicted result. It is the unexpected that makes you think the hardest. If there is any tendency in these data, it is one opposite to the 'fear of success' prediction since the women were slightly more negative about John's success. The chi-square test, being nondirectional, tests for either possibility: for more negative response to John or for more negative response to Anne, or in general for any kind of difference from a flat no-relationship pattern. So if the chi-square does turn out to be significant, we have some confidence that the two variables are related but we do not know how they are related; we must examine the data to see. Again, this is similar to analysis of variance where we have to examine the means to see what a significant difference among them consists of. The percentage table is a good place to start.

Degrees of Freedom for Chi-Square

In earlier tests the degrees of freedom were based on N, because a larger sample size meant more reliable estimates and thus less extreme critical values. Here, we find that the number of degrees of freedom does not depend on N at all but instead on the size of the table or $(R - 1)(C - 1)$. Why? The chi-square compares observed to expected values cell by cell, so what really matters is the number of comparisons or the number of cells. So why not just R times C instead of $(R - 1)(C - 1)$? Consider the simplest possible table again, a two by two table like our response to success table. Suppose we know any one cell value: it doesn't matter which, let's say it is the Anne low cell. We also know the marginals, which are given throughout. So we have:

	High	Low	Total
John			128
Anne		96	117
Total	56	189	245

What do we know about the three blank cells? Everything! For example, the John low cell must be $189 - 96 = 93$; all the remaining cell values are fixed once we know the value of any one cell. So we really only have one independent comparison of observed and expected values. And the $(R - 1)(C - 1)$ formula tells us that we have one degree of freedom. Here is an illustration with a larger table:

			Total
5	10	?	20
10	5	?	25
10	10	?	25
?	?	?	15
Total 30	30	25	85

Once we fill in six cells, like the six filled in above for example, we know what the other cells must be. So we have six degrees of freedom; and $(R - 1)(C - 1) = 3 \times 2 = 6$.

Chi-Square Assumptions

As with any confirmatory test, chi-square can be used appropriately only if some assumptions about the data are met. First, the data must consist of randomly selected, independently measured cases. Secondly, the expected values must be large enough. 'Large enough' depends on the size of the table primarily:

1 For 2 × 2 tables, the expected values in each cell should be 10 or more.
2 For tables larger than 2 × 2, the mean of the expected values should be six or more for tests at the 5 per cent level; for tests at more demanding levels, like 1 or 0.1 per cent, the minimum mean expected value should be somewhat higher.

These requirements for expected values are something new, so let's try to get a feel for them by looking at the simple 2 × 2 case again. In our example this assumption was met easily, since the smallest expected value was 26.74. Suppose it was not met. Suppose we were doing a little trial run with fewer respondents and got this table of expected values:

	High	*Low*	*Total*
John	2.5	9.5	12
Anne	2.5	9.5	12
	5	19	24

Now, no matter what the observed values are, they must be at least a bit different from the expected values. Further, the last step in preparing cell values for chi-square is to divide through by the expected values; so if the expected values are small, such artifactual $O - E$ differences get even more exaggerated. The net effect is that the chi-square value can be increased a bit by arithmetic constraints that have nothing to do with the relationship between the two variables. The same sort of problem comes up in tables larger than

2×2, except that the effect is not quite as serious because it is spread over more cells, so the minimum mean expected value can be lower.

Suppose the expected values are too small? If the table is larger than 2×2 you can *collapse* the table; combine some of the categories with small marginals (and thus small expected values) to get bigger expected values. Try to do so in some sensible, non-arbitrary way without peeking at the observed values.

Let's go through another, larger example. This will let us illustrate the details that are a bit different for larger tables, while reviewing the overall chi-square procedure.

A Larger Example: Ice Hockey Violence

Ice hockey has the reputation of being a violent sport. Michael Smith (1979), in a survey of amateur players in Toronto, Canada, explored some of the reasons for the violence. Table 14.11 looks at the relationship between players' ages and their perceptions of their coach's approval of fighting, based on answers to the question: 'Are there any situations you can imagine in which your coach would approve of punching another player?' Low = approves in no situation; medium = approves in one or two situations; high = approves in three or four situations.

Clearly a change in age might lead to a change in the (perceived) coaches'

Table 14.11   Player age and coaches' approval of punching

Player age	Low	Medium	High	Total
12–13	123	28	15	166
14–15	115	59	22	196
16–17	51	47	32	130
18–21	28	26	58	112
Total	317	160	127	604

Table 14.12   Player age and coaches' approval of punching (percentaged)

Player age	Low	Medium	High	Total	N
12–13	74	17	9	100%	166
14–15	59	30	11	100%	196
16–17	39	36	25	100%	130
18–21	25	23	52	100%	112
Total	317	160	127		604

approval of violence, but the reverse is not possible, so age (the row variable) is the independent variable and we percentage along rows. The results are in Table 14.12. Comparing the youngest players to the oldest gives %diffs of 49 for low approval and −43 for high approval, both major differences. Something is going on in this table.

Putting that something into words is easy here: the older the player, the higher the coaches' approval of punching fellow players. But interpretation is trickier. First we must ask what actually grows: (a) the coaches' approval, or (b) the players' perception of this. Perhaps (b) is true because the players themselves accept violence more as they grow older. The players may be responding to growing pressure from other sources (like spectators or parents), or may feel more confident in fights as they get older and bigger, or they may accept norms of violence more and more as they have longer exposure to hockey sub-culture. Or perhaps (a) is true and the coaches give greater approval of violence for older players who are stronger and are expected to meet adult male expectations of toughness. Perhaps both are true; perhaps every subgroup in the ice hockey world expects more macho behaviour and rougher competition from older boys, and these expectations reinforce each other.

Statistical Test

First we check the assumptions. We expect that the sample survey of Toronto amateurs was competently done, and we have a random sample of independently observed cases. Next we consider the expected values: are they large enough? The table is larger than 2×2 so we would like a mean expected value of six or more. Dividing the grand total by the number of cells gives:

$$\frac{N}{RC} = \frac{604}{3 \times 4} = 50.3$$

which is more than enough. Let us also decide to use a 5 per cent significance level. With degree of freedom $(R - 1)(C - 1) = 6$, our critical value is 12.595. H_0: the row and column variable are not related in the universe; H_1: the row and column variables are associated in the universe. Table 14.13 shows the computations.

Summing the computations gives chi-square $= 119.98$, well above the critical value of 12.592, and the relationship is significant at the 5 per cent level. (Indeed it is significant at much more demanding levels, including the 0.001 level, which has a critical value of 22.457 for 6 degrees of freedom.)

Significance and Strength: Measures of Association

So far we've learned to use the chi-square test to answer one major question: is there a significant relationship between the row and column variables? Are the

Table 14.13   Finding chi-square for coaches' approval of fighting

| Age | Coaches' approval | | | |
	Low	Medium	High	Total
	Expected values			
12–13	87.12	47.97	34.90	165.99
14–15	102.87	51.92	41.21	196.00
16–17	68.23	34.44	27.33	130.00
18–21	58.78	29.67	23.55	112.00
Total	317.00	160.00	126.99	603.99
	Observed − expected			
12–13	35.88	−15.97	−19.90	0.01
14–15	12.13	7.08	−19.21	0
16–17	−17.23	12.56	4.67	0
18–21	−30.78	−3.67	34.45	0
Total	0	0	0.01	0.01
	(Observed − expected)²/expected			
12–13	14.78	5.80	11.35	
14–15	1.43	0.97	8.95	
16–17	4.35	4.58	0.80	
18–21	16.12	0.45	50.40	

observed values different from the ones we would expect if there is no relationship, so different that we think there probably is a relationship? This is of course a very important question and one we must know how to answer, but there are other questions just as important; perhaps most important is the question, 'How strong is this relationship?'

This is the question that %diff tries to answer, and much of the time it does a pretty good job. It is usually easy to calculate, it makes intuitive sense and it is easy to communicate. But there are a few problems with it. For example, when we constructed a hypothetical table showing the strongest possible relationship (Table 14.9), the %diff was 44, indicating a major difference. But if it is as strong as it can possibly be, why is the %diff not 100? Without worrying about the mathematics here, the maximum %diff can be 100 in a 2×2 table only when the marginals are related in particular ways. And the more the marginals deviate from such a relation, the smaller the maximum %diff will be. Imagine, for example, conducting research on ways to make people more politically active, getting more people to contribute to and work for their political party. At the present time perhaps 5 per cent of the population does so (we are guessing), but of the, say, 200 people in your hypothetical experiment, 12.5 per cent got involved – two and a half times as many – WOW! But it is not much of a

%diff. This is a serious problem – it doesn't mean that %diff is worthless, but it does mean that we need more than one measure in our tool box.

What about chi-square? That isn't a per cent-based measure so you might expect to handle this problem better. It turns out that it is not only not immune to what we might call the 'marginals problem', it is subject to what might be an even more serious problem – how large chi-square can be depends on sample size.

Let's look at a few examples to show how significance and strength differ and why. Earlier we looked at the proportion of negative sentences in stories written by females about John or Anne, getting this summary picture:

	High	Low	
John	35	93	128
Anne	21	96	117
	56	189	245

$$\chi^2 = 3.057 \quad \text{n.s.}$$

This value for χ_1^2 is not significant at the 5 per cent level. Now let's suppose that someone with plenty of time on his or her hands decides to replicate this study with a sample size ten times larger, and happens to find a relationship that is identical except that everything is multiplied by ten:

	High	Low	
John	350	930	1280
Anne	210	960	1170
	560	1890	2450

$$\chi^2 = 30.57 \quad P < 0.01$$

Note that the chi-square gets multiplied by ten too. If we had doubled all the numbers in the table, the chi-square would have doubled; if we had tripled the numbers, the chi-square would have tripled, and so on. This hypothetical increase in sample size can affect the significance level even if the strength of the relationship stays the same. This is similar to what we found for the correlation coefficient in the previous chapter: if the N is large enough, even a very weak r can be significant, so strength and significance are not exactly the same thing. For chi-square too, strength and significance are two separate though related questions.

Now we know how to ask if the relationship in our sample is significant, if it is likely also to be present in the universe from which the sample was taken: that is the question chi-square deals with. But what of strength? We can use chi-square for this if we can only remove chi-square's dependence on N. One very easy way to do this is to find

$$\phi = \sqrt{\frac{\chi^2}{N}}$$

(ϕ is the Greek letter pronounced 'fie'.)

In our little example, for the first (the real) table

$$\sqrt{\frac{\chi^2}{N}} = \sqrt{\frac{3.057}{245}} = \sqrt{0.012} = 0.11$$

while for the imaginary replication with increased N,

$$\sqrt{\frac{\chi^2}{N}} = \sqrt{\frac{30.57}{2450}} = \sqrt{0.012} = 0.11$$

Whether we have 245 cases or 2450, this figure suggests that the relationship between negative sentences in stories and gender of person written about is a weak one, which fits with a common-sense look at the table. Thus ϕ is the kind of thing we want a measure of association between two variables to be: it suggests how strongly the variables are related whatever sample size we happen to have.

As long as there are either two rows or two columns in the table, the theoretical maximum for ϕ is 1.0. This is useful for two reasons. It is possible to compare the strength of relationship in tables of different sizes, and as well, such numbers are easier to make sense of. Unfortunately, when both dimensions of the table are greater than two, ϕ loses this desirable property. Just a slight modification, however, gives us Cramer's V, which does have the useful range, 0–1.0;

$$\text{Cramer's } V = \sqrt{\frac{\chi^2}{N}(S - 1)}$$

where S = either R or C, whichever is smaller.

If the row or column variable has just two categories then the smaller of $(R - 1)$ and $(C - 1)$ is $2 - 1$, so V is the same as ϕ. In bigger tables, there is a difference. For the Smith example:

$$V = \sqrt{\frac{\chi^2}{N}(S - 1)} = \sqrt{\frac{119.98}{604\,(3 - 1)}} = \sqrt{0.099} = 0.315$$

So there is a highly significant but moderate relationship between age and approval of fighting. Cramer's V does a good job of coping with the sample size problem of chi-square (ϕ is a special case of Cramer's V). But the 'marginals problem' that we encountered with %diff remains a problem for V as well. We won't prove this for you, but if you are interested, compute ϕ for the 'strongest possible' section of Table 14.9. We need a measure that combines the best features of %diff, simple to compute and understand, like V, independent of sample size, but also independent of the marginals.

There is a class of measures of association called PRE measures, which stands for 'proportional reduction of error'. There are many such measures but we will only consider two. For 2 × 2 tables, one of the best and simplest PRE measures is Yule's Q. If we simply label the counts in the cells of the 2×2 table as

a b
c d

then:

$$Q = \frac{ad - bc}{ad + bc}$$

This measure varies from -1.0 (if either a or d is zero) to $+1.0$ (if b or c is zero) and is equal to 0 where the row variable tells you nothing about the column variable, where row and column are independent. If we calculate Q for the three Anne–John tables we get, for the strongest possible table

$$(72 \times 0 - 117 \times 56)/(72 \times 0 + 117 \times 56) = -1.0$$

for the no-relationship table

$$(99 \times 27 - 90 \times 29)/(99 \times 27 + 90 \times 29) = 0.01$$

and for the original table

$$(93 \times 21 - 96 \times 35)/(93 \times 21 + 96 \times 35) = -0.26$$

With only slight exceptions, these measures are consistent with what we should reasonably expect – the no-relationship table with Q nearly 0 (rounding error prevents Q from being exactly zero), a perfect value of 1.0 or -1.0 where the relationship is as strong as possible, and for the original table, where the relationship is modest, a modest Q.

If your table is larger than 2×2, there is a variety of PRE measures. One of the simplest of these measures is called lambda, which literally measures how much your guesses about the dependent variable are improved by knowing the value of the independent variable. Consider again Smith's data on ice hockey violence in Table 14.10; if you had to guess to what extent a player would believe that his coach approved of punching, but didn't know the players' ages, your best guess would be 'low' because that's the largest column marginal. You'd be right 317 times and wrong $160 + 127 = 287$ times. However, if you know the player's age, you can do better than this. You would still guess 'low' if the player was in one of the three youngest groups since the low column is the largest cell entry in each of the first three rows. That guess would be correct $123 + 115 + 51 = 289$ times and incorrect $28 + 15 + 59 + 22 + 47 + 32 = 203$ times. But if the player was in the oldest group, the best guess is 'high', right 58 times and wrong 54. Overall, then, knowing which row a person is in (here, knowing the player's age) enables you to make a better guess of the column, reducing the number of errors made from 287 to 257. To make this a *proportional* reduction of error measure, we need to find the proportion of errors we 'save'. More formally, if $E(0)$ is the number of errors when row is unknown, and $E(1)$ is the number of errors given the row: lambda $= (E0 - E1)/E0 = (287 - 257)/287 = 0.10$. Lambda can range from 0, where knowing row tells you nothing about column, to 1.0, a perfect relationship where knowing row tells you everything about column. In the example above, the lambda of 0.10 indicates a modest relationship. There are many PRE measures, most of them pretty easy to compute, but this measure probably comes closest to our intuitive understanding of PRE.

Exploratory and Confirmatory

Tabular analysis, either the more exploratory percentage analysis of bivariate or multivariate tables or the more confirmatory chi-square analysis, is the commonest choice for most questionnaire data. In fact, even high-quality ordinal data that might well be analysed using regression techniques are frequently analysed this way. We've discussed some of the problems of chi-square and derived measures, but the major problem is conceptual. All that these measures tell you is if something is going on inside the table; to find out what you must look, and the percentage table is one of the places to look and look hard. Percentage tables are also useful as a way of learning if the variables are related causally and, if so, how.

Using the Computer

The chi-square test is easy in MINITAB. For the Smith data on hockey violence:

ROW	LOW	MEDIUM	HIGH
12–13	123	28	15
14–15	115	59	22
16–17	51	47	32
18–21	28	26	58

MTB> CHIS C1–C3

	C1	C2	C3	Total
1	123	28	15	166
	87.12	43.97	34.90	
2	115	59	22	196
	102.87	51.92	41.21	
3	51	47	32	130
	68.23	34.44	27.33	
4	28	26	58	112
	58.78	29.67	23.55	
Total	317	160	127	604

ChiSq = 14.775 + 5.802 + 11.350 +
       1.431 + 0.965 + 8.956 +
       4.350 + 4.583 + 0.796 +
      16.119 + 0.454 + 50.397 = 119.979
$df = 6$
MTB> stop

This shows each cell having two values. The top value is the observed frequency while the bottom value is the expected frequency. Immediately below the table, after the heading 'ChiSq' you will find values that tell you how much each cell in the table contributes to the total chi-square statistic. To find out whether the value is significant use a table like Table A.5 (page 372) to find the CV for the given df. To get V, take

$$\sqrt{\frac{\chi^2}{N(S-1)}} = \sqrt{\frac{119.98}{604 \times 2}}$$

Running percentage tables, on the other hand, is not something that MINITAB does as well as some other statistics packages. It is easy enough if you begin with data that have been entered casewise; that is, 604 rows, with age in C1 and coaches' support of violence in C2. Then:

> MTB> TABLE C1 C2;
> SUBC> ROWPERCENT

will give you the zero order table. To control for C3, say, the main command will be TABLE C1, C2, C3. If you prefer percentaging down the columns instead of across rows, use COLPERCENT. However, if you begin with the table itself, as here, you can use the 'TABLE' command, but you will have to do your own percentaging.

APPENDIX: Calculating %diff for Tables With Three or More Rows

When there are more than two rows, the possible comparisons are increased. Consider the following abstract table where the letters represent counts.

	High	Medium	Low	Total
High	a	b	c	$a+b+c$
Medium	d	e	f	$d+e+f$
Low	g	h	i	$g+h+i$

If we merely want to compare some pair of rows, say the high row to the low row, the procedure is just like the case with two rows and many columns. For example, we could compare the percentage that is high on the column variable for high row versus low row, or

$[a/(a + b + c) - g/(g + h + i)] \,(100)$ (i.e. subtract one proportion from the other then multiply by 100)

to get the %diff. But if you want to compare the high row versus medium plus low row, again on the high column, the comparison is:

$[a/(a + b + c) - (d + g)/(d + e + f + g + h + i)] \,(100)$

In short, we can't just add percentages from different rows unless the row marginals are identical. Fortunately, much of the software that does tabular analysis can either compute such %diffs for you or at least make it easy to combine row (and column) categories through a recode command.

HOMEWORK

1 The following data on Wisconsin, USA, high school seniors in 1957 came from Sewell and Shah (1968). Table 14.14 examines a random sample of 9007 respondents cross-classified by intelligence test score and college plans.

Analyse the data including a brief explanation of why you chose to percentage the table as you did.

2 Table 14.15 from the same study further cross-classifies the respondents by gender.

(a) Is gender related to college plans? To IQ?

(b) Use an arrow diagram to describe a possible causal relationship among these three variables.

(c) Test your model and discuss.

3 Table 14.16 contains three tables, each based on responses by the same players to different questions. In each table there are 166 players aged 12–13,

Table 14.14

College plans	Students' intelligence test score			
	High	Medium	Low	Total
Yes	1669	929	405	3003
No	1344	2088	2572	6004
Total	3013	3017	2977	9007

Table 14.15   IQ and college plans, by sex: Wisconsin high school seniors

College plans	Boys' IQ			Girls' IQ		
	High	Medium	Low	High	Medium	Low
Yes	923	504	214	746	425	191
No	565	948	1234	779	1140	1338

196 aged 14–15, 130 aged 16–17, 112 aged 18–21. The data are from the Smith (1979) study, based on a sample of Toronto amateur players. The question format was: 'Are there any situations you can imagine in which [   ] would approve of punching another player?'

Low = no situation, Med = one or two, High = three or four.

Choose any two of the tables, percentage appropriately, find χ^2 and V, and discuss.

Table 14.16 Approval of ice hockey fighting

Player's age	Mother's approval			Own approval			Teammates' approval		
	Low	Med	High	Low	Med	High	Low	Med	High
12–13	148	13	5	90	41	35	38	38	90
14–15	167	23	6	73	76	47	22	53	121
16–17	105	18	7	17	64	49	5	34	91
18–21	84	20	8	19	27	66	10	15	87

THIRD REVIEW
Y by X Analysis

Let us remind you of the importance of organic and sensibly limited analyses. Do not try a hectic mixture of attacks on the data hoping they will somehow make sense at the last minute; pick a core topic and follow through on it in some orderly way, commenting as you go. For example, you might choose a dependent variable on which to focus Y by X analysis, explore a promising independent variable, examine residuals for suggestions about other possible independent variables, then do a corresponding confirmatory analysis, and finally compare the two approaches. This would follow the order of the preceding chapter quite closely. Or you might start with confirmatory statistics and use exploratory methods to enrich this analysis. Don't just look at one combination of variables after another until one looks terrific; even a weak relationship can be interesting, and you are not going to be marked on the strength of relationships (that depends on reality, not on you!).

1 Table R3.1 presents data on voter behaviour (per cent left-wing and per cent turn-out) for 24 areas of Vancouver by income and year. The 24 areas are grouped into East Side (areas 1–13) and West Side (areas 14–24), a familiar local distinction. During much of the period from 1958 to 1966, Vancouver had municipal parties that were identifiable as left, right or centre. These data can be attacked in a variety of ways, e.g. your dependent variable can be left-wing vote for any year, turn-out for any year or a combination of either of these over all years, or something else that makes sense to you. Similarly, your predictor variable might be mean income or something else that makes sense to you.

2 Table R3.2 looks at per capita GNP and percentage of married women using contraception (this includes women whose husbands practise contraception) for 40 randomly selected countries in 1983. Before beginning your Y by X analysis, you will want to consider (and discuss) the causal ordering of these two variables. These data can also be set up as a table and analysed using tabular techniques. If you choose to analyse the data in this fashion, it would be useful to also do a brief Y by X/regression analysis and compare the results.

Table R3.1 Left-wing vote and turn-out in Vancouver

Area	Mean income 1961	Left-wing vote (%)					Turn-out (%)				
		1958	1960	1962	1964	1966	1958	1960	1962	1964	1966
1	2751	28	26	16	29	24	20	26	27	24	22
2	3315	37	30	18	34	27	22	25	29	26	25
3	3422	33	28	16	32	27	24	28	33	30	27
4	3864	35	29	15	36	28	32	35	44	42	39
5	3865	26	24	11	26	22	31	35	44	38	34
6	3865	36	31	13	32	27	33	37	43	38	32
7	3974	33	31	15	33	28	29	35	43	40	36
8	4003	36	29	15	35	28	33	35	42	39	37
9	4173	35	29	13	30	27	32	36	44	42	36
10	4186	36	31	14	32	29	29	33	41	38	34
11	4299	32	27	11	28	25	32	34	44	40	34
12	4383	28	23	11	26	22	34	36	48	43	40
13	4594	34	29	12	29	26	33	42	45	41	35
14	3589	20	18	10	20	19	26	28	32	27	26
15	3785	24	20	10	23	20	28	29	38	34	30
16	3786	22	19	10	22	19	25	27	33	30	27
17	4233	19	15	9	18	17	28	28	35	33	29
18	4558	21	17	9	22	18	33	37	47	41	39
19	4640	24	18	9	21	20	32	36	47	40	32
20	5701	16	13	7	16	14	44	54	66	58	50
21	5908	18	15	8	19	17	40	44	54	48	43
22	6267	15	9	8	15	12	41	46	60	55	47
23	7066	12	10	6	13	11	45	51	65	59	53
24	8477	9	8	5	12	10	40	40	58	52	48

Source: Ewing (1972).

Table R3.2   Wealth and contraception

	GNP per capita	% of married women using contraception
Ethiopia	110	2
Mali	140	1
Zaire	140	3
Nepal	160	7
Niger	190	1
Uganda	230	1
India	260	35
China	310	71
Kenya	310	17
Haiti	320	7
Sri Lanka	360	55
Pakistan	380	11
Indonesia	540	50
Philippines	660	48
El Salvador	710	34
Egypt	720	30
Zimbabwe	760	27
Peru	1000	41
Jamaica	1150	51
Chile	1700	43
Brazil	1720	50
Portugal	1970	66
Mexico	2040	48
Poland	2100	75
Hungary	2100	74
Yugoslavia	2120	55
Spain	4440	51
Hong Kong	6330	80
Italy	6420	78
Singapore	7260	71
UK	8570	77
France	9760	79
Japan	10630	56
Belgium	8610	85
Netherlands	9520	75
Finland	10770	80
Sweden	11860	78
Norway	13940	71
USA	15390	76
Switzerland	16330	70

Source: World Development Report (1986).

Section IV
Using Two Independent Variables

In the previous sections we learned how to work with one independent variable, X, and one dependent variable, Y. We have learned how to deal with the effect of X on Y under many different conditions. X and Y can each be numerical or categorical; our general style can be exploratory or confirmatory; the variables can have various levels, shapes and spreads. Let us remind you of what we have so far (Table IV.1).

We even know how to use these methods for a numerical X or Y that is far from normal (we can almost always transform or sub-batch).

Suppose that we now want to examine the effects of two independent variables on Y? Most social variables – if not all – are the product of many causes working together, not the result of just one.

This section is devoted to ways of predicting a numerical Y from two X variables in combination. First, we see how to combine two categorical Xs. Chapter 15 shows how to assess the effects of two independent variables, which can be categorical or ordinal, summarizing either by means or by medians. Chapter 16 shows one way to fit effects of the two variables in combination, or

Table IV.1

Variable type		Statistical techniques	
Independent (X)	Dependent (Y)	Exploratory	Confirmatory
categorical	numeric	batch analysis (Ch. 2 to 6)	t-test, Z-test and one-way anova (Ch. 8 to 10)
numeric	numeric	Y by X (Ch. 11, 12)	linear regression (Ch. 13)
categorical	categorical	tabular analysis (Ch. 14)	chi-square test (Ch. 14)

interaction effects. Then Chapter 17 presents the basic confirmatory approach, two-way analysis of variance. In the second half of this section we work with two numeric X variables. Chapter 18 adds a second X to the exploratory Y by X techniques, while Chapters 19 and 20 give the analogous confirmatory tools.

It is also possible to handle all the other combinations, although we will not try to cover the techniques here. A numeric X and a categorical X with a numeric Y? You just combine Y by X and sub-batching, follow your common sense. In confirmatory statistics you can use dummy variable regression or a kind of anova–regression hybrid called analysis of covariance. Two categorical Xs and a categorical Y? Extensions of chi-square and related methods can be used here. In general, it is pretty hard to come up with a data set for which no standard technique exists, as there are lots of techniques available. The ones we give here are the ones most widely used. To read most journal articles, or handle most simple research problems, you may never need more.

Finally, the techniques presented here can be easily extended to handle three or more independent variables. They can also be seen as closely related techniques. Indeed, all of them are special applications of one approach, the 'general linear model'.

15
Elementary Analysis

We already know how to look at the effect of one categorical X on a numeric Y: divide up the Y values into batches, with each batch corresponding to a category of X, and find the batch levels. For example, we batched suicide rates (Y) by age groups (X) and found that the level of suicide increased with age. Now we extend this to the situation where two categorical independent variables together determine the level of Y.

First we make a table, like Table 15.1. The two categorical X variables are the row and column variables. The column variable in Table 15.1 is the number of children in the household; the row variable is the number of earners in the household. The Y or dependent variable is the proportion of families in each constellation that live below the poverty line. So 33 per cent of families with no earners and no children have an income (welfare, retirement benefits, rents, investment income, etc.) that places them below the poverty level. This is a very straightforward type of table that you have probably seen before. It may look similar to a chi-square table but it's quite different. In a chi-square table there are two variables and the cell entries are the counts for each cross-classification. Here we have three variables, because the entries are scores on Y. This type of table is often referred to as a 'two-way' table.

In this chapter we will look at two methods of analysing this kind of table; the two methods have the same goal, but one uses means and the other uses medians. Although the means analysis is not resistant, we will start with it because it is much simpler to compute. In this chapter and the next we think of both methods as exploratory approaches, although the use of means will turn up again in the confirmatory version.

Elementary Analysis Using Means

Let's put off thinking about the row variable 'number of earners' for a moment. Each of the columns can be viewed as a batch of three numbers; for example, the left hand column consists of proportions of childless families below the poverty line. To find the effect of number of children on poverty, we just have

Table 15.1 A simple two-way table: percentage of families below the poverty line, by number of earners and number of children in the household

Number of earners	Children in household			
	0	*1–2*	*3–4*	*5+*
0	33	70	89	88
1	14	20	28	41
2+	4	6	12	25

Source: From the cumulative US General Social Survey (James A. Davis, personal communciation).

to find the level of each column; that is, average over the rows. Going from the category 'no children' to the category 'five or more', the column means are 17, 32, 43 and 51.33. If we look closely at these four numbers, we can see several interesting things. First, the column means increase as number of children increase; that is, the more children, the greater the 'risk' of living in poverty (no parent will be surprised by this). But what is perhaps surprising is that the column-to-column differences, the 'marginal cost' of an additional child, declines with more children. So going from no children to one or two increases the risk of poverty by 15 per cent $(32 - 17)$ while going from three or four to five (or more) only increases that risk by 8.33 per cent, little more than half as much. We can make the effect of number of children a little easier to see by setting aside the level of these numbers, their mean, which is also the grand mean of the cell entries of the original table, giving us column effects rather than column means:

$$\bar{\bar{Y}} = \text{grand mean} = \text{mean of all the } Y \text{ cell entries}$$
$$= \text{mean of the column means}$$
$$= \text{mean of the row means}$$

Here $\bar{\bar{Y}} = \dfrac{17 + 32 + 43 + 51.33}{4} = 35.83$

For the first column:

column mean − grand mean = $17 - 35.83 = -18.83$

Thus, families with no children were nearly 19 per cent less likely than average to live in poverty. The rest of the column means and column effects, the grand mean $\bar{\bar{Y}}$ and the first set of residuals (each observation − column mean) are to be found in Table 15.2.

Now what might be going on with these residuals? The first thing to look for is the possible effect of the other variable: the row variable in this case. (We could have started with the rows and then gone to columns; the final result would be the same when using means.) Once again, to see the effect of the row

Table 15.2 Percentage of families below the poverty line: column means removed

Number of earners	Number of Children			
	0	1–2	3–4	5+
0	16	38	46	36.67
1	−3	−12	−15	−10.33
2+	−13	−26	−31	−26.33
Column mean	17	32	43	51.33
Column effect	−18.83	−3.83	7.17	15.5 $Y = 35.83$

variable we find the row means. We could do this just as we did for the columns: go back to Table 15.1, find row means and subtract the grand mean. But we get exactly the same answer a little more quickly if we just find the row effects, or the means of the residuals in Table 15.2; then we don't have to bother removing the grand mean, which we took out in the previous step when we removed column means. So, for example, we find the row effect for 'no earners' by finding

$$\frac{16 + 38 + 46 + 36.67}{4} = 34.17$$

which tells us that the 'no earner' families ran a much higher risk of poverty than the other families. If we follow the somewhat longer route of returning to Table 15.1, we find the row mean

$$\frac{33 + 70 + 89 + 88}{4} = 70$$

and then we subtract the grand mean to get the row effect: $70 - 35.83 = 34.17$, the same result. That's one big reason why using means is so handy computationally: you can get the same result in several different ways. Table 15.3 gives the row effects, as well as the column effects we found earlier.

Table 15.3 Full means analysis

Number of earners	Number of Children				Effect
	0	1–2	3–4	5+	
0	−18.17	3.83	11.83	2.5	34.17
1	7.08	−1.92	−4.92	−.25	−10.08
2+	11.08	−1.92	−6.92	−2.25	−24.08
Effect	−18.83	−3.83	7.17	15.5	35.83 = Y

What is the effect of the row variable 'number of earners'? Not surprisingly, it is very large – families with no earners are more than 34 per cent more likely than average to live in poverty, while families with two or more earners are more than 24 per cent less likely than average to be in that position. This means that the variable 'number of earners' makes a total difference of more than 58 per cent $(34.17 - (-24.08))$. And most of that difference is between 'no earners' and 'one earner' (over 44 per cent). That families with no earners are highly likely to live in poverty should not surprise us. But why would the second (or third!) earner make so much less of a difference? Given that where there are two or more earners in a family, one of them is likely to be a woman, and given further that women are generally paid only two-thirds of what men are paid, the marginal contribution of the second earner may well be modest. So while both the row and column variables are important in predicting risk of poverty, the row variable 'number of earners' seems to be the stronger predictor (it makes more of a difference, as evidenced by the range of effects).

Naturally we go on to find the residuals. Again it saves time to go to Table 15.2, not Table 15.1:

Final residual
= Y − column mean − row effect
= $Y - \bar{\bar{Y}}$ − column effect − row effect

The first formula is faster at this stage than the second and is of course the same thing. For example, consider families with no earners and no children. From Table 15.2 we find that the residual from the grand mean and column effect is 16, the row effect is 34.17, so the final residual is $16 - 34.17 = -18.17$, which is entered in Table 15.3 in the appropriate cell.

Please note that Table 15.3, the full means analysis with $\bar{\bar{Y}}$ and column and row effects removed, is the same thing as the table we started with, Table 15.1. We have broken the original numbers down into their components or elements but we have not changed them. The elements are the pieces that make up our overall fit:

$\bar{\bar{Y}}$ = overall size of the cell entries
Column effect = the effect on Y of being in one column rather than another; the column means minus the grand mean
Row effect = the effect on Y of being in one row rather than another; the row means minus the grand mean

as well as residuals from the fit:

Residual = whatever is left over after fitting the above; the observed values in the cells minus grand mean, column effect and row effect.

In Table 15.3 these various elements making up Y are separated and clearly displayed. $\bar{\bar{Y}}$ goes in the lower right corner; effects go in the margins of the table (means can be put there too, largely for the benefit of those who like means better than effects); and the residuals go in the cells. At a glance we can see what the effects of the row and column variables are, and whether the row or the column variable appears to be stronger. If we put the elements together again, we get right back to our original table. For example, the upper right cell has a residual of 2.5, a row effect of 34.17, a column effect of 15.5, and the grand mean is 35.83. Putting all these components together,

$$2.5 + 34.17 + 15.5 + 35.83 = 88$$

What We Have Done So Far

We have outlined a very simple procedure that lets us look at the effects of two categorical X variables on a numeric Y variable. In doing an elementary analysis, you usually do all the arithmetic first and then discuss. The arithmetic is easy: start with one of the Xs, find and remove its means; find the grand mean and then remove it from the first X's means to get effects; then find and remove the effects of the second X variable. This is just addition and subtraction and very fast to do. Sometimes people get a little mixed up at first in removing effects: they forget when to add and when to subtract. You may find it helpful to remind yourself that you want to fit some aspect of the data, say a row effect; when you have this fit, you move it *out* of the main body of the table and *into* the margins of the table where it can be clearly seen. So if a row effect is -0.1, you put -0.1 in the margin and subtract -0.1 from the entries in that row (subtracting -0.1 is the same as adding 0.1 to all the entries).

Because you are working with means, there are lots of arithmetic checks you can make. The grand mean should be the mean of the row means and the mean of the column means. The row and column effects should add up to zero. The residuals in any row or column of the final table should add up to zero. Of course, all these 'shoulds' are true within rounding error.

The interpretation of row and column effects is pretty much the same as interpreting batch levels in the old days when we only had one X. So far, the only new wrinkle we have seen is that the strength of effects of the two Xs can be roughly compared: the stronger X is the one with effects of wider range. We will see a real wrinkle in the next chapter, where we see how to work with combinations of the two X variables as well as looking at their effects separately as we do here.

Beyond the Basic Fit: Using the Residuals

We have a fit:

$$Y = \bar{\bar{Y}} + \text{column effect} + \text{row effect}$$

Naturally, we want to know how good a fit this is. As always with a numeric Y, we compare the midspread of the residuals from the fit to the midspread of the original Y. In an elementary analysis, the original Y values come from the cells of a table like Table 15.1 and the residuals from the cells of a table like Table 15.3. In our example,

$$\frac{dq\ Y'}{dq\ Y} = \frac{10.52}{50.25} = 0.21$$

which suggests that the fit does a good job of explaining Y. A careful look at Table 15.3 shows that the residuals are generally small compared to the effects, giving a similar impression.

Well, that's all the more reason to look hard at the residuals, a good idea in any case. In numerical form, as in Table 15.3, the residuals can be rather hard to see because there is too much detail; the larger the table, the harder it can be to see patterns in the residuals. To make things more visual we make a 'plot' of the residuals by replacing the numbers with symbols. Table 15.4 shows how we would define these symbols, using the poverty example.

The plotted residuals are given in Table 15.5, which is called a coded table. We can see at a glance that all the residuals beyond the midbox are in the first

Table 15.4   Symbols from a stem and leaf

lower far outlier	M		
lower outlier	=	−1	8
lower adjacent	−	−1	
q_L, q_U, or in	.	−0	6
between	.	−0	42110
	.	0	23
upper adjacent	+	0	7
	+	1	11
upper outlier	#		
upper far outlier	P		

$$q_L = -4.25$$
$$q_U = 6.27$$
outliers: −18

Table 15.5   Coded table of residuals from means analysis

Earners	Children			
	0	*1–2*	*3–4*	*5+*
0	=	.	+	.
1	+	.	−	.
2+	+	.	−	.

and third columns. The no-earner/no-children cell is far lower than the additive model predicts; in fact, it is an outlier. Interestingly, the no-earner/3–4 children cell is much higher than the model predicts, the largest positive residuals in the table. It makes some intuitive sense that the 'none–none' cell should be different because it is likely to include different sorts of people from the rest of the table (retired elderly, for example), but what is so magical about three or four children? Let's hold off thinking too hard about this until after the next section, where we introduce resistant analysis of two-way tables.

Getting a Resistant Analysis: Median Polish

So far, so good: now we have an easy and sensible approach to pulling apart the two-way table. But what about this business of using means? This is hardly the best thing for exploratory work! Our row and column effects will lack resistance if they are based on mean levels of row and column values after the grand mean Y is gone. And our residuals will tend to be rather bland (remember, if there is an unusual case then it will affect the mean strongly and the oddball case will not look as odd as it would if a more resistant level were used). Furthermore, because the residuals in each row and column must sum to zero, one extreme observation, like the 'none–none' cell, will artifactually create other large residuals in that row and column. Thus, we can't tell which of the other coded residuals are noteworthy and which are artifactual. More generally, use of the mean has a flattening effect on residuals, which makes residuals less helpful for generating further insights.

Let's try using medians instead of means. The basic idea is the same, breaking Y up into systematic components, but the components will be resistant levels instead of means. This work can be done by hand, but it is best avoided where possible, especially for larger tables. It is a lot more work – the means analysis is essentially a two-step procedure (remove column effects and row effects) while the median polish may require several iterations to get a solution. Checking the means analysis is easy: row effects and column effects must sum to zero, and so must the residuals in each row and column, so spotting

Table 15.6 Median polish of poverty data

Earners	Number of Children				Effect
	0	1–2	3–4	5+	
0	−30.000	0.500	12.000	−0.500	49.0
1	0.000	−0.500	0.000	1.500	0.0
2+	4.500	0.000	−1.500	0.000	−14.5
Effect	−10.25	−3.75	3.75	15.25	24.25

errors is easy. But a median analysis doesn't have these built-in checks – it is easy to make errors and hard to find them. Fortunately, many statistical packages do a median polish quickly and easily. These provide not only the full table consisting of grand level, row and column effects and residuals, but also a coded table and other useful things that we will want for the next chapter. In Table 15.6 we provide a median polish of the poverty data.

With median analysis, as with means analysis, we have broken Y up into elements, which can be added up to give us the original Y again. The difference is that the components of the fit are resistant components after a median polish has been done. What kind of difference is this?

Means Analysis versus Median Polish

Now we have two versions of the data in Table 15.1: we have a means analysis in Table 15.3 and a median analysis in Table 15.6. How do they compare? We expected to see differences in the residuals especially, with the residuals from medians being more clear-cut. The two sets of residuals are compared in Table 15.7; clearly there is a great difference of the kind expected.

In the median analysis, ten of the residuals are on the lower zero stems (with seven of them at zero) and the remaining two are substantially separated from this clump. In the means analysis, only one residual is zero, only one is separated, and the rest are generally indistinct. These differences are summarized reasonably well by the dq ratios; for the means analysis, this is 0.21, quite good. For the medians analysis, it is 0.03, indicating a super fit.

What about the patterns of effects and residuals in the two approaches? Are we getting much the same story from the two analyses? It is usually best to

Table 15.7   Residuals from means versus medians

Y', means analysis		Y', median polish
	−3	0
	−2	
	−2	
8	−1	
	−1	
6	−0	
42110	−0	10000
32	0	00014
7	0	
11	1	2
$q_L = -4.25$		$q_L = -0.50$
$q_U = 6.27$		$q_U = 1.25$

Table 15.8   Coded table of median polish residuals

	0	1–2	3–4	5
0	M	.	P	.
1	.	.	.	+
2+	#	.	–	.

analyse these tables 'from the outside in', looking first at the fit, Tables 15.3 and 15.6, and then at the residuals, Tables 15.5 and 15.8. The fit sums up the basic impact of the X variables through row and column effects (the overall level is generally not very interesting).

The broad messages of the effects from the two analyses are similar – the risk of poverty *increases* with greater numbers of children, and *declines* with greater numbers of earners. Some of the finer-grained comparisons are also pretty comparable. For both analyses, going from no earners to one makes an enormous difference: a decrease in risk of 44.25 per cent in the means analysis and 49 per cent when we use medians. Adding one or more additional earners only decreases the risk by about 14 per cent using means or medians. Looking at column effects, the messages are a bit more different. The range of the column effects in the median polish is quite a bit lower than it is in the means analysis, with a range of 25.5 per cent compared to 34.33 per cent in the means analysis, suggesting a lower marginal cost for additional children. Furthermore, we observed for the means analysis that childless families ran a *much* lower risk of poverty than those with children, the risk increasing by 15 per cent $(-18.83 - (-3.83))$ going from the 'none' column to the 'one-or-two' column. This is the largest difference between adjacent columns, with the inter-column difference declining with additional children. The median analysis, in contrast, suggests that going from no children to one or two still increases the risk of poverty, but by only 6.5 per cent. Moreover, the risk *increases* with additional children (7.5 and 11.5 per cent from column two to three, and three to four, respectively). If we look back at the original table with this in mind, the median results look truer to the data, and make rather more sense.

Finally, consider the residuals. Generally, residuals from a median analysis will have nicer properties than those from means. The small residuals are smaller while the large ones will be larger – more different from the rest, where those from the means analysis are flatter. This is especially marked in this data set. Moving now to a more detailed examination of the residuals, there are several interesting things to be seen.

At first glance the residuals from the means analysis look simpler with the first and third columns containing nothing but coded residuals. But part of this simplicity is really an artifact – the very large negative residual in the zero–zero cell has 'forced' large positive residuals in the first column and first row – the residuals have to add to zero, after all. The coded residuals from the median polish are found in the first and third columns (plus one small adjacent in column four). But these residuals focus our attention very sharply on the 'none–none' cell and also the 'none–three to four' cell. The 'none–none' cell is of special interest because, as we suggested earlier, these families appear to be a very different kind of poor from the rest: inadequately pensioned retirees, jobless young, the sick and injured, etc. The large *negative* residual suggests that this is a good category to be in ('good' here meaning low risk) but the risk may appear to be low because the two-way analysis compares them to unemployed single parents who are likely to make up much of the rest of the first row. The other outlier in the first row is more difficult to understand. What is so special about three or four children, compared to more or fewer children? Perhaps there are special welfare provisions that come into force when an earnerless family has a fifth child. More likely, perhaps there are few cases in the sample of no earner–many children families and what we are seeing is just small-sample fluctuation. Clearly, further research is called for.

The final outlier in this table is the two-earner/no-children cell. This is the smallest cell in the original table – how can it generate one of the largest positive residuals? Look at the fitted value for this cell. When we add the common value, the row effect and the column effect, the sum is negative! As a result, we are guaranteed to get a positive residual. Here is another instance of the linear model making a prediction that, logically, is impossible but makes perfect sense in the context of the model. But looking past this oddity, this cell does raise an interesting question: why would we find any families with several earners and no children living in poverty? Who are these people? Seasonal workers? People operating in a barter economy rather than a cash economy? Here again, we need more research. We have been seeing one of the strengths of the median polish in action. The residuals obtained can be so clear that they focus our attention on only a few genuinely unusual cases that we can look hard at.

By the way, it is very common for students who are new to this technique to get mixed up when discussing the residuals and to confuse them with the main effects, or even the original table entries. They represent differences between the original values and predictions based on the main effects.

Fertility in Ireland: a More Complex Table

Let's try going through a larger, more complex example in detail. The data are adapted from Kennedy (1973: in particular see Table 6, page 95). The original sources are Irish census reports.

In Table 15.9 Y is the average number of children born alive per woman aged 25–29 at marriage and married for 20–24 years (thus the women have had roughly equal time in which to have children). The row variable is the status of the husband's occupation. The column variable is the most complex, being a combination of religion and part of Ireland: Catholics in Northern Ireland and in the Republic of Ireland, non-Catholics in the North and in the Republic. At first, this might seem like jamming two variables together; but we will soon see that the combination of place and religion may well be thought of as a variable in its own right.

The median polish is given in Table 15.10 and the coded table in Table 15.11. We will discuss row effects, then column effects, and then residuals from the fit.

Table 15.9 Average number of children

Occupational status of husband	Catholics NI	Catholics RI	Non-Catholics NI	Non-Catholics RI
Upper	4.02	3.80	2.13	2.19
Middle	4.14	3.91	2.20	2.44
Lower	4.82	4.33	2.65	2.81
Agriculture	5.25	4.57	3.37	3.08

Source: Kennedy (1973: 95).

Table 15.10 Median polish of Irish fertility data

	Catholics NI	Catholics RI	Non-Catholics NI	Non-Catholics RI	Effect
Upper	−0.11	0.03	0.02	−0.02	−0.35
Middle	−0.11	0.02	−0.02	0.11	−0.23
Lower	0.11	−0.02	−0.04	0.02	0.23
Agriculture	0.12	−0.20	0.27	−0.12	0.65
Effect	1.14	0.78	−0.88	−0.78	Common = 3.34

Table 15.11 Coded table for median analysis

	Catholics NI	Catholics RI	Non-Catholics NI	Non-Catholics RI	Row effects
Upper	−	.	.	.	−0.35
Middle	−	.	.	+	−0.23
Lower	+	.	.	.	0.23
Agriculture	+	−	+	−	0.65
Column effects	1.14	0.78	−0.88	−0.78	−3.34

Effects of class (row effects)

The picture is a pleasantly simple one: the higher the class the fewer the children. Those higher in the class structure are generally more educated, and hence may be more exposed to modern values stressing the importance of birth control. Perhaps more important is access to birth control: successful birth control requires some knowledge, money and medical supplies. These sources are more available to the wealthier (especially in the Republic of Ireland, where birth control, despite recent modifications to the law, is not fully legal at the time of writing). Further, some people may actively desire and try to get large families. Perhaps this is why the agricultural row effects are so high: children can be very useful as cheap labour around a farm. Religious prohibitions on some birth control techniques may be most effective for farm people too, since people in rural areas tend to be more regular in performance of religious obligations.

Effects of place and religion (column effects)

The order of column effects is C/NI, C/RI, NC/RI, NC/NI. The columns are complex, really, being combinations of place and religion, so let's break interpretation up into easy stages.

Religion alone   Here we compare the first two columns (Catholics) to the second two (non-Catholics) and find that the Catholics have more children. This is no surprise: we have already alluded to Catholic prohibitions on many forms of birth control. The sheer size of the difference between Catholics and non-Catholics is worth noting. Even the gap between the lower Catholic effect and the higher non-Catholic effect (0.78 versus -0.78 or a difference of 1.56) is far larger than the gap between the largest and smallest row effects (-0.35 versus 0.65 or a difference of 1.0). Clearly religion makes much more difference to child-bearing than class does in Ireland. This suggests that the Catholics, at least, may be quite religiously observant. Is it possible that ties based on religion are stronger and better organized than those based on class?

Place alone   Here we compare the first and third columns (Northern Ireland) to the second and fourth (Republic of Ireland). Well, it is not just a simple matter of level difference, of one place having a higher number of children than the other: NI effects are 1.14 and -0.88, RI effects are 0.78 and -0.78. There is no great level difference here, but there is a *spread* difference: the two NI values are more different from each other than the two RI values are. In other words, religion appears to make more of a difference in Northern Ireland. This brings us to the third step of column interpretation of these data.

Place and religion together   Religion makes more difference in Northern Ireland. Why? Well, as we all know, tension between Catholics and Protestants in Northern Ireland has been great for many years. Probably the Catholics and non-Catholics there live much more separated lives than those in the Republic, which could intensify within-group similarity and between-group differences. Hostility may even lead some Catholics in the North to prefer larger families as a way to capture the North by getting a majority of the votes (at least, this policy has been advocated by some people). There may also be a status effect here as well, since the Catholics of the North are poorer than the Protestants and less powerful and so on. Some of the effects of class were removed by the row effects, but the rows only deal with one aspect of class and there may be a bit left over.

Religion matters more in the North. Does place matter more for one religion than for the other? Clearly so. Being in Northern Ireland rather than the Republic makes a big difference for Catholics (1.14 versus 0.78, or a difference of 0.36) but not such a big difference for non-Catholics (-0.88 versus -0.78, or a difference of -0.10). This suggests that the social situations of Catholics in the two places differ more. All of the factors in child-bearing so far suggested could be relevant here. Further ideas could be developed. For example, the NC/RI and C/NI groups are both minorities, and both have relatively high numbers of children compared to majorities of the same religion. Could this be some sort of response to powerlessness?

Residuals (plotted cell entries)   What a nice simple picture! We see that the basic additive model (observation = overall level + row effect + column effect) is fine except for one row and one column where it is very poor. The agricultural row is poorly fitted (even worse than it looks, perhaps, since one residual was nearly an outlier). The first column is poorly fitted as well, though not as poorly as the bottom row. What might be happening?

In general, it is not surprising that the agricultural row stands out; rural life is quite different from urban so we would expect rural people to differ in many ways from city dwellers. Getting down to specifics, we see that the number of children is relatively high in Northern Ireland and relatively low in the Republic (relative to the additive fit, that is). Perhaps farming is more modernized in the Republic so that children are less useful for labour; or perhaps those in agricultural work in the Republic are less well off so that children can't be supported as well.

For the Catholics of Northern Ireland column residuals we again have a nice simple pattern, with the wealthier Catholics having fewer children and the poorer having more than the additive model predicts. This is an accentuated version of the overall status effects summarized in the row effects. Why does status make more difference for Catholics in Northern Ireland than for other groups? Perhaps lower status C/NI people are doubly disadvantaged (they are poor as well as being underdogs in a very tense conflict) so they have especially poor access to birth control information and devices.

The Fit Overall

We seem to have done a pretty good job of squeezing the juice out of these numbers. The row and column effects were strong (very large compared to the residuals) and suggested several reasonable interpretations. We have very little unexplained material left.

We can evaluate the additive fit in the usual way:

$$\frac{dq\ Y'}{dq\ Y} = \frac{0.18}{1.79} = 0.10$$

The ratio indicates that the fit works very well here. Class, place, and religion have strong effects on the number of children for Irish women. We can suggest some reasons for the few deviations from these effects.

Exploratory and Confirmatory

The means version of elementary analysis is directly related to two-way analysis of variance, which is coming up soon. Means analysis is very useful indeed in figuring out what the two-way anova is telling you. On the other hand, we have just seen that the median polish of a means analysis may be essential for a clear, resistant interpretation. Both should be done and thought about.

The exploratory tools in this chapter and in Chapter 16 are very important for interpreting the two-way anova results, much as exploratory thinking was essential for interpreting one-way anova results. Most of the terms mean the same thing in either approach: 'grand means', 'row effect', 'residual', 'additive fit', etc., are all terms used in confirmatory work.

Using the Computer

The format for entering data is the same for both the means analysis and median polish. The data are entered in a single column, C1. Row and column identifiers are entered in C2 and C3 respectively. For the poverty data, this would look like:

```
DATA  ROW   COLUMN
C1    C2    C3
33    1     1
70    1     2
89    1     3
88    1     4
```

To look at the data in table form:

```
MTB> TABLE C2 C3;
SUBC> DATA C1.
```

To get residuals for a *means analysis*:

> MTB> TWOWAY C1 C2 C3 C4 C5

This is the command for two-way analysis of variance. All we will use here is C4, the residuals. Then:

> MTB> TABLE C2, C3;
> SUBC> DATA C4.

This sets your residuals into a table.

To obtain row and column means and fitted values you can either do the work by hand, or use the TWOWAY subcommands:

> SUBC> MEAN C2 C3;
> SUBC> ADDITIVE.

For a median polish:

> MTB> MPOL C1 C2 C3 C4;
> SUBC> EFFECTS COMMON K1 ROW EFFECTS C5 COL EFFECTS C6.

This tells MINITAB to:

(a) do a median polish on the *Y* values in C1
  ● rows are in C2, columns in C3,
  ● put residuals in C4;
(b) store the effects
  ● the common value, or overall median, is a constant and is stored in a special constant space labelled with a K,
  ● row effects will be found in column 5, listed from top row (row 1) to the last,
  ● column effects will be found in C6, from first to last.

The full median polish is now obtained by:

> MTB> TABLE C2 C3;
> SUBC> DATA C4.

This tables the residuals; C5 and C6 provide row and column effect respectively and grand level/common is in K1.

To get the coded table for either the means analysis or the median polish:

> MTB> CTABLE C4 C2 C3

HOMEWORK

1 Table 15.12 looks at life expectancy at birth by race and sex, and when born. These figures are taken from 'current life tables', or tables based on current

Table 15.12   Average life expectancy, continental USA

Race and sex	Year of birth				
	1929–31	1939–41	1949–51	1959–61	1971
White males	59.12	62.81	66.31	67.55	68.3
White females	62.67	67.29	72.03	74.19	75.6
Other males	47.55	52.26	58.91	61.48	61.2
Other females	49.51	55.56	62.70	66.47	69.3

Source: US Department of Health, Education and Welfare (1968, 1974).

death rates. For example, a while male born in 1971 is given a life expectancy of 68.3 years; that is the average length of life if death rates at all ages stay at the 1971 values. No doubt these death rates will not stay the same, so the figure 68.3 summarizes the experience of men of all ages who died in 1971 rather than predicting what a boy born in 1971 can expect over his lifetime. Do a median polish. What effect does the row variable have? Why? What effect does the column variable have? Why? Which variable seems to have the stronger effect? How well does the combined fit, overall level plus row effect plus column effect, account for Y? Do you see any striking patterns or oddities in the residuals? If so, what's going on?

2   Table 15.13 examines rates of still-birth in Scotland by year and social class (from I = high to V = low). Median polish these data and discuss the output using the guidelines in example 1.

Table 15.13   Stillbirths by year and social class

Year	Class				
	I	II	III	IV	V
1970	128	104	137	158	167
1971	83	109	128	133	181
1972	77	106	129	153	178
1973	74	85	112	135	162
1974	86	93	115	135	172
1975	78	77	112	129	144
1976	71	90	91	119	95

Source: Registrar General of Scotland (1978).

16
Interaction Effects in Elementary Analyses

In Chapter 15 we learned a simple and effective way of analysing two-way tables, elementary analysis, which breaks each observation up into the sum of the overall level, row effect, column effect and residual. This is a very useful fit when it works, because it is easy to work with numerically and easy to interpret. But sometimes the simple additive fit works poorly. This can indicate that the Xs are poor predictors of Y. But it can also result from good predictors that don't work together in a purely additive way. If so, we need a new approach. First, we'll return to the Irish fertility example to illustrate the general difference between the simple additive fit of Chapter 15 and the slightly more complex fit used here. Then we will turn back to the Vancouver voting data (Table R3.1, p. 263) to develop a technique for handling this complication.

Additive Fits and Interaction Effects

We now know how to make an additive fit: we isolate the effect of each of the independent variables on the dependent variable. Their sum is the fit, and the difference between an observation and this fit is, of course, the residual. Finding these effects is easy in a means analysis, and the computer makes a median polish easy as well. When we look at, for example, the non-Catholic/ Northern Ireland effect (Table 15.9), status effects don't enter into the value we find; they are 'averaged out' of the column values, appearing separately as row effects. To see the effect of the two variables combined we just add their separate effects together: row effect + column effect. The column effect stays the same whatever row we are working on, and vice versa; for example, we add in −0.88 for NC/NI whether we are finding the fit for high status husbands or agricultural husbands or whatever. Now this is fine as long as the effect of being non-Catholic in Northern Ireland is the same for all status groups. Is it? Pretty much so, as we can see from the residuals for this column, which are small on the whole. The additive fit works pretty well there.

It does not work as well in some other parts of the table, however. For example, we saw that the C/NI column had comparatively extreme residuals:

negative residuals for higher status groups and positive residuals for lower status groups. There is something systematic and interesting going on that the additive fit is missing. It is not missing the overall effect of C/NI, which is accurately summed up in the column effect. Nor is it missing the overall effects of the various statuses found in the row effects. The problem is that these overall effects don't quite describe the Catholics in Northern Ireland. If they are of higher status, they have somewhat fewer children than row effect + column effect predicts; if they are of low status, they have somewhat more children than the additive fit suggests. To predict these figures accurately we really need to make one fit for higher status C/NI and another for lower status C/NI: a different fit for different combinations of the two independent variables.

This is the kind of thing meant by interaction. There are lots of ways to define interaction, with all the versions meaning much the same thing. Interaction effects are present to the extent that the effect of one variable depends on the value of another. In the fertility example, the effect of C/NI depended in part on what status level was involved. Or, to put the same thing another way, the effects of status weren't exactly the same for Catholics in Northern Ireland as they were for the other groups: status made a bit more difference for C/NI than for C/RI, NC/NI or NC/RI. There was also a possibly interesting interaction effect in the 'agricultural' row, where agricultural women had more children in the North, and fewer in the Republic, than the additive model indicated.

You can see that being able to deal with interaction effects is important. It is somewhat more difficult than straightforward elementary analysis, but still easy enough. The ability to recognize and handle some common kinds of interaction effects is an important skill for the data analyst. Interactions add a layer of complexity to two-way analysis, at least conceptually, but they are easy enough technically. In this chapter we will learn how to look for, fit and interpret one type of interaction, the 'opposite-corner pattern'. This pattern is quite common, is easy to recognize, is generally interpretable and can be of substantial theoretical interest.

Vancouver Left-Wing Voting

The Vancouver vote data we look at here are patterns of left-wing voting in five municipal elections (see Table 16.1, adapted from Table R3.1). The column variable is election year, from earlier to later; the row variable is area, from lower to higher income as reported from the 1961 census. These 'areas' were formed by averaging sets of districts together, since 24 districts are more than we could handle comfortably. For both the East and West sides, districts were classified as high, medium or low as regards income, trying to follow natural breaking points. Then the mean percentage left-wing vote for districts in an area was found and entered in Table 16.1. (There are many other ways we

Table 16.1   Left-wing vote by income and time

Area, low to high income	Election year					mean income ($)	Range ($)
	1958	1960	1962	1964	1966		
East low	33	28	17	32	26	3163	2751–3422
West low	22	19	10	22	19	3713	3589–3785
East medium	34	29	14	32	27	4017	3864–4186
West medium	21	17	9	20	18	4377	4233–4640
East high	31	26	11	28	24	4425	4299–4594
West high	14	11	7	15	13	6684	5701–8477

Table 16.2   Left-wing vote: median polish

	1958	1960	1962	1964	1966	Effects
East low	0.75	0.25	−0.75	1.50	−1.00	5.5
West low	−1.75	−0.25	0.75	0.00	0.50	−3.0
East medium	0.75	0.25	−4.75	0.50	−1.00	6.5
West medium	−0.75	−0.25	1.75	0.00	1.50	−5.0
East high	1.25	0.75	−4.25	0.00	−0.50	3.0
West high	−2.75	−1.25	4.75	0.00	1.50	−10.0
Effects	7.50	0.00	−10.00	2.75	−0.75	22.25

could have constructed districts, and measures for them, of course.) The median polish of the data is in Table 16.2.

First we look at the additive fit: the row effects, or the overall impact of the row variable (area), and the column effects, or the overall impact of the column variable (year). From the column effects we see that the percentage left-wing vote varied quite a bit from election to election, with 1962 being something of a disaster for the left (see Ewing, 1972, for details). An analysis of the column effects will not be attempted since this would require too much specific information (on candidates and issues, for example).

The row effects show an eye-catching pattern that we can discuss: every East district effect is positive and every West district effect is negative. That is, the East side is more left-wing, even for those districts with incomes close to those of some West districts. If we look closely we can also see that, for East districts alone or West districts alone, higher income generally goes with lower left-wing vote. Thus two kinds of things are going on here. First, income is inversely related to left-wing voting as one would expect (left-wing policies being more oriented to the interests of those with lower incomes). Thus the less wealthy East side is more left-wing. Secondly, there is an East–West difference

above and beyond wealth; perhaps campaign strategies or community structures are different in the two districts.

Overall, the additive fit makes a lot of sense: there are swings from
election to election (column effects) and both low income and East side
placement go with higher left-wing vote (row effects). How well does this
additive fit do? The dq of the original Y values in Table 16.1 is 14, and the dq of
$Y' = Y -$ (common + row effect + column effect) (see Table 16.2) is 1.562,
giving an excellent dq ratio of 0.11.

Even when the additive fit is good, it is worthwhile to look for possible
interaction patterns that may make the fit even better and add to the
understanding of how the variables are related. To look for interaction, we
look for meaningful patterns in the residuals, which are plotted in Table 16.3 to
make looking easier. There are some striking individual residuals, two lower
outliers and one upper, and some pretty substantial adjacents, but it is hard to
see any simple patterns. Well, a lot depends on how the data are arranged. In
Table 16.3 the rows and columns are arranged in a 'natural' ordering: columns
by time, areas by income. So if interaction effects were linked to time or income
we would be able to see them; but if they are linked to something else, this sort
of ordering probably makes them harder to see. Obviously we need to try
different row and column arrangements making some other kind of sense;
another arrangement may reveal a simple pattern in the residuals that is hidden
in Table 16.3.

Let's try re-ordering the rows. We know income *per se* does not fully
explain area effects: being on the East or West side matters a lot too. Instead of
ordering rows by income, let's try ordering them by row effects, from the most
left-wing area to the least left-wing area. A little quick recopying gives us Table
16.4. This new order of rows happens to make a lot of sense: now it is clearer
than ever both that the East is more left-wing and that rising income mostly
goes with declining left-wing vote. And look what happens to the residuals!
They are much simpler: the East and West residuals are almost exact opposites.

Re-ordering the rows by effect size seems to be helping, so let's try it on
columns as well. We arrange the columns of Table 16.4 and get Table 16.5,

Table 16.3 Residuals plotted, 'natural order'

	1958	1960	1962	1964	1966	Effect
East low	.	.	.	+	−	5.5
West low	−	.	.	.	.	−3.0
East medium	.	.	=	.	−	6.5
West medium	.	.	+	.	+	−5.0
East high	+	.	=	.	.	3.0
West high	−	−	#	.	+	−10.0
Row effect	4.50	0.0	−10.00	2.75	−0.75	22.25

Table 16.4   Re-ordering Table 16.3 by row effect size

	1958	1960	1962	1964	1966	Effect
West high	−	−	#	.	+	−10.00
West medium	.	.	+	.	+	−5.00
West low	−	.	.	.	.	−3.00
East high	+	.	=	.	.	3.00
East low	.	.	.	+	−	5.50
East medium	.	.	=	.	−	6.50
Effect	4.50	0.0	−10.00	2.75	−0.75	22.25

Table 16.5   Effect order version of Table 16.3

	1962	1966	1960	1964	1958	Effect
West high	#	+	−	.	−	−10.00
West medium	+	+	.	.	.	−5.00
West low	.	.	.	.	−	−3.00
East high	=	.	.	.	+	3.00
East low	.	−	.	+	.	5.50
East medium	=	−	.	.	.	−6.50
Effect	−10.00	−0.75	0.0	2.75	4.50	22.25

going from the election lowest in percentage left-wing vote (1962) to the highest (1958). Now the pattern is very simple indeed: we tend to have negative residuals in the upper right and lower left and positive residuals in the other two quadrants. In a simplified form to help underline the pattern, the table blocked out schematically looks something like this:

Low left area	+	−
High left area	−	+
	Low left	High left
	election	election

We seem to have found a pattern, all right. What does it mean? First we just want to get the pattern into words to help in thinking about it. In an election with a high left-wing vote, the highly left-wing areas have positive residuals and the areas with a low left-wing vote have negative residuals; that is, the high left-wing areas are more left-wing and the low left-wing areas are even less left-wing than the additive model predicts. The differences between areas are heightened. On the other hand, when an election shows a relatively low vote for the left then the high left areas are voting left less and the low left areas are voting left more than the model predicts, which means they are more alike than the additive model would suggest. You might find it helpful to connect this verbalization with the raw data in Table 16.1. In the left's worst year, 1962, the difference between the most and least left-wing area is 10 per cent (17 − 7); in the left's best year, 1958, the difference between the most and least left area is 20 per cent (34 − 14). The greater the support for the left, the more different the areas are in left-wing vote. This is clearly an interactive effect not an additive one, since it sums up the way one independent variable (area) has different effects given different values of another dependent variable (election).

Why might this pattern happen? Perhaps it stems from the fact that percentage left-wing vote is rather low in Vancouver in this time period, only about 22 per cent overall, so most of the time few people expect the left-wing candidates to be very important. But when there is a swing leftward, as in 1958, the possibility of a left-wing victory is taken more seriously and both left and right voters respond more vigorously, the former voting left in the hopes of a victory, the latter voting right in order to prevent such a victory, and the centre losing ground. In elections where the left does poorly, on the other hand, people in left-wing areas may stay home or vote for the least unappealing right-wing or centrist candidate with a chance to win; while those in right-wing areas may venture to vote for left-wing candidates they like as individuals, knowing they will not be part of a left majority. Thus the differences between left and right get muted.

So we have found a pattern, put it into words and generated a possible explanation for it. How about fitting it? The general pattern is that the residuals are (mostly) positive when the effects for row and column have the same sign

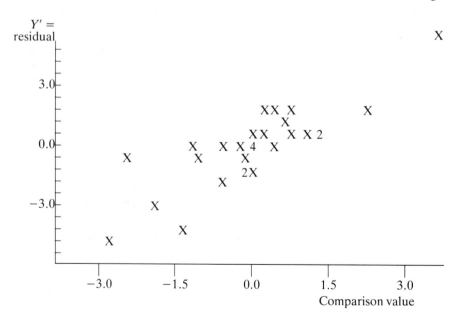

Figure 16.1   Plot of interaction fit

and negative when one effect is positive and the other negative. In short, we can predict the signs of the residuals fairly well by multiplying the signs of the relevant rows and columns. This suggests that the residuals are multiplicatively related to their associated effects – that we can predict the size as well as the sign of each residual by multiplying its row effect by its column effect. This can be done by hand. It involves multiplying each row effect by each column effect, keeping the resulting product linked to the appropriate residual. Then a resistant line can be used to fit the table of products to the table of residuals. This is not a horrible task if the table is small, but for larger tables it is a lot of work and errors are easy to make. Fortunately, most computer packages that do a median analysis also provide *comparison values*. With one useful exception, comparison values are just row effect × column effect, or *RC*. The exception is that all of the products are divided by the common value from the median polish. This makes absolutely no difference when it comes to fitting the residuals because it just involves dividing everything by a constant, so the plots and quality of fit are exactly the same. But later in the chapter, when we consider transformation as a way of treating interactions, we will find that there is a powerful advantage to defining comparison values in this way.

The plot of the residuals by comparison values is in Figure 16.1. As you can see, there isn't much slope but the fit is fairly tight – a cucumber, so it should do a reasonable job of accounting for the spread of the residuals. Fitting a resistant line, we get:

$$Y' = 0.95 \, (\text{comp}) - 0.25$$

How much has this multiplicative fit added to what the two-way analysis had told us about Vancouver voting? Here again, this amounts to asking how big the residuals are, but now the residuals come from two analytic steps (a median polish and a Y by X analysis of the residuals) rather than one, and are symbolized Y''. As before, the dq-ratio is a useful guide to goodness of fit; the smaller Y'' is, compared to the initial residuals, Y', the more the addition of the multiplicative interaction term has helped. In this instance, $dq(Y'') = 1.21$, where $dq(Y') = 1.56$ and the ratio $dq(Y'')/dq(Y') = 0.78$. We conclude from this that the addition of a multiplicative interaction term to the basic additive fit has been an improvement, though not a big one – we have explained about a quarter of the spread of Y'. We can also ask how much of the original data remains unexplained after both the additive and interactive fits. This suggests looking at $dq(Y'')/dqY = 0.086$, which is very good.

Combining Additive Fits and Interaction Fits

We have just seen that we can find, explain and fit an interaction effect for the left-wing voting example. This effect can be added to the original additive model to get a more complete fit for Y. Thus we go from the basic additive fit,

$$Y = \text{common} + \text{row effect} + \text{column effect}$$

to the interaction fit:

Y = common + row effect + column effect + b(comp)

To evaluate the interaction fit against the simpler additive fit without interaction, we can look at two things. First is the overall strength of each one or

$$\frac{dq\,(Y')}{dqY}$$

for the basic additive fit, compared to

$$\frac{dq\,(Y'')}{dqY}$$

for the basic additive fit with interaction included. Second is how much the interaction fit explains of the residuals not explained by the basic fit, or

$$\frac{dq\,(Y'')}{dq\,(Y')}$$

Consider the first kind of comparison for our example: we get a dq ratio of 0.11 for the basic fit and a dq ratio of 0.086 for the basic fit plus interaction. The fit is very good with or without interaction and perhaps the interaction fit does not seem to make much difference. However, if we find

$$\frac{dq\,(Y'')}{dq\,(Y')} = 0.78$$

as above, we see that the interaction fit explains a fair amount of what the basic fit did not explain. The basic fit was very good, so the interaction fit was left little to work on; of that little we have explained nearly a quarter, which is not bad.

We conclude that the strongest influences on percentage left-wing vote in our table are year and area effects; there is a modest interaction effect as well. The interaction takes the form of a heightened difference between left and non-left areas in years with higher leftward trends, and a reduced difference in years when the left is weak.

Other Interaction Fits

The interaction fit just illustrated is often useful, but it is not the only kind of interaction fit; there are other fits for other interaction patterns. First, consider one very mild variation. Suppose the block of residuals looks like this:

	Column effect	
Row effect	Low	High
High	+	−
Low	−	+

Table 16.6   Residential segregation

City	Census year		
	1940	1950	1960
Jacksonville	94.3	94.9	96.9
Atlanta	87.4	91.5	93.6
Dallas	80.2	88.4	94.6

Source: Taeuber (1965).

Note: The segregation index ranges from 0 to 1, 0 if black and white people are evenly distributed over residential areas and 1 if all black people live in black neighbourhoods and all whites in white neighbourhoods.

Table 16.7   Median analysis of Table 16.6

	1940	1950	1960	Row effects
Jacksonville	3.5	0	−0.1	1.3
Atlanta	0	0	0	−2.1
Dallas	−4.1	0	4.1	−5.2
Column effects	−4.1	0	2.1	$Md_Y = 93.6$

At first glance, this looks like the left-wing voting example, but there's an important difference. In the earlier example, positive residuals came in cells where row and column effects had the same sign. Here the same sign effects give negative residuals, while the opposite sign effects give positive residuals.

Consider Table 16.6, which gives residential segregation indices for three southern US cities for three census years. Since this is a small example, we can easily do a median analysis by hand, as in Table 16.7. The row effects show some city-to-city difference in residential segregation, and the column effects show that segregation increased from 1940 to 1960 (this did not happen in all cities). The residuals show the sort of pattern sketched just above: the large positive residuals occur in cells with high row effect and low column effect or vice versa, while the one large negative residual occurs in a cell going with row and column effects that are both very low. The higher the rates are, the more alike they are. Probably we have a simple ceiling effect here, since the segregation index cannot be more than 100 and these values are very close to that. How can we fit this? Easily: use comparison values again, expecting to get a negative b instead of a positive one.

Sometimes interaction effects show up clearly, with rows and columns in some order other than effect order. For example, our voting data could have shown some strong time patterns in the residuals, although as it happens they didn't. In such a case one might want to handle interaction by using Y' as a dependent variable and time as the independent variable, e.g. $Y' = b \times$ (election year). Often we forget the importance of geography: physical location, natural barriers (mountains, rivers, etc.), and having allies or enemies for neighbours are all often important in analysing interaction effects, so plotting on a map may help. Sometimes a few rows or columns show a pattern of residuals related to time or income or some other variable; then you might fit the residuals for those rows or columns only, trying to explain why they depart from the additive fit and the rest of the table does not. (A strategy like this might help in the homework example in Chapter 15.)

So far we have talked about interaction fits that use basic Y by X methods to add on another layer of explanation:

$$Y' = b(RC)$$
$$\text{or} \quad Y' = b(\text{time})$$
$$\text{or} \quad Y' = b(\text{income}), \text{etc.}$$

Such strategies plus a little ingenuity will give useful results surprisingly often.

Another broadly useful strategy is – surprise – transformation. Earlier we described the percentage left-wing vote interaction in this way: the areas are more different in their percentage left-wing vote in election years with higher leftward swing. If you think about that for a moment, and/or look at the numbers, you'll see this is the same as saying: the columns with larger Y levels have larger Y spreads. Similarly rows with higher Y levels have larger Y spreads. We would like these spreads to be evened up, so that the column variable has the same sort of effect whatever the row and vice versa. And, as we have often seen, a covariation of level and spread can usually be removed with transformation.

How do we choose a useful transform? This is the great advantage of comparison values – when we fit a resistant line between Y' and the comparison values, the slope provides guidance here, in the same way the slope of log level/log spread did in Chapter 6. Here our slope was found to be 0.95, very

Table 16.8 Median analysis of logged data

	1958	1960	1962	1964	1966	Effect
East low	−0.003	0.004	0.072	0.003	−0.022	0.108
West low	−0.018	−0.004	0.003	0.000	0.002	−0.053
East medium	0.008	0.016	−0.015	0.000	−0.009	0.110
West medium	0.003	−0.011	−0.003	0.000	0.019	−0.094
East high	0.025	0.026	−0.062	0.000	−0.002	0.053
West high	−0.049	−0.076	0.013	0.000	0.003	−0.219
Effect	0.078	0.000	−2.85	0.059	−0.006	1.336

Table 16.9   Coded table of residuals from median analysis of logged data

	1958	1960	1962	1964	1966
East low	.	.	P	.	−
West low	−	.	.	.	.
East medium	+	+	−	.	.
West medium	.	−	.	.	+
East high	#	#	M	.	.
West high	M	M	+	.	.

$$\frac{dq Y'}{dq Y} = \frac{0.014}{0.301} = 0.05$$

close to 1.0, which suggests using logs. We transform (the original Y values, of course) and make a second median polish (Tables 16.8 and 16.9, Figure 16.2).

You can see that there is virtually no slope in this plot, that is, we have pretty well removed the interaction. Here we see how powerful a tool transformation can be for dealing with interaction. Not only do we have a simpler representation for our data – just row and column effects with no interaction term – but the simple additive fit for log (Y) gives us a much better

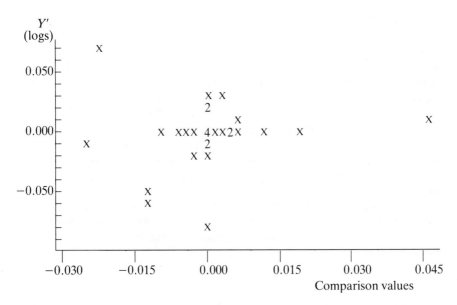

Figure 16.2   Plot of residuals versus comparison values for median analysis of logged data

dq ratio than the additive plus interaction fit for raw *Y*. In short, after logging *Y* we end up with data that are almost perfectly additive.

In this chapter, we have used insights gained from looking hard at interaction to make some interesting speculations about left-wing voting patterns in Vancouver. These speculations could turn out to be correct or incorrect. The point is that interesting ideas were generated: by looking hard at interaction, we came up with ideas we might well have missed otherwise. Once we have them, we can decide whether they look worth testing.

We did some critical thinking (if not formal hypothesis testing) for one of our interpretations with turn-out data. If it is true that a leftward swing makes left-wing voters hopeful and right-wing or centrist voters worried, surely it should make them more likely to vote; so in this case a higher percentage of left-wing votes in an election should go with higher turn-out. Does it? Just the opposite! The percentage left-wing vote is high when turn-out is low. This suggests a second interpretation: the number of people voting left is fairly steady (perhaps, again, a committed minority?); it is the number voting for the right or centre that varies. So a larger turn-out means a smaller percentage left-wing vote: the same numbers of left-wing votes, roughly, but increased numbers of non-left-wing votes. If this view is correct, the best the left can hope for is a deadly dull campaign, so that most of the opposing voters will stay home. That's quite a provocative speculation. And how about . . .? Well, enough's enough.

Recapitulation

In working with interaction effects, the first step is to see what they are. Begin with a means or median polish analysis to find a basic additive fit and residuals from it. Then look for patterns in the residuals. Patterns may emerge in a few special parts of the table, as in the Irish fertility data perhaps. Or there may be an overall pattern visible with rows or columns in effect order.

Once you have seen a pattern, the next step is to put it into words and then try to explain it. This is the hardest step, at least when you first try it, but with some practice you'll be able to come up with interpretations. We've whipped up several possibilities for the left-wing voting interaction to give you some ideas of the kinds of things you can come up with.

The interaction pattern should also be fitted numerically. The procedures we illustrated are best for interaction patterns that show an opposite corner effect. The effect ordering pattern should look like either of the following simplified forms:

Effect		
High	+	−
Low	−	+
Effect	Low	High

Effect
High   −   +
Low   +   −

Effect   Low   High

We can handle either of these by transforming the original data or making an interaction fit:

$$Y' = b(\text{comparison})$$

Suppose the data do not look so neat? Then you might try fitting Y' to some new variable, like time or income or geography. Finally, you might decide that the Y' values should not be further fitted in any way because these residuals are very small and unsystematic. Small unpatterned residuals may be nothing more than measurement error, so that fits based on them are meaningless (this is sometimes called 'overfitting'). However, most people stop too soon rather than too late in explaining residuals. It is usually a good idea to keep trying to reduce the spread of the residuals for as long as your resources permit; this is especially useful in exploratory work.

Using the Computer

There is only one new bit of computer output in this chapter: comparison values. The comparison value is defined as

$$\frac{(\text{row effect}) \times (\text{column effect})}{\text{common value}}$$

Comparison values can be obtained from MINITAB with a subcommand of MPOLISH

```
MTB> MPOLISH C1 C2 C3 RESIDS IN C4 FIT IN C5;
SUBC> EFFECTS COMMON IN K1, ROW EFF IN C6, COL EFF IN C7;
SUBC> COMPARISON IN C8.
```

Again you can find the dq ratio ingredients with DESCRIBE, and get both the raw and coded residuals in table form with TABLE and CTABLE just as described for means analysis and median polish in Chapter 15.

HOMEWORK

For your homework, choose either Table 16.10 or Table 16.11. Table 16.10 is adapted from Molotch and Lester's (1975) study of newspaper coverage of a large oil spill in Santa Barbara, California. By examining the most detailed

Table 16.10   Percentage of occurrences covered by selected newspapers

Newspaper and Region	Period ending			
	21 Feb 69 (1)	30 Jun 69 (2)	1 Dec 69 (3)	31 Dec 70 (4)
San Francisco Chronicle (California)	63.6	18.2	31.0	16.7
New York Times (East)	50.0	10.9	8.6	0.0
Washington Post (East)	36.3	14.6	1.8	3.4
Atlanta Constitution (South)	18.2	5.5	6.9	0.0
Boston Globe (East)	22.7	3.7	3.5	0.0
New Orleans Times Picayune (South)	9.1	7.3	1.8	0.0

Source: Molotch and Lester (1975); © University of Chicago.

coverage, that in the local paper, Molotch and Lester made a list of occurrences connected with the spill during four time periods. Then 19 other papers (of which we show only every third) were examined for the same four time periods; for each period, the percentage of occurrences reported in a given paper was found.

Table 16.11 examines the effects of education and secular trending on average income. For whichever data set you choose, try transforming as well as fitting comparison values to the residuals to see how well each copes with the interaction. Compare the two results.

Table 16.11   The relationship between income ($100) and education in four post-war years

Schooling	1946	1949	1956	1958
Elementary	20	24	31	31
Some high school	25	32	45	46
High school	29	38	54	56
Some college	37	44	64	70
4+ years college	45	62	85	92

Source: Miller (1961); data for USA.

17
Two-way Analysis of Variance

By now we know how to look very hard at a two-way table. We can break up an observation Y into its components: observation = grand mean + row effect + column effect + interaction + residual. We can display these components clearly, whether separately or together, and we can interpret them in an orderly way. This is a very useful set of skills for exploratory work and will continue to be important for making sense of a confirmatory analysis. The confirmatory tools are all we lack and we will begin to learn them in this chapter.

Once again our basic problem is making inferences about a universe from a sample. If we already have data about the universe (as in the Irish fertility example from Chapter 15) then we don't need statistical tests. We simply interpret the results with elementary analysis and report our conclusions about trends in the universe. But if our data are from a sample, we must use a test to tell us whether the apparent patterns are likely to be merely random sampling fluctuations or whether there is probably a similar pattern in the universe we want to make inferences about. We want to make decisions about three things: effects of the row variable, effects of the column variable, and interaction between row and column variables. It is possible that none of these is significant, that any one is, that any two are, or that all three are.

The confirmatory technique that we begin with here is two-way analysis of variance, which is a fairly straightforward extension of one-way analysis of variance but with a few extra wrinkles. The basic idea is the same. Remember that in one-way anova we used an F-test:

$$F = \frac{\text{MS between}}{\text{MS within}} = \frac{\text{how much the means vary about the grand mean}}{\text{how much they would be expected to vary by chance}}$$
$$\text{alone}$$

We had just one independent variable, the various categories or groups, and all we had to do was compare the magnitude of the differences among these groups to the size of differences we could expect to get from random sampling fluctuations if the groups were not 'really' different (i.e. not different in the universe). We estimated these chance differences by looking at the variability of observations within groups. When the observed differences are much larger than chance, the F-ratio is large, and we can reject the null hypothesis, H_0, which asserts that there is no difference among group means, in favour of H_1.

The problem we deal with here involves the same kind of logic but because Y is now seen as being made up of three components, row, column and interaction effects, three ratios will be needed. We find the observed variability of effects of each component, and compare these mean squares to estimates of how big they would be by chance. Thus, all three tests are based on the same principle we used in one-way anova and each is computed in an analogous way.

Two-way anova is a standard part of every major statistics package, so you may never have to do one by hand. However, seeing the hand work can be a real aid to understanding, so in this chapter we work through an example entirely by hand.

An Example: Experimenter Expectations

Table 17.1 reports some experimental data which we will use to illustrate the new procedure. This table is obviously just another two-way table. There is a row variable (O_1, O_2, O_3), a column variable (E_1, and E_2) and a Y variable reported in the cells. The only new feature is that each cell has 18 Y observations, while the tables we have worked with in previous chapters had just one case (often a mean) per cell. Note that a 'row' is a category of the row variable. So in Table 17.1 we have three rows; that is, O_1 and O_2 and O_3. We have two columns, E_1 and E_2. Finally, we have six cells: O_1E_1, O_1E_2, O_2E_1, O_2E_2, O_3E_1, O_3E_2. The numbers inside the cells (replications) do not count as rows or columns because their arrangement within cells is irrelevant and arbitrary. They are batches: they could be arranged in any convenient way in any order, as long as they are in the correct cell.

The data in Table 17.1 come from an experiment by Adler (1973) designed to find out about 'experimenter effects', or biases stemming from the experimenter's expectations. There is a great deal of evidence showing that researchers are not completely objective, that they tend to see what they expect to see. Moreover, in some as yet undetected way, researchers seem able to communicate their expectations to their subjects. This problem is of concern in many disciplines, medicine for one, and has been studied increasingly by social psychologists. In Adler's study, several research assistants acted as experimenters. They showed pictures of people's faces to respondents who were asked to estimate how successful or unsuccessful the people were. Thus the experiment seemed to be a study of physical appearance. In fact, it was not; the pictures used were all average-looking as far as successful appearance goes. The averageness was established by showing various pictures to judges beforehand and choosing only pictures that were judged to belong to moderately successful people.

What was really being studied was the experimenters and the different ratings they might get out of their respondents if they (the experimenters) had

Table 17.1 Experimenter effects

Outcome stressed	E_1 Expect high ratings			E_2 Expect low ratings		
O_1 'good' data	25	0	−16	−25	−20	−2
	5	11	−6	−23	−24	12
	42	−2	−13	−28	−24	−8
	14	4	−22	−22	−22	−17
	19	6	9	−22	−23	−30
	13	−3	−6	−10	−19	−22
O_2 'scientific' data	−19	5	−13	6	−22	−5
	−24	−1	−1	−5	7	−5
	−4	−9	−3	14	14	−9
	−24	−5	−11	−11	15	3
	0	−6	−6	14	−6	−5
	−4	4	−4	−5	9	6
O_3 'no stress'	−26	−21	−10	−12	−4	20
	−1	−19	−37	−4	−10	9
	22	−12	0	13	−3	−8
	3	9	−10	−27	−11	8
	−26	−9	−6	−7	2	−6
	4	−27	−11	−20	−9	6

different expectations of what the respondents would do. In a way, the research assistants/experimenters were really the subjects here! The experimenters' expectations form the column variable: some were told that their respondents were likely to give high success ratings (E_1) and some were told that their subjects were likely to give low success ratings (E_2). In fact, there was no reason for the subjects to differ: they were randomly assigned to E_1 or to E_2 experimenters, and they were all rating pictures with approximately the same average appearance of success. So if E_1 ratings are different from E_2 they differ because of the experimenters' expectations.

Adler pushed this idea a bit further by also giving the experimenters different kinds of instructions: these instructions form the row variable. One-third of the experimenters were instructed to try to get 'good' data (O_1), one-third were instructed to try to get 'scientific' data (O_2), and one-third were just told what to do without any stress on the kind of results they should try for (O_3). These may seem like small variations, but small changes in wording can often have big effects on how people behave in an experiment or interview. So the instructions given to the experimenters could affect the way they conducted the experiment, which in turn could affect the ratings given by respondents.

Each cell is made up of the 18 respondents (replications) who were interviewed by experimenters with the same instructions and the same expectations. The table entries, Y, are the ratings given by the respondents, but differences from row to row and column to column will tell us about the experimenter effects. If the experimenters' expectations and/or instructions have effects on subject ratings, then the ratings will differ from cell to cell; if not, all the cells will have roughly the same levels. The rating scale went from $+10$ to -10, and the pictures used were rated at about zero in the pretest.

Before we test the effects of expectation, instruction and their interaction, let us note just what kind of two-way anova we are dealing with. We will present the procedures for tests appropriate when:

1 There is more than one case per cell.
2 The number of cases in each cell is the same (18 in our example).
3 The row and column categories are fixed, not random; we will say more about this later in this chapter.

In other cases (e.g. when there are unequal numbers of cell entries) the procedures need to be modified. We will tell you where to find such modifications if you need them, but for now we'll stick with the simplest case. We will begin by showing how this kind of analysis is done, discussing assumptions later.

Computing Two-way Analysis of Variance

As in one-way analysis of variance, it turns out to be very handy to calculate some basic sums of squares and then to use them to construct the sums of squares and mean squares needed for our F-tests. Four of the basic sums (A, B, C_{col} and C_{row}) are essentially the same as the ones used in one-way anova. There is one new basic sum (D), which we need because two-way anova is slightly more complex. To keep the formulae for A to D straight, we need some subscripts:

Part of table	Subscript	
rows	i	Note that i goes from one to r; that is, the number of rows in r. In our case $r = 3$.
columns	j	j goes from one to c, which is the number of columns; in our example, $c = 2$.
cells	k	k goes from one to n, the number of replicates in each cell; in our example $n = 18$.

Thus Y_{ijk} is the kth entry in the cell in row i and column j. Finally, N is the total number of entries in the table; this is the number of rows times the number of columns times the number of replications:

$$N = rcn = 108, \text{ in our case}$$

A pragmatic note: most of these sums involve adding up the table entries in

Table 17.2   Cell totals for Table 17.1

	E_1	E_2	Row totals
O_1	80	-329	-249
O_2	-125	15	-110
O_3	-177	-63	-240
Column totals	-222	-377	Grand total = -599

various ways, so it is handy to have cell totals. These can be combined as needed, rather than having to add up the same numbers over and over again.

Table 17.2 gives cell totals, row totals, column totals and grand totals for Table 17.1. For example, the 80 for the O_1E_1 cell is the total of the 18 cases in that cell; the row total for O_1 is $(80 - 329) = -249$, which is the total of all the entries in that row; the column total for E_1 is $(80 - 125 - 177) = -222$, the total of all the entries in that column; and the grand total is $(-249 - 110 - 240) = (-222 - 377) = -599$, the total of all the entries in the table. Now we are ready to give the formulae and their verbal interpretations.

$$A = \sum_{i=1}^{r} \sum_{j=1}^{c} \sum_{k=1}^{n} Y_{ijk}^2$$

In words: square each entry separately and then add up the squares. In our example,

$$A = 25^2 + 0^2 + (-16)^2 + (-25)^2 + \ldots + (-9)^2 + 6^2$$

$$= 24\,101$$

$$B = \frac{1}{N} \left(\sum_{i=1}^{r} \sum_{j=1}^{c} \sum_{k=1}^{n} Y_{ijk} \right)^2$$

In words: add up all the entries, square this total, and divide by the number of entries. So in our example,

$$B = \frac{1}{108} (25 + 0 - 16 - 25 \ldots - 9 + 6)^2$$

$$= \frac{(-599)^2}{108}$$

$$= 3322.232$$

$$C_{col} = \frac{1}{nr} \sum_{j=1}^{c} \left(\sum_{i=1}^{r} \sum_{k=1}^{n} Y_{ijk} \right)^2$$

In words: go through the table column by column this time. For each column, add up all the entries in the column and then square the column total. Finally, add up the squared totals and divide by nr, the number of entries in each column. In our example,

$$C_{col} = \frac{1}{54}[(-222)^2 + (-377)^2]$$

$$= \frac{191\,413}{54}$$

$$= 3544.685$$

$$C_{row} = \frac{1}{nc} \sum_{i=1}^{r} \left(\sum_{j=1}^{c} \sum_{k=1}^{n} Y_{ijk} \right)^2$$

In words: go through the table row by row, add up the entries in each row; square each row total; then add up the squared totals and divide by nc, the number of entries per row. In our example,

$$C_{row} = \frac{1}{36}[(-249)^2 + (-110)^2 + (-240)^2]$$

$$= \frac{131\,701}{36}$$

$$= 3658.361$$

Clearly C_{col} and C_{row} are much the same idea; C_{col} does for columns what C_{row} does for rows.

$$D = \frac{1}{n} \sum_{i=1}^{r} \sum_{j=1}^{c} \left(\sum_{k=1}^{n} Y_{ijk} \right)^2$$

In words: go through the table cell by cell. Add up the entries in each cell; square these cell totals; add up the squared totals and divide by n, the number of entries in each cell. In our example,

$$D = \frac{1}{18}[(80)^2 + (-329)^2 + (-125)^2 + (15)^2 + (-177)^2 + (-63)^2]$$

$$= \frac{165\,789}{18}$$

$$= 9210.5$$

Computing *F*-Ratios

Now that we have these basic sums, we can plug them into very simple formulae to get the sums of squares, mean squares and *F*-ratios needed for our test. The formulae are summarized in Table 17.3. Let's go through the main features of this table to help clarify what's going on.

First of all, in every *F*-test we have MS within as the denominator of the *F*-ratio. That is because the MS within is our basic standard of comparison; it is

Table 17.3   Basic two-way anova table (fixed categories)

Source of variance	Sum of squares	df	Mean squares	F-ratio
Rows	$C_{row} - B$	$r - 1$	$\dfrac{C_{row} - B}{r - 1}$	$\dfrac{\text{MS rows}}{\text{MS within}}$
Columns	$C_{col} - B$	$c - 1$	$\dfrac{C_{col} - B}{c - 1}$	$\dfrac{\text{MS cols}}{\text{MS within}}$
Interaction	$B + D - C_{row} - C_{col}$	$(r - 1)(c - 1)$	$\dfrac{B + D - C_{row} - C_{col}}{(r - 1)(c - 1)}$	$\dfrac{\text{MS interaction}}{\text{MS within}}$
Within cell	$A - D$	$rc(n - 1)$	$\dfrac{A - D}{rc(n - 1)}$	
Total	$A - B$	$N - 1$		

the size of difference we could expect just by sampling fluctuations, even when there is nothing happening in the universe. Basically, MS within is the 'average' variance of cell batches. Like the error or within term in the simpler one-way case (Chapter 10), within-cell variance has nothing to do with the effects of the independent variables, for row and column are constant for all replications within each cell. So differences inside cells should reflect differences just due to 'error': sampling fluctuations, measurement error, the effects of other unmeasured independent variables, etc. Within-cell differences represent the magnitude of differences we can expect even if the row and column variables have no effect, so row effects or column effects or interaction effects must be greater than this before we can take them seriously.

So our basic strategy, once again, will be to compare observed variations in row, column or interaction effects to the chance expectation: MS within. We will use three ratios:

$$\frac{\text{MS rows}}{\text{MS within}} = \frac{\text{differences between rows}}{\text{differences we expect if } H_0 \text{ true}}$$

$$\frac{\text{MS columns}}{\text{MS within}} = \frac{\text{differences between columns}}{\text{differences expected if } H_0 \text{ true}}$$

$$\frac{\text{MS interaction}}{\text{MS within}} = \frac{\text{differences between cells after row and column differences are gone}}{\text{differences expected if } H_0 \text{ true}}$$

In each case H_0 has the same general form:

For rows, H_0 says: there are no differences in Y from row category to row category in the universe.

For columns, H_0 says: there are no differences in Y from column category to column category in the universe.

For interaction, H_0 says: after row and column means are removed, there are no differences in Y from one combination of row and column categories to another combination, in the universe.

In short, H_0 asserts that there are no real differences in the universe, and the apparent differences in our data could reasonably have arisen from mere chance fluctuations. MS within gives us our estimate of what to expect if H_0 is true; we will reject H_0 only if our observed differences are significantly greater than MS within.

We sum up observed differences between rows (MS rows) by finding $C_{row} - B$ and dividing by the degrees of freedom, $r - 1$ (the number of rows less one). We saw earlier that C_{row} is a row-by-row computation. If you work through a lot of algebra, this short computing form of MS rows turns out to be approximately a weighted form of the variance of the row means about the grand mean, just as MS within turns out to be approximately the variance within cells.

We sum up the column differences (MS columns) by finding $C_{col} - B$ divided by the degrees of freedom $C - 1$ (the number of columns less one). This is the same idea as MS rows, of course; similarly MS columns is approximately the weighted variance of column means around the grand mean.

Finally, we come to MS interaction. This is approximately the variance of the cell-to-cell residuals after the grand mean, row effect and column effect have been removed. This turns out to be $D - (C_{row} + C_{col} - B) = B + D - C_{row} - C_{col}$. If the basic additive fit predicts the cell means perfectly there will be no interaction: as the basic fit works more poorly the size of the interaction term will increase, just as we saw in the exploratory analysis.

F-Tests for the Adler Data

Let's work our example, and then look harder at the data to interpret what the numbers mean. We have the basic numbers A, B, C_{col}, C_{row} and D; we know r, c, n. So we just need to plug these into the basic anova table, Table 17.3, which

Table 17.4 Anova table for Table 17.1

Source	Sum of squares	df	MS	F-ratio
Rows	336.129	2	168.065	1.151
Columns	222.453	1	222.453	1.524
Interaction	5329.686	2	2664.843	18.254
Within cell	14890.5	102	145.985	
Total	20778.768	107		

gives us Table 17.4. Next we consult an *F*-table to find out whether the *F*s are large enough for it to be unlikely that they have happened if H_0 is true. The size of the critical value for *F* depends on the degrees of freedom and the significance level chosen. For the significance level we might as well use the familiar 0.05; the degrees of freedom can be read off from the basic table for our example, Table 17.4. For example, the *F*-ratio for rows is based on MS rows divided by MS within, so the numerator has two *df* and the denominator has 102 *df*, which is the case for all three ratios. For the *F* for columns, the *df* for the numerator is one; for the *F* for interaction the *df* for the numerator is 2. Looking at our table for critical F-values at the 5 per cent level, we find:

Critical values for *F*, 5 per cent
Rows $F_{2,102} = 3.07$
Columns $F_{1,102} = 3.92$
Interaction $F_{2,102} = 3.07$

If we compare these critical values to the computed *F*s for our data, we see that only the *F* for interaction exceeds the critical value. We cannot reject H_0 for rows and columns; that means that different instructions (rows) made no overall difference to the subjects' ratings (*Y*), and different expectations (columns) made no overall difference either. But we can reject the H_0 for interaction, which means that particular combinations of instruction and expectations probably did have an effect on the ratings.

But what combinations? What is happening here? The *F*-test can't tell us; we have to look at our data to figure it out. The original data in Table 17.1 are not helpful because there are too many numbers. We want to figure out interaction effects, which are differences between cells that row and column effects can't explain, so we don't really need the 18 replications. Let's take trimeans of each of the 18 replications in each cell of Table 17.1 and median polish them – a doubly resistant analysis. The elementary analysis gives visual support for the *F*-test results. On row effects, those instructed to get 'scientific data' got higher ratings than others, while the 'good data' subjects got lower scores, but neither of these effects are very large compared to some of the residuals. The column effects are a bit odd, with positive expectancy subjects giving lower ratings than negative expectancy subjects, but again not by much. It looks like the 'scientific data' subjects and perhaps also the 'no stress' subjects may have 'bent over backwards' trying to avoid bias, and ended up overdoing it. Much the same thing in a slightly weaker form occurs in the third row, where the experimenters were given instructions without stress on any special kind of outcome. Only the instructions stressing 'good data' produce the classic experimenter effect, perhaps because the instruction implies that there is a correct answer (high ratings or low ones) so an experimenter who doesn't get these correct results is not doing it right.

Let's go through the residuals in Table 17.5 systematically to interpret interaction effects. The first row reports results for those experimenters told to get 'good data'. We see that those expecting to get higher ratings got them (15.55 for those expecting high ratings versus −15.55 for those expecting low

Table 17.5   Resistant analysis of Table 17.1

	Cell trimeans		
	E_1 (high)	E_2 (low)	Effects
O_1 ('Good' data)	4.0	−21.3	
O_2 ('Scientific' data)	−5.3	0.5	
O_3 ('No stress')	−10.3	−3.5	
O_1	15.55	−15.55	−1.75
O_2	0	0	4.50
O_3	−0.50	0.50	0.00
Effects	−2.9	2.9	−6.90
dq ratio: $\dfrac{8.52}{14.43} = 0.59$			

ratings). The stress on 'good data' seems to produce a strong experimenter effect, with the experimenter getting what she expects to get. The second and third rows show virtually negligible residuals.

Assumptions in Two-way Anova

Like all confirmatory statistics, two-way analysis of variance is based on a set of assumptions about the data. They should be checked before starting an analysis, although we report them afterwards here for clarity of presentation. We look at three assumptions.

First, in each cell the data should be normally distributed. This is surely no surprise. Most of the powerful and useful statistics assume normality. As in one-way anova, this assumption can be stretched if n (the number of cases per cell) is large. The larger the number of replications, the more non-normality you can put up with. If you have a close call to make, and you are unsure about whether your n is big enough to make up for patent straggling, consult an expert.

In our example, we have $n = 18$, which is not bad; we could accept a fair bit of straggle without seriously bending this assumption. In fact, we do not have much to accept: the stems and leaves of the six cell distributions (Table 17.6) show pretty balanced patterns. Some of the stems and leaves are not quite symmetric (O_1E_2 straggles up, for example) but, on the whole, they are quite pretty.

What do you do if your data have pronounced departures from normality? If the cell stems and leaves show straggle in the same direction, it is easy: transform the data. If most cells straggle strongly in one direction, but a few straggle strongly in the other, you're probably safe after transforming, but it

Table 17.6   Cell stems and leaves

O_1E_1	4	2		O_1E_2	1	2
	3				0	
	2	5			−0	28
	1	4931			−1	970
	0	50469			−2	32204423258
	−0	2366			−3	0
	−1	63				
	−2	2				
O_2E_1	0	045		O_2E_2	1	4445
	−0	4411349566			0	67936
	−1	319			−0	5565595
	−2	44			−1	1
					−2	2
O_3E_1	2	2		O_3E_2	2	0
	1				1	3
	0	3490			0	2986
	−0	196			−0	4743986
	−1	92001			−1	201
	−2	6617			−2	70
	−3	7				

stems: tens
leaves: units

may be useful to talk to an expert. If the cells straggle seriously about half and half up and down, and cell sizes are fairly small, you probably need expert advice.

Secondly, in each cell the data should have equal variances. Again, this is familiar from one-way anova. And again, although the assumption is important it can be relaxed if the number of entries in each cell is equal.

In our example, the cell variances are:

	E_1	E_2
O_1	237.2	106.1
O_2	71.4	109.3
O_3	216.7	135.2

The largest variance (237.2) and the smallest (71.4) are in a ratio of about three to one. If the cell sizes are unequal, a ratio of three to one would be barely acceptable; a much larger disparity would be too great. In fact, our cell sizes are equal, so we could tolerate even a bit more inequality among the variances. Since only very rough similarity of variances is required given equal cell sizes, we do not really need to go through the labour of computing all those variances: a rougher and faster comparison of spread is fine. For example, we could look at the midspreads and ranges:

	dq	Range		dq	Range
O_1E_1	19	64	O_1E_2	7	42
O_2E_1	10	29	O_2E_2	14	37
O_3E_1	21	59	O_3E_2	16	47

The midspreads vary a fair bit (O_3E_1 has a dq three times as large as that of O_1E_2) and the ranges somewhat less (the range of O_1E_1 being about twice that of O_2E_1). Thus the faster spread measures give an impression in the same ballpark as the variance (close enough when cell sizes are equal); but we probably should look at variances if cell sizes are unequal. With large, equal cell sizes, even a look at the stems and leaves needed to check normality can be enough. (Here we could look at Table 17.6.)

What can you do if your cell variances are very unequal and you do not have equal numbers in each cell? Transformation can help here too, if cell variances happen to be related to cell levels. Recall the log of spread versus log of level plot for finding the best transformation, which we used in Chapter 6. You could use this again, plotting each cell as a point to find the appropriate transformation. Log sd by log mean would be suitable. If this doesn't work, consult that expert. Moral: plan ahead and get equal cell sizes.

Thirdly, errors (or the things not explained by the row, column and interaction variables) should be independent. In practice, this means that each case should be gathered and measured independently so that the datum for one case is not a function of the datum for another. The best way to ensure this is to use randomization; randomly assign people (or factories or whatever you are studying) to cells; apply the row and column variables as called for; then measure the dependent variable to fill in the cells with Y values and do the analysis. Be sure to measure each case separately; for example, do not let one subject see another's reaction before giving her own.

For example, when Adler did the study we have used as this chapter's example, she had a pool of subjects, who were randomly assigned to a combination of treatments. She also had a pool of experimenters who were randomly assigned to instruction and expectation conditions.

Randomization right at the start, followed by experimental manipulation of the independent variables, is a very powerful strategy that has many statistical (and other) advantages. Do it whenever you can; and if you can't do it, approximate it as much as you can. (A useful source on these matters is Cook and Campbell, 1979.)

Alas, this lovely strategy is very hard or impossible in most 'natural' experiments where you must take the category assignments as they come. For example, we don't decide (in Chapter 15) what religion our Northern Irish are going to have. Still, we can make sure that data gathered for one cell are not tied to data gathered for another cell if we use our heads. For example, suppose one of our variables (row or column) was sex and we were looking at its effects on aggression. Suppose further that we sampled some men for the male category, and then used their wives to fill in the female category. Obviously this will create problems. Spouses tend not to be independent of each other, so the male and female aggression rates in this imaginary table would be far from independent. To get a more accurate comparison of the sexes, we would have to sample men and women separately – independently. Then the third assumption would be satisfied and it would make sense to use anova.

All in all, analysis of variance is a very robust technique. The assumptions do not have to be met perfectly, and can be met fairly imperfectly if a little advance planning has produced: (a) ample entries in each cell; (b) equal numbers of entries in each cell; (c) entries based on randomly sampled, independently measured cases.

Some Special Problems

What do you do if the data you have are suitable for analysis of variance (categorical X_1 and X_2 and numerical Y) but the practical details are messy? What if you do not have equal numbers in each cell? What if you have only one case per cell? And what happens when the categories are random instead of fixed? There are two essential points here. First of all, you can still do analysis of variance; it is a very flexible technique. Secondly, however, you can't do it in exactly the way we have done it here. The formulae have to be modified. The modifications are not hard for the most part and you can find them in many standard books (e.g. Guilford, 1954; Snedecor, 1956; Winer, 1962).

We will say no more about having just one case per cell or having unequal numbers in the cells; if these happen, you will not have any trouble telling. But the next issue, the difference between fixed and random categories, is less obvious so we will go over it.

Fixed and Random Categories

As mentioned earlier, our discussion so far holds only for two-way analyses with row and column variables whose categories are fixed, not random. If the categories are fixed, inferences are made only about the categories directly studied in the anova table. If the categories are random, they are chosen to represent a whole range of possible categories and inferences are made for that whole range, including categories not in the anova table itself. This is a tricky distinction at first. In making it, you may find it helpful to ask yourself whether the variables were measured as categories from the start or whether they were based originally on numeric variables made into categories. So far, we have seen just categorical Xs. In Chapter 15, we looked at fertility by variables like religion and residence. In this chapter we've looked at positive versus negative expectation by type of instructions. All these are fixed categories: when we finish our analysis, we would expect to make inferences just from these categories and no others.

Suppose, however, that our independent variables were originally measured on interval scales, and that we had 'sampled' on these scales to obtain the table's categories. For example, suppose that to induce expectation on the part of our experimenters/subjects we had prepared a tape that we played under their pillows while they were asleep. Suppose, further, that we could play this tape for any length of time from, say, four minutes to nine hours. We might end up comparing the effects of eight, four and two hours of exposure, but when we finish our analysis we would want to talk about exposure time as a continuous variable with eight, four and two hours as convenient representative levels. Now we are talking about random categories. In other words, if the various levels we actually study show strong effects as we hope, then we will conclude that our variable in general works the same way. If we have sampled our categories well, then they are likely to represent all possible categories and what is true in our study is likely to be true for the variable in general.

In one-way analysis of variance we did not stress fixed versus randomly chosen categories because the distinction does not make much practical difference there. But it makes a lot of difference in two-way anova. Since random categories involve not one but two layers of random selection, with an ambitious attempt to generalize to universes of subjects and universes of categories, it is a somewhat more demanding affair than fixed categories. The tests are tougher. Tougher on the data, that is, not on you; you do no more arithmetic work for random categories than for fixed ones. In fact, you find the same basic quantities (A to D) and the same mean squares; the way these mean squares fit together in F-tests is a little different, however. Should one or both of your independent variables have random categories, look up the modified procedures in Guilford (1954), Snedecor (1956), Winer (1962) or another such source. Watch out for the conventional terminology, which is far from intuitive. If both independent variables have fixed categories (the case we treat here), it is conventional to say that we have two variables with 'fixed effects' and a 'model one' analysis of variance. If one or both variables have randomly selected categories, conventional usage refers to 'random effects' and 'model two' analysis of variance.

Exploratory and Confirmatory

By now you can see the full set of analogies between exploratory and confirmatory approaches to two-way tables. Both approaches break Y up into row, column and interaction components; the exploratory components are resistant levels and the confirmatory components are means. Both offer ways in which the effects of the row and/or column variables can be evaluated. In exploratory statistics the strength of overall fit (row and column effects, or those plus interaction effects) is evaluated by comparing differences of quartiles. In confirmatory, each of the three possible parts of the fit (row, column, interaction) is tested. There are also confirmatory measures of the strength of each of these components (rather like r^2), although we have not gone into them here. Both approaches need eye-work: there is no way to interpret a means or a median analysis without looking hard at it.

Finally, the two approaches work very well together. One can do resistant analysis to develop ideas for later testing on fresh data, or one can do analysis of variance first and then interpret with exploratory approaches. The exploratory approaches supplement the confirmatory well in yet another way: they help us to tell if the confirmatory analysis has been pulled off by a few extreme cases.

Using the Computer

The general command for two-way anova with equal number of cases in each cell in MINITAB is TWOWAY, the same command we used in Chapter 15 to get the computer to do most of a means analysis. The input format is the same as was described there, data in C1, row identifier in C2 and column identifier in C3. The command

        MTB> TWOWAY C1 C2 C3 C4 C5

gives the analysis of variance table and all mean-squares as well as confidence intervals for each row and column. You do have to calculate F-ratios yourself, however.

If you also want row and column means and/or the cell-by-cell additive fits, the subcommands

        SUBC> MEAN C2 C3;
        SUBC> ADDITIVE.

will provide them.

HOMEWORK

The data in Table 17.7, from the Atkinson and Polivy (1976) study, examine the effects of 'insult (with and without apology)' and 'opportunity to retaliate' on depression ratings for female subjects. (See notes on the Atkinson and Polivy study in the second review.)

Do a two-way analysis of variance for these data. Do not forget to examine the assumptions first. Both independent variables have fixed categories here. Do not forget to discuss the anova results together with a median polish.

Table 17.7 Female depression as a function of insult, apology and retaliation

	No retaliation		Retaliation	
Insult/no apology	66	70	141	72
	78	57	64	78
	89	52	73	51
	75	41	59	78
	96	69	77	41
Insult/apology	70	107	57	69
	73	57	60	57
	68	42	41	122
	52	55	49	46
	69	44	39	39

FOURTH REVIEW
Two-way Analysis

Here we present two *very* different sets of data. The first set, on Canadian labour force participation by age and sex for nine consecutive years (Table R4.1) *can* be analysed using confirmatory tools (treat the years as independent replications and ignore the fact that each number represents *many* thousands of cases) but exploratory techniques are probably more appropriate.

Table R4.1 Labour force participation rates (percentages) by year, age group and sex

	15–19	*20–24*	*25–44*	*45–64*	*65–69*	*70+*
Males						
1975	54.6	85.0	95.6	87.0	29.9	11.0
1976	52.6	85.1	95.7	85.7	25.4	9.8
1977	54.1	85.2	95.5	85.4	25.1	9.2
1978	54.8	85.9	95.8	85.8	23.5	9.6
1979	57.1	86.4	96.0	85.5	24.4	9.1
1980	57.8	86.4	95.6	85.2	23.5	8.9
1981	58.2	86.5	95.7	84.8	21.9	8.9
1982	53.7	84.4	94.6	83.5	22.6	8.2
1983	52.9	84.3	94.3	83.0	21.2	7.9
Females						
1975	47.4	67.0	52.3	39.4	9.6	2.3
1976	47.0	67.4	53.6	41.0	7.8	2.2
1977	46.7	68.9	55.4	41.5	8.5	2.0
1978	48.0	70.3	58.7	42.6	7.8	2.7
1979	50.8	71.3	60.0	43.6	8.2	1.9
1980	52.1	73.0	62.3	44.5	8.3	2.1
1981	53.0	72.9	65.1	45.3	8.0	2.6
1982	50.5	73.1	65.7	45.5	8.3	2.2
1983	50.1	74.0	67.3	46.3	7.4	3.1

Source: Statistics Canada *Labour Force Annual.*

The second data set, in Table R4.2, examines the effects of mothers' smoking and drinking behaviour during pregnancy on children's cognitive development. These data are a part of a larger study by Peter Fried (1983). Here, the independent variables are 'smoking' (smokers/non-smokers) and 'alcohol consumption' (low/medium/high). Cognitive development is the dependent variable, measured at 60 months (the measure is the McCarthy Scale of Children's Ability, with higher scores indicating greater development). This table can be analysed with both exploratory and confirmatory tools.

Table R4.2 Cognitive development as a function of mothers' smoking and drinking during pregnancy

	Alcohol Consumption					
	Low		Medium		High	
Non-smokers						
	129	146	124	126	79	118
	128	120	117	131	133	118
	110	126	139	109	125	89
	139	134	123	137	126	138
	130	139	125	126	109	124
	96	110	112	121	105	112
	111	150	147	114	137	144
	104		121		127	
	125		117		136	
	122		121		138	
	106		150		119	
Smokers						
	132	112	145	146	138	116
	120	112	115	138	124	129
	122	119	116	60	109	129
	141	125	106	110	118	110
	114	120	136	105	143	110
	95	110	115	118	95	88
	119		117		126	
	126		114		106	
	119		101		126	
	127		111		108	
	140		102		88	
	113		110		117	

Source: P. Fried, personal communication.

18
Getting More from Residuals

Having rounded out our collection of tools for two categorical independent variables and a numeric Y, we now move on to tools for two numeric variables and a numeric Y. At this point you might want to look back to the introduction to Section IV to get your bearings.

One of the basic strategies of the good data analyst is the scrutiny of residuals. Many of the techniques of exploration were designed just to make it easier to spot suggestive residuals. This is the single best way of pushing research further, of getting just a bit more out of a body of data.

We have pointed out that one of the pay-offs from making a numeric fit is precisely being able to get residuals so that further explanatory factors can be more easily sought. You have done enough poring over residuals by now to know that possible further factors can easily be suggested with some hard looking and a bit of thought. But when you've thought of them, what next? Thus far, we are rather short on methods for pursuing residuals from Y by X analysis.

We need ways to make fits involving more than one numeric explanatory variable at a time. Virtually every social phenomenon has many causes, so for any Y we should be able to work with several Xs.

Furthermore, bringing in additional variables offers the genuine advantage of clarifying causality by helping us to understand how the variables fit together. This is closely tied to the ideas of multivariate tabular analysis, introduced in Chapter 14. Let's begin with a familiar procedure, a simple Y by X analysis.

Consider the data in Table 18.1 on infant mortality rates (IMR) by GNP per capita (GNP/PC), for 18 middle income countries (a sample of middle income countries for which all the relevant data are available, from the *World Development Report*, 1986). It is reasonable to expect GNP/PC to predict IMR, because the greater a country's GNP/PC, the greater the *potential* for satisfying basic human needs. Here, this might include not only access to medical facilities and pre- and peri-natal care, but also more basic needs like safe drinking water, adequate sanitation, etc. Figure 18.1 gives the plot of IMR by GNP/PC. It is easy to see that the relationship here is curvy. Since the log of

Table 18.1　GNP/PC and IMR for 18 randomly selected middle income countries

	GNP/PC	IMR
Mauritania	450	133
Lesotho	530	107
Yemen Arab Republic	550	155
Philippines	660	49
El Salvador	710	66
Egypt	720	94
Nicaragua	860	70
Dominican Republic	970	71
Ecuador	1150	67
Guatemala	1160	66
Paraguay	1240	44
Jordan	1570	50
Brazil	1720	68
Panama	1980	25
South Korea	2110	28
Argentina	2230	34
Greece	3770	16
Trinidad-Tobago	7150	22

Source: World Bank (1986).

X is one way to handle this curve and GNP is a variable that usually responds well to logging we try the log (let's call log GNP/PC 'wealth') and replot (Figure 18.2). When we calculate the resistant line, the half-slope ratio suggests that there is no longer enough curve to bother with:

$$Y = -112.4X + 298 \text{ (half-slope ratio} = 1.215) \text{ } dq\text{-ratio} = 0.51$$

The dq ratio suggests a moderate fit.

Wimberley (1990), in his analysis of Third World mortality, examines a variety of factors expected to influence infant mortality. One important factor is education, for several reasons. Education is likely to affect economic growth through the enhancement of human capital. Further, as education becomes more nearly universally available, income inequality might be expected to decline. This, together with the previous point, should reduce infant mortality by improving life chances generally. Lastly, improved education should also have effects at a personal level, by raising the general knowledge level about nutrition, hygiene, sanitation, etc.

The definition we have chosen for education is, 'the number enrolled in secondary school as a percentage of the appropriate age group' (Table 18.2).

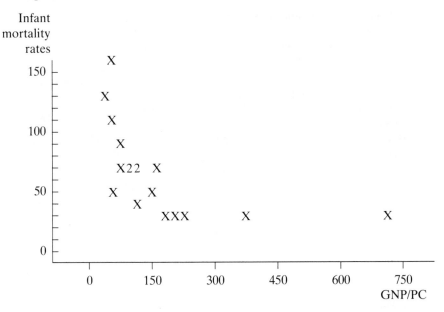

Figure 18.1   Infant mortality rates plotted against gross national product per capita (1984)

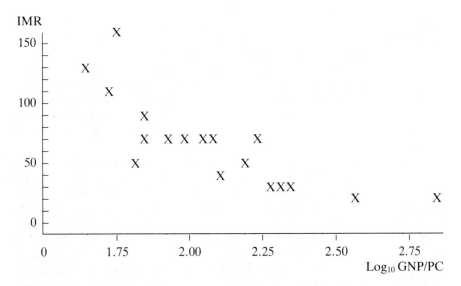

Figure 18.2   Infant mortality rates versus wealth ($\log_{10}$ GNP/PC)

Table 18.2 Education scores for the sample of
18 countries

Mauritania	12
Lesotho	19
Yemen Arab Republic	9
Philippines	63
El Salvador	24
Egypt	58
Nicaragua	43
Dominican Republic	45
Ecuador	53
Guatemala	16
Paraguay	36
Jordan	78
Brazil	42
Panama	59
South Korea	89
Argentina	60
Greece	82
Trinidad-Tobago	70

Broadly, we want to see how well the new variable 'education' can account for the residuals, what remains of IMR after controlling for wealth. This sounds familiar and easy – just fit a resistant line. Well, it is easy but there is a wrinkle. Conceptually, the problem here is that our new Y variable is a set of residuals, IMR with the linear effects of wealth fully removed. The X variable, on the other hand, almost certainly includes some effects of wealth – how could it not? Our Y and X variables, then, have different status with respect to this third variable. So in order usefully to compare these two variables, we have to clear away some underbrush – remove the linear effects of wealth from education too. This necessitates fitting wealth to education to get residuals from education with wealth held constant. This is more easily done than said, so let's get on with it.

First, let's look at Figure 18.3, the plot of IMR against education without controls (often called a 'zero-order relationship', which is similar to the language of multivariate tabular analysis in Chapter 14 – in the same way, we speak of first-order relationships, etc.). This plot appears somewhat curvy (the half-slope ratio is 0.30, supporting the impression of curviness), so it may be useful to transform. We prefer to transform education rather than IMR because we already have a linear relationship between raw IMR and wealth. If we transform IMR in the relationship with education, we will have to use the same form of IMR against wealth, which will probably no longer be straight. Figure 18.4 plus a few tries indicates that the square of education will be a satisfactory transform. The plot in Figure 18.4 is straight enough, with a

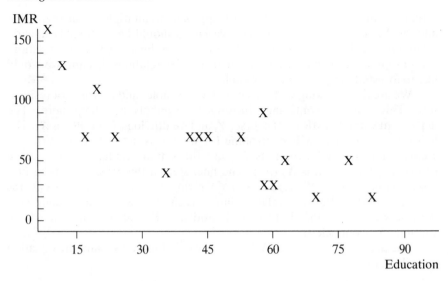

Figure 18.3   IMR versus education

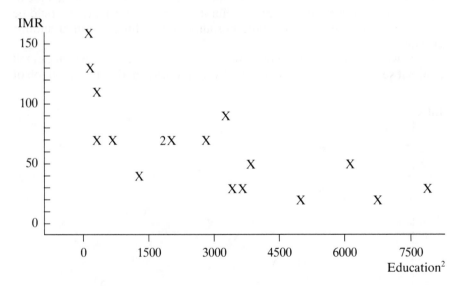

Figure 18.4   IMR versus education (transformed by squaring)

half-slope ratio of about 1.5, in the discretionary range. The relationship, though, is modest in strength (the *dq* ratio = 0.96).

Technically, since we make virtually no use of the zero-order relation between IMR and education, you might wonder why we have bothered transforming to make the plot more linear. There are two reasons for this. One is that this procedure is an exploratory approach to multiple linear regression and, as the name suggests, predictor variables should be reasonably linearly related to the dependent variable. Secondly, non-linear zero-order relationships are likely to result in non-linear first-order relationships and we would like to forestall this problem, if possible.

We are now working with two predictor variables and a variety of residual sets. This can get confusing. Introducing symbols can help here. The dependent variable IMR is, of course, Y, and wealth, $\log_{10}$ GNP/PC, is X_1. The first set of residuals, IMR controlling for wealth, is designated $Y'(X_1)$. The second predictor, education, is X_2 and the set of residuals of education controlling for wealth is $X_2'(X_1)$. The final step in this procedure is to fit a resistant line between $Y'(X_1)$ and $X_2'(X_1)$, giving the new residuals $Y''(X_1X_2)$ as a product of the first-order relationship (it is easier to keep this straight now because we can see that both sets of residuals, Y' and X_2', have the same variable, X_1, controlled).

The plot of $Y'(X_1)$ versus $X_2'(X_1)$ is given in Figure 18.5 and the equation describing the line is:

$$Y' = -0.003X_2' + 2.29$$

which says that if all countries had the same level of wealth, then an increase of one unit in X_2' (where education is calibrated in per cent-squared) would be associated with a decrease in infant mortality rate of three one-thousandths: virtually nil.

As we noted earlier, we have several dq ratios now, each of which can tell us about some aspect of the fit. Wealth by itself does a moderately good job of

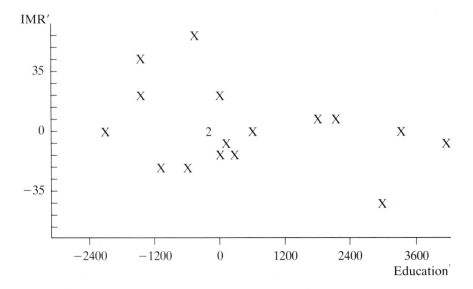

Figure 18.5   IMR versus education, fully controlling for wealth

predicting IMR, with a *dq*-ratio of 22.54/44.25 = 0.51. We now have two ways of determining the extra effect of education: $dqY''/dqY' = 24.99/22.54 = 1.11$, which says that, looking only at that part of IMR that wealth doesn't account for, education does a poor job of adding to our knowledge. The other is $dqY''/dqY = 24.99/44.25 = 0.56$. This ratio looks at the effect of both wealth and education on IMR just like the *dq* ratio from a median polish, and tells us that wealth and education together predict IMR no better than using wealth alone (the *dq* ratio is larger with the two variables than with wealth alone).

What do we conclude from all this? First, a country's per capita gross national product is generally an important predictor of IMR. No surprise; we observed earlier that increasing wealth also increases the potential for satisfying basic needs. But the moderate *dq*-ratio suggests that simply raising a nation's GNP doesn't automatically improve health standards (IMR is generally viewed as one of the most sensitive measures of health-care quality). Other factors must also be implicated. We examined a promising one: education. While its strength was in the expected direction (with or without controls for wealth), its effect, especially at the first-order level, was very modest. (Wimberley (1990), with a different and larger sample and a more complex equation, showed a stronger role for education, though the findings were generally similar.) Perhaps this negative finding should not surprise us, however. It is very likely that wealth causes both education and IMR (where 'cause' is interpreted in the same way as for multivariate analysis), so controlling for wealth would result in the IMR–education relationship diminishing or disappearing.

How might we go about pushing this analysis further? One way is to look at existing theory and/or research. Here again, Wimberley's (1990) discussion is likely to be useful. In his analysis, he considers a number of additional factors pertinent to IMR in developing countries, one of the more suggestive being penetration by multinational corporations. Another way is to look hard at the last set of residuals, *Y''*. As we noted earlier, a set of residuals is just a batch to which the simple techniques of batch analysis are appropriate. We can start by identifying the larger ones. The three in Table 18.3 that stand out are Yemen (49), Philippines (−38) and Trinidad-Tobago (38). The Trinidad-Tobago residual, on closer examination, is far less impressive than the other two. Because its GNP/PC is so much higher than that of the other countries in the sample, its predicted IMR is −16! So *any* reasonable IMR must give a large positive residual. We decide to set this case aside and focus on the other two countries. A thoughtful scan of the *World Development Report* may help.

First, Yemen Arab Republic: in common with women in many Arab states, Yemeni women have far poorer access to education than men (male enrolment in primary schools in 1983 was more than five times as high as female enrolment). Perhaps women have lower status than men and hence poorer life chances generally. If so, this might translate into unsatisfactory pre- and post-natal care. Perhaps poorer access to education can result in inadequate knowledge about nutrition and sanitation. A second interesting statistic for Yemen AR is that almost 37 per cent of central government expenditure in

Table 18.3 IMR residuals fully controlling for
wealth and education

Mauritania	18.5
Lesotho	0.1
Yemen Arab Republic	48.8
Philippines	−38.2
El Salvador	−27.9
Egypt	8.7
Nicaragua	−12.1
Dominican Republic	−5.5
Ecuador	−0.1
Guatemala	−8.1
Paraguay	−24.3
Jordan	5.6
Brazil	14.9
Panama	−17.1
South Korea	1.4
Argentina	−2.8
Greece	10.5
Trinidad-Tobago	38.3

1983 went for defence, the highest in the world for that year. With so much of
their small GNP going into defence, there would be little left for health and
social services.

The Philippines, in contrast, had high and virtually equivalent rates of
primary (and higher) education for males and females while their defence
expenditure was about average for middle income countries. In addition, the
long-term American military presence in the country might perhaps have
resulted in improved health care and sanitation. Of course, these two countries
differ in myriad ways, but such easily interpretable differences can offer a
useful starting point for further analysis.

Controlled Relationships

We have seen that the technique for finding the relationship between two
variables with a third controlled is easy enough, just a common-sense use of old
techniques. Thinking about relationships with controls is a bit harder, because
it is less familiar. Here we will underline the difference between a relationship
without a third variable controlled and the same relationship with such
controls. We will also discuss interpretation of controlled relationships a bit,
and point out some of the problems that can arise.

First, it is vital to understand that the relationship here between education
(X_2) and IMR (Y) is not the same as that between X_2' and Y', the same two

variables having controlled for a third, here wealth. A relationship may change greatly, slightly or not at all when a third variable is held constant.

As one illustration of this, compare the IMR–education relationship with wealth controlled in Figure 18.4 with that of the zero-order relationship between the same two variables. As it happens, both are negative and neither is strong. But after wealth is controlled, the relationship becomes much weaker. So in the zero-order plot, the common component of wealth had the effect of appearing to strengthen the relationship. Now our interpretation must be modified; that something about wealth has an impact on education and something (perhaps the same 'something') about wealth has an impact on IMR, but in hypothetical middle income countries with approximately the same level of wealth, we would expect virtually no relationship between education and IMR. This is worth thinking about!

We cannot give any general rules for interpreting relationships with controls, since each case is a little different and must be thought through on its own, but we will give some suggestions about one use of controls in the next chapter when we discuss controls and causality briefly. Here we will just caution you not to control too freely. For example, suppose you are investigating the possible relationship of urban experience and modern attitudes. You find that urban dwellers are more modern in outlook than rural dwellers. You suspect that this is just because the urban dwellers have higher status so you control status and then look again. If urban dwellers are still more modern, it is not simply because of status – we have removed this – it has something to do with urban life. But suppose you push this further and control for mobility, variety of interpersonal contacts, access to the mass media, and so on. Such variables may well be related to modern attitudes, and the urban–rural difference may well vanish when these variables are controlled. After all, in many ways these variables *are* the urban–rural difference! What is a city, if not a place where people move around a lot and meet lots of varied people and are bombarded by the media and so on? You may be controlling the urban–modern relationship for urbanism itself, which is not helpful. As Stouffer (1962: 267) notes, if we are not careful we are 'likely to "partial out" elements in such a way as to remove much of the commonly understood meaning from a particular index'.

Conclusions and Comments

We have added to our understanding of a dependent variable by bringing in a second independent variable. We did so without anything really new by way of technique. Instead, we used familiar Y by X methods plus common sense. An important step here was the plotting of the zero-order relationship between IMR and education. This made it possible to see the curviness in the plot and transform, perhaps avoiding curviness in the first-order plot. If the first-order plot is found to be curvy in spite of these precautions, it is still possible to go back to the zero-order relationships and try a different transform. It is a mistake to try to transform residuals. In general, it is more likely for variables to have linear relationships if they have the same shape and more likely for variables to have non-linear relationships if their shapes are very different; but this is not a hard and fast rule by any means. Keep plotting and thinking as you go, and you will be able to cope with most surprises the data have for you.

We added the second independent variable by linear fitting, because the second variable was a numeric one. But this is only one possibility of many. We saw still another possibility in Chapter 16, where the first layer of fit was two-way, with categories as the row and column variables, while the residuals were analysed by Y by X methods: we fitted the residuals to a multiplicative interaction term (comparison values). It was noted that we could as easily have fitted the residuals to some new numeric variable such as time. Fits can be mixed. Use whatever combination of techniques, in whatever order, seems promising to you.

We have seen how useful it can be to work in an additional layer of fit. But how far should this process be pushed? When should one stop adding new layers of fit? There are several criteria and you have to make your choices in line with your own feelings about the data. One criterion is 'stop when there is nothing left to explain'. The dq ratio is helpful here: if it is pretty close to zero, then there is not much of Y left to worry about. You don't expect the ratio to get right down to zero, by the way: almost always there are some Y residuals left, either because of measurement error with no systematic explanation or because of the effects of some variable not covered by your data. If you keep pushing on regardless, trying to get all of Y explained, you can get overfitting, which happens when you have milked so much out of the data that there is nothing left but random error. Fitting tiny errors is not likely to do you much good. On the other hand, don't give up too soon. An additional layer can often produce interesting insights even when Y is substantially explained. Usually it is worthwhile to push as far as you can, stopping when you get silly-looking results (often a sign of overfitting). Now, often you never get to use the 'nothing left to explain' criterion because other issues enter earlier. First, and most common, you may run out of time. Secondly, you may run out of potential Xs. You may have looked at everything you feel is worth looking at.

How do you choose independent variables for further layers of fit? You may choose the variable that you think should be most closely related to Y (you may think this because you have a hunch, or because you know there are theories or research that predict X is important for Y). If you are short of ideas about causes of Y, you may plot a few interesting-looking possibilities and see which one has a relationship to Y that is strong and makes sense (there is little point in using a fit that you cannot explain, since your understanding of Y is not increased much that way). This last approach can cause problems though. A very common one is the search for the perfect fit, where several imperfect but suggestive fits may be passed over in favour of continuing the search for the 'best'. Remember: if you are engaging in this kind of search, it is probably because you don't really understand the process you're investigating all that well. But a few suggestive exploratory fits can increase your understanding and make it easier for you to locate those better variables as a result. Of course, some of the ideas you try out will lead nowhere; but, as you should realize by now, this has advantages. Finding that a given X has nothing to add can actually be very useful. For one thing, you learn what to rule out; in addition, the very poorness of the fit may lead to very interesting questions (most commonly, 'it should have/was supposed to work; why didn't it, and what can I learn from that?').

Exploratory and Confirmatory

The exploratory techniques in this chapter are directly parallel to the confirmatory technique partial correlation, the topic of the next chapter. The parallels will be discussed there. In both exploratory and confirmatory statistics, the strategy of controlling one variable (or more) while examining a relationship between two others is not confined to Y by X methods.

HOMEWORK

Table 18.4 Homicide rates (per 100 000 population) and correlates, Canadian provinces and territories, 1981

Province	Homicide rate	% British	% Native (first peoples)	1980–1 structural poverty index
Newfoundland	0.6	92.2	0.6	−1.26
Prince Edward Island	0.8	77.0	0.4	−1.66
Nova Scotia	1.1	72.4	0.8	−1.25
New Brunswick	2.3	53.5	0.7	−1.33
Quebec	2.9	7.6	0.7	0.77
Ontario	1.9	52.6	1.0	−0.78
Manitoba	3.9	36.9	5.9	−0.74
Saskatchewan	2.9	38.3	5.7	−0.22
Alberta	3.4	43.5	2.7	0.22
British Columbia	4.0	51.0	2.4	0.22
Yukon	4.5	43.6	14.8	2.67
Northwest Territories	11.5	22.4	51.2	3.38

Source: Lenton (1989).
The structural poverty index is a combination of IMR and proportion of families without income. It is given in standardized form (using the mean and standard deviation). Higher index values mean higher levels of structural poverty.

The data in Table 18.4 contain 1981 homicide rates (per 100 000) and three correlate variables for the Canadian provinces and territories. Explore the relationship between homicide rates and any two of the three predictor variables. You will want to use one of the chosen two as a control variable and look at the first-order relationship between the dependent variable and the predictor. How does it differ from the zero-order relationship? Assess the strength of the relationship and discuss.

19
Partial Correlations and Causality

In Chapter 11 we learned how to make a exploratory Y by X fit with one independent variable, and in Chapter 18 we learned how to go further by looking at the relationship between Y and a second independent variable with the first independent variable controlled. In this chapter we continue with the confirmatory parallels to the exploratory material used so far. We have already seen, in Chapter 13, how to make a confirmatory Y by X fit with one independent variable: we use linear regression, which is strongly parallel to exploratory Y by X. Here we learn how to measure the strength of the relationship between Y and X_2 with X_1 controlled, or partial correlation. This is strongly parallel to the exploratory approach, except that we focus on the strength of the fit, rather than the fit itself.

To compute the partial correlation between two variables with a third controlled, one follows the same basic steps as in the previous chapter. The effects of the control variable, here X_1, are removed. That is, find $X'_2 = X_2 - (b_2 X_1 + a_2)$ and $Y' = Y - (b_1 X_1 + a_1)$; but this time the bs and as are found via linear regression, the confirmatory fitting method, rather than the exploratory Y by X. This having been done, all we need is the regression between X'_2 and Y':

$$Y' = b_3 X'_2 + a_3$$

The correlation that goes with this fit is the partial correlation of X_2 and Y with X_1 held constant.

We will also show a faster way to compute a partial correlation by hand, with a computing formula. Finally, we will look at spurious correlation and causality, the regression analogue of material we treated in multivariate tabular analysis.

An Example of Partial Correlation

To underline the parallels between partial correlation and the approach used in Chapter 18, let's continue with the IMR data used there. Again, let us consider the relationship between IMR and education with wealth held constant. We begin, as we did in Chapter 18, by removing the linear effects of wealth from both IMR and education, with wealth and education transformed in the same way as before. The regression equation between wealth and IMR is:

$$Y = -97.1X_1 + 268 \ (r^2 = 0.648)$$

giving the residuals $Y' \ (X_1)$.

Next, we find the residuals from education holding wealth constant, as before. The residuals X_2' come from the equation

$$X_2 = 5123X_1 - 7862 \ (r^2 = 0.46)$$

Finally, we calculate the regression line between Y' and X_2', with X_1 fully controlled. This equation is:

$$Y'(X_1) = -0.005X_2' \ (X_1) + 0 \ (r^2 = 0.14)$$

which also provides the final residuals, $Y''(X_1X_2)$. This equation is very close to the exploratory fit, where the estimate of the slope was -0.003. One important difference between the two fits is the assessment of their strength; the r^2 suggests a modest association, while the exploratory results, with a dq-ratio greater than 1.0, suggests that the inclusion of education adds little or nothing to our understanding of IMR.

There are three useful points that are illustrated by this example. First, in confirmatory regression, adding another predictor variable, even a worthless one, can never make r^2 smaller. Second, this example is a strong reminder that the dq ratio only measures changes in the spread of the middle half of the data, so improvements outside the quartiles don't get picked up by this measure. Third, you must be careful with the critical value for the t-ratio associated with the slope between two sets of residuals – the computer 'assumes' that the proper number of degrees of freedom will be $n - 2$, but when we controlled for X_1 we lost another degree of freedom, so the proper number of dfs here is $n - 3$.

The IMR example also gives us some feeling for the importance of exploration in multiple regression analysis. Finding appropriate functional forms for our predictor variables, the log of wealth and the square of education, was an important step in our analysis. Both of the plots after transforming were more nearly regular ovals of points, better satisfying regression assumptions, which also hold for partial correlation. (Review Chapter 13 to refresh your memory on these assumptions.)

The confirmatory analysis also permits us to measure the strength of the IMR–education fit with wealth controlled in a useful, widely accepted way. In Chapter 13, we encountered two strength measures associated with a regression line; the simple correlation, r, and r^2, the proportion of variance accounted for by the linear fit (which also happens to be the square of the correlation). We use comparable measures for relationships with one or more variables controlled. The correlation between $Y'(X_1)$ and $X_2(X_1)$, a partial correlation, can be obtained in a variety of ways. When you have a computer output from the regression in hand, an easy way is just to take the square root of r^2, here 0.14, and attach the sign of the slope (in this case, the slope is negative). This gives us -0.37, which indicates a modest relationship, as before.

The computations for the partial correlation can be done by hand, from scratch. It is, after all, just a correlation and the same equation that was used in Chapter 13 can equally well be used here. But don't round too soon. You get residuals by removing systematic variation from a variable. Consequently, residuals contain less systematic variation but about the same random error as the original data. So if you round too casually, you may lose an important part of the systematic variance that remains. However, computers are good at running regressions so it will rarely be necessary to do such work by hand.

What we have calculated is called the partial correlation of IMR and education holding wealth constant, or alternatively, the first-order correlation (similar to the language of multivariate tabular analysis). As noted earlier, this comes out of a set of regressions and so should meet the assumptions of regression. The quick-and-dirty way to check the assumptions is just to look hard at the plot in Figure 19.1. While it isn't perfect, most of the points would be included in a fairly smooth oval 'envelope'. Looking more closely at the plot, however, we see that the spread is greater on the left side of the plot than on the right. There are too few points here for anything more than speculation. But it is striking that for those countries whose education residuals are greater than zero (greater access to education than wealth predicts), improvements in universality of education are associated with some reduction in IMR. In contrast, for those countries with poorer education than wealth would predict, the negative residuals, there appears to be virtually no relationship between

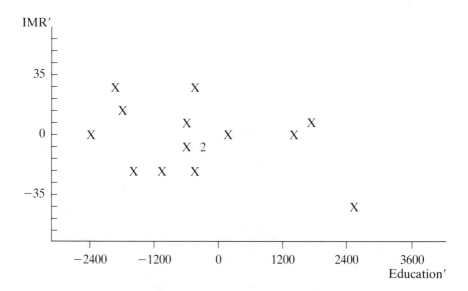

Figure 19.1   The plot of IMR versus education, with wealth controlled

education and IMR. This suggests that, first, how a country spends its money may be as important as how much it has to spend and, secondly, structural barriers to education may be one of the keys to understanding IMR.

This plot of IMR and education with the linear effects of wealth held constant is, like the regression equation, quite similar to its exploratory parallel. Both plots were produced in the same way, so what we see is the way these variables would be expected to relate if all the countries had the same level of wealth. These data are pretty well behaved, which is why the exploratory and confirmatory lines are so similar.

We will not discuss these results further since the patterns are so similar to those found in exploration. But it is worth noting that, for both analyses, the IMR–education relationship is substantially weakened after holding wealth constant – the r^2 drops from 0.46 to 0.14. Of course, controlling one variable will not always weaken the ties between other variables. As we have seen with multivariate tabular analysis, ties can be strengthened, weakened, reversed or unaffected by such controls. About the only way to find out what will happen is to try it and see, to control your X_1 and look at X_2' and Y'.

Finding Partial Correlations Directly

Controlling a variable is so useful that we would like to do it often, so it would be nice if we could do it quickly. The procedure we just used has some advantages (it uses nothing new, it is visual at every step, and one can clearly see what is happening) but it is rather indirect. Fortunately there is a simple formula for computing the partial correlation directly from the zero order correlations:

$$\text{partial correlation} = r_{X_2Y.X_1} = \frac{r_{X_2Y} - (r_{X_2X_1})(r_{YX_1})}{\sqrt{1 - r_{X_2X_1}^2}\ \sqrt{1 - r_{YX_1}^2}}$$

There is a bit of new notation here, so let's go through it part by part:

$r_{X_2Y.X_1} =$ This is a common notation for the partial correlation of X_2 and Y with X_1 controlled.

$r_{X_2Y} - (r_{X_2X_1})(r_{YX_1})$ This top part of the $r_{X_2Y.X_1}$ formula just puts simple correlations together, and does so in a reasonable way. You start with the r for X_2 and Y, the relationship before controlling for X_1; then you remove (subtract) the correlation of X_1 with Y multiplied by the correlation of X_1 with X_2. This makes sense since the idea is to remove the effects of X_1.

$\sqrt{(1 - r_{X_2X_1}^2)}\ \sqrt{(1 - r_{YX_1}^2)}$ This bottom part of the $r_{X_2Y.X_1}$ formula is also based on simple correlations and also makes sense. We know that $1 - r^2$ tells us how much of a dependent variable is not explained: so here we have the amount of X_2

that X_1 does not explain and the amount of Y that X_1 does not explain. This product tells us how much action remains after X_1 is controlled. It is a kind of norming or standardizing factor, which ensures that our partial correlation will go from -1 to $+1$ just like a correlation of raw data.

The partial correlation formula is another one of those things which are easier to do than explain: plugging in the numbers is no trouble. In our example,

$$r_{X_2Y.X_1} = \frac{(-0.71) - (0.68)(-0.81)}{\sqrt{1 - 0.68^2} \ \sqrt{1 - 0.81^2}} = \frac{-0.16}{0.43} = -0.37$$

This is the same figure we got by the longer, but numerically identical, route of finding and correlating X'_2 and Y'.

Significance Testing for Partial Correlations

Since the partial correlation is a correlation, a correlation between residuals, we can treat it as such; most importantly, we can test the significance of a partial correlation in almost exactly the same way as we test a simple correlation. Find

$$F_{1,N-3} = \left[\frac{r^2_{X_2Y.X_1}}{1 - r^2_{X_2Y.X_1}} \right] (N - 3)$$

Once again we find the ratio of explained to unexplained variance (the partial r^2 over one minus the partial r^2) and multiply it by the degrees of freedom, here $N - 3$. The only new wrinkle as compared to the simple correlation procedure in the earlier chapter is this: the degrees of freedom become 1 and $N - 3$ instead of 1 and $N - 2$. We have 'used up' one more degree of freedom because we have two predictors here (X_1 is invisible but still involved).

We will continue to work with the IMR example, not only for continuity with the exploration, but also because the data set is appropriate for confirmatory analysis. The cases are independent and randomly selected. The squared partial correlation between IMR and education, with wealth held constant, is $r^2_{x_2y.x_1} = 0.14$ so

$$F_{1,15} = \frac{0.14}{1 - 0.14}(15) = 2.44$$

The critical value for F with 1 and 15 dfs is 4.54, so this partial correlation is not significantly different from zero at the 0.05 level. Again, the confirmatory results mirror the exploratory results in the previous chapter. What began as a robust zero-order relation between IMR and education became substantially weaker after controlling for wealth, although it didn't vanish. What we have done here with regression and correlations is strongly analogous to our use of multivariate analysis for clarifying causality. This form of statistical control can be enormously useful for interpreting causality.

Related Variables and Causal Relationships

We can all think of instances where variables appear to be related but causation is absent ('I just have to leave my umbrella at home and it starts to rain!'). Let's look at a few examples of spurious correlations.

Earlier, we mentioned the relationship between thumb length and reading speed (you can win 'beer bets' with this, and you thought statistics didn't have practical applications . . .). The explanation we offered for this oddity is that as age increases, so too do both reading speed and thumb length.

Therefore, if we control for age, the correlation between thumb length and reading speed will disappear. We can sum up the situation in a little diagram with arrows representing causal relationships, marking the arrows with a + if the relationship is positive and a − if the relationship is negative:

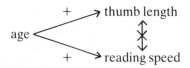

Age is causally related to both thumb length and reading speed: both are by-products of maturation. Thumb length and reading speed are in no way causally related to each other (the broken arrow between them). However, thumb length and reading speed are positively correlated because each is related to age. Spurious relationships can be identified easily if you have information about the variable that is affecting the spurious pair; control for this variable and see if the relationship disappears.

Let's consider another example: the per capita expenditure on alcoholic beverages over time has a strong positive relationship with the average salary of clergymen. This sounds as though the only way we can keep people sober is to keep the clergy poor. This is probably false, and we'll assume that clerical income has no causal effect on expenditure on alcohol. It is barely possible that there is some causal link in the other direction, however: perhaps increased expenditure on alcohol leads to increased social problems and thus to increased demand for clerical services. But the most likely possibility is that this is a spurious correlation again. After all, both salaries and luxury expenditures tend to be related to overall wealth in the society. We could have something like this:

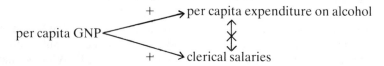

If this model is correct, then controlling per capita GNP should wipe out the correlation between clerical salaries and spending on alcohol.

Partial Correlations and Causality: An Example

Let's look at a small example including actual correlations so that we can see how partial correlations help in clarifying possible causal connections. Turning once again to the World Handbook (1964), we find that death rates per 1000 population are inversely related to urbanization ($r = -.33$). Urbanization here is defined as the percentage of population residing in communities with a population in excess of 20 000. Now, there are many ways that this could be causally meaningful, for example, there are usually more doctors and hospitals, better sanitation, etc., in urban areas, but even these are actually aspects of another variable, general wealth. After all, hospitals and sewage systems are perquisites of the wealthy countries, and so is a large urban population. A high rate of urbanization implies that a sizeable proportion of the population has been freed from primary production. Let's examine how per capita GNP is correlated with the other variables.

The correlation matrix in Table 19.1 is a conventional, compact way to present correlations among variables and is especially handy if a lot of variables are involved. The main diagonal, upper left to lower right, gives correlations of variables with themselves; all these correlations are 1.0, of course, so they are often omitted. The area above the main diagonal is left blank because the entries there would just repeat the information given below the main diagonal (remember, correlations are symmetric).

The model we are suggesting is one where national wealth is the underlying cause of both an increase in urbanization and a decrease in the death rate; e.g.

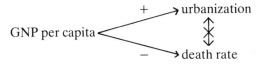

Table 19.1   A correlation matrix

	GNP per capita	Death rate per 1000	Urbanization
GNP per capita	1.0		
Death rate (per 1000)	−0.41	1.0	
Urbanization	0.71	−0.33	1.0

If this is true, then the correlation between urbanization and death rate should vanish when GNP per capita is controlled. Let's try it. Plugging in the correlations we get:

$$r_{UD.G} = \frac{-0.33 - (-0.41)(0.71)}{\sqrt{1 - (-0.41)^2} \ \sqrt{1 - (0.71)^2}} = -0.06$$

It does virtually vanish. This is strong support for the model. However, it is also conceptually possible for an alternative causal structure to be at work here: wealth could be causing urbanization, as before, but city life might just be safer, for the reasons mentioned above as well as others. Then the model would look like this:

$$+ \qquad\qquad\qquad -$$

GNP per capita $\longrightarrow$ urbanization $\longrightarrow$ death rate

If this model is correct then GNP per capita and death rate should have a zero partial because they are linked only through urbanization, the intervening variable. If this model is correct, the $r_{GD.U}$ should vanish. Let's try it.

$$r_{GD.U} = \frac{-0.41 - (0.71)(-0.33)}{\sqrt{1 - (0.71)^2} \ \sqrt{(1 - (-0.33)^2}} = -0.27$$

It is clear from this that the first model, in which wealth causes both urbanization and reduced death rate, is definitely preferable to this one.

What about the IMR example? Is the IMR–education linkage also spurious? You might think so, for two reasons. After controlling for wealth, the partial correlation is not significantly different from zero, and all the examples here have been of spurious relationships. However, while the partial relationship is much weaker than the zero-order one, it doesn't vanish, but rather, at 0.14, is of moderate size. This outcome is more consistent with a diagram like the following:

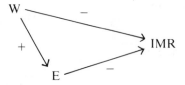

This diagram depicts wealth as having strong direct effects on both education and IMR while education has a modest effect on IMR net of wealth.

In general, partial correlations can be very helpful in examining alternative causal possibilities, for those that do not conform to the observed partials can be eliminated. Perhaps there will be more than one plausible view that does match the observed partials; if so, turn to theory or consider the roles of some further variables. Simon (1954) describes some of the conclusions that can be drawn from partial correlations if a few simple assumptions are met. We will not go into this further here, but will just remind you not to jump to conclusions about causal relationships. It is possible for two variables to be correlated but to have no causal connection to each other. It is also true that two variables can seem unrelated, having a zero-order correlation of zero, for example; yet when a third variable is controlled, their causal connection becomes manifest.

Exploratory and Confirmatory

We have seen that the exploratory and confirmatory techniques for making a second linear fit are directly analogous. In both cases, the dependent variable Y' (the residuals from Y controlling for X_1) is fitted to the new variable X'_2 (X_2 with the linear effect of X_1 removed). This control of X_1 in both Y and X_2 clears away the underbrush, thus clarifying the $X_2 - Y$ relationship. The exploratory and confirmatory procedures are exactly the same, except for the kind of linear fit (exploratory or confirmatory) that is used.

When the controlled relationship between Y' and X'_2 is examined, the amount of Y' unexplained by X'_2 is

$$\frac{dq\ Y''}{dq\ Y'}$$

in the exploratory analysis, and is

$$1 - r^2_{X_2Y.X_1}$$

in the confirmatory analysis.

Using the Computer

Of the two ways to get partial correlations, the more familiar route is to run a series of regressions. This approach uses only the familiar MINITAB instruction REGR (see Chapter 13 to refresh your memory). If you prefer to use the formula involving zero-order correlations, you will need a correlation matrix. MINITAB makes this easy: if your variables are in C1, C2 and C3, the command is

    MTB> CORR C1–C3

HOMEWORK

For Chapter 18's homework, you found a second layer of fit in an exploratory fashion. Now do the confirmatory equivalent. Examine two alternative causal patterns that might exist among your variables. Make diagrams of these, compute the appropriate partial correlations and discuss. If your data set is a random sample, do the appropriate significance tests.

20
Multiple Regression

In Chapters 18 and 19 we presented ways to examine situations involving two independent variables by looking at the effects of each in sequence. The process consisted of first making an ordinary linear fit for X_1 with both X_2 and Y, then looking at the relationship between X_2 and Y with X_1 controlled. Both exploratory and confirmatory approaches were given. These are useful techniques, but they do not tell us all we might like to know about two independent variables. In particular, they do not show us how the two can work together to make a combined fit for Y. *Multiple regression* is a confirmatory technique that combines X_1 and X_2 to predict Y using both variables at once. There are exploratory parallels to multiple regression (sometimes called 'robust regression') but they go a bit beyond the quick and easy paper-and-pencil exploratory methods we have stuck to in this book. So rather than introduce more complex exploratory procedures, we'll point out ways that exploratory thinking can be combined with multiple regression procedures.

We will begin the chapter by describing the simplest kind of multiple regression, in which two independent variables are added together to make a combined fit. This is actually quite a familiar idea. Recall what we did in two-way elementary analysis. We predicted Y from a simple combination of the row variable and the column variable:

Y = row effect + column effect + overall level

For basic multiple regression, the effects of two independent variables are added together in a similar way:

$Y = b_1 X_1 + b_2 X_2 + a$

To make such a fit we have to find values for b_1, b_2 and a; the multiple regression computations are designed to find values which minimize the sum of the squared residuals from the fit (this is the 'least squares criterion' again, the same one used in simple linear regression in Chapter 13). We will describe the role and meaning of b_1, b_2 and a, but we will give only a few formulae for computing such values and these formulae will be left to an optional appendix at the end of the book. While the computations for most multiple regressions are simple in principle, they are very time-consuming in practice, so that the work is almost always done by computer. Every statistical package has a multiple regression program that is easy to use.

Once made, a multiple regression fit can be evaluated with a *multiple correlation coefficient*, which turns out to be just a special use of the correlation we met in Chapter 13. The test for a multiple correlation is also very similar to the test for a simple correlation as done in Chapter 13.

With basic multiple regression under your belt, it is easy to move on to a few simple and very useful variations. These extensions include making a curvy fit, making interaction fits, using categorical variables and working with additional independent variables.

Combining Two Variables

Let's start with two independent variables added together (a 'linear combination' of two independent variables):

$$Y = b_1 X_1 + b_2 X_2 + a$$

We said above that the 'effect' of X_1 is added to the 'effect' of X_2, just as row and column variables are added in two-way analysis. Here the 'effect' of each variable is worked in through the *regression weights* or the b_i values by which the X variables are multiplied. These weights are analogous to slopes in simple linear regression:

b_1 = the change in Y for a unit change in X_1, holding X_2 constant
b_2 = the change in Y for a unit change in X_2, holding X_1 constant

The new wrinkle here, compared to simple linear regression, is the part about holding the other independent variable constant. Why do we do that? Well, $b_1 X_1$ should reflect the separate, distinct effect of X_1 on Y, while $b_2 X_2$ should reflect the separate, distinct effect of X_2; then we can add $b_1 X_1$ and $b_2 X_2$ together without duplication, without adding the same effect in twice.

Consider the infant mortality example again. We want to find the equation

$$IMR = b_1 \text{ (logged GNP/PC)} + b_2 \text{ (squared education)} + a$$

in order to determine the best additive combination of wealth and education for predicting IMR, a question we have so far not attempted to answer. The equation turns out to be:

$$Y = -72.3 X_1 - 0.00483 X_2 + 230 \ (r^2 = 0.697)$$

(If you would like to know how to calculate these numbers by hand, look at Appendix A.) What does this equation tell us? First, when education is held constant, wealth is inversely related to IMR (the negative weight tells us this). Secondly, when wealth is held constant, education similarly is inversely related to IMR. It is also worth noting that the weight for X_2 is exactly the same, within rounding error, as that obtained in Chapter 19 from the regression between $Y'(X_1)$ and $X_2'(X_1)$.

The regression weights tell us the direction of each Xs effect on Y with the other X controlled. Do they tell us any more? Unfortunately, no. It is especially important to note that they do not tell us the strength of each independent variable's separate effect on Y. This can be a problem because it is very tempting to think that the bs do reflect strength. For example, in the fit above it looks as though wealth is enormously more important than education because its weight is so much larger in absolute value (-22.3 versus -0.0048, quite a difference). However, we just can't draw this conclusion: the problem is that the bs depend in part on how strongly each variable is related to Y, and also in part on the difference between the scale of Y and the scale of that X. In our example, wealth has a much smaller spread than does education, so wealth must be multiplied by a large b just to get $b_1 X_1$ into the same sort of units as Y.

We noted that the same sort of problem cropped up in simple linear regression in Chapter 13. At that time we pointed out that a linear fit could be made with standardized versions of X and Y to get a fit directly reflecting the real strength of relationship between X and Y: if Y^* and X^* are the standardized variables, the fit between them is just

$$Y^* = rX^*$$

Standardizing eliminates the scale differences that can make interpretation of slopes misleading, leaving a nice simple picture involving nothing but the strength of the relationship. Why not try the same thing with multiple regression?

The Standardized Fit

We begin by standardizing all the variables used in the multiple regression:

$$Y^* = \frac{Y - \bar{Y}}{sd_Y}$$

$$X^*_1 = \frac{X_1 - \bar{X}_1}{sd_{X_1}}$$

$$X^*_2 = \frac{X_2 - \bar{X}_2}{sd_{X_2}}$$

Then we do the same regression over again with the standardized variables to get a standardized multiple regression fit with standardized weights:

$$Y^* = b_1{}^* X_1{}^* + b_2{}^* X_2{}^*$$

What should these new standardized regression weights be like? We still want to combine X_1 and X_2 to make a good combined fit predicting Y. How much weight should we give to each of the independent variables? Surely that should now depend only on how strongly they are related to Y. Take X_1, for instance. The more impact X_1 has on Y, aside from X_2's impact, the more weight X_1 should get. Similarly, the weight given to X_2 reflects the strength of X_2's effect on Y, with the effects of X_1 held constant. X_1 is held constant when considering X_2, and vice versa, so that the weights for each independent variable reflect the separate, distinct effect it has on Y. Then these distinct effects can be added up to get the overall fit above, in which

b_1^* = the effect of X_1^* on Y^*, holding X_2^* constant
b_2^* = the effect of X_2^* on Y^*, holding X_1^* constant

These b^*s sound a lot like partial correlations, and indeed if you look in Appendix A you will see that the formulae look very similar to those for partial correlations, although the differences are important. A partial correlation, for example, must range from $+1$ to -1, while b^* can lie outside that range. By looking at these b^* values one can immediately see both the relative importance of the X variables and the direction of their effects. Because $\bar{Y}^*$, $\bar{X}_1^*$ and $\bar{X}_2^*$ are all equal to zero, a^* is also zero, always.

Let's consider IMR again. When IMR, wealth and education are standardized, the linear multiple regression fit for predicting IMR from the other two variables is

$$Y^* = -0.600X_1^* - 0.303X_2^*$$
$$(t\text{-scores} = -2.10 \quad -1.57)$$

Now this means: IMR* = -0.600 wealth* -0.303 education*

1 When wealth is held constant, education has a negative effect on IMR; we see this from the negative b_2^*, -0.303, for education. This is the same thing we learned from the raw weight b_2, and also from the partial correlation found in Chapter 19.
2 When education is held constant, wealth has a negative effect on IMR; we see this from the negative weight -0.600 for wealth.
3 Wealth has about twice the effect of education; we see this from both the b^* values, and from the t-scores. We could not see anything like this from the unstandardized regression.

Regression equations with standardized variables and standardized weights are easy to interpret because the weights mean what they appear to mean. We often prefer to work with standardized variables and regression weights.

We should emphasize that the unstandardized and standardized versions of a regression are the same fit. It is often easier to make sense of the standardized version, though, and we prefer it for that reason. On the other hand, the raw weights are also very useful. For example, Inkeles and Smith (1974) report a study of individual modernity in six developing nations. They wanted to know, among other things, the extent to which people are modernized through modern work experience; that is, through working in a factory. They can and do report results using standardized weights, but they also report results using raw weights, in part because the raw weights have a clear interpretation: one can compare the modernity gained from a year of education to the modernity gained by a year of factory work.

Evaluating the Fit as a Whole

The fit described above combines two independent variables in the way that best predicts Y. The criterion for a good fit is the same as it was for simple linear regression: the squared residuals are minimized. The residuals are just

$$Y' = Y - (b_1X_1 + b_2X_2 + a)$$
$$= \text{observation} - \text{fit}$$

Since multiple regression is designed to minimize squared residuals for all the data points, it will not be very resistant. Even though residuals from non-resistant fits are not entirely satisfactory, they are better than nothing. And since most computer programs are equipped to print out and plot residuals, you should request and scrutinize them as a standard practice.

As always, we want some measure of how well the fit is working, of how close the predicted values $\hat{Y}$ are to the actual Y values. Well, we have two sets of numbers and we want to see how well they are related; why not just correlate them? The correlation of observed Y values and the $\hat{Y}$ values predicted from two or more X variables is called a *multiple correlation* and symbolized as a capital R (to distinguish it from simple correlations using just one X). R goes from 0 to 1.0: if $R = 0$ there is no linear relationship between X_1 or X_2 or their additive combination and Y, while if $R = 1.0$ then X_1 and X_2 predict Y perfectly. A multiple correlation, unlike the r for just one independent variable, cannot be negative. Again the easiest thing to interpret is the squared multiple correlation. R^2 for the IMR example is 0.70, which means that a linear combination of wealth and education explains 70 per cent of the variation in IMR. Wealth alone explained 65 per cent and education alone explained 50 per cent, so we haven't done a lot better using the two variables together than we could have done using them separately. This is partly because while wealth and education are both strongly related to IMR, they are also strongly related to each other ($r = 0.68$), so they duplicate their effects a great deal.

A Significance Test for R^2

There is a very simple test for R^2 that is very much like the F-tests for simple linear regression and for partial correlation.

The null and alternate hypotheses are:

H_0: $R^2 = 0$. In the universe, X_1 and X_2 have no linear effects on Y.
H_1: $R^2 > 0$. In the universe, X_1 and X_2 have a combined linear effect on Y.

To do the test find

$$F_{2,N-3} = \frac{R^2}{(1-R^2)} \frac{(N-3)}{2}$$

if you have two independent variables. Later in the chapter, we will see how this formula can be generalized. For the IMR example

$$Y^* = -0.600X_1^* - 0.303X_2^*$$
$$R^2 = 0.70$$

so the observed F-value is

$$F_{2,15} = \frac{0.70}{0.30} \left(\frac{15}{2}\right) = 17.27$$

The critical value for $F_{2,15}$ at the 0.05 level is 3.58, so our F is much too high for H_0 to be retained.

As always, the test is based on some assumptions about the data which should be considered ahead of time. Technically, the assumptions apply to the sub-batches of Y defined by combinations of values of X_1 and X_2: given any (X_1,X_2) combination, Y should be normal, and the spread of Y should be the same for every (X_1,X_2) combination. Now this is a hard set of assumptions! It is hard to visualize, and also hard to check.

Fortunately multiple regression, like the other confirmatory techniques in this book, is very robust. The assumptions need only be met roughly; so they only have to be checked roughly. One reasonable approach is to plot Y by each of the independent variables and check to see whether the plots are roughly

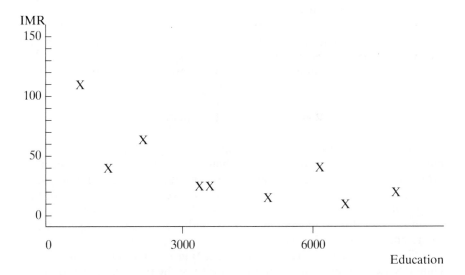

Figure 20.1a   IMR/education for high wealth

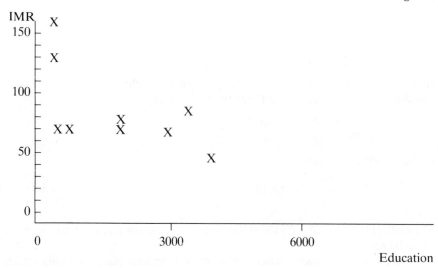

Figure 20.1b   IMR/education for low wealth

oval; this is easy to do and is worthwhile for other reasons as well, like checking for curvilinear relationships. We have already seen, in Chapters 18 and 19, that the plots of IMR by log GNP/PC and IMR by (enrolment in secondary school)^2 look fine. You can refine this approach a bit by plotting Y against one independent variable with the other held constant, for example as in Figure 20.1, where we plot IMR by education twice: once for wealth high, once for wealth low. Both the plots look very roughly oval. The plots are also useful for other reasons, as we will see shortly.

The data should also be based on a random sample, as always. This does hold for this set of data, which was randomly selected from the set of middle income countries in the *World Development Report* (1986), although there could be unknown biases in the way the World Bank classified the countries.

Interpreting Multiple Regressions: More Examples

Since multiple regressions are mostly done by computer, people working with multiple regression spend most of their time interpreting regression fits provided for them by the computer or by a research article. To help you get used to reading multiple regression equations, we'll give a few more of them along with interpretations in words. The IMR example had two negative weights, so we'll present examples where both weights are positive as well as where one is positive and one negative.

First consider some regressions predicting occupational prestige in the United States and in Canada. In both countries, the prestige ratings of a large set of occupations have been found by asking a sample of people to rate occupations. Duncan (1961) argued that prestige in the USA should be related to the income and education of people in an occupation. He developed measures of X_1 (occupational income) and X_2 (occupational education) and used these to predict Y (the occupation's prestige rating). He found this equation (using raw weights):

$$Y = 0.59X_1 + 0.55X_2 - 6.0 \qquad R^2 = 0.83$$

Later, Blishen and McRoberts (1976) found a similar multiple regression for Canada, using Canadian ratings of occupations and income and education measures based on the 1971 Canadian census. Rounding their equation to two significant digits to keep it parallel to Duncan's, it is:

$$Y = 0.30X_1 + 0.37X_2 + 12.0 \qquad R^2 = 0.84$$

What are these two equations saying? First, in both of them the weights for income and education are positive: the prestige of an occupation is higher if the people in it are better paid and better educated. Secondly, the pattern of weights looks roughly similar in both equations, suggesting that the under-pinnings of prestige may be similar in both countries; this would be plausible given that the two nations are culturally and economically related. Thirdly, both fits are very good, with over 80 per cent of prestige explained by income and education combined. We cannot be sure of the relative importance of education versus income in determining prestige, since these are raw re-gression weights (it turns out that education and income are roughly equal in their effects). Why did we give raw weights? Only raw weights were reported by Blishen and McRoberts, because these weights were used for prediction. The multiple regression was done using only 85 occupations (there is a limit to the number whose prestige can be rated in practice) while there are many hundreds reported in the census. The prestige of the remaining occupations can be estimated from the regression equation and the income and education information in the census.

A variable can be a predictor in one analysis and dependent in another. We have just seen income used to predict prestige; Stolzenberg (1975) tries to predict income. His Y is the median earnings of people in an occupation. To predict this, he uses $X_1 =$ median years of schooling and $X_2 =$ years of specific vocational preparation needed to perform the occupation's work at an average level (X_2 was based on ratings by experts; all the data came from the US census). He found:

$$Y = 391.5X_1 + 412.1X_2 - 49.1 \qquad R^2 = 0.22$$

It is no surprise to find that occupations with more highly educated people and with more training requirements are better paid. It is more interesting to see that years of general schooling (X_2) have a positive effect on income even when specific job training is held constant and vice versa; both general and specific education go with increased earnings. However, together they explain only 22 per cent of the variation in occupational income, so other independent variables should be considered.

Chase-Dunn (1975) uses multiple regression in a very different way from the previous authors. He is interested in the effects of 'investment dependence', the 'profits made by foreign direct investment in the "host" country', on the rate of economic development. The effects could be positive (because investment stimulates economic growth by providing new capital) or negative (because foreign investment is a form of foreign control and exploitation that will hinder development rather than foster it). In any case, looking at the simple relationship between investment dependence and development clearly won't do; for example, if we find they are positively correlated, does that mean investment leads to development or does it mean more developed countries attract more investment? To clarify the causal position, Chase-Dunn used data from two points in time. Using logged GNP per capita to measure development, he looked at

1970 development $= b_1$ (1950 development) $+$
$\qquad\qquad\qquad b_2$ (1950–5 investment dependence) $+ a$

The 1950 development is included because countries more developed in the past are usually more developed in the present, aside from other factors like investment; by including past development in the regression we control for it. Then we can see what effect past investment dependence has on changes in development. The regression fit was:

$$Y = 1.32X_1 - 0.097X_2 - 0.17$$

(The R^2 is not given but is described as 'high'.) The weight for 1950 development is both positive and over 1.0, which suggests that development tends to increase over time: the countries with high GNP per capita in 1950 have even higher GNP in 1970. No surprise there. On the other hand the weight for 1950–5 investment dependence is negative, suggesting that countries with heavier foreign investment in the past have lost ground in development compared to others. The author uses other measures of development and finds the same result: investment dependence tends to hamper development.

Some Extensions of the Simple Case

Now that we know how to use two independent variables in a multiple linear regression, we can push the idea just a bit further to get ways of making curvilinear fits, using categories, working with additional X variables, and working with interaction. All of these are very useful capabilities: often the data are not linear, the variables are poorly measured, Y is related to more than two other variables or the independent variables have non-additive effects. We have already seen some examples of curvy relationships in Chapter 12 and of interaction effects in Chapter 16.

Fitting a Curved Relationship

Back in Chapter 12 we showed how to use transformations to straighten out one kind of curve: a curve with just one bend that is always increasing or always decreasing. Once the curve is straightened, either confirmatory or exploratory fits can be made. Fine, but what if the curve is a U or J shape, so it is not always increasing or always decreasing? Then we have to make this kind of fit:

$$Y = b_1X_1 + b_2X_1^2 + a$$

which will fit any one-bend curve well enough, even a U or J. In the exploratory chapter we left things there, since working with transformations was enough for one chapter: we did not show you how to make an exploratory fit of the form above, although this can be done fairly easily.

With multiple linear regression, making a fit like this is extremely easy. What difference is there between this fit and the one we just made earlier in the chapter? That is, what difference is there between

$$Y = b_1X_1 + b_2X_1^2 + a \text{ (curve fit)}$$

and

$$Y = b_1X_1 + b_2X_2 + a \text{ (regression with two independent variables)}$$

where X_2 is just X_1^2? It should be clear that there is no difference to the computer. So let's do that. We make a curvilinear fit by doing a multiple regression of a special kind; everything we said about multiple linear regression earlier still goes.

Let's consider our example again. Suppose we want to predict IMR with wealth, and we want to know whether the fit should be linear or curvilinear. We must choose between these two equations:

$$Y = bX_1 + a \qquad \text{linear fit}$$
$$Y = b_1X_1 + b_2X_1^2 + a \qquad \text{curvilinear fit}$$

Let us consider the relationship between IMR and GNP/PC (untransformed):

$$Y = -0.143X + 88.2 \ (r^2 = 0.37)$$

so using raw GNP/PC to predict IMR gives a moderate fit. If we use X^2 to take account of the fact that the relationship is curvy we get:

$$Y = -0.580X + 0.0006X^2 + 129 \ (R^2 = 0.66)$$

which accounts for nearly twice the variance of the linear fit, enough of an improvement to prefer the second equation, in spite of its greater complexity. In this example, the confirmatory results agree with our earlier exploratory look at the relationship between IMR and GNP/PC; it did look quite curved, and the confirmatory work agrees that there is substantial curvature. Once again, there is no substitute for looking at the plot. You may be able to see a curvilinear pattern right away, or you may see something even more complex.

Generally, then, we prefer the curvilinear fit to the linear if the X^2 term adds 'substantially' to the R^2. How much is 'substantial'?

One criterion is statistical significance: use the curvilinear fit if the R^2 for the curvilinear fit is significantly greater than the r^2 for the linear fit. Most computer packages for multiple regression provide this or equivalent information for you.

This raises an interesting question. The second equation actually accounts for a bit more of the variance than did the equation using only wealth; that is, the log of GNP/PC. Which equation should we prefer, and why? One consideration is the appropriateness of the transform. Here the X^2 term is an omnibus treatment that always works for one-hump curves and, consequently, tells us nothing about the process that underlies the data. In contrast, the log transform is associated with a process of cumulative growth, which is relevant to issues related to a nation's wealth. Secondly, other things being equal, we prefer the simpler representation, here one predictor rather than two. But 'other things being equal' is not very well defined. So if you must decide between, say, a one-variable equation and one using two or even more predictors, rather than just looking at the size of the associated R^2, you may prefer to use R^2 (adj). This is also part of the multiple regression output. Unlike R^2, which can only get larger with the addition of predictors, R^2 (adj) also takes account of how many predictors are being used and can get smaller if a poor predictor is added.

Using More than Two Independent Variables

Multiple linear regression with three or more X variables is very much like regression with two X variables. Suppose we are using three predictors: X_1, X_2 and X_3. The fit is

$$Y = b_1X_1 + b_2X_2 + b_3X_3 + a$$

The formulae for the bs get more complicated because more variables are involved, but the basic idea remains the same. Each slope gives the change in Y with a change in one independent variable, with all the other independent variables held constant. For example, b_1 is the change in Y given a unit change in X_1, holding X_2 and X_3 constant. If the unstandardized variables are used, the bs are not good guides to the relative importance of the variables because, as before, they include a scale correction. If the standardized versions of Y, X_1, X_2 and X_3 are used, then the b^*s do reflect the relative strength of each X's contribution to the combined prediction for Y. The fit as a whole, or $Y = b_1X_1 + b_2X_2 + b_3X_3 + a$, is the 'best' possible, where 'best' means that the squared residuals are minimized. Finally, the multiple correlation R is the correlation between the predicted values $\hat{Y}$ (or $b_1X_1 + b_2X_2 + b_3X_3 + a$) and the observed values of Y, as before. The test for R is modified a bit to allow for the fact that more variables are involved. Let k be the number of independent variables involved in a regression. Then the null hypothesis $R^2 = 0$ can be tested with

$$F_{k,n-k-1} = \frac{R^2}{1 - R^2} \left(\frac{N - k - 1}{k} \right)$$

If $k = 1$, we get the familiar formula for r^2 in a simple regression with just one predictor. If $k = 2$, we get the formula for the R^2 for two independent variables given earlier in this chapter.

Let us return to the six-nation study of individual modernity (Inkeles and Smith, 1974) for an example. What makes people more modern in their attitudes, more open to new experience and ready for change, more ready to hold opinions and respect those of others, more oriented to the future, more comfortable with time scheduling, more confident in their ability to control their own lives, more ambitious, more favourable towards technical skill, more informed about modern industry, and so on? An overall measure of modernity was used as the major dependent variable and was compared to many combinations of independent variables. One of the more important was the combination of education, mass media exposure and factory experience; each of these should increase modernity by increasing a person's exposure to modern ideas and modern experiences. Separately, each is positively related to modernity. But how do they work in combination? Consider the standardized regression for factory workers in Argentina, for example:

modernity* = 0.48 (education)* + 0.24 (mass media exposure)*
+ 0.20 (factory experience)*

We can easily see that each of the three variables makes a contribution to modernity, even with the other two variables controlled. Education is clearly the most important single influence on modernity but mass media and factory work are also important.

This six-nation study is an excellent example of how useful numeric fits can be in summarizing information. The same regression as shown for Argentina was run for Chile, Bangladesh, India, Israel and Nigeria. It would be rather hard to get an overall feeling for all this just using plots; but it is easy with a summary table of the regression weights for all six regressions (Inkeles and Smith, 1974: Table 19-2). The results for all six nations can be quickly seen to be similar. This is a rather surprising and interesting result, suggesting that the processes of individual modernization are similar even in nations with very dissimilar social structures.

Using Interaction Terms

Suppose we suspect that a simple linear combination of X_1 and X_2 may not do justice to the situation because X_1 and X_2 have interactive effects, where interaction means the same thing here as it did in two-way analysis of variance or elementary analysis; the effects of X_1 are different for different values of X_2 or vice versa. In Figure 20.1, which we claimed would come in handy for more than checking regression assumptions, we see clear indication of an interaction effect. The effect of education is quite different for differing levels of wealth. Where wealth is high, the slope between education and IMR is about half as great as where wealth is low, -0.01 versus -0.02. Clearly the combination of the two variables is important.

How could we work this into our regression fit procedures? Once again we can draw on what we learned in elementary analysis. There we found that interaction could often be fitted to the comparison values, essentially $RC = $ (row effect) $\times$ (column effect). Why not do the same for regression and fit interaction with the multiplicative term X_1X_2? To create this interaction term, multiply the two predictors together case by case (if a computer is doing the work, just multiply the two variables). Then, the new variable X_1X_2 is treated just as if it were any new predictor, say X_2. When we add this predictor to X_1 and X_2, we get:

$$Y = -139X_1 - 0.046X_2 + 0.0195X_1X_2 + 362 \ (R^2 = 0.79)$$
$$(t\text{-values} \quad -4.34 \quad\quad -2.95 \quad\quad 2.68)$$

There are several things to note in this equation. First, b_1 and b_2 are quite different after the interaction term is added. This will nearly always happen – in fact, sometimes even the sign of the slopes will change. Second, the t-scores indicate that all three predictors make a significant contribution, which is not always the case. Third, the multiplicative interaction term is not only significantly different from zero, it also adds almost 10 per cent to R^2, which is quite a lot. Finally, you may find it surprising that the sign for the interaction term is positive, where both other slopes are negative. This is because the curve is slightly 'hollow upward' – the residuals from the two-variable regression tend to be positive for both low and high values of X_1 and X_2 and negative for intermediate values. Why should high wealth–high education countries have higher than predicted IMR? We observed earlier that the Trinidad-Tobago residual was at least partly artifactual. Other high wealth countries like Greece (also a high education country) are probably being underpredicted for similar reasons.

Dummy Variable Regression

So far in our discussion, we have found multiple regression to be an enormously flexible tool: with enough cases, we can use an almost limitless number of predictors, each implicated linearly, curvilinearly or interactively, and still the analysis will be technically quite simple. However, there are analyses that we might want to do that don't seem possible; for example, there are a variety of categorical variables whose effects would be interesting to measure, but the only variables we know how to work with are essentially numeric. For instance, the relationship of gender to earnings is interesting, important and complex – and would be ideal for multiple regression, but gender is a category. Perhaps we are interested in unemployment in various regions of the country or language retention of Inuit compared to other native people, or the effects of education and 'collar colour' (blue, white or pink) on income, or. . . . We can easily think of dozens of interesting but non-numeric variables that we would like to use in regression. What can be done?

Actually, like many things about multiple regression, the solution is simple. Any category that we can code 0, 1 will work as a predictor, usually called a *dummy variable*. To illustrate let's look at a few artificial examples using gender as a dummy variable.

To start, consider a hypothetical and very simple two-sample *t*-test problem on gender and body weight, where males average 155 pounds and females 125 pounds.

Males	Females
151	121
153	123
155	125
157	127
159	129

A *t*-test yields a highly significant *t*-score of 15.0.

Now for something completely different. First, put all of the weights into one column, then create a second column consisting of a code for gender; say 1 if male, 0 if female (the reverse code will work just as well, as we shall see). Now, a regression of gender on weight gives the equation $Y = 30X + 125$. If we break this down we get

$$Y_m = 30\,(1) + 125 = 155 \text{ for males}$$
$$Y_f = 30\,(0) + 125 = 125 \text{ for females}$$

the mean weights for the two groups. Moreover, the *t*-value for b is (you guessed it!) 15.0. Thus, in its simplest form, dummy variable regression is just a basic *t*-test in disguise.

If we look at a slightly more complicated example we can begin to see how useful this approach might be. Let's look at the effects of both gender (X_2) and, say, years of experience (X_1) on earnings (Y). First, assume that gender and experience don't interact.

Taking 1 if female and 0 if male, our equation is

$$Y = a + b_1X_1 + bX_2$$

or, for males

$$Y = a + b_1X_1 + 0$$

and for females

$$Y = a + b_1X_1 + b_2 = (a + b_2) + b_1X_1$$

In this case, the intercept (here starting salary) is different for males and females, with b_2 probably negative. However, income returns for each year of experience are the same (see Figure 20.2**a**). Not very realistic? Well, a slightly more complicated equation can tell us if male and female earnings are affected differently by experience. That is to say, it can measure the extent to which

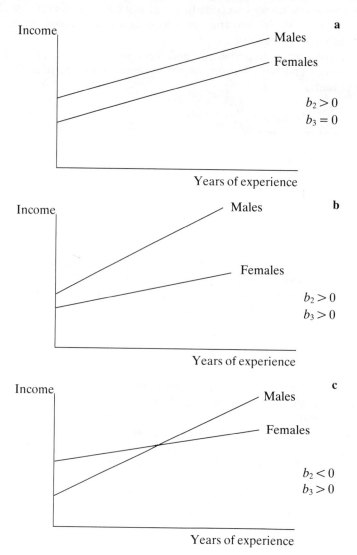

Figure 20.2   Hypothetical regression of income by gender and experience

gender and experience interact. In the past, we have looked for systematic interaction by creating a new variable (let's call it X_3), which is the product of the two (or more!) variables. We can do that here. Our variables are:

X_1 = years of experience;
X_2 = gender (0 if male, 1 if female);
X_3 = X_1X_2 (which is zero for males but years of experience, X_1 for females)

The equation is of the form;

$$Y = a + b_1X_1 + b_2X_2 + b_3X_3$$

Since, for the males, X_2 and X_3 are both zero, the male equation is

$$Y = a + b_1X_1$$

while for females

$$Y = a + b_1X_1 + b_2 + b_3X_1$$

The regression weight b_2, as in the previous case, is part of the intercept, the gender difference in starting salary. In the same way, b_3 is the gender difference in annual raises. Collecting terms in the female equation gives:

$$Y = a + b_2 + (b_1 + b_3)X_1.$$

As before, if b_2 is significantly different from 0, then the difference in male and female starting salaries is statistically reliable, while if b_3 is significantly different from zero, then the gender differences in annual salary increments are significant. Figure 20.2**b** shows the case where both males' starting salaries and annual increments are greater than females'. The plot in Figure 20.2**c** depicts a situation where females have higher entry salaries but lower annual increments. So we see that one or more dummy variables can be added to a multiple regression equation just like any numeric variable, and similarly for interaction effects. However, in order to see clearly the additive and multiplicative effects of such variables, it is important to simplify the equation as we have done above. Now, let us turn to a real example.

In Chapter 16, we looked at left-wing vote in Vancouver by income level and 'side' of city for several elections. We noted that, holding income constant, East siders were more left-wing than West siders. It would be interesting to see if voter turn-out also was affected by 'side' as well as income. In Table 20.1 we have mean income (from the 1961 census) and voter turn-out (TO) for the 1964 civic election for each of Vancouver's 24 districts.

Some preliminary exploration indicates that income and turn-out are related directly, but the relationship is curvy. A little trial and error finds that the negative inverse of income is satisfactorily linear with turn-out. This form of income is X_1. Side of the city is the dummy variable X_2. Let us define this as 1 if West side, 0 if East side. This results in the equation:

$$Y = 182X_1 - 3.9X_2 + 80.6 \qquad R^2 = 0.85$$

Simplifying, we get, for the West side,

$$TO = 182X_1 + 76.7$$

and, for the East side,

$$TO = 182X_1 + 80.6$$

There are several things to note here. First, holding income constant, East side districts have nearly 4 per cent greater electoral turn-out than West side districts ($b_2 = -3.9$). Secondly, the fit is very good indeed ($R^2 = 0.85$). Thirdly, a t-score is given for each regression weight, making it easy to tell which predictors make a significant contribution. Here, the t-scores are 10.08 for X_1,

Table 20.1   Vancouver municipal voting

District	Mean income (1961)	Turn-out (1964)
East side		
1 Strathcona	2751	24
2 Woodland	3315	26
3 Mt Pleasant	3422	30
4 Grandview	3864	42
5 Riley Park	3865	38
6 Kingsway	3865	38
7 Cedar Cottage	3974	40
8 New Brighton	4003	39
9 Fraserview	4173	42
10 Collingwood	4186	38
11 Sunset	4299	40
12 Little Mountain	4383	43
13 Newport	4594	41
West side		
14 Burrard	3589	27
15 Kitsilano North	3785	34
16 Fairview	3786	30
17 West End	4233	33
18 Kitsilano South	4558	41
19 Marpole	4640	40
20 Dunbar	5701	58
21 Pt Grey	5908	48
22 Arbutus	6267	55
23 Kerrisdale	7066	59
24 Shaughnessy	8477	52

Source: Ewing (1972).

and -2.06 for X_2, with 21 degrees of freedom. We selected an α-level of 0.1. At this level, both slopes are significantly different from zero, meaning that both variables make a statistically reliable contribution.

We have seen that income (transformed) and city side combine additively to predict electoral turn-out well. Do they also combine interactively? To examine this, we created the multiplicative term X_1X_2 and ran the three-variable regression. As it happens, the interaction does not quite make a significant contribution ($t = 1.33$, $df = 20$), so we deleted it and conclude that a unit change in income affects turn-out roughly equally for both sides of the city.

Thus far, we have looked only at the simplest sort of dummy variable: where the predictor has just two levels, male–female, East side–West side, etc. But there are many interesting categorical variables with more than two levels that we would like to use as predictors; for example, region of the country, job 'collar colour', work environment, personality type, political preference, religion. . . . Well, you get the idea.

Working with this kind of dummy variable is no more complicated conceptually than what we have just discussed. But there are a few unfamiliar issues that must be addressed. Let us begin with a simple artificial example and use it to pull some of these issues out. Consider the effect of religion on birthrate. To keep this as simple as possible, we examine just three religions, Protestant, Catholic and Jewish, and discuss without data. In order to treat religion as a predictor, we need *two* dummy variables, X_1 and X_2. We define the first dummy variable, X_1, as

1 if Protestant, 0 otherwise,

and X_2 is defined as

1 if Catholic, 0 otherwise.

It doesn't matter which categories are coded 1 and which 0, but it does matter that there is one more category than the number of dummy variables. If we had used a third variable for Jews here, then knowing any two of the X values would permit us to predict the third perfectly. This is an instance of the problem of collinearity, where some or all of the predictors are very highly correlated. Recall the earlier discussion of b_2 in multiple regression: what a particular variable tells us about Y, net of the other predictors. Well, in the situation above, the third variable can tell us nothing after controlling for the other two.

The general equation, then, is

$$Y = a + b_1X_1 + b_2X_2$$

For Protestants, $X_1 = 1$ and $X_2 = 0$, so this simplifies to:

$$Y = a + b_1 \text{ (for Protestants)}$$

For Catholics, the equation simplifies to

$$Y = a + b_2 \text{ (for Catholics)}$$

For Jews, where both X_1 and X_2 are zero, $Y = a$. You can see that a little addition will give the information we want on religious differences in birthrates. The t-scores tell us which, if any, of the differences is reliable.

Another unfamiliar thing about dummy variable predictors is the plots they produce. Whether you examine the Y by X plots or the residuals versus X, what you see is not the familiar roughly oval data 'vegetable', but rather 'candlesticks', where all the points are heaped at $X = 0$ and $X = 1$. The best we can do about regression assumptions here is to check to see if the spreads of the candlesticks are roughly equal.

You might be wondering how dummy variables can possibly work. Recall that the slope answers the question: how much does Y change for every unit change in X? By coding, say, gender 0/1, we represent it as a one-unit difference so b now indexes how much of a difference gender makes for income, or whatever. The models can and should get more complicated, but the basic idea remains simple. In short, dummy variables are usually straightforward and permit you to answer important questions. So get comfortable with them because they belong in your tool box.

High Influence Points

We have mentioned a number of times that least squares regression is not very resistant to unusual observations. This is a good time to elaborate briefly on this. We use the term 'leverage point' or 'high influence point' for a point that markedly affects the outcome of a regression. Leverage points can affect slope, level or R^2. We have already seen (Figure 13.1) a 'leverage point' dramatically effect the slope of a line. Such slope changers are the most familiar kinds of influential observations and perhaps the most troublesome. Slope changers can be identified by two general characteristics:

(a) they are well off the fitted line;
(b) they are among the most extreme points on X, either high or low. Any *one* of the circled points in Figure 20.3**a** would affect the slope.

There are two other kinds of influential observations that we will want to know about, intercept changers and R^2 changers. The intercept-changing observations again have two general properties:

(a) they, like the slope changers, are well off the fitted line;
(b) they have middling values on X. Either of the circled points in Figure 20.3**b** would affect the intercept.

The observations that affect R^2 overmuch are those that substantially increase the range of X – remember, we observed earlier that the 'quality' of the fit, the R^2, is roughly the ratio of the length of the data 'vegetable' to its thickness. So making the vegetable longer will increase R^2. Thus, the two characteristics of the R^2-changing observation are:

(a) the points are on or close to the fitted line;

(b) they have *very* extreme values on X. The circled points in Figure 20.3c are R^2 changes.

In addition, there are other, subtler sorts of influential observations, but they are beyond the scope of this discussion.

We have identified the problem but what now? First is locating influential points – now that you know what to look for, careful examination of residual plots is one of your best bets. In addition, several statistical packages identify points that are particularly influential. The R^2 changers really have to be identified at the exploratory stages, however.

Having located the problem observations, what can be done about them? Well, they are outliers and we know how to handle those; often transforming

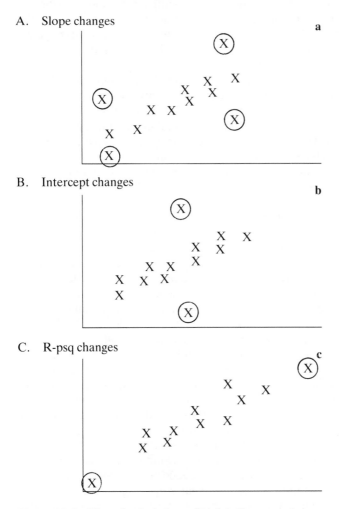

A. Slope changes

B. Intercept changes

C. R-psq changes

Figure 20.3 Hypothetical plots of high influence points

will help. We don't throw them away, but we do give them special attention, perhaps even set them aside. Setting points aside in a regression context might mean running your regression twice, once with and once without the unusual points (of course, informing your readers about your procedure). More generally, the variety of exploratory techniques and thinking are invaluable here in using such points to help you push your analysis further.

Exploratory and Confirmatory

Obviously the confirmatory and exploratory materials tie in with each other in many ways in multiple regression problems. A multiple regression may be run as a test of ideas developed in an exploratory analysis. If so, remember that the data used for the test must be a new set of data. Often, if you have lots of cases, it's a good idea to explore a modest subset of the cases and then do the confirmatory work on the rest.

When doing exploratory work, there is no limit to the number of fits you can try with a modest subset of data (or rather, the only limits are those set by your judgement, interest and available time). But in confirmatory work it is best to make just a few simple fits if you have a small number of cases. Overly complex fits can look very impressive quite artificially. To give an extreme example, suppose you have just two cases and you make a Y by X fit: naturally the fit is perfect, since the two points can be connected with a straight line. Similarly, three cases can be perfectly fitted with two X variables, four cases with three X variables, and so on.

In less extreme cases there are no hard and fast rules governing how complex a fit is justifiable for how many cases. You must use your judgement, much as we suggested in Chapter 12 when we said that choosing a curved or straight fit depended on a number of things, including the sample size and the strength of the fit. In the IMR example, we used only 18 cases in order to keep the arithmetic simple; then we made a large number of fits with as many as three predictors. We have probably done more with those data than is entirely safe from a confirmatory point of view. It would be a good idea to take the fit or fits we like the best and test them anew on the cases we left out.

Before a multiple regression is run, the confirmatory assumptions should be tested, which involves exploratory thinking in checking approximate normality of the residuals. After a regression is run, exploratory thinking comes in again when you try to interpret the results. For example, interpreting an interaction term may be a lot easier if you use a little of the data to make a plot like that of Figure 20.1. You should always get all the plots that your computer program can be persuaded to give so you can see the relationships; often one quick look will alert you to the distorting influence of a few extreme cases, or will make it clear that a curve fit was needed at some point. We will not go into plots in more detail here because what you can get depends on the program that has been made available to you. Whatever statistical package you are using, it is always possible to get the residuals from the regression and these should be carefully examined. First, you can plot the residuals against the fit and against each of the predictors; this will often suggest modifications in the fit if they are needed. Secondly, you can look over the extreme residuals for ideas about new variables that may be worth examining.

These uses of exploratory thinking are the same ones we became used to for simple linear regression; but they are even more important for multiple regression because it is easy to be seduced by the computer, to take its print-out at face value instead of looking hard at the data to check the analysis.

Finally, there is a way to use multiple regression itself in a somewhat exploratory way. This procedure is called *stepwise regression*: most statistical packages have this option. Stepwise regression proceeds by steps in a way very similar to the exploratory layer-of-fit approach. In the first step of one approach, the machine runs a regression with just one independent variable: the one that does the best job in one-variable regression, which means the one with the biggest simple correlation (the biggest r). At the second step, the machine runs another regression with two variables: the one from the first step plus the one that adds the most to that (this means the one with the biggest partial correlation with the first-step independent variable controlled). At the third step, the machine examines the independent variables not yet used and again adds in the one that improves the R^2 the most. This process may be continued; at each step, the independent variable with the most to add is added to the fit. The process stops when there are no more independent variables or whenever there are no more that raise the R^2 enough to bother with. The program also does a significance test on the increase in R^2 from each new variable. This is a useful procedure if you have a lot of possible independent variables and are not sure which combination will do the best job in predicting Y. Stepwise regression can meaningfully be used in an exploratory spirit, as a way to get into the data quickly and get started thinking about them. But it is no substitute for thinking up meaningful explanations! Because the criteria for adding variables are completely statistical, stepwise regression can sometimes give rather peculiar results. Thus, after you have digested the stepwise results, you may well decide that the regression you want is a slightly different one, one with a more theoretically compelling mix of variables – even if the theoretically interesting version has a somewhat smaller R^2.

Multiple regression is a flexible and widely used technique. We have dealt with a few of the more familiar uses of the approach. There are many other useful extensions of multiple regression that you will meet in later courses and more advanced texts.

Using the Computer

The MINITAB command for multiple regression with *two* predictors is:

MTB> REGR C2 2 C1 C3

This tells the program to regress Y (C2) on *two* predictors, X_1 (C1) and X_2 (C3). For the dummy variable example on voter turn-out:

The regression equation is

C2 = 84.4 + 182 C1 − 3.85 C3[1]

Predicator	Coef[2]	Stdev	t-ratio[3]
Constant	84.376	4.818	17.51
C1	181.68	18.02	10.08
C3	−3.851	1.873	−2.06

s = 3.846 R^2 = 84.9%[4] R^2 (adj) = 83.5%[5]

Analysis of Variance[6]

SOURCE	DF	SS	MS
Regression	2	1745.25	872.63
Error	21	310.58	14.79
Total	23	2055.83	

SOURCE	DF[7]	SEQ SS
C1	1	1682.73
C3	1	62.52

Unusual Observations[8]

Obs.	C1	C2	Fit	Stdev. Fit	Residual	St. Resid
20	−0.180	58.000	47.823	1.241	10.177	2.80R
24	−0.120	52.000	58.724	1.914	−6.724	−2.02R

R denotes an obs. with a large st. resid.

The multiple regression output is similar to that for linear regression. The exception is an extra table under analysis of variance.

1 The multiple regression equation is:

$Y = 182X_1 − 3.85X_2 + 84.4$

2 The intercept is 84.4, the slope of b_1 = 182 and the slope of b_2 = −3.85.
3 The *t*-ratio or *t*-value allows us to evaluate whether each of the independent variables is contributing significantly to the regression. The critical value for the *t*-value must first be determined by specifying the degrees of freedom (in this case df = 21), level of significance (we will use 0.10) and direction of the test (two-tailed). According to Table A.3 the *CV* for this *t*-value is 1.721. The actual *t*-value for C1 is 10.08 and for C3 is −2.06. Both X_1 and X_2 have a statistically reliable effect at $p = 0.1$.
4 R^2 is also called the coefficient of determination. Here R^2 is 0.849 which means 84.9 per cent of Y is explained by known X values. Generally the higher the R^2 the stronger the relationship.
5 R^2 (adj) has been adjusted for the number of degrees of freedom and is an estimate of R^2 in the population.

6 This documents the source of measurements in the corresponding columns. There are two sources: regression and error.
7 This section of the analysis of variance table allows us to calculate how much of the variance is accounted for by each of the x variables. The total sum of squares due to regression (1745.25) is split into that part due to X_1 (1682.73) and that part due to X_2 (62.52).
8 In this section of the output, two kinds of unusual observations are identified if present. Here, there are two instances of unusual observation, both labelled R. This notation identifies them as outliers from the batch of residuals. Cases labelled with an X are high influence points of one sort or another.

HOMEWORK

Return to the 1981 Canadian homicide data (Table 18.4).
1 Use the same two predictor variables from your Chapter 18 and Chapter 19 homework and run multiple regressions for both the raw and standardized variables. Compare these results to those obtained earlier.
2 Explore the third variable – the one you have not yet used. Try the three-variable regression and compare the results to those from the earlier two regressions using two predictors.
3 For any pair of predictors you choose, try a multiplicative interaction fit and discuss.

FIFTH REVIEW
An Exploration of the Causes of Rape

The data in Table R5.1, from Baron and Strauss (1989) include US state-by-state rape rates for 1980 as well as information on five variables that can be argued to be causally important. The variables are

1 *Rape* Rate per 100 000 of rapes known to and reported by the police, as given in the Uniform Crime Reports.
2 *Poverty* Proportion of the population of each state that is living at or below the official poverty level.
3 *Unemployment* Percentage of civilian labour force unemployed, a₃ defined by the US Bureau of the Census.
4 *Percentage of women relative to men who are administrators in non-farm occupations* The median here is just above 50 per cent, indicating that, in the average state, half as many women as men are employed as administrators.
5 *Median income of females as a proportion of the median income of males* The median value of this statistic is just under 60 per cent, which indicates that in the average state women employed full-time earn not quite 60 per cent of what full-time employed males earn.
6 *Violent TV viewing index* A reflection of the size of the audience in each state for the six most violent TV shows in 1980.

Construct a 'reasonable' multiple regression model with rape rates as the dependent variable. Test it and discuss residuals. You may choose to begin your analysis with exploration or theory as you prefer. However you prefer to go, your analysis should include exploration, confirmation, residual analysis and a discussion of process.

Table R5.1

State	Rapes/ 100 000	% popn below poverty level	% unemployed	% women/ % men non-farm admin.	Md income females/Md income males	Violent TV
AL	30.0	17.9	7.5	51.1	56.8	186
AK	62.5	10.1	9.8	64.4	63.9	–
AZ	45.2	12.4	6.2	58.2	58.8	109
AR	26.7	18.7	6.9	45.8	61.6	173
CA	58.2	11.3	6.6	57.3	61.2	118
CO	52.5	10.2	5.0	53.1	60.1	153
CT	21.6	8.7	4.7	37.7	59.0	132
DE	24.2	11.9	6.3	41.6	58.3	158
FL	56.9	13.0	5.1	55.7	60.5	154
GA	44.3	16.4	5.9	49.0	52.0	208
HI	34.7	10.0	4.7	59.4	59.2	115
ID	22.4	12.7	8.0	57.6	58.9	179
IL	26.9	11.5	7.2	46.6	56.6	170
IN	33.1	9.8	7.8	45.2	55.6	163
IA	14.3	9.4	5.0	56.9	58.5	153
KS	31.5	10.2	4.0	43.6	59.9	160
KY	19.2	18.4	8.5	58.2	57.1	185
LA	44.5	18.9	6.0	49.6	53.2	223
ME	12.9	12.9	7.6	52.3	63.5	149
MD	40.1	9.9	5.8	50.6	61.9	171
MA	27.3	9.8	5.1	44.8	62.5	116
MI	46.6	11.1	11.0	47.6	56.7	153
MN	23.2	9.3	5.4	50.0	58.4	152
MS	24.6	24.5	7.2	49.7	60.1	185
MO	32.6	12.4	6.9	57.1	57.6	160
MT	21.0	12.4	8.3	60.0	55.7	200
NE	23.2	10.4	3.7	43.1	58.6	135
NV	67.2	8.5	5.9	70.6	61.6	125
NH	17.3	8.7	4.8	42.5	59.3	–
NJ	30.7	9.7	6.7	47.0	57.5	–
NM	43.4	17.4	7.1	61.3	58.3	162
NY	30.9	13.7	7.1	44.2	64.3	139
NC	22.7	14.6	5.5	37.7	66.0	206
ND	9.5	12.8	5.3	43.8	57.0	155
OH	34.3	10.5	8.0	48.5	56.5	169
OK	36.3	13.3	4.1	56.9	58.4	166
OR	41.5	11.3	8.3	64.7	58.5	133
PA	23.0	10.5	7.4	44.6	58.3	139
RI	17.1	10.3	7.0	37.7	59.5	108
SC	37.5	15.9	6.1	52.1	64.6	226
SD	12.5	16.1	4.9	47.1	61.7	165
TN	37.4	17.0	7.4	52.1	59.3	199
TX	47.3	14.9	4.0	54.7	57.7	167
UT	27.7	10.7	5.5	47.0	54.2	159
VT	29.1	11.4	6.3	50.6	64.4	146
VA	27.4	11.5	5.0	52.2	62.2	163
WA	52.7	10.2	7.4	60.0	57.3	131
WV	15.8	14.5	8.5	50.3	51.4	189
WI	14.9	8.5	6.6	49.1	58.6	164
WY	28.6	8.0	4.1	51.5	50.2	179

Source: Brown and Strauss (1989) © Yale University Press.

Appendices

Appendix A: Background Maths

Negative Numbers

You may have gotten a little rusty at working with negative numbers. You'll need to work with them easily because we use them a great deal; for example, we often remove fits by subtraction, as in Table 4.3. The all-purpose guideline is: an even number of negative signs preceding a number makes it positive, an odd number makes it negative. So if you are subtracting a positive number (often a level) from a larger positive number, it is simple subtraction; e.g.

$$10 - 6 = 4$$

However, if you subtract a number from a smaller number you get a negative answer, like this:

$$4 - 6 = -(6 - 4)$$
$$= -(2)$$
$$= -2$$

That is, you find what the answer would be if the order of subtraction were reversed; then put a minus sign in front of it. Sometimes you will subtract negative numbers from positive numbers such as

$$6 - (-4)$$

Now there are two minus signs in a row, and an even number of minus signs makes the number positive. So

$$6 - (-4) = 6 + 4$$
$$= 10$$

Finally, you may subtract a negative number from a negative number, as in

$$-10 - (-4) \quad \text{or} \quad -2 - (-4)$$

Just take it in stages, first simplifying:

$$-10 + 4 \qquad\qquad -2 + 4$$
$$= -6 \qquad\qquad\quad = 2$$

In a string of signs the plus signs don't count, e.g.

$$-10 + (-6) = -10 - 6 = -16$$

For practice, check some of our subtractions in Tables 4.3 and 4.5. For example, the dq of the standardized summary values for the youngest batch is

$$dq = q_U - q_L = 0.3 - (-0.7) = 0.3 + 0.7 = 1.0$$

Similar rules apply for multiplications involving minus signs. An odd number of negative values multiplied together gives a negative result, for example

$$(-6)(-8)(-2) = -96 \quad \text{and} \quad -(6)(8)(2) = -96$$

An even number of negative values multiplied together gives a positive result, for example

$$(6)(-8)(-2) = +96$$

Finally, the same idea goes for division:

$$\frac{6}{12} = 0.5 \qquad \frac{-6}{12} = -0.5 \qquad \frac{-6}{-12} = 0.5$$

Significant Digits

The basic idea of significant digits is familiar to all of us. If someone says, 'I make £10 469.00 a year', then we know that he is giving us a very exact report of his income (perhaps because he has just filled out his income tax form, or just moved to a new salary level; otherwise he would not be likely to know his salary so exactly). But if he says, 'I make ten thousand a year', he can mean anything between nine thousand and eleven thousand. In the first case he has given us his income to five significant digits (10 469) or five digits that give us information beyond mere magnitude; he implies that he really has measured his income to the pound. In the second case he gives us his income with only two significant digits (the 10 in ten thousand) plus an indication of magnitude (the thousand in ten thousand); the implication is that he only knows his income to the nearest thousand.

We can usually recognize degrees of accuracy in words, but they are not always so clear in numbers unless we use the appropriate way of recording the numbers. For example, how many significant digits are there in this income figure: £15 000? There is no way to be sure. Perhaps there are only two (1 and 5) because income is known only to the nearest thousand. Perhaps there are three (1, 5 and the first 0) because income is known to the nearest hundred; or perhaps there are four or even five. To avoid such ambiguity, the number of significant digits should be clearly indicated in some way. You owe this to your readers; they have the right to know how accurately your data have been measured, or how many significant figures are justified.

You can indicate the accuracy of measurement in words, for example by putting 'to the nearest thousand' or 'to the nearest hundred' at the bottom of a table of income figures. Do not report more significant figures than are justified. For example, if you know your income data are accurate to the nearest hundred then a figure like £54 943.00 is quite wrong because it gives the misleading impression that it is accurate to the penny. The figure should be reported as £54 900 with detailed information only to the hundreds.

The accuracy of measurement can also be indicated by reporting the numbers in a form often used by scientific workers. In this form a number is broken into two parts: a set of significant digits plus a power of ten which gives the magnitude of the number. The significant digit part is generally written with one digit to the left of the decimal place. For example, consider again an income of £54 943 where income is measured only to the hundreds with any accuracy. This number would be written

$$5.49 \times 10^4.$$

The first part, 5.49, gives all the significant digits justified by our accuracy of measurement: three of them. The second part gives the order of magnitude so that we can tell 54 900 from 5490 (which is 5.49×10^3) or from 549 (which is 5.49×10^2) and so on. The ambiguity mentioned above is easy to handle now. If we have an income figure of £15 000, the number of significant digits can be easily recorded. Say there are three; then we write 1.50×10^4. Say there are five; we write 1.5000×10^4.

Finding the right power of ten is easy: move the decimal place as many places over as necessary, and the number of places moved is the power of ten needed. If you move to the left, the power is positive. For example, above we found

$$\underset{4\ 3\ 2\ 1}{15000.} = 1.50 \times 10^4$$

If we have to move to the right, the power of ten is negative. For example, suppose we are recording the number 0.0015, with two significant digits:

$$\underset{1\ 2\ 3}{0.0015} = 1.5 \times 10^{-3}$$

(Remember, 10^{-3} is $\dfrac{1}{10^3}$ or $\dfrac{1}{1000}$ or 0.001.)

Finally, note that we have been talking mostly about rules for presenting the original data. Values computed from the data may be reported to one or two more significant digits than the data themselves. In the process of computing these values (like the means and variances introduced in Chapter 3) lots of detail should be kept until the final figure is found; this avoids rounding error. Avoiding rounding error is usually less important in exploratory work than in confirmatory.

Appendix B: Some Proofs

Proof that total sum of squares is the sum of the 'within' and the 'between' sums of squares

The sum of squares from which the variance is computed is

$$\sum_i\sum_j(x_{ij} - \bar{\bar{x}})^2 = (N - 1)\,\text{VAR}$$
$$= \sum_i\sum_j[(x_{ij} - \bar{x}_i) + (\bar{x}_i - \bar{\bar{x}})]^2$$

That is, we've just added and subtracted the means of each group. This equals, by expanding the squared expression,

$$\sum_i\sum_j(x_{ij} - \bar{x}_i)^2 + \sum_i\sum_j(\bar{x}_i - \bar{\bar{x}})^2 + 2\sum\sum(x_{ij} - \bar{x}_i)(\bar{x}_i - \bar{\bar{x}}) \qquad (1)$$

Now the first term is just the sum of squares within groups; the second term is the sum of deviations of the group means from the grand mean, the between groups sum of squares. What about the third term,

$$2\sum_i\sum_j(x_{ij} - \bar{x}_i)(\bar{x}_i - \bar{\bar{x}})?$$

Now $(\bar{x}_i - \bar{\bar{x}})$ is the sum of each group mean minus the grand mean and when summing over j it is a constant. So the formula above becomes

$$2\sum_i[(\bar{x}_i - \bar{\bar{x}})\sum_j(x_{ij} - \bar{x}_i)]$$

The last term here, $\sum_j(x_{ij} - \bar{x}_i)$ is just the sum of the deviations of a batch of observations about the batch's mean, and that sum *must* equal zero (you might want to refresh your memory by looking at Chapter 3). In fact, the other term, too, must equal zero, but it doesn't really matter; as long as one of them equals zero the whole product equals zero. Consequently, (1) becomes

$$\sum_i\sum_j(x_{ij} - \bar{\bar{x}})^2 = \sum_i\sum_j(x_{ij} - \bar{x})^2 + \sum_i\sum_j(\bar{x}_i - \bar{\bar{x}})^2$$

or the total SS = within groups SS + between groups SS.

Formulae for Two Independent Variables

Earlier we said that we would have an optional appendix showing how bs and R are computed when two independent variables are used. We include these formulae because some people like to know what the computer is up to, or like to read formulae to get a mathematical sense of what multiple regression does. Other people find formulae no help at all or find them deeply counter-productive. Read this section or not, accordingly. We will give no formulae for more complex multiple regressions (with three X variables, for example), not because the formulae are difficult but because they get very cumbersome.

Standardized Regression Weights

The computations for b_i^* are quite straightforward and require nothing but the set of zero-order correlations:

$$b_1^* = \frac{r_{YX_1} - r_{YX_2}r_{X_1X_2}}{1 - r^2_{X_1X_2}}$$

In the text, the formulae for the standardized regression weights were described as being quite similar to those for the partial correlations. Compare b_1^* to the formula for $r_{YX_1.X_2}$:

$$r_{YX_1.X_2} = \frac{r_{YX_1} - r_{YX_2}r_{X_1X_2}}{\sqrt{1 - r^2_{X_1X_2}}\ \sqrt{1 - r^2_{YX_2}}}$$

As you can see, the formulae are identical in the numerators but rather different in the denominators. b_2^* is computed in an exactly analogous way.

Unstandardized Regression Weights

Let's look at the formula for b_1, the unstandardized coefficient for X_1:

$$b_1 = \frac{sd_Y}{sd_{X_1}} b_1^*$$

This equation is built up of sensible and familiar pieces. One part of b_1 is scale correction.

$$\frac{sd_Y}{sd_{X_1}}$$

gets from X_1's spread to Y's. First X_1's spread is removed (divided by) and then Y's spread replaces it (multiplied by).

If Y and X are standardized then $sd_Y^* = sd_{X_1}^* = 1$, so we get back to b_1^* as the regression weight.

Scale includes level as well as spread; level differences are fixed up through a, which is (as usual) simple to find:

$$a = \bar{Y} - b_1\bar{X}_1 - b_2\bar{X}_2$$

If we are using standardized variables they all have zero means, so a is zero too.

Appendix C: Statistical Tables

Table A.1   Random sampling numbers

15 77 01 64 69	69 58 40 81 16	60 20 00 84 22	28 26 46 66 36	86 66 17 34 40
85 40 51 40 10	15 33 94 11 65	57 62 94 04 99	05 57 22 71 77	99 68 12 11 14
47 69 35 90 95	16 17 45 86 29	16 70 48 02 00	59 33 93 28 58	34 32 24 34 07
13 26 87 40 20	40 81 46 08 09	74 99 16 92 99	85 19 01 23 11	74 00 79 41 63
10 55 33 20 47	54 16 86 11 16	59 34 71 55 84	03 48 17 60 13	38 71 23 91 83
05 06 67 26 77	14 85 40 52 68	60 41 94 98 18	62 20 94 03 71	60 26 45 17 92
65 50 89 18 74	42 07 50 15 69	86 97 40 25 88	14 17 73 92 07	93 11 93 15 15
59 68 53 31 55	73 47 16 49 79	69 80 76 16 60	58 53 07 04 53	66 94 94 18 18
31 31 05 36 48	75 16 00 21 11	42 44 84 46 84	83 20 49 17 12	21 93 34 61 16
91 59 46 44 45	49 25 36 12 07	25 90 89 55 25	83 47 17 23 93	99 56 14 60 16
63 59 73 21 67	80 00 25 58 25	72 06 12 86 74	54 79 70 85 88	71 58 21 98 48
89 72 47 46 94	78 56 10 65 97	84 79 42 31 49	94 15 41 13 09	45 43 03 82 81
70 51 21 03 18	50 21 99 49 73	06 99 19 24 96	39 43 10 14 12	94 08 55 54 70
14 15 99 60 44	62 72 38 18 36	63 92 61 55 93	77 66 82 10 91	81 51 67 01 47
92 46 90 39 99	64 08 00 97 27	54 96 63 40 54	34 70 27 48 18	68 59 91 83 32
81 23 17 13 01	37 57 92 16 34	15 80 90 25 64	67 77 29 95 84	80 84 84 87 22
87 54 42 46 56	28 89 02 06 98	59 90 74 13 38	98 66 23 20 23	90 55 31 83 48
74 73 84 98 13	11 48 25 33 39	27 36 08 99 57	60 42 88 68 25	22 89 67 83 16
94 55 14 00 97	32 51 92 47 03	92 33 73 20 21	29 77 37 06 98	64 63 34 31 43
69 21 94 26 20	73 90 70 92 76	49 14 60 34 43	90 51 72 11 07	75 94 19 49 40
82 36 36 89 29	87 70 08 71 98	49 00 89 89 99	29 08 02 72 32	68 16 29 82 19
25 06 22 30 87	87 44 48 90 91	38 53 10 60 29	40 07 58 97 84	09 04 33 56 72
82 37 97 60 92	76 39 17 84 34	67 65 52 89 90	62 97 04 33 81	91 27 56 46 35
83 71 07 22 15	17 55 56 82 62	88 83 86 38 14	63 89 39 81 90	25 62 58 68 87
73 13 79 15 12	18 34 22 24 75	56 47 45 22 81	30 82 38 34 52	57 48 30 34 17
91 28 00 57 30	92 12 38 95 21	15 70 78 50 88	01 07 90 72 77	99 53 04 34 73
33 47 55 62 57	08 21 77 31 05	64 74 04 93 42	20 19 09 71 46	37 32 69 69 89
56 66 25 32 38	64 70 26 27 67	77 40 04 34 63	98 99 89 31 16	12 90 50 28 96
88 40 52 02 29	82 69 34 50 21	74 00 91 27 52	98 72 03 45 65	30 89 71 45 91
87 63 88 23 62	51 07 69 59 02	89 49 14 98 53	41 92 36 07 76	85 37 84 37 47
32 25 21 15 08	82 34 57 57 35	22 03 33 48 84	37 37 29 38 37	89 76 25 09 69
44 61 88 23 13	01 59 47 64 04	99 59 96 20 30	87 31 33 69 45	58 48 00 88 48
94 44 08 67 79	41 61 41 15 60	11 88 83 24 82	24 07 78 61 89	42 58 88 22 16
13 24 40 09 00	65 46 38 61 12	90 62 41 11 59	85 18 42 61 29	88 76 04 21 80
78 27 84 05 99	85 75 67 80 05	57 05 71 70 21	31 99 99 06 96	53 99 25 13 63
42 39 30 02 34	99 46 68 45 15	19 74 15 50 17	44 80 13 86 38	40 45 82 13 44
04 52 43 96 38	13 83 80 72 34	20 84 56 19 49	59 14 85 42 99	71 16 34 33 79
82 85 77 30 16	69 32 46 46 30	84 20 68 72 98	94 62 63 59 44	00 89 06 15 87
38 48 84 88 24	55 46 48 60 06	90 08 83 83 98	40 90 88 25 26	85 74 55 80 85
91 19 05 68 22	58 04 63 21 16	23 38 25 43 32	98 94 65 35 35	16 91 07 12 43
54 81 87 21 31	40 46 17 62 63	99 71 14 12 64	51 68 50 60 78	22 69 51 08 37
65 43 75 12 91	20 36 25 57 92	33 65 95 48 75	00 06 65 25 90	16 29 34 14 43
49 98 71 31 80	59 57 32 43 07	85 06 64 75 27	29 17 06 11 30	68 70 97 87 21
03 98 68 89 39	71 87 32 14 99	42 10 25 37 30	08 27 75 43 97	54 20 69 93 50
56 04 21 34 92	89 81 52 15 12	84 11 12 66 87	47 21 06 86 08	35 39 52 28 99
48 09 36 95 36	20 82 53 32 89	92 68 50 88 17	37 92 02 23 43	63 24 69 69 91
23 97 10 96 57	74 07 95 26 44	93 08 43 30 41	86 45 74 33 78	84 33 38 79 78
43 97 55 45 98	35 69 45 96 80	46 26 39 96 33	60 20 73 30 79	17 19 08 47 28
40 05 08 50 79	89 58 19 86 48	27 98 99 24 08	94 19 15 81 29	82 14 35 88 93
66 97 10 69 02	25 36 43 71 76	00 67 56 12 69	07 89 55 63 31	50 72 20 33 36

Source: A. Hald (1952) *Statistical Tables and Formulas.* New York: John Wiley & Sons, Inc. Reprinted by permission of John Wiley & Sons, Inc.

Table A.2 The standardized normal distribution

Z	.00	.01	.02	.03	.04	.05	.06	.07	.08	.09
.0	.5000	.4960	.4920	.4880	.4840	.4801	.4761	.4721	.4681	.4641
.1	.4602	.4562	.4522	.4483	.4443	.4404	.4364	.4325	.4286	.4247
.2	.4207	.4168	.4129	.4090	.4052	.4013	.3974	.3936	.3897	.3859
.3	.3821	.3783	.3745	.3707	.3669	.3632	.3594	.3557	.3520	.3483
.4	.3446	.3409	.3372	.3336	.3300	.3264	.3228	.3192	.3156	.3121
.5	.3085	.3050	.3015	.2981	.2946	.2912	.2877	.2843	.2810	.2776
.6	.2743	.2709	.2676	.2643	.2611	.2578	.2546	.2514	.2483	.2451
.7	.2420	.2389	.2358	.2327	.2297	.2266	.2236	.2206	.2177	.2148
.8	.2119	.2090	.2061	.2033	.2005	.1977	.1949	.1922	.1894	.1867
.9	.1841	.1814	.1788	.1762	.1736	.1711	.1685	.1660	.1635	.1611
1.0	.1587	.1562	.1539	.1515	.1492	.1469	.1446	.1423	.1401	.1379
1.1	.1357	.1335	.1314	.1292	.1271	.1251	.1230	.1210	.1190	.1170
1.2	.1151	.1131	.1112	.1093	.1075	.1056	.1038	.1020	.1003	.09853
1.3	.09680	.09510	.09342	.09176	.09012	.08851	.08691	.08534	.08379	.08226
1.4	.08076	.07927	.07780	.07636	.07493	.07353	.07215	.07078	.06944	.06811
1.5	.06681	.06552	.06426	.06301	.06178	.06057	.05938	.05821	.05705	.05592
1.6	.05480	.05370	.05262	.05155	.05050	.04947	.04846	.04746	.04648	.04551
1.7	.04457	.04363	.04272	.04182	.04093	.04006	.03920	.03836	.03754	.03673
1.8	.03593	.03515	.03438	.03362	.03288	.03216	.03144	.03074	.03005	.02938
1.9	.02872	.02807	.02743	.02680	.02619	.02559	.02500	.02442	.02385	.02330
2.0	.02275	.02222	.02169	.02118	.02068	.02018	.01970	.01923	.01876	.01831
2.1	.01786	.01743	.01700	.01659	.01618	.01578	.01539	.01500	.01463	.01426
2.2	.01390	.01355	.01321	.01287	.01255	.01222	.01191	.01160	.01130	.01101
2.3	.01072	.01044	.01017	$.0^2 9903$	$.0^2 9642$	$.0^2 9387$	$.0^2 9137$	$.0^2 8894$	$.0^2 8656$	$.0^2 8424$
2.4	$.0^2 8198$	$.0^2 7976$	$.0^2 7760$	$.0^2 7549$	$.0^2 7344$	$.0^2 7143$	$.0^2 6947$	$.0^2 6756$	$.0^2 6569$	$.0^2 6387$

Table A.2 (continued)

Z	.00	.01	.02	.03	.04	.05	.06	.07	.08	.09
2.5	$.0^2 6210$	$.0^2 6037$	$.0^2 5868$	$.0^2 5703$	$.0^2 5543$	$.0^2 5386$	$.0^2 5234$	$.0^2 5085$	$.0^2 4940$	$.0^2 4799$
2.6	$.0^2 4661$	$.0^2 4527$	$.0^2 4396$	$.0^2 4269$	$.0^2 4145$	$.0^2 4025$	$.0^2 3907$	$.0^2 3793$	$.0^2 3681$	$.0^2 3573$
2.7	$.0^2 3467$	$.0^2 3364$	$.0^2 3264$	$.0^2 3167$	$.0^2 3072$	$.0^2 2980$	$.0^2 2890$	$.0^2 2803$	$.0^2 2718$	$.0^2 2635$
2.8	$.0^2 2555$	$.0^2 2477$	$.0^2 2401$	$.0^2 2327$	$.0^2 2256$	$.0^2 2186$	$.0^2 2118$	$.0^2 2052$	$.0^2 1988$	$.0^2 1926$
2.9	$.0^2 1866$	$.0^2 1807$	$.0^2 1750$	$.0^2 1695$	$.0^2 1641$	$.0^2 1589$	$.0^2 1538$	$.0^2 1489$	$.0^2 1441$	$.0^2 1395$
3.0	$.0^2 1350$	$.0^2 1306$	$.0^2 1264$	$.0^2 1223$	$.0^2 1183$	$.0^2 1144$	$.0^2 1107$	$.0^2 1070$	$.0^2 1035$	$.0^2 1001$
3.1	$.0^3 9676$	$.0^3 9354$	$.0^3 9043$	$.0^3 8740$	$.0^3 8447$	$.0^3 8164$	$.0^3 7888$	$.0^3 7622$	$.0^3 7364$	$.0^3 7114$
3.2	$.0^3 6871$	$.0^3 6637$	$.0^3 6410$	$.0^3 6190$	$.0^3 5976$	$.0^3 5770$	$.0^3 5571$	$.0^3 5377$	$.0^3 5190$	$.0^3 5009$
3.3	$.0^3 4834$	$.0^3 4665$	$.0^3 4501$	$.0^3 4342$	$.0^3 4189$	$.0^3 4041$	$.0^3 3897$	$.0^3 3758$	$.0^3 3624$	$.0^3 3495$
3.4	$.0^3 3369$	$.0^3 3248$	$.0^3 3131$	$.0^3 3018$	$.0^3 2909$	$.0^3 2803$	$.0^3 2701$	$.0^3 2602$	$.0^3 2507$	$.0^3 2415$
3.5	$.0^3 2326$	$.0^3 2241$	$.0^3 2158$	$.0^3 2078$	$.0^3 2001$	$.0^3 1926$	$.0^3 1854$	$.0^3 1785$	$.0^3 1718$	$.0^3 1653$
3.6	$.0^3 1591$	$.0^3 1531$	$.0^3 1473$	$.0^3 1417$	$.0^3 1363$	$.0^3 1311$	$.0^3 1261$	$.0^3 1213$	$.0^3 1166$	$.0^3 1121$
3.7	$.0^3 1078$	$.0^3 1036$	$.0^4 9961$	$.0^4 9574$	$.0^4 9201$	$.0^4 8842$	$.0^4 8496$	$.0^4 8162$	$.0^4 7841$	$.0^4 7532$
3.8	$.0^4 7235$	$.0^4 6948$	$.0^4 6673$	$.0^4 6407$	$.0^4 6152$	$.0^4 5906$	$.0^4 5669$	$.0^4 5442$	$.0^4 5223$	$.0^4 5012$
3.9	$.0^4 4810$	$.0^4 4615$	$.0^4 4427$	$.0^4 4247$	$.0^4 4074$	$.0^4 3908$	$.0^4 3747$	$.0^4 3594$	$.0^4 3446$	$.0^4 3304$
4.0	$.0^4 3167$	$.0^4 3036$	$.0^4 2910$	$.0^4 2789$	$.0^4 2673$	$.0^4 2561$	$.0^4 2454$	$.0^4 2351$	$.0^4 2252$	$.0^4 2157$
4.1	$.0^4 2066$	$.0^4 1978$	$.0^4 1894$	$.0^4 1814$	$.0^4 1737$	$.0^4 1662$	$.0^4 1591$	$.0^4 1523$	$.0^4 1458$	$.0^4 1395$
4.2	$.0^4 1335$	$.0^4 1277$	$.0^4 1222$	$.0^4 1168$	$.0^4 1118$	$.0^4 1069$	$.0^4 1022$	$.0^5 9774$	$.0^5 9345$	$.0^5 8934$
4.3	$.0^5 8540$	$.0^5 8163$	$.0^5 7801$	$.0^5 7455$	$.0^5 7124$	$.0^5 6807$	$.0^5 6503$	$.0^5 6212$	$.0^5 5934$	$.0^5 5668$
4.4	$.0^5 5413$	$.0^5 5169$	$.0^5 4935$	$.0^5 4712$	$.0^5 4498$	$.0^5 4294$	$.0^5 4098$	$.0^5 3911$	$.0^5 3732$	$.0^5 3561$
4.5	$.0^5 3398$	$.0^5 3241$	$.0^5 3092$	$.0^5 2949$	$.0^5 2813$	$.0^5 2682$	$.0^5 2558$	$.0^5 2439$	$.0^5 2325$	$.0^5 2216$
4.6	$.0^5 2112$	$.0^5 2013$	$.0^5 1919$	$.0^5 1828$	$.0^5 1742$	$.0^5 1660$	$.0^5 1581$	$.0^5 1506$	$.0^5 1434$	$.0^5 1366$
4.7	$.0^5 1301$	$.0^5 1239$	$.0^5 1179$	$.0^5 1123$	$.0^5 1069$	$.0^5 1017$	$.0^6 9680$	$.0^6 9211$	$.0^6 8765$	$.0^6 8339$
4.8	$.0^6 7933$	$.0^6 7547$	$.0^6 7178$	$.0^6 6827$	$.0^6 6492$	$.0^6 6173$	$.0^6 5869$	$.0^6 5580$	$.0^6 5304$	$.0^6 5042$
4.9	$.0^6 4792$	$.0^6 4554$	$.0^6 4327$	$.0^6 4111$	$.0^6 3906$	$.0^6 3711$	$.0^6 3525$	$.0^6 3348$	$.0^6 3179$	$.0^6 3019$

Source: A. Hald (1952) *Statistical Tables and Formulas*. New York John Wiley & Sons, Inc. Reprinted by permission of John Wiley & Sons, Inc.

Table A.3   Critical values for *t* significance test

df (N − 1)	0.4 0.8	0.25 0.5	0.1 0.2	0.05 0.1	0.025 0.05	0.01 0.02	0.005 0.01	0.001 One tail 0.002 Two tails
1	0.325	1.000	3.078	6.314	12.706	31.821	63.657	318.31
2	.289	0.816	1.886	2.920	4.303	6.965	9.925	22.326
3	.277	.765	1.638	2.353	3.182	4.541	5.841	10.213
4	.271	.741	1.533	2.132	2.776	3.747	4.604	7.173
5	0.267	0.727	1.476	2.015	2.571	3.365	4.032	5.893
6	.265	.718	1.440	1.943	2.447	3.143	3.707	5.208
7	.263	.711	1.415	1.895	2.365	2.998	3.499	4.785
8	.262	.706	1.397	1.860	2.306	2.896	3.355	4.501
9	.261	.703	1.383	1.833	2.262	2.821	3.250	4.297
10	0.260	0.700	1.372	1.812	2.228	2.764	3.169	4.144
11	.260	.697	1.363	1.796	2.201	2.718	3.106	4.025
12	.259	.695	1.356	1.782	2.179	2.681	3.055	3.930
13	.259	.694	1.350	1.771	2.160	2.650	3.012	3.852
14	.258	.692	1.345	1.761	2.145	2.624	2.977	3.787
15	0.258	0.691	1.341	1.753	2.131	2.602	2.947	3.733
16	.258	.690	1.337	1.746	2.120	2.583	2.921	3.686
17	.257	.689	1.333	1.740	2.110	2.567	2.898	3.646
18	.257	.688	1.330	1.734	2.101	2.552	2.878	3.610
19	.257	.688	1.328	1.729	2.093	2.539	2.861	3.579
20	0.257	0.687	1.325	1.725	2.086	2.528	2.845	3.552
21	.257	.686	1.323	1.721	2.080	2.518	2.831	3.527
22	.256	.686	1.321	1.717	2.074	2.508	2.819	3.505
23	.256	.685	1.319	1.714	2.069	2.500	2.807	3.485
24	.256	.685	1.318	1.711	2.064	2.492	2.797	3.467
25	0.256	0.684	1.316	1.708	2.060	2.485	2.787	3.450
26	.256	.684	1.315	1.706	2.056	2.479	2.779	3.435
27	.256	.684	1.314	1.703	2.052	2.473	2.771	3.421
28	.256	.683	1.313	1.701	2.048	2.467	2.763	3.408
29	.256	.683	1.311	1.699	2.045	2.462	2.756	3.396
30	0.256	0.683	1.310	1.697	2.042	2.457	2.750	3.385
40	.255	.681	1.303	1.684	2.021	2.423	2.704	3.307
60	.254	.679	1.296	1.671	2.000	2.390	2.660	3.232
120	.254	.677	1.289	1.658	1.980	2.358	2.617	3.160
∞	.253	.674	1.282	1.645	1.960	2.326	2.576	3.090

Source: Table III of Fisher and Yates: *Statistical Tables for Biological, Agricultural and Medical Research*, published by Longman Group Ltd, London (previously published by Oliver and Boyd, Edinburgh); reproduced by permission of the authors and publishers.

Table A.4   Critical values for F, $\alpha = 0.05$

	df for between																		
df for within	1	2	3	4	5	6	7	8	9	10	12	15	20	24	30	40	60	120	∞
1	161.4	199.5	215.7	224.6	230.2	234.0	236.8	238.9	240.5	241.9	243.9	245.9	248.0	249.1	250.1	251.1	252.2	253.3	254.3
2	18.51	19.00	19.16	19.25	19.30	19.33	19.35	19.37	19.38	19.40	19.41	19.43	19.45	19.45	19.46	19.47	19.48	19.49	19.50
3	10.13	9.55	9.28	9.12	9.01	8.94	8.89	8.85	8.81	8.79	8.74	8.70	8.66	8.64	8.62	8.59	8.57	8.55	8.53
4	7.71	6.94	6.59	6.39	6.26	6.16	6.09	6.04	6.00	5.96	5.91	5.86	5.80	5.77	5.75	5.72	5.69	5.66	5.63
5	6.61	5.79	5.41	5.19	5.05	4.95	4.88	4.82	4.77	4.74	4.68	4.62	4.56	4.53	4.50	4.46	4.43	4.40	4.36
6	5.99	5.14	4.76	4.53	4.39	4.28	4.21	4.15	4.10	4.06	4.00	3.94	3.87	3.84	3.81	3.77	3.74	3.70	3.67
7	5.59	4.74	4.35	4.12	3.97	3.87	3.79	3.73	3.68	3.64	3.57	3.51	3.44	3.41	3.38	3.34	3.30	3.27	3.23
8	5.32	4.46	4.07	3.84	3.69	3.58	3.50	3.44	3.39	3.35	3.28	3.22	3.15	3.12	3.08	3.04	3.01	2.97	2.93
9	5.12	4.26	3.86	3.63	3.48	3.37	3.29	3.23	3.18	3.14	3.07	3.01	2.94	2.90	2.86	2.83	2.79	2.75	2.71
10	4.96	4.10	3.71	3.48	3.33	3.22	3.14	3.07	3.02	2.98	2.91	2.85	2.77	2.74	2.70	2.66	2.62	2.58	2.54
11	4.84	3.98	3.59	3.36	3.20	3.09	3.01	2.95	2.90	2.85	2.79	2.72	2.65	2.61	2.57	2.53	2.49	2.45	2.40
12	4.75	3.89	3.49	3.26	3.11	3.00	2.91	2.85	2.80	2.75	2.69	2.62	2.54	2.51	2.47	2.43	2.38	2.34	2.30
13	4.67	3.81	3.41	3.18	3.03	2.92	2.83	2.77	2.71	2.67	2.60	2.53	2.46	2.42	2.38	2.34	2.30	2.25	2.21
14	4.60	3.74	3.34	3.11	2.96	2.85	2.76	2.70	2.65	2.60	2.53	2.46	2.39	2.35	2.31	2.27	2.22	2.18	2.13
15	4.54	3.68	3.29	3.06	2.90	2.79	2.71	2.64	2.59	2.54	2.48	2.40	2.33	2.29	2.25	2.20	2.16	2.11	2.07
16	4.49	3.63	3.24	3.01	2.85	2.74	2.66	2.59	2.54	2.49	2.42	2.35	2.28	2.24	2.19	2.15	2.11	2.06	2.01
17	4.45	3.59	3.20	2.96	2.81	2.70	2.61	2.55	2.49	2.45	2.38	2.31	2.23	2.19	2.15	2.10	2.06	2.01	1.96
18	4.41	3.55	3.16	2.93	2.77	2.66	2.58	2.51	2.46	2.41	2.34	2.27	2.19	2.15	2.11	2.06	2.02	1.97	1.92
19	4.38	3.52	3.13	2.90	2.74	2.63	2.54	2.48	2.42	2.38	2.31	2.23	2.16	2.11	2.07	2.03	1.98	1.93	1.88
20	4.35	3.49	3.10	2.87	2.71	2.60	2.51	2.45	2.39	2.35	2.28	2.20	2.12	2.08	2.04	1.99	1.95	1.90	1.84
21	4.32	3.47	3.07	2.84	2.68	2.57	2.49	2.42	2.37	2.32	2.25	2.18	2.10	2.05	2.01	1.96	1.92	1.87	1.81
22	4.30	3.44	3.05	2.82	2.66	2.55	2.46	2.40	2.34	2.30	2.23	2.15	2.07	2.03	1.98	1.94	1.89	1.84	1.78
23	4.28	3.42	3.03	2.80	2.64	2.53	2.44	2.37	2.32	2.27	2.20	2.13	2.05	2.01	1.96	1.91	1.86	1.81	1.76
24	4.26	3.40	3.01	2.78	2.62	2.51	2.42	2.36	2.30	2.25	2.18	2.11	2.03	1.98	1.94	1.89	1.84	1.79	1.73
25	4.24	3.39	2.99	2.76	2.60	2.49	2.40	2.34	2.28	2.24	2.16	2.09	2.01	1.96	1.92	1.87	1.82	1.77	1.71
26	4.23	3.37	2.98	2.74	2.59	2.47	2.39	2.32	2.27	2.22	2.15	2.07	1.99	1.95	1.90	1.85	1.80	1.75	1.69
27	4.21	3.35	2.96	2.73	2.57	2.46	2.37	2.31	2.25	2.20	2.13	2.06	1.97	1.93	1.88	1.84	1.79	1.73	1.67
28	4.20	3.34	2.95	2.71	2.56	2.45	2.36	2.29	2.24	2.19	2.12	2.04	1.96	1.91	1.87	1.82	1.77	1.71	1.65
29	4.18	3.33	2.93	2.70	2.55	2.43	2.35	2.28	2.22	2.18	2.10	2.03	1.94	1.90	1.85	1.81	1.75	1.70	1.64
30	4.17	3.32	2.92	2.69	2.53	2.42	2.33	2.27	2.21	2.16	2.09	2.01	1.93	1.89	1.84	1.79	1.74	1.68	1.62
40	4.08	3.23	2.84	2.61	2.45	2.34	2.25	2.18	2.12	2.08	2.00	1.92	1.84	1.79	1.74	1.69	1.64	1.58	1.51
60	4.00	3.15	2.76	2.53	2.37	2.25	2.17	2.10	2.04	1.99	1.92	1.84	1.75	1.70	1.65	1.59	1.53	1.47	1.39
120	3.92	3.07	2.68	2.45	2.29	2.17	2.09	2.02	1.96	1.91	1.83	1.75	1.66	1.61	1.55	1.50	1.43	1.35	1.25
∞	3.84	3.00	2.60	2.37	2.21	2.10	2.01	1.94	1.88	1.83	1.75	1.67	1.57	1.52	1.46	1.39	1.32	1.22	1.00

Source: Table V of Fisher and Yates: *Statistical Tables for Biological, Agricultural and Medical Research*, published by Longman Group Ltd. London (previously published by Oliver and Boyd, Edinburgh); reproduced by permission of the authors and publishers.

Table A.5 Critical values for chi-square

df	Probability													
	.099	.98	.95	.90	.80	.70	.50	.30	.20	.10	.05	.02	.01	.001
1	$.0^3157$	$.0^3628$	.00393	.0158	.0642	.148	.455	1.074	1.642	2.706	3.841	5.412	6.635	10.827
2	.0201	.0404	.103	.211	.446	.713	1.386	2.408	3.219	4.605	5.991	7.824	9.210	13.815
3	.115	.185	.352	.584	1.005	1.424	2.366	3.665	4.642	6.251	7.815	9.837	11.341	16.268
4	.297	.429	.711	1.064	1.649	2.195	3.357	4.878	5.989	7.779	9.488	11.668	13.277	18.465
5	.554	.752	1.145	1.610	2.343	3.000	4.351	6.064	7.289	9.236	11.070	13.388	15.086	20.517
6	.872	1.134	1.635	2.204	3.070	3.828	5.348	7.231	8.558	10.645	12.592	15.033	16.812	22.457
7	1.239	1.564	2.167	2.833	3.822	4.671	6.346	8.383	9.803	12.017	14.067	16.622	18.475	24.322
8	1.646	2.032	2.733	3.490	4.594	5.527	7.344	9.524	11.030	13.362	15.507	18.168	20.090	26.125
9	2.088	2.532	3.325	4.168	5.380	6.393	8.343	10.656	12.242	14.684	16.919	19.679	21.666	27.877
10	2.558	3.059	3.940	4.865	6.179	7.267	9.342	11.781	13.442	15.987	18.307	21.161	23.209	29.588
11	3.053	3.609	4.575	5.578	6.989	8.148	10.341	12.899	14.631	17.275	19.675	22.618	24.725	31.264
12	3.571	4.178	5.226	6.304	7.807	9.034	11.340	14.011	15.812	18.549	21.026	24.054	26.217	32.909
13	4.107	4.765	5.892	7.042	8.634	9.926	12.340	15.119	16.985	19.812	22.362	25.472	27.688	34.528
14	4.660	5.368	6.571	7.790	9.467	10.821	13.339	16.222	18.151	21.064	23.685	26.873	29.141	36.123
15	5.229	5.985	7.261	8.547	10.307	11.721	14.339	17.322	19.311	22.307	24.996	28.259	30.578	37.697
16	5.812	6.614	7.962	9.312	11.152	12.624	15.338	18.418	20.465	23.542	26.296	29.633	32.000	39.252
17	6.408	7.255	8.672	10.085	12.002	13.531	16.338	19.511	21.615	24.769	27.587	30.995	33.409	40.790
18	7.015	7.906	9.390	10.865	12.857	14.440	17.338	20.601	22.760	25.989	28.869	32.346	34.805	42.312
19	7.633	8.567	10.117	11.651	13.716	15.352	18.338	21.689	23.900	27.204	30.144	33.687	36.191	43.820
20	8.260	9.237	10.851	12.443	14.578	16.266	19.337	22.775	25.038	28.412	31.410	35.020	37.566	45.315
21	8.897	9.915	11.591	13.240	15.445	17.182	20.337	23.858	26.171	29.615	32.671	36.343	38.932	46.797
22	9.542	10.600	12.338	14.041	16.314	18.101	21.337	24.939	27.301	30.813	33.924	37.659	40.289	48.268
23	10.196	11.293	13.091	14.848	17.187	19.021	22.337	26.018	28.429	32.007	35.172	38.968	41.638	49.728
24	10.856	11.992	13.848	15.659	18.062	19.943	23.337	27.096	29.553	33.196	36.415	40.270	42.980	51.179
25	11.524	12.697	14.611	16.473	18.940	20.867	24.337	28.172	30.675	34.382	37.652	41.566	44.314	52.620
26	12.198	13.409	15.379	17.292	19.820	21.792	25.336	29.246	31.795	35.563	38.885	42.856	45.642	54.052
27	12.879	14.125	16.151	18.114	20.703	22.719	26.336	30.319	32.912	36.741	40.113	44.140	46.963	55.476
28	13.565	14.847	16.928	18.939	21.588	23.647	27.336	31.391	34.027	37.916	41.337	45.419	48.278	56.893
29	14.256	15.574	17.708	19.768	22.475	24.577	28.336	32.461	35.139	39.087	42.557	46.693	49.588	58.302
30	14.953	16.306	18.493	20.599	23.364	25.508	29.336	33.530	36.250	40.256	43.773	47.962	50.892	59.703

For larger values of df, the expression $\sqrt{2x^2} - \sqrt{2df} - 1$ has the Z-distribution; see Table A.2.
Source: Table IV of Fisher and Yates: *Statistical Tables for Biological, Agricultural and Medical Research*, published by Longman Group Ltd, London (previously published by Oliver and Boyd, Edinburgh); reproduced by permission of the authors and publishers.

References

Adler, N. E. (1973) 'Impact of prior sets given experimenters and subjects on the experimenter expectancy effect', *Sociometry*, **36**, 113–26.

Atkinson, C. and Polivy, J. (1976) 'Effects of delay, attack, and retaliation on state depression and hostility', *Journal of Abnormal Psychology*, **85** (6), 570–6.

Babbie, E. (1986) *Understanding Ourselves*. Belmont, CA: Wadworth.

Baron, L. and Strauss, M. A. (1989) *Four Theories of Rape in American Society*. New Haven, CT: Yale University Press.

Blishen, B. R. and McRoberts, H. A. (1976) 'A revised socioeconomic index for occupations in Canada', *Canadian Review of Sociology and Anthropology*, **13**, 71–9.

Brownlee, K. A. (1960) *Statistical Theory and Methodology in Science and Engineering*. New York: Wiley.

Caplovitz, D. with Single, E. (1974) *Consumers in Trouble: A Study of Debtors in Default*. New York: Free Press of Glencoe.

Chase-Dunn, C. (1975) 'The effects of international economic dependence on development and inequality: a cross national study', *American Sociological Review*, **40**, 720–38.

Cook, T. D. and Campbell, D. T. (1979) *Quasi-Experimentation*. Chicago: Rand McNally.

Cuddy, M. (1989) 'Predicting sexual abuse from dissociation, somatization, and nightmares', PhD dissertation, York University Department of Psychology.

Dominion Bureau of Statistics (1969) *1961 Census of Canada*. Cat. 92–539 (Bull. 1.1–10) and Cat. 98–529 (Bull. SX-15). Ottawa: DBS.

Duncan, O. D. (1961) 'A socio-economic index for all occupations', in A. J. Reiss (ed.) *Occupations and Social Status*. New York: Free Press.

Ewing, A. (1972) 'Socioeconomic status and voting behaviour in Vancouver', MA thesis, Carleton University Department of Sociology.

Fried, P. (1983) *Pregnancy and Life Style Habits*. New York: Stoddart.

Gallup, G. (1972) 'Opinion polling in a democracy', in J. M. Tanur *et al.* (eds) *Statistics: A Guide to the Unknown*. San Francisco: Holden-Day.

Gove, W. R. and Tudor, J. F. (1973) 'Adult sex roles and mental illness', *American Journal of Sociology*, **78**, 812–35.

Guilford, J. P. (1954) *Psychometric Methods*, 2nd edn. New York: McGraw-Hill.

Hays, W. L. (1981) *Statistics*, 3rd edn. New York: Holt.

Huff, D. (1954) *How to Lie with Statistics*. New York: Norton.

Information Please Almanac (1988) Boston: Houghton-Mifflin.

Inkeles, A. and Smith, D. H. (1974) *Becoming Modern*. Cambridge, MA: Harvard University Press.

Kennedy, R. E. Jr (1973) 'Minority status and fertility', *American Sociological Review*, **38**, 85–96.

Kish, L. (1965) *Survey Sampling*. New York: John Wiley & Sons.

Kuhn, T. S. (1970) *The Structure of Scientific Revolutions*, 2nd edn. Chicago: University of Chicago Press.

Lenton, R. L. (1989) 'Homicide in Canada and the US: a critique of the Hagan thesis', *Canadian Journal of Sociology*, **14**, 163–78.

Levine, A. and Crumrine, J. (1975) 'Women and the fear of success: a problem in replication', *American Journal of Sociology*, **80**, 964–75.

Link, R. F. (1972) 'Election night on television', in J. M. Tanur *et al.* (eds) *Statistics: A Guide to the Unknown*. San Francisco: Holden-Day.

Luce, S. R. (1974) 'Classroom behaviors as predictors of achievement', MA thesis, Carleton University.

Myles, J. (1984) *Old Age in the Welfare State*. Boston: Little, Brown.

Miller, H. (1961) 'Money value of education', *Occupational Outlook Quarterly*, **5**, 3–10.

Maccoby, E. E. (1960) 'Effects upon children of their mothers' outside employment', in N. W. Bell and E. F. Vogel (eds) *A Modern Introduction to the Family*. Toronto: Macmillan.

Molotch, H. and Lester, M. (1975) 'Accidental news: the great oil spill as local occurrence and national event', *American Journal of Sociology*, **81**, 235–60.

Registrar General of Scotland (1978) *Annual Report of the Registrar General of Scotland: Part I, Mortality Statistics*. Edinburgh: HMSO.

Rosenberg, M. (1968) *The Logic of Survey Analysis*. New York: Basic Books Inc.

Russett, M. M., Alker, H. R. Jr, Deutsch, K. W. and Lasswell, H. D. (1964) *World Handbook of Political and Social Indicators*. New Haven, CT: Yale University Press.

Sewell, W. H. and Shah, V. P. (1968) 'Social class, parental encouragement, and educational aspirations', *American Journal of Sociology*, **73**, 559–72.

Simon, H. A. (1954) 'Spurious correlation: a causal interpretation', *Journal of the American Statistical Association*, **49**, 467–79.

Smith, M. (1979) 'Towards an explanation of hockey violence', *Canadian Journal of Sociology*, **4**, 105–24.

Snedecor, G. W. (1956) *Statistical Methods*, 5th edn. Ames, IA: Iowa State College Press.

Statistics Canada (1973) *1971 Census of Canada*. Cat. 92–708, vol. 10, part 1 (Bull. 1.1–8). Ottawa: DBS.

Stolzenberg, R. M. (1975) 'Occupations, labor markets and the process of wage attainment', *American Sociological Review*, **40**, 645–65.

Stouffer, S. (1962) *Social Research to Test Ideas*. New York: Free Press of Glencoe.

Sudman, S. (1976) *Applied Sampling*. New York: Academic Press.

Taeuber, K. E. (1965) 'Residential segregation', *Scientific American*, **213** (2), 12–19.

Taylor, C. L. and Hudson, M. C. (1972) *World Handbook of Political and Social Indicators*, 2nd edn. New Haven, CT: Yale University Press.

Tukey, J. W. (1977) *Exploratory Data Analysis*. Reading, MA: Addison-Wesley.

United Nations Statistical Office (1976) *United Nations Statistical Yearbook, 1975*. New York: United Nations.

US Department of Health, Education and Welfare (1968) *United States Life Tables 1959–61*. Washington, DC: National Center for Health Statistics.

US Department of Health, Education and Welfare (1974) *Facts of Life and Death*. Rockville, MD: National Center for Health Statistics.

Weil, A. T., Zinberg, N. E. and Nelson, J. M. (1968) 'Clinical effect of marijuana in men', *Science*, **162**, 1234–42.

Whiting, J. M. and Child, I. L. (1962) *Child Training and Personality*. New Haven, CT: Yale University Press.

Whiting, J. M., Kluckhohn, R. and Anthony, A. (1958) 'The function of male initiation ceremonies at puberty', in *Readings in Social Psychology*, 3rd edn. New York: Holt, Rinehart and Winston.

Wimberley, D. W. (1990) 'Investment dependence and alternative explanations of Third World mortality: a cross cultural study', *American Sociological Review*, **55** (1), 75–91.

Winer, B. J. (1962) *Statistical Principles in Experimental Design*. New York: McGraw-Hill.

World Bank (1980) *World Development Report, 1980*. Washington, DC: World Bank.

World Bank (1986) *World Development Report, 1986*. New York: Oxford University Press.

World Health Organization (1974) *World Health Statistics Annual, Volume 9, 1971*. Geneva: WHO.

Zajonc, R. B. (1968) 'The attitudinal effects of mere exposure', *Journal of Personality and Social Psychology*, **9**, monograph supplement, 1–27.

Zeisel, H. and Kalven, H. Jr (1972) 'Parking tickets and missing women: statistics and the law', in J. M. Tanur *et al.* (eds) *Statistics: A Guide to the Unknown*. San Francisco: Holden-Day.

Index